Education, Equity,

Volume 4

Series Editors
George W. Noblit, University of North Carolina at Chapel Hill, USA
William T. Pink, Marquette University, Milwaukee, USA

Editorial Board
Belmira Bueno, University of São Paulo, Brazil
Rattana Buosonte, Naresuan University, Phitsanulok, Thailand
Li Manli, Tsinghua University, Beijing, China
Allan Luke, Queensland University of Technology, Brisbane, Australia
Jane Van Galen, University of Washington, Bothell, USA

More information about this series at http://www.springer.com/series/13055

Michelle D. Young • Sarah Diem
Editors

Critical Approaches to Education Policy Analysis

Moving Beyond Tradition

Editors
Michelle D. Young
Curry School of Education
University of Virginia
Charlottesville, VA, USA

Sarah Diem
Department of Educational Leadership
  and Policy Analysis
University of Missouri
Columbia, MO, USA

ISSN 2364-835X　　　　　　　　ISSN 2364-8368　(electronic)
Education, Equity, Economy
ISBN 978-3-319-81929-7　　　　ISBN 978-3-319-39643-9　(eBook)
DOI 10.1007/978-3-319-39643-9

© Springer International Publishing Switzerland 2017
Softcover reprint of the hardcover 1st edition 2016
This work is subject to copyright. All rights are reserved by the Publisher, whether the whole or part of the material is concerned, specifically the rights of translation, reprinting, reuse of illustrations, recitation, broadcasting, reproduction on microfilms or in any other physical way, and transmission or information storage and retrieval, electronic adaptation, computer software, or by similar or dissimilar methodology now known or hereafter developed.
The use of general descriptive names, registered names, trademarks, service marks, etc. in this publication does not imply, even in the absence of a specific statement, that such names are exempt from the relevant protective laws and regulations and therefore free for general use.
The publisher, the authors and the editors are safe to assume that the advice and information in this book are believed to be true and accurate at the date of publication. Neither the publisher nor the authors or the editors give a warranty, express or implied, with respect to the material contained herein or for any errors or omissions that may have been made.

Printed on acid-free paper

This Springer imprint is published by Springer Nature
The registered company is Springer International Publishing AG Switzerland

Foreword

During the three years of my phased retirement (2005–2008) from a career that began as a teaching-principal in 1958, I co-taught a course at The University of Texas at Austin, *critical policy analysis*, with Michelle Young, one of this book's editors. The other editor, Sarah Diem, was a student in that class, as were some of the contributors to this volume. And you might say I, too, was a student in that class. So, before we get into this book, *Critical Approaches to Education Policy Analysis: Moving Beyond Tradition*, and what I believe is truly a seminal contribution to our field and an experience that brought a whole lot of meaning to my career, let me tell you about my earlier dalliances with this notion of *critical policy analysis*. I believe there were critical turns in the paths I took that challenged me to dig beneath the obvious and search for answers to what works throughout my career.

By the time I left the comfort of my Downeast Maine hometown for faraway California, like my great grandfather[1] nearly a 100 years earlier, I had been a teaching-principal in a three-room schoolhouse and the first principal of a relatively large middle school established in a recently vacated high school. I had also completed my master's degree and was headed for a doctorate and an uncertain future at Stanford University. I was the ripe old age of 27. I mention this beginning to a 50-year professional career, not because it's of much importance to the reader but because of how it shaped my thinking about how policies and decisions get made in our field and perhaps planted the seeds for my earliest courtship with critical policy analysis.

If you have ever lived in a small town, you truly understand the notion, "It takes a village to raise a child." Imagine a 21-year old entering a school as a teacher and a principal for the first time with two experienced middle age women who exuded excellence in the classroom. The school was a wooden framed building built by members of the community, and it served as a community center for the school club. The national Parent-Teacher Association (PTA) was anathema to parents and friends of the school because once school business and any organized program were

---

[1] *My great grandfather, Wallace Scribner, and his brother Charles were lumberjacks and arrived in California not long before Stanford University was established in 1891.*

over, out came the bingo (beano) cards and the gambling began. The PTA did not permit such behavior.

Add to this my undergraduate professors, several with degrees from Columbia University where they were steeped in John Dewey's approach to "individual differences (ID)" and "unit planning." Their worldviews heavily influenced my approach to teaching. The ID approach to delivering instruction to students, individually and in small and large groups, was perfect for the multigrade situation. Moreover, students participated in planning weekly, monthly, and even semester-long interdisciplinary units around topics they chose collectively, sometimes spontaneously, because of some unforeseen event.

During this first experience, I was the consummate listener, everyone was engaged in the process, and opinions and ideas were shared. It was a great beginning, learning how creativity in policy and decision-making takes place in the context of the work.

I am certain my second experience as the first principal of a relatively large middle school with an entirely new student body, a whole new teaching staff, and a community wrought with skepticism about the disruption their children were perceived to be undertaking had a lot to do with how I viewed policy and decision-making in the workplace, not to mention, my later brush with critical policy analysis. My stance was *this is not my problem, this is our problem,* and *we* set out to organize a new curriculum with block scheduling and large and small group instruction, a brand-new faculty and student governance system, and the creation of parental involvement strategies that involved parents in all aspects of the school. The bottom line was to provide opportunities for every party to have a voice and play a role in creating new policies for a new school situation, and my role naturally evolved, as an initiator, instigator, and facilitator of the talent that surrounded me.

The third early influence can only be described as "cultural exasperation" or "a clash of cultures." My arrival at Stanford University as a new kid on the block was like sprinting as fast as one can move into an oncoming 18-wheeler. I had no idea what challenges a university of Stanford's stature would present for me. For example, it attracted a different kind of student than the laid-back Mainers who surrounded me during my earlier degrees, it provided an environment that fostered competition over collaboration, and it fostered a top-down approach to leadership and a new language that included theoretical frameworks, hypotheses making and testing, heuristics, and structural-functional systems analysis. It would take too long to tell how I adapted to all this, but all I can say is it was not easy.

I became good at developing conceptual frameworks, building models, and generating hypotheses. All of these because my natural instincts and earlier experiences taught me three rather compelling habits. First, I always tried to comprehend the big picture, rather than become burdened by details. Second, one might attribute this to a small amount of paranoia, but I learned early to never take anything at face value, to always look beyond the obvious for a deeper meaning. I have found this to be especially useful if what you encounter appears to be the indisputable, undeniable, and unmistakable *truth*. Third, very early in life, economic circumstances required that I move frequently to different locations. I think this may have contributed to how I learned to adapt and be flexible. I tend *not* to see each new situation or condition, concern, or controversy before me as black or white, either/or, or a two-sided issue; rather, I approached the experiences life put in my path as many-sided and worthy of continued scrutiny, critique, patience, tolerance, equitableness, and humanity.

These earliest personal accounts had a lot to do with what Young and Diem reference in their introduction to this volume. For example, concerns about the differences between policy rhetoric and practice reality; about how policies and decisions emerge; about how power is distributed; and about the effects of how policies and decisions impact inequities and the development of humane and democratic contexts were inherent in my early socialization.

One last vignette, in the early 1970s, we instituted an Urban Educational Policy and Planning Program at UCLA, where I was a faculty member. It was considered highly successful as a portal for a diverse group of students from East Los Angeles, Watts, and throughout the city, and we provided in-service, preservice, and mid-career educational experiences, as well as preparation for the professorship. Around two decades later at The University of Texas at Austin, I worked with my colleagues to develop an Educational Policy and Planning Program concentrating on research and preparing still another new cadre of educational researchers. At UCLA where we had the Center for the Study of Educational Evaluation, our focus was on policy evaluation, alternatives, and practices. In contrast, our approach at UT was interdisciplinary, with a program made up of core faculty steeped in discourse theory, critical ethnography, critical race theory, queer legal theory, and feminist analyses. The UT policy students received a markedly different preparation for their careers as policy scholars.

When 15 years after the establishment of the UT policy program I found myself co-teaching with one of the program's first graduates, I welcomed the challenge to explore and share "what counts as critical policy analysis." I continued to view myself as "a willing student" in this final classroom experience of my career. As noted, I learned firsthand some of the elemental premises of what have become known as critical policy analysis through life experiences, and I expanded my thinking through my engagement with the scholars and students with whom I have worked over the course of my career. Thus, this book, at least in some measure, not only makes a significant contribution to our field as it currently exists, it represents a meaningful capstone to my career.

Finally, this book and its authors not only resonate with me on an intellectual level but also on a personal level. I have been blessed to have either known the authors as students or colleagues, played a small part in their professional development, coauthored and collaborated on projects with them, or in a few instances come to know them through their outstanding contributions to the field (Oh yes, I was there when one of them was born!).

I hope you enjoy this book, as I did, and also I hope it helps you to think deeply about how these new perspectives in our field challenge us to see the big picture, penetrate beyond the obvious, and remain flexible and open to the new and unexpected.

Austin, TX, USA   Jay D. Scribner

Preface

In the spring 2007 semester at The University of Texas at Austin, we were both fortunate to be a part of a course (as professor and student) aptly titled *critical policy analysis*, where each week we examined the complexities surrounding the policy process through a critical perspective. Frank Fischer's text, *Reframing Public Policy: Discursive Politics and Deliberative Practices*, served as our foundational reading for the semester, and through his writings we were exposed to the methodological, theoretical, and political approaches to policy research that are working to challenge the dominant, traditional models in policy studies. Additional readings by scholars across the globe operating under the growing umbrella of CPA supplemented Fischer's text and guided us through our exploration of multifaceted and often convoluted policy contexts. Each week introduced a different policy framework and a new set of policy theorists. Yet while we recognized an increasing number of scholars being drawn to CPA work, and we understood our own attraction to the work, we were unable to locate an attempt to capture the state of this policy subfield. We were interested in developing a stronger understanding of who was influencing this work, what theories and methods were being utilized in critical policy analyses, and what rationales scholars gave for engaging in critical policy work, particularly within the field of education.

Before the semester closed, several members of the class interested in CPA came together to conduct a study that sought to examine the methods, tools, theories, paradigms, and influential people and experiences informing the work of critical policy analysis. Our intent was to build a deeper understanding of nontraditional approaches to policy work, critical policy analysis, and the methodological approaches used to do this work. The first step in this project included conducting a series of focus group discussions around CPA through a World Café Conversation at the 2008 University Council for Educational Administration (UCEA) Annual Convention. We felt that a World Café Conversation would be an ideal venue to discuss CPA as the World Café process itself is created to bring people together around important questions where people have the capacity to work together, share knowledge, and ignite innovation to emerge ideas and perspectives through the power of conversations.

The focus of the CPA World Café session was what "counts" as CPA (and what doesn't). We hoped to attract and create a network for scholars who were interested in building on knowledge of CPA in filling the gaps of the current political dichotomy between "traditional" and "critical" camps of policy analysts in the educational leadership and policy fields. In the session, members of our research team facilitated a conversation at each table (4–5 people per table) as participants discussed and came to a consensus around this policy analysis approach. Questions asked during the World Café discussion included: How do you define critical policy analysis? What and who has informed this definition? Has your understanding/definition changed over time? How does critical policy analysis differ from other approaches for policy analysis? What is significant about critical policy analysis? What is the value added of doing a critical policy analysis compared to more traditional policy analyses?

The World Café session helped give us a better sense of how US-based educational leadership and policy scholars were conceptualizing CPA and utilizing it in their own research. It also helped shape the next phase of our data collection, which included a series of 19 in-depth oral history interviews with scholars who were identified as using critical theoretical frameworks in their policy scholarship. The scholars we interviewed represented a diverse group of researchers at the early and later stages of their academic careers, each of whom discussed with us why and how they conduct critical policy analyses. We presented our initial findings of this research project at the 2010 American Educational Research Association Annual Meeting, which resulted in our CPA network expanding further.

As we worked to finalize our project for publication, we found ourselves in multiple conversations that emphasized the importance of providing guidance around what counts as CPA and how CPA is done. As a result, we reached out to critical educational policy scholars who utilize different theoretical approaches in their scholarship, some who assisted us in our initial CPA project at The University of Texas at Austin, and asked them to contribute a piece to a special issue proposal we were working on for the *International Journal of Qualitative Studies in Education*. Thanks to the support from QSE's editor and a CPA scholar himself, Jim Scheurich, we were able to share a collection of CPA scholarship representing five different theoretical approaches to educational policy, including queer legal theory, feminism, critical race theory, postmodernism, and critical discourse analysis. The QSE special issue was an initial attempt to provide the education field with a better understanding of how CPA is employed in educational policy research and specifically how theory connects to research design and methods. The authors of the special issue presented their research in a symposium session at the 2013 AERA Annual Meeting, which Jolanda Voogd from Springer attended. As the end of the session, she approached us to discuss the possibility of a publication based on the presentations—thank you, Jolanda!

The possibility of contributing an edited volume on critical policy analysis was simultaneously exciting and daunting as such a book, we felt, was long overdue. Yet we were overwhelmed with encouragement and gratitude when the contributors of this volume expressed their immediate excitement around the opportunity to be involved in such a project. We were even more grateful when the contributors extended themselves to being a part of two CPA sessions at the 2015 AERA Annual Meeting that were highly attended, as well as sessions at the 2014 and 2015 UCEA Annual Conventions. We have found these symposiums to be important venues for gaining critical feedback on our work as well as for expanding our network of CPA colleagues. The attendance at all of the CPA sessions at AERA and UCEA throughout the years has deepened our commitment to the work as more and more scholars are searching for a way to situate their own scholarship within CPA but may not have the tools yet to do so. Perhaps more importantly, through this work we have had the opportunity to develop strong, intellectually stimulating relationships with our colleagues, who have pushed our thinking and work to places we couldn't have gone alone.

Needless to say, this volume presented here represents many years of work and commitment on the part of a number of people we are deeply indebted to. Along with the authors in this volume, we would like to thank Erin Atwood, Margaret Grogan, Pei-Ling Lee, Patricia López, Catherine Lugg, Katherine Cummings Mansfield, Jason Murphy, Jim Scheurich, and Angela Valenzuela for their CPA contributions over the years. We would also like to thank Helen van der Stelt at Springer for her patience and assistance throughout the publication process. Thank you to Jill Blackmore for her contribution to the book and Jay D. Scribner or who us Longhorns refer to as Dr. J. Dr. J has been a mentor to both of us as students and now professors and paved the way for our current work. We would also like to thank our former colleagues and professors at The University of Texas at Austin for providing a setting where critical scholarship is valued and expected.

Finally, we acknowledge and thank our families and dear friends who have stood by and supported us throughout our careers. Their encouragement has been crucial to all stages of this project, and we are forever grateful. Similarly, we acknowledge each other as general editors for the hard work and mutual support essential to an effective editorial partnership.

Columbia, MO, USA	Sarah Diem
Charlottesville, VA, USA	Michelle D. Young

Contents

Introduction: Critical Approaches to Education Policy Analysis........... 1
Michelle D. Young and Sarah Diem

Part I Emphasis on Methods

**Critically Examining Policy Workers and Policy Work Within
State Boards of Education** 19
Michelle D. Young and Amy Luelle Reynolds

**A Critical Policy Analysis of the Politics, Design,
and Implementation of Student Assignment Policies** 43
Sarah Diem

Public Educational Policy as Performance: A Queer Analysis.............. 63
Michael P. O'Malley and Tanya A. Long

**The Politics of Student Voice: Conceptualizing a Model for
Critical Analysis**... 83
Anjalé D. Welton, Tiffany O. Harris, Karla Altamirano,
and Tierra Williams

**When Parents Behave Badly: A Critical Policy Analysis
of Parent Involvement in Schools**... 111
Erica Fernández and Gerardo R. López

A Feminist Critical Policy Analysis of Patriarchy in Leadership 131
Catherine Marshall, Mark Johnson, and Torrie Edwards

Part II Emphasis on Theory

**Silent Covenants in the Neoliberal Era: Critical Race
Counternarratives on African American
Advocacy Leadership in Schools** 155
Chandra Gill, LaTasha L. Cain Nesbitt, and Laurence Parker

Policy Enactments and Critical Policy Analysis: How Institutional Talk Constructs Administrative Logics, Marginalization, and Agency 175
Rodney S. Whiteman, Brendan D. Maxcy, Erica Fernández, and Samantha M. Paredes Scribner

Ontario's Fourth 'R': A Critical Democratic Analysis of Ontario's Fund-'R'aising Policy 193
Michelle Milani and Sue Winton

Examining the Theater of "Listening" & "Learning" 215
Bradley W. Carpenter

Utilizing Michel De Certeau in Critical Policy Analysis 243
Curtis A. Brewer and Amanda Bell Werts

Policy Studies Debt: A Feminist Call to Expand Policy Studies Theory ... 261
Wanda S. Pillow

Afterword 275

Index 283

Contributors

Karla Altamirano Parkland College, Champaign, IL, USA

Jill Blackmore Faculty of Arts and Education, Deakin University, Burwood, VIC, Australia

Curtis A. Brewer Department of Educational Leadership and Policy Studies, The University of Texas at San Antonio, San Antonio, TX, USA

Bradley W. Carpenter Department of Educational Leadership and Policy Studies, University of Houston, Houston, TX, USA

Sarah Diem Department of Educational Leadership and Policy Analysis, University of Missouri, Columbia, MO, USA

Torrie Edwards School of Education, University of North Carolina, Chapel Hill, NC, USA

Erica Fernández Department of Educational Leadership, Neag School of Education, University of Connecticut, Storrs, CT, USA

Chandra Gill Blackacademically Speaking, Chicago, IL, USA

Tiffany O. Harris Department of Education Policy, Organization and Leadership, University of Illinois, Champaign, IL, USA

Mark Johnson School of Education, University of North Carolina, Chapel Hill, NC, USA

Tanya A. Long Counseling, Leadership, Adult Education and School Psychology Department, Texas State University, San Marcos, TX, USA

Gerardo R. López Department of Educational Leadership and Policy, College of Education, The University of Utah, Salt Lake City, UT, USA

Catherine Marshall School of Education, University of North Carolina, Chapel Hill, NC, USA

Brendan D. Maxcy Department of Educational Leadership and Policy Studies, Indiana University—Purdue University Indianapolis, Indianapolis, IN, USA

Michelle Milani Faculty of Education, York University, Toronto, ON, Canada

LaTasha L. Cain Nesbitt Department of Educational Policy Organization and Leadership, College of Education, University of Illinois at Urbana-Champaign, Champaign, IL, USA

Michael P. O'Malley Counseling, Leadership, Adult Education and School Psychology Department, Texas State University, San Marcos, TX, USA

Laurence Parker Department of Educational Leadership and Policy, College of Education, University of Utah, Salt Lake City, UT, USA

Wanda S. Pillow Department of Education, Gender Studies/Education Culture and Society, University of Utah, Salt Lake City, UT, USA

Amy Luelle Reynolds Department of Leadership, Foundations and Policy, University of Virginia, Charlottesville, VA, USA

Samantha M. Paredes Scribner Department of Educational Leadership and Policy Studies, Indiana University—Purdue University Indianapolis, Indianapolis, IN, USA

Jay D. Scribner Department of Educational Administration, The University of Texas at Austin, Austin, TX, USA

Anjalé D. Welton Department of Education Policy, Organization and Leadership, University of Illinois, Champaign, IL, USA

Amanda Bell Werts Reich College of Education, Appalachian State University, Boone, NC, USA

Rodney S. Whiteman Department of Educational Leadership and Policy Studies, Indiana University, Bloomington, IN, USA

Tierra Williams Southern Illinois University, Carbondale, IL, USA

Sue Winton Faculty of Education, York University, Toronto, ON, Canada

Michelle D. Young Curry School of Education, University of Virginia, Charlottesville, VA, USA

Introduction: Critical Approaches to Education Policy Analysis

Michelle D. Young and Sarah Diem

Our purpose in this book is twofold. The main purpose is to discuss the methodological implications of critical approaches to educational policy analysis. A second purpose of the book is to provide concrete examples, and thus road maps, for engaging in critical policy analysis. Neither of these purposes can be achieved without an introduction to the basic ideas in this approach. We therefore devote this chapter to introducing some of the basic elements of critical policy analysis (CPA), including some of the fundamental ontological and epistemological claims as well as their implications for investigating educational policy. From this starting point, the reader will then find a variety of ways that other critical policy scholars have chosen to pursue this work.

Critical policy analysis is not a homogeneous movement in social science. There are many different perspectives and developments. For example, some authors foreground methods in their work, and others discuss CPA from a philosophical perspective, while others ground their analyses in policies and policy contexts. Although the studies collected within this volume explore, build upon, and extend the work of CPA, the intention of the book is not a contribution to the philosophical debates concerning critical perspectives; rather, we focus on the methodological implications of critical perspectives in policy research and offer the reader a number of examples of critical policy analyses.

M.D. Young (✉)
Curry School of Education, University of Virginia, Charlottesville, VA, USA
e-mail: mdy8n@virginia.edu

S. Diem
Department of Educational Leadership and Policy Analysis, University of Missouri, 202 Hill Hall, Columbia, MO 65211, USA
e-mail: diems@missouri.edu

One assumption of this book is that theory and method are interrelated. We have found a tendency within the policy community to think about the theoretical part of policy analysis as separate from the more practical part, the empirical and methodological details, as if theory is something that is applied only after data has been collected. However, theory and method should not be treated as two separate issues or stages in a process. It is our contention that theory and method should be considered simultaneously. Policy analysis is, by its very nature, theoretical; that is, it requires theorizing about the objects of study. Thus, this book seeks to demonstrate the interrelated nature of theory and method.

1 Critical Policy Analysis as Critique

One of the drivers behind the development of CPA was a critique of the positivist approach to policy analysis—an approach that has dominated the field since its inception (Diem and Young 2015; Young 1999). Researchers began to question the very nature of policy, its formation, and assumptions about its impact. As such questions emerged and evolved, scholars questioned the way policy was traditionally thought of, examined, and analyzed.

Traditional policy analysis is often characterized as theoretically narrow, relying first and foremost upon positivist notions of reality and knowledge, such as functionalism and rationalism (Levinson et al. 2009; Nagel 1984). As Ball (1994a) noted, "educational policy studies have tended to spawn a growing number of concepts which are primarily descriptive, and which are dislocated from any coherent explanatory or predictive framework" (p. 1). Many traditional policy analysts have viewed policy-making as a deliberate process, undertaken by a bounded set of actors, who use research and reason to ensure the best possible policy outcomes (Rist 1994). Indeed, elsewhere we have identified four key tenets of traditional approaches to policy analysis. These include the following:

1. Traditional policy researchers, who are concerned with planning, adoption, implementation, examination, and/or evaluating educational changes or reforms, tend to view change or reform as a deliberate process that can be planned and managed.
2. Traditional policy researchers generally view behavior as goal-driven and that rational individuals will weigh the costs, benefits, and subsequent outcomes of a given action or strategy.
3. Traditional policy researchers believe they are capable of obtaining, accumulating, and understanding the knowledge necessary for identifying and deciding between policy solutions and planning for implementation and evaluation and that this information can be expressed to others.
4. Traditional policy researchers assume they can effectively evaluate policies, policy alternatives, and practices and then based on these evaluations are able to identify and ameliorate problems (Diem et al. 2014).

As these assumptions demonstrate, the locus of concern was primarily placed at what was considered to be the end of the policy-making process: the policy, the implementation of the policy, and/or the impact of the policy (Ball 1994a). Though, as Levinson et al. (2009) point out, this focus was implemented "with an eye toward policy reformulation and/or the reform of local structures for policy implementation" (p. 768).

As part of the policy studies field, educational policy research has tended to operate within a traditionalistic (i.e., positivist) paradigm and reflects a group of taken-for-granted assumptions, norms, and traditions that institutionalize conventional ontological, epistemological, and methodological traditions (Diem et al. 2014; Young 1999). The four assumptions listed above are identifiable in policy research theories and approaches such as systems theory and analysis, structural analysis, cost-benefit analysis, information technology approaches, decision theory, problem-solving frameworks, technicist models, and political models (Adams 1991; Becker 1986; deLeon and Vogenback 2007; Dunn 1994; Levin 1988; McDonnell 2009; Troyna 1994; Weimer and Vining 2011). The result is a circumscribed set of research findings, garnered through a restricted grouping of theory and method (Diem et al. 2014; Young 1999).

Over the last 30 years, however, a growing number of policy researchers have shifted from traditional approaches and used critical frameworks to interrogate both the beliefs and practices associated with traditional work as well as the policies, insights, and recommendations that result from such work (McDonnell 2009). Levinson et al. (2009) refer to this as the "first generation of critical policy research" (p. 774). Work from the United Kingdom by Stephen Ball (1991, 1993, 1994b) and in the United States by Michael Apple (1982) and Tom Popkewitz (1997, 2000) has been particularly influential. These scholars problematized the rational approach associated with traditional educational policy research, elucidated the role of power and ideology in the policy process, and broke new ground for critical policy scholars.

Importantly, during the same period of time that scholars struggled with and perforated the boundaries of traditional policy studies, the study of educational policy moved beyond the borders of individual countries to the consideration of global trends and the imposition of educational policies cultivated in primarily western countries in developing nations (Ball 1998). Some of the more troubling global trends under examination have included the tightening of control on students, educators, administrators, and the schooling process through national-level educational policies (Levinson 2005). Although one could argue that these trends are completely unrelated, it is interesting that as power and control in education became increasingly consolidated and as the movement toward accountability and consolidation marched across the globe, a growing number of educational policy scholars, dissatisfied with traditional frameworks, began using critical frameworks in their analyses (Diem et al. 2014). We do not see these trends as merely coincidental. Rather, it is our contention that developments in critical educational policy analysis are a response to conditions in education, just as they signal an important shift in the field.

2 The Basic Elements of Critical Policy Analysis

Within the educational policy realm, scholars have studied, critiqued, and offered alternative strategies for examining a variety of educational policy issues (e.g., Brewer 2014; Lipman 2004; Mosen-Lowe et al. 2009; Young 1999), and they have offered a variety of new perspectives and approaches. Examples include Marshall (1997) and Taylor's (1997) use of discourse theory to critically examine educational policy and its impact, Young's (2003) critical analysis of state-level policy work on Iowa's leadership crisis, Levinson's (2005) use of critical policy ethnography to study policy appropriation in Mexico, and Brewer's (2008, 2014) examination of federal policy histories and microhistories. Other examples include Ball and Junemann's (2012) examination of new philanthropies and policy networks in educational policy-making; Winton and Brewer's (2014) use of microhistory and cultural history to analyze policy-relevant political events; Carpenter et al. (2014) analysis of policy vocabularies within federal and state education reform policies concerning the evaluation of public school leaders; Atwood and López's (2014) utilization of critical race theory to question everyday racial politics; Lugg and Murphy's (2014) employment of queer theory and queer legal theory as a means to understand institutional and cultural practices that frame sex, gender, class, and race in education that can lead to policy changes that benefit all students, teachers, and staff; and Mansfield et al. (2014) critical feminist analysis of STEM policies in education.

In our analyses of critical policy work in education, we have found that scholars tend to focus their work around five critical concerns. These include the following:

1. Concern regarding the difference between policy rhetoric and practiced reality
2. Concern regarding the policy, its roots, and its development (e.g., how it emerged, what problems it was intended to solve, how it changed and developed over time, and its role in reinforcing the dominant culture)
3. Concern with the distribution of power, resources, and knowledge as well as the creation of policy "winners" and "losers"
4. Concern regarding social stratification and the broader effect a given policy has on relationships of inequality and privilege
5. Concern regarding the nature of resistance to or engagement in policy by members of nondominant groups (Diem et al. 2014)

As the above concerns illustrate, critical policy researchers have explored policy roots and processes; how policies that are presented as reality are often political rhetoric; how knowledge, power, and resources are distributed inequitably (e.g., Flyvbjerg 1998); how educational programs and policies, regardless of intent, reproduce stratified social relations; how policies institutionalize inequality; and how individuals react to policy and policy processes (e.g., Street 2001).

Three additional similarities mark the work of critical educational policy scholars. First, critical policy researchers tend to pay significant attention to the complex systems and environments in which policy is made and implemented. Indeed, CPA scholars tend to take time to provide the historical and/or cultural context of the policy issue under examination. Recognizing that the development of policy is "an extremely complex, often contradictory process," critical policy researchers work to capture the full complexity of policy contexts, those involved, and the evolution of policy over time (Weaver-Hightower 2008, p. 153).

Second, critical policy researchers emphasize the inextricable nature of theory and method. Critical policy researchers see theorizing as a vital part of methodology, and, as such, it is a central feature in the planning of a research project. Theory impacts the identification of the research topic or problem, it impacts the way the researcher thinks about the problem, and it impacts the questions that she/he asks about the issue. Indeed, every attempt to make sense of the world around us begins with our notions, conceptualizations, and theories about it. In the case of analysis, which involves close examination and distinguishing among various components or aspects of a data set, body of knowledge, etc., we engage in judgments regarding what patterns we attend to and how we go about separating and examining. We always have a perspective, and therefore our observations are always undertaken from a perspective. Yet, as Danermark et al. (2002) point out, "the all-important significance of concepts and conceptualization in all production of knowledge is generally a downplayed field in books on methodology" (p.15). This is not the case for most critical policy scholars; rather, most CPA scholars begin with the assumption that our different ways of seeing and thinking about phenomena determine what we see. From this point of view, CPA scholars, as you will see in this volume, take great care in delineating the perspectives they bring to their work and how those perspectives inform how they do research (i.e., their methods).

This brings us to the third similarity marking the work of critical policy researchers. Given the nature of their policy questions and perspectives, critical policy scholars are more likely to use qualitative research approaches than quantitative approaches in their work (deLeon and Vogenback 2007; Denzin and Lincoln 2005; Levinson et al. 2009). To be clear, we are not arguing that CPA scholars never use quantitative methods or a mixture of methods drawn from what the field has designated as qualitative and quantitative. Indeed, there is no single or correct critical policy analysis method. However, our observation has been that the majority of CPA work is qualitative in nature (Diem et al. 2014) and that this body of scholarship does provide guidance for others doing or hoping to do work of this nature.

Importantly, the preceding review of literature of traditional and critical approaches to policy analysis is not intended to be exhaustive. Rather, it is provided to draw attention to the general contours of traditional and critical approaches, as we have come to understand them, as a way of orienting the reader to the focus of our research project.

3 Outline of the Book

Due to the introductory character of the book, we have included a set of chapters by authors who engage in CPA, and we have asked that they share an example of their work that makes the theoretical and methodological connections clear—clear enough for a novice researcher to develop a keen understanding of what CPA is and what conducting one involves. We hope that we have been able to achieve a balance between the task of simplifying and the need to do justice to the complexity of engaging in critical policy research.

Chapter authors use a variety of theoretical and experiential perspectives, including perspectives drawn from critical theory, critical race theory, feminism, post-structuralism, and queer theory, among others. The methods used to explore questions emerging from these perspectives include discourse analysis, document analysis, historical approaches, in-depth interviews, and critical policy ethnography. Their work reflects the tendency of CPA scholars to emphasize methods that explore below the surface of what to understand and why. Finally, and perhaps most importantly, the authors demonstrate how method flows from the framework in use by the researcher.

We have organized the book into two primary sections: a focus on methods and a focus on theory. Although each of the studies articulates a theoretical framework and a methodological approach, they are emphasized to varying degrees in the chapters. The first set of studies, chapters "Critically Examining Policy Workers and Policy Work Within State Boards of Education", "A Critical Policy Analysis of the Politics, Design, and Implementation of Student Assignment Policies", "Public Educational Policy as Performance: A Queer Analysis", "The Politics of Student Voice: Conceptualizing a Model for Critical Analysis", "When Parents Behave Badly: A Critical Policy Analysis of Parent Involvement in Schools" and "A Feminist Critical Policy Analysis of Patriarchy in Leadership", emphasize methods, while the studies in the second section of the book, chapters "Silent Covenants in the Neoliberal Era: Critical Race Counternarratives on African American Advocacy Leadership in Schools", "Policy Enactments and Critical Policy Analysis: How Institutional Talk Constructs Administrative Logics, Marginalization, and Agency", "Ontario's Fourth 'R': A Critical Democratic Analysis of Ontario's Fund-'R'aising Policy", "Examining the Theater of "Listening" & "Learning"", "Utilizing Michel de Certeau in Critical Policy Analysis" and "Policy Studies Debt: A Feminist Call to Expand Policy Studies Theory", accentuate theory. We do this not as a way to divorce methods from theory, as critical policy scholars see the clear link between the two. Rather, similar to Wolcott's (1994) presentation of the distinction between description, analysis and interpretation, we believe separating the chapters in this way provides insight into how the authors situate her/his own research within the CPA terrain. As Wolcott states (1994) in his discussion on qualitative research:

> By no means do I suggest that the three categories–description, analysis, and interpretation–are mutually exclusive. Nor are the lines clearly drawn where description ends and analysis begins, or where analysis becomes interpretation. ...I do suggest that identifying and distinguishing among the three may serve a useful purpose, especially if the categories can be regarded as varying emphases that qualitative researchers employ to organize and present data. (p. 11)

We agree with Wolcott's assertion that qualitative data does not need to fit in the same manner within "all" of these categories, just as CPA work may differ in its attention to methods and theory. Thus, we present this volume as a way to make sense of the two to better inform the education policy field about the methodological and theoretical perspectives used in critical policy analysis.

Chapter two, "Critically Examining Policy Workers and Policy Work Within State Boards of Education" by Michelle Young and Amy Reynolds, outlines a set of critical policy studies focused on State Boards of Education, a policy entity that has received scant attention from the research community, traditional and critical alike. They open with an overview of inquiry on state boards, the majority of which is offered through a traditional perspective. The remainder of the chapter is divided into three sections that outline inquiry projects focused on state boards. The first project outlined is a critical historical analysis, a core strategy of critical theorists interested in the historical roots and evolution of institutions, norms, and beliefs. The second relies on the work of scholars like Marshall and Young (2013) to examine the power and authority of state boards and individual members using a feminist critical policy perspective. The third project relies on the analytical work of scholars like and Ball (2008) and Rhodes (1997), who employ network analysis to examine state boards as policy actors and the governing models they work with.

In chapter three, "A Critical Policy Analysis of the Politics, Design, and Implementation of Student Assignment Policies", Sarah Diem provides a critical policy analysis of three present-day school desegregation policies that use a number of factors in assigning to schools to achieve diversity. As school districts are growing increasingly segregated, and legal and political environments favor race-neutral or color-blind approaches to addressing the continued racial disparities in education, Diem's analysis sheds light on how school districts generate methods of student assignment to achieve racial diversity while not being race-conscious. She pays particular attention to how the politics surrounding student assignment policies (local, state, and federal) has an impact on their design and implementation. By utilizing a CPA approach to analyzing these policies, Diem is able to illustrate the complexities behind the development of the policies, how and why decisions were made when designing the policies, and the (un)intended consequences of the policy implementation process.

Chapter four, "Public Educational Policy as Performance: A Queer Analysis" by Michael O'Malley and Tanya Long, analyzes the recent case of the first school district in Texas to adopt domestic partnership benefits, inclusive of same sex couples, in order to understand and theorize the processes influencing LGBTQ-inclusive educational policy. They conducted a content analysis of print media articles that reported on the development and implementation of the policy in order to map the public process through which the policy was negotiated and adopted in the district. The chapter illustrates "the value of queer theory as an intellectual tool for problematizing and interrupting normalizing assumptions inscribed in specific educational policies that have the material effect of fostering inequity across multiple manifestations of difference."

Using a critical framework when analyzing education policy enables the exploration of the voices of those typically not heard in traditional policy contexts and processes (Diem et al. 2014). In chapter five, "The Politics of Student Voice: Conceptualizing a Model for Critical Analysis," Anjalé Welton, Tiffany

Harris, Tierra Williams, and Karla Altamirano argue and focus on the potential of as well as the obstacles to developing educational policy that is informed by student youth voice. In their study, they examined a high school class focused on social justice education where students actively researched, made decisions, identified problems, collected and analyzed data, and provided recommendations for school improvement and transformation. The chapter shows how institutionalized structures and practices and hierarchies of power can impede students' attempts to have their voices heard when it comes to school improvement decisions. However, the authors argue that youth voice in the school improvement process "has the potential to be one of the most authentic, democratic forms of engaging in public policy" as "when students have a voice in school policy they can be the architects of their own educational trajectories."

In chapter six, "When Parents Behave Badly: A Critical Policy Analysis of Parent Involvement in Schools," Erica Fernández and Gerardo López problematize the current discourse around traditional norms of parental involvement in schools by examining the power dynamics associated with parental involvement and how the meaning of such involvement is not only defined and prescribed for parents but also delimited within school spaces. They employ tools from critical race theory and Latino critical race theory, specifically the concept of counterstories, to illustrate the conflicts that emerge when an organized group of Latino parents challenges traditional conceptualizations of parental involvement activity set forth by the school's administration. Their CPA of parental involvement is critical in a time when parental engagement is on the rise in public schools as it helps us understand the types of involvement that become privileged and ingrained in schools and, subsequently, how these defined ways of involvement then marginalize certain populations of parents and lead to them being labeled as uninvolved in their children's educational experiences.

CPA scholars seek to understand the distribution of power and how policies can work to reinforce or reproduce social injustices and inequalities (Diem et al. 2014). In the last chapter in section one, chapter "A Feminist Critical Policy Analysis of Patriarchy in Leadership," Catherine Marshall, Mark Johnson, and Torrie Edwards examine the persistence of male dominance in education leadership roles, looking specifically at how cultural and political discourses play a role in undermining women's positions in education. They utilize a feminist critical policy analysis to uncover and deconstruct masculine tropes within dominant narratives on educational leadership. Through their analysis, they are able to demonstrate the nuances and complexity of patriarchy as it exists within a predominantly female professional field.

The chapters in the second half of the book shift our focus to the theoretical significance in critical policy analysis studies. In chapter eight, "Silent Covenants in the Neoliberal Era: Critical Race Counter-Narratives on African American", Chandra Gill, LaTosha Cain Nesbitt, and Laurence Parker problematize the current color-blind and context-blind educational policy context and its implications on educational opportunity. Specifically, in their chapter, "Silent Covenants in the Neoliberal Era: Critical Race Counter-narratives on African American Advocacy in

Schools," they argue for the need of critical race theory in providing an alternative critical policy lens that centers racial perspectives on policies and challenges the contemporary context-blind policy discourse. They use counter-narratives of African American leaders within a community to understand how they viewed the shifting policy discourse from desegregation to an emphasis on testing and accountability and "call out" the harmful effects of current color-blind and context-blind policy contexts "that create an image of policy development in schools that will 'fix' the achievement gap with students of color."

In chapter nine, Rod Whiteman, Brendan Maxcy, and Samantha Scribner's chapter, "Policy Enactments and Critical Policy Analysis: How Institutional Talk Constructs Administrative Logics, Marginalization, and Agency," is based upon the CPA assumption that policy analysis moves beyond technical-rational analysis of policy design, implementation, and measurable, quantifiable outcomes (Diem et al. 2014; Fischer 2003). Specifically, they examine the role of institutions in structuring interactions between school administrators and historically marginalized communities. Their framework includes an institutionally structured micropolitical orientation to critical policy analysis, which allows them to focus on policy enactments and the relationship between institutionally contingent language and micropolitical negotiations within schools. They apply this framework through a secondary analysis of three ethnographic studies to illustrate how when historically marginalized communities assert their collective interests in their school communities, they find themselves in positions where they have to negotiate the institutional logic and language of school administration.

In chapter ten, "Ontario's Fourth 'R': A Critical Democratic Analysis of Ontario's Fund'r'aising Policy," Michelle Milani and Sue Winton use a critical democratic lens to examine how fundraising policy in Ontario, Canada, is undermining the ideals of critical democracy in its public schools. They pay particular attention to what is occurring in the fundraising policy's contexts of influence, text production, and practice in order to ascertain whether the policy supports equity, inclusion, participatory decision-making processes, and knowledge inquiry and critical mindedness. The findings of their critical policy analysis illustrate the contradictory nature of fundraising and critical democratic commitment to equality, equity, social justice, and community as it shifts the responsibility of funding education from the public to the private domain. Milani and Winton suggest that Ontario's fundraising policy must be eliminated from the public school system and the government must adequately fund schools if critical democracy is to be achieved.

In chapter eleven, "Examining the Theater of 'Listening' and 'Learning'," Bradley Carpenter looks beyond the analysis of language and focuses on how dominant discourses are constructed through the performance of politics. Specifically, Carpenter seeks to ameliorate the limitations of traditional policy studies by utilizing Hajer's (2003, 2005, 2006) argumentative discourse analysis to provide a unique approach to the analysis of deliberative policy-making. He describes how, unlike the traditional framing of the "Listening & Learning" tour as a tool for informing the developing of federal educational policy, the political performances of the Obama/Duncan Administration in their "Listening & Learning" tour acted in coordination with neoliberal and globalized discourses to codetermine the authoring of the Title I School Improvement Grant of 2009.

The twelveth chapter of the volume, "Utilizing Michel de Certeau in Critical Policy Analysis" by Curtis Brewer and Amanda Werts, explores Michel de Certeau's concept of consumption in every day as an analytical tool for critical policy analysis in education. Brewer and Werts build off of the idea of policy enactment and argue that foregrounding the concept of everyday practices can work to assist educators in understanding their simultaneous roles as active democratic subjects and governed subjects. By offering an additional theoretical guide for the critical study of policy enactment, including a hypothetical application of the approach, Brewer and Werts hope that educators might be able to locate possibilities for radical forms of democracy in the current standardized education context.

In chapter thirteenth, "Policy Studies Debt: A Feminist Call to Expand Policy Studies Theory," Wanda Pillow discusses the "policy debt" occurring in education. Using a feminist policy analysis and, in particular, a women of color (WOC) feminist epistemology, as a lens, Pillow interrogates policy studies in the face of this debt. Pillow outlines and applies four characteristics of WOC feminist epistemology to the issue of improving young mothers' access to schools in order to illustrate the impacts of policy debt by those facing it as well as those charged with fixing it. Through this analysis, she asks the reader to question our responsibilities as policy studies scholars, to consider what we are doing to face and respond to our policy debt, and to examine the tools we are using to disrupt and perform praxis in policy settings.

4 Conclusion

[T]he undoubted value of these analyses lies in their attempt to problematize policy through several of its 'levels' or 'dimensions' or 'moments' of activity and effect; and in their insistence on continuing to ask basic sociological questions about the relationship between educational practices and social inequalities. (Ball 1994a, p. 2)

This book offers a window into the work of critical policy analysis. It captures a variety of theoretical and experiential perspectives, including perspectives drawn from critical theory, critical race theory, feminism, post-structuralism, and queer theory, among others, and it foregrounds the methodological implications of critical approaches to educational policy analysis. The methods used to explore questions emerging from these perspectives include discourse analysis, document analysis, historical approaches, in-depth interviews, and critical policy ethnography. We consider these pieces to be important exemplars of CPA and the efforts of CPA scholars to engage in critique, to interrogate the taken for granted, and to use social theory to reveal what otherwise might have been left unseen.

There are, without question, critical policy perspectives and research approaches that are not represented herein. The book is intended to serve as an introduction to critical policy analysis (CPA) for those less familiar to the approach, and as such, the contributing authors take care to articulate road maps for conducting CPA as they present their work. Thus, our focus is to promote depth of understanding of a slice of the critical policy work under way, rather than to survey the critical policy field comprehensively.

The weakness of much contemporary policy work lies in perspective—in a failure to explore outside the traditions of the field. Much educational policy work continues to operate inside traditional frameworks, while policy project designs, methods, analysis, and representations are generated by traditional assumptions, language, and politics. It is our hope that the work included in this volume will foster a break with tradition and assist educational scholars in their efforts to think, conceptualize, and analyze educational policy issues from critical perspectives.

References

Adams, D. (1991). Planning models and paradigms. In R. V. Carlson & G. Awkerman (Eds.), *Educational planning: Concepts, strategies, and practices* (pp. 5–20). New York: Longman.
Apple, M. (1982). *Education and power*. London: Routledge.
Atwood, E., & López, G. (2014). Let's be critically honest: Towards a messier counter story in critical race theory. *International Journal of Qualitative Studies in Education, 27*(9), 1134–1154.
Ball, S. J. (1991). *Politics and policy making in education*. London: Routledge.
Ball, S. J. (1993). What is policy? Texts, trajectories, and toolboxes. *Discourse: Studies in the Cultural Politics of Education, 13*(2), 10–17.
Ball, S. J. (1994a). At the cross-roads: Education policy studies. *British Journal of Educational Studies, 42*(1), 1–5.
Ball, S. J. (1994b). *Education reform: A critical and post-structural approach*. Buckingham: Open University Press.
Ball, S. J. (1998). Big policies/small world: An introduction to international perspectives in education policy. *Comparative Education, 34*(2), 119–130.
Ball, S. J. (2008). New philanthropy, new networks and new governance in education. *Political Studies, 56*, 747–765.
Ball, S. J., & Junemann, C. (2012). *Networks, new governance and education*. Bristol: Policy Press.
Becker, G. (1986). The economic approach to human behavior. In J. Elster (Ed.), *Rational choice* (pp. 108–122). Oxford: Basil Blackwell.
Brewer, C. A. (2008). *Interpreting the policy past: The relationship between education and antipoverty policy during the Carter administration*. Unpublished doctoral dissertation, The University of Texas at Austin, Austin, TX.
Brewer, C. A. (2014). Historicizing in critical policy analysis: The production of cultural histories and microhistories. *International Journal of Qualitative Studies in Education, 27*(3), 273–288.
Carpenter, B. W., Diem, S., & Young, M. D. (2014). The influence of values and policy vocabularies on understandings of leadership effectiveness. *International Journal of Qualitative Studies in Education, 27*(9), 1110–1113.
Danermark, B., Ekstrom, M., Jakobsen, L., & Karlsson, J. C. (2002). *Explaining society: Critical realism in the social sciences*. New York: Routledge.
deLeon, P., & Vogenback, D. M. (2007). The policy sciences at a crossroads. In F. Fischer, G. J. Miller, & M. S. Sidney (Eds.), *Handbook of public policy analysis: Theory, politics, and methods* (pp. 3–14). Boca Raton: Taylor & Francis Group.

Denzin, N. K., & Lincoln, Y. S. (2005). Introduction: The discipline and practice of qualitative research. In N. K. Denzin & Y. S. Lincoln (Eds.), *The SAGE handbook of qualitative research* (3rd ed., pp. 1–32). Thousand Oaks: Sage.

Diem, S., Young, M. D., Welton, A. D., Mansfield, K. C., & Lee, P. (2014). The intellectual landscape of critical policy analysis. *International Journal of Qualitative Studies in Education, 27*(9), 1068–1090.

Dunn, W. N. (1994). *Public policy analysis: An introduction*. Englewood Cliffs: Prentice Hall.

Fischer, F. (2003). *Reframing public policy: Discursive politics and deliberative practice*. New York: Oxford University Press.

Flyvbjerg, B. (1998). *Rationality and power: Democracy in practice*. Chicago: The University of Chicago Press.

Hajer, M. A. (2003). A frame in the fields: Policymaking and the reinvention of politics. In M. A. Hajer & H. Wagenaar (Eds.), *Deliberative policy analysis: Understanding governance in the network society* (pp. 88–112). Cambridge: Cambridge University Press.

Hajer, M. A. (2005). Rebuilding ground zero: The politics of performance. *Planning Theory and Practice, 6*(4), 445–464.

Hajer, M. A. (2006). Doing discourse analysis: Coalitions, practices, meaning. In M. van den Brink & T. Metze (Eds.), *Words matter in policy and planning: Discourse theory and method in the social science* (pp. 65–74). Utrecht: Koninklijk Nederlands Aardrijkskundig Genootschap.

Levin, H. M. (1988). Cost-effectiveness and educational policy. *Educational Evaluation and Policy Analysis, 10*(1), 51–69.

Levinson, B. A. U. (2005). Programs for democratic citizenship education in Mexico's Ministry of Education: Local appropriations of global cultural flows. *Indiana Journal of Global and Legal Studies, 12*(1), 251–284.

Levinson, B. A. U., Sutton, M., & Winstead, T. (2009). Education policy as a practice of power: Theoretical tools, ethnographic methods, democratic options. *Educational Policy, 23*(6), 767–795.

Lipman, P. (2004). *High stakes education: Inequality, globalization, and urban school reform*. New York: RoutledgeFalmer.

Lugg, C. A., & Murphy, J. P. (2014). Thinking whimsically: Queering the study of educational policy-making and politics. *International Journal of Qualitative Studies in Education, 27*(9), 1183–1204.

Mansfield, K. C., Welton, A. D., & Grogan, M. (2014). "Truth or consequences": A feminist critical policy analysis of the STEM crisis. *International Journal of Qualitative Studies in Education, 27*(9), 1155–1182.

Marshall, C. (1997). Dismantling and reconstructing policy analysis. In C. Marshall (Ed.), *Feminist critical policy analysis: A perspective from primary and secondary schooling* (pp. 1–39). London: The Falmer Press.

Marshall, C., & Young, M. D. (2013). Policy inroads undermining women in education. *International Journal of Leadership in Education, 16*(2), 205–219.

McDonnell, L. M. (2009). A political science perspective in education policy analysis. In G. Sykes, B. Schneider, & D. N. Plank (Eds.), *Handbook of education policy research* (pp. 57–70). New York: Routledge.

Mosen-Lowe, L. A. J., Vidovich, L., & Chapman, A. (2009). Students "at-risk" policy: Competing social and economic discourses. *Journal of Education Policy, 24*(4), 461–476.

Nagel, S. S. (1984). *Contemporary public policy analysis*. Birmingham: The University of Alabama Press.

Popkewitz, T. S. (1997). A changing terrain of knowledge and power: A social epistemology of educational research. *Educational Researcher, 26*(9), 18–29.

Popkewitz, T. S. (Ed.). (2000). *Educational knowledge: Changing relationships between the state, civil society, and the educational community*. Albany: State University of New York Press.

Rhodes, R. A. W. (1997). *Understanding governance: Policy networks, governance, reflexivity and accountability*. Buckingham: Open University Press.

Rist, R. (1994). Influencing the policy process with qualitative research. In N. K. Denzin & Y. S. Lincoln (Eds.), *Handbook of qualitative research* (pp. 545–557). Thousand Oaks: Sage.

Street, S. (2001). When politics becomes pedagogy: Oppositional discourse as policy in Mexican teachers' struggles for union democracy. In M. Sutton & B. A. U. Levinson (Eds.), *Policy as practice: Toward a comparative sociocultural analysis of educational policy* (pp. 145–166). Westport: Ablex.

Taylor, S. (1997). Critical policy analysis: Exploring contexts, text and consequences. *Discourse: Studies in the Cultural Politics of Education, 18*(1), 23–35.

Troyna, B. (1994). Reforms, research, and being reflexive about being reflective. In B. Troyna & D. Halpin (Eds.), *Researching education policy: Ethical and methodological issues* (pp. 1–14). London: Falmer.

Weaver-Hightower, M. B. (2008). An ecology metaphor for educational policy analysis: A call to complexity. *Educational Researcher, 37*(3), 153–167.

Weimer, D., & Vining, A. R. (2011). *Policy analysis*. Upper Saddle River: Longman.

Winton, S., & Brewer, C. A. (2014). People for Education: A critical policy analysis. *International Journal of Qualitative Studies in Education, 27*(9), 1091–1109.

Wolcott, H. F. (1994). *Transforming qualitative data: Description, analysis, and interpretation*. Thousand Oaks: Sage Publications, Inc.

Young, M. D. (1999). Multifocal educational policy research: Toward a method for enhancing traditional educational policy studies. *American Educational Research Journal, 36*(4), 677–714.

Young, M. D. (2003). The leadership crisis: Gender and the shortage of school administrators. In M. D. Young & L. Skrla (Eds.), *Reconsidering feminist research in educational leadership* (pp. 265–278). Albany: SUNY Press.

Young, M. D., & Diems, S. (2014). Putting critical theoretical perspectives to work in educational policy. *International Journal of Qualitative Studies in Education, 27*(9), 1063–1067.

Part I
Emphasis on Methods

> It is time now to worry about something that has been implicit throughout the discussion of methodology... those mysterious procedures by which you transform what you see and hear into intelligible accounts. (Agar 1980, p. 189)

By comparison with the numerous texts on policy analysis, few focus on critical policy analysis or more qualitative approaches to policy analysis and interpretation. Given the varied approaches to this work, one might reasonably expect a number of texts charting these processes.

The chapters included in part one represent critical policy work that emphasize the methods of CPA, though what makes an analysis count as more methodological than theoretical is not only a matter of degree but one of opinion. Depending on one's readings of these pieces, they could certainly be recategorized as each piece emphasizes the connection between theory and method. Different researchers have different purposes, and to achieve these different purposes, they may utilize different approaches and types of analysis.

Before moving forward, it is important to differentiate the analysis in critical policy analysis from traditional notions of analysis, wherein analysis reflect a rather perfunctory use of theory and a concern for being correct. Rather, critical policy analysis straddles the line between theory-based analysis and interpretation.

> I do not jump to broad or aesthetically satisfying interpretations unless I feel I have a handle on my topic. My interpretations are never offered as mere conjecture. To my own satisfaction, I personally must believe that I am almost getting it right, but it is not the sam kind of rightness that is associated with [traditional] analytical claims-making. (Wolcott 1994, p. 175)

How chapter authors approached their critical analytical-interpretive work, like the methods they used to gather their data, differed depending on their theoretical frameworks and research purpose.

The chapters included in this part, which were described in greater detail in the introduction, present six different methodological approaches to CPA. In reverse order, Chap. 7, "A Feminist Critical Policy Analysis of Patriarchy in Leadership," Marshall, Johnson, and Edwards use a discourse analysis approach informed by feminist critical theory to to uncover and deconstruct masculine tropes within dominant narratives on educational leadership. Also using a form of discourse analysis, Fernández and López, in Chap. 6, problematize the current discourse around traditional norms of parental involvement in schools. In conducting their analysis, they employ tools from Critical Race Theory and Latino Critical Race Theory, specifically the concept of counter-stories, which differentiates their use of discourse analysis from Marshall and her colleagues who focus on hegemony.

Similarly, in Chap. 4, "Public Educational Policy as Performance: A Queer Analysis," O'Malley and Long, use a content analysis approach to read and reread print media articles that reported on the development and implementation of a policy focused on domestic partnership benefits, inclusive of same sex couples. As they mapped the process through which the policy was negotiated and adopted, they used queer theory to problematize normalizing assumptions embedded within the policy documents as well as the media articles concerning the policy in question.

In contrast, in Chap. 5, Welton, Harris, Williams and Altamirano analyze "The Politics of Student Voice: Conceptualizing a Model for Critical Analysis," through direct engagement. As participant observers, the student and faculty team, analyzed documents, conducted interviews, and conducted participant observations in an effort to both work for school improvement and transformation and to explore how institutionalized structures, practices and hierarchies of power impede students' attempts to have their voices heard when it comes to school improvement decisions. Also using interviews, observations and the examination of policy documents, Diem, in Chap. 3, shares a critical policy analysis of three present-day school district desegregation policies. Diem pays particular attention to the relationship of the politics surrounding student assignment policies (local, state, and federal) and the design and implementation districts' policies.

Finally, in Chap. 2, Young and Reynolds, outline three critical policy studies focused on State Boards of Education, each of which suggests a different methodological approach. The first study, which involves a historical analysis of state boards highlights the utility of discourse analysis and engaging in comparative case studies. The second study, which focuses on the individuals who serve on state boards, suggests content analyses of policy and media documents as well as interviews. The third project, which positions board members as policy actors, emphasizes the utility of interviews, discourse analysis, and network analysis.

This book is based on our experiences as researchers and teachers, which has involved doing and teaching about a variety of qualitative methods for conducting research on policy and practice. Our work has persuaded us of the value of exemplars that provide insight into how research unfolds. Specifically, it is helpful to not only read quite a few strong examples of this work but also to read pieces that open up the black box of critical policy methodology. The pieces included in this part of the book strive to make clear the methods used to produce their findings and arrive at their conclusions.

References

Agar, M. H. (1980). *The professional stranger: An informal introduction to ethnography.* New York: Academic.

Wolcott, H. F. (1994). *Transforming qualitative data: Description, analysis, and interpretation.* Thousand Oaks: Sage Publications, Inc.

Critically Examining Policy Workers and Policy Work Within State Boards of Education

Michelle D. Young and Amy Luelle Reynolds

Abstract This chapter outlines a set of critical policy studies focused on State Boards of Education, a policy entity that has received extremely little attention from the research community, traditional and critical alike. The chapter opens with an overview of research that has been conducted on state boards, the majority of which is offered through a traditional perspective. The remainder of the chapter is divided into three sections that outline inquiry projects focused on state boards. The first sub-section outlines a critical historical analysis, a core strategy of critical theorists interested in the historical roots and evolution of institutions, norms, and beliefs. The second sub-section explores how critical feminist theory could be used to examine the power and authority of state boards and individual members. The third sub-section suggests an analysis of state boards as policy actors, including governing models, policy roles, responsibilities and authorities, and policy actor interactions and networks.

Keywords Methods • Theory • Data sources • Historical analysis • Critical feminism • Critical ethnography

1 Introduction

When headlines like "Texas State Board of Education Candidate is a Creationist Who Thinks Obama Was a 'Male Prostitute'" scroll across one's computer, one might wonder who sits on state boards of education, how they obtain their positions, and what kind of influence they wield on education in their state (Mehta 2016). Interestingly, a thorough review of the research literature in education yields little more than superficial answers to such questions. State Boards of Education (SBOEs), we found, are significantly underrepresented within the educational research literature. Even within sub-fields that focus on the politics of and policy in education, SBOEs make only minor appearances. Why is that?

M.D. Young (✉) • A.L. Reynolds
Curry School of Education, University of Virginia, Charlottesville, VA, USA
e-mail: mdy8n@virginia.edu

© Springer International Publishing Switzerland 2017
M.D. Young, S. Diem (eds.), *Critical Approaches to Education Policy Analysis*,
Education, Equity, Economy 4, DOI 10.1007/978-3-319-39643-9_2

SBOEs are described in many state constitutions as policy making entities; however, few state boards engage in policy making directly. State constitutions and state statutes, which set the legal basis for SBOEs, are wildly diverse across the US, meaning that state governance of education is diverse as well. Nonetheless, all but three of the 50 states (Minnesota, New Mexico, and Wisconsin) and the District of Columbia currently have state boards, and in the majority of cases, the efforts of state boards are overshadowed by state legislators, governors and chief state school officers.

State boards are located in a critical nexus between the public and legislators, governors, and state agencies. Although each board is unique and its structure and function has been subject to different sets of changes and limitations, in some states they wield a significant source of influence over public education. The Kansas Evolution Hearings that took place from May 5–12, 2005, and the Texas state boards' revision of the state's social studies curriculum in 2010, serve as excellent examples of how a state board can implement policies that dramatically alter what educators are authorized to teach in their classrooms (Klein 2015; Slevin 2005). Nonetheless, few scholars have engaged in close examinations of these entities, their make up, or the broader implications of their influence over time.

This chapter places state boards in the center of a larger set of questions on Critical Policy Analysis (CPA), including: How is CPA done? What questions does it engage? What counts as a CPA framework? As such, this chapter attempts to demystify both CPA and state boards by thinking through the design of several critical policy analyses of SBOEs. In his book, *Transforming Qualitative Data*, Harry Wolcott (1994) uses the analogy of "*postholing*" to describe the difficulty of teaching about qualitative methods (p. 381). Like Wolcott, faced "with the inevitable challenges of too much to take in and too little in the way of available resources or time," we have chosen to focus on three approaches to the study of SBOEs (p. 381). Subsequent chapters in this book then provide additional examples of CPA, utilizing a wide variety of theories and methods.

2 Why State Boards of Education?

A comprehensive search of educational databases (e.g. EBSCO, Google Scholar, Web of Science, and the Sage Collection) using search terms including "state boards of education," "state education agencies," "chief state school officers," and "state governance" yielded few studies that substantively addressed SBOEs, and the majority of pieces we did locate were derived from organizational reports from the 1990s or earlier. Furthermore, many of the studies we identified simply aimed to catalog information about the structural features of SBOEs, and almost all of the studies were descriptive, going no further than charting the structure, authority or make up of boards. For example, an article by Kysilko (2011) in a National Association of State Boards of Education (NASBE) publication provides an overview of SBOE history and their roles in education policy. The first SBOEs,

Kysilko noted, emerged in the early 1800s as citizen groups organized at the state level for the purpose of administering public education. However, as Kysilko (2011) and Timar (1997) attest, SBOEs have evolved a great deal since this time.

In addition to charting the history of state boards, efforts have been made to understand the roles, governance models, and influence of state boards. The earliest robust study of SBOEs we identified was Campbell and Mazzoni's (1974) report for the Educational Governance Project (1972–1974) at Ohio State University, funded by the US Office of Education. The researchers purposefully selected 12 states and examined the governance models used in each state as well as the purpose and influence of the board. Other researchers, similarly mapped the governance models used in each of the states, including the McCarthy et al. (1993) ECS report on this topic. Finally, several scholars, including Henig (2013), have included SBOEs within broader examinations of trends in educational governance.

Our review of the literature revealed that, when SBOEs have been examined, the studies have utilized a traditional, realist perspective. The literature on SBOEs takes their existence and purpose for granted, it describes and categorizes, but seldom questions the claim that SBOEs serve an important representative function within public education. Rarely do scholars interrogate the purpose of state boards and whether they are fulfilling their purpose. Moreover, scholars seldom critically examine the people who populate state boards or interrogate their background or selection for the board, or make the public aware of the work in which these boards are engaged. In fact, the paucity of literature focused on SBOEs would indicate that very few questions are asked about them at all, making SBOEs one of the most understudied policy making entities in the field of education.

In contrast to the research community, the media has taken a fairly strong interest in the work of state boards, particularly the role of state boards in setting curriculum standards. For example, a Google search for "news coverage of state boards of education, 2015" yielded over 20,900,000[1] results and Burnette (2016) of *Education Week* frequently covers the work of SBOEs in its State EdWatch blog. Many of the news stories focused on the boards' approval of new state tests, curriculum standards, and accountability systems; the membership of the board or their choice of a new chief state school officer; or clashes concerning state standards or who controls state departments. What is clear from the media coverage is state boards are involved in shaping the public education system across the US, which makes them an appropriate of focus of critical policy inquiry.

In this chapter, we map a CPA agenda focused on SBOEs. The agenda we suggest approaches SBOEs from multiple critical perspectives and suggests a variety of data collection and analysis approaches, highlighting relationships "between theory 'in the clouds' and empirical materials 'on the ground'" (Weis and Fine 2004, p. xvi)

---

[1] This search was conducted on April 10, 2016. Approximately 30 % of the results pointed to news posted on SBOE websites.

that have the potential to reveal more about the nature and impact of these little-understood state level policy entities. As such this chapter provides a guide not only to the study of SBOEs but also for designing a critical policy analysis project. We begin our project with an overview of CPA as we understand and make use of it, and then we move into a discussion of the methods used by critical policy scholars. Subsequently, we present several approaches to the critical analysis of the work, membership, and influence of SBOEs.

3 Critical Policy Analysis: Theory and Method

- What is CPA?
- How is CPA done?
- What questions does CPA engage?
- What counts as a CPA framework?

These questions prompted the development of this book as well as the contents of this specific chapter. Although as Diem and Young (2015) point out "Critical policy analysis is not a homogeneous movement in social science" (p. 839), the scholarship associated with this genre have a number of discernable attributes. Nonetheless, the range of critical policy strategies is broad as are the frameworks used by critical policy scholars.

CPA scholars have drawn on a variety of critical perspectives and methods in their exploration of policies, policy contexts, policy processes, policy communities, and policy impact. Examples include Marshall (1997) and Taylor's (1997) use of discourse theory to critically examine educational policy and its impact; Young's (2003) critical analysis of state-level policy work on Iowa's leadership crisis; Maguire's (2007) examination of gender and movement in social policy; and Braun et al. (2011) research on policy enactments. More recent examples include Ball and Junemann's (2012) examination of new philanthropies and policy networks in educational policymaking; Winton and Brewer's (2014) use of microhistory and cultural history to analyze policy relevant political events; Carpenter et al. (2014) analysis of federal and state policy vocabularies; and Mansfield et al. (2014) critical feminist analysis of STEM policies in education.

Importantly, while the work of CPA scholars is not homogenous, there are distinguishable themes. Diem et al. (2014) identified five such themes, including an interest in:

1. The difference between policy rhetoric and practiced reality;
2. Policy, its roots, and its development (e.g., how it emerged, what problems it was intended to solve, how it changed and developed over time, and its role in reinforcing the dominant culture);
3. The distribution of power, resources, and knowledge and the creation of policy "winners" and "losers;"

4. Social stratification and the broader effects of policy on relationships of inequality and privilege; and
5. The nature of resistance to or engagement in policy by members of non-dominant groups. (Diem et al. 2014)

In undertaking such work, critical policy researchers rely on theoretical perspectives informed by poststructural frameworks, critical theory, feminist theories, queer theories, and critical race perspectives, among others.

Diem and Young (2015) identified several other commonalities among the work of critical policy analysts, including a focus on the relationship between theory and method. According to Young (1999), the "research frame one uses dictates, to a large extent, the way one identifies and describes policy problems, the way one researches these problems, the policy options one considers, the approach one takes to policy implementation, and the approach taken for policy evaluation" (Young 1999, p. 681). In other words, the theory one uses to explore a given research problem, has significant implications for the way the researcher thinks about the problem; it impacts the questions that s/he asks and the methods used to investigate those questions (Diem et al. 2014; Diem and Young 2015; Young 1999).

This is not to say that there is a specific critical policy method. According to Morrow and Brown (1994), "the selection of methodological techniques is not deterministic" (p. 200). Indeed, CPA scholars use a variety of data collection strategies, as demonstrated through the chapters in this book, including: observations, interviews, key informant testimonies, mass media analysis, document analysis, examination of statistical databases, and literature reviews. However, while there is no a priori rejection of nor a requirement for any particular method or technique, there are methodological affinities. Indeed, CPA scholars, given the nature of their policy questions and perspectives, are more likely to use qualitative research approaches than quantitative approaches, which provide an opportunity for deeper engagement with their research subject (e.g., persons, policies, discourses) (deLeon and Vogenback 2007; Denzin and Lincoln 2005; Morrow and Brown 1994).

According to Diem and Young (2015) "concentrated looking," which involves the collection and examination of "contextualizing information, policy texts, observations and interviews," is a distinguishing feature of CPA (p. 845). Similarly, Bowe et al. (1994) argue that critical policy scholars "look in a more concentrated fashion and question what is happening... to reveal and critically assess the 'carefully managed, prescribed viewpoints' that may be emerging" (p. 76). Critical analytical techniques often include historical reconstruction, deconstruction, ethnographic interpretation, and theory-based analysis. Paired with these analytic techniques, critical scholars also engage in self-reflexive practices and discursive reading and re-reading of data, the intent of which is to interrogate not only the data but their own sense-making. Through such techniques, critical scholars engage in "intensive explication," which involves questioning the taken-for-granted, interrogating policy constructions, searching for epistemological roots, and identifying and explaining deep patterns by "empirically lifting into view the underlying semantic, socio-cultural, and structural relations that are constitutive of historically unique actors, mediations, and systems" (Morrow and Brown 1994, p. 212).

4 Critical Policy Analysis Approaches to the Study of SBOEs

> The problem here is not so much that some methods are intrinsically "appropriate" and others not, so much as "what is or isn't appropriate can only be decided by reference to judgments about the nature of the thing to be explained." (Sayer 1992, p. 232)

We opened this chapter by pointing to the lack of research, particularly critical research, focused on state boards. From the existing literature on SBOEs we have learned that the first SBOEs emerged in the early 1800s as citizen groups organized at the state level for the purpose of administering public education (Kysilko 2011). However, their authority was limited due to the strong tradition of democratic localism that pervaded public education at the time. This appeared to change following World War I (WWI), when district consolidation and the professionalization of careers in education led to greater centralization in education, and a more significant role for SBOEs. At this time, there was little decision-making competition for the board.

While the majority of reports we identified included fairly simple reviews of SBOE data, some also contributed more analytical sense making based on the politics, values and concerns of a given time period. For example, Beach and Will (1955) and Deffenbaugh and Keesecker (1940) noted that the role of SBOEs changed following World War II (WWII) as outside groups took interest in education, namely as a means of bolstering national defense at the outset of the Cold War. These authors note that the language and tone used to discuss the purpose of SBOEs, and education writ large, from this era make apparent the sense of urgency around education to protect American ideals. Later educational historians suggest that this influx of outside interest in education policy may have marked the beginning of a sea change in education governance. In his book, *The End of Exceptionalism in American Education*, Henig (2013) proposed that the special legal status of educational policy entities like SBOEs, intentionally insulated from politics and general-purpose government, gradually eroded, followed by the emergence of "education governors," the increasing role of the federal government in education, and the creation of new education positions and committees, which have often take on powers previously held by SBOEs and chief state school officers (CSSOs).

These historical studies provide useful information about state boards. These accounts, however, are caught, as any story is caught, within a particular way of viewing the world, actors, purpose, need, etc. "The paradigm through which policy studies operates involves time-worn assumptions, norms, and traditions that have been institutionalized and thus are accepted by most researchers as the appropriate way to undertake educational policy research" (Young 1999, p. 678). As such, traditional historical accounts of SBOEs, such as those shared above, were "garnered through a confined and circumscribed grouping of and method" and, thus, are able to present only partial stories–stories that do not critique, stories that consider policy problems to be natural, stories that view policy work as value-free, stories that "view the knowledge necessary for planning and evaluation as obtainable, objective, and communicable" (Young 1999, p. 678).

As argued above and as evident throughout this book, there are a variety of perspectives and methods that are put to work by critical policy scholars. In CPA, like in many research approaches, a research design connects a study's focal issue, to the selection of theory, the development of research questions, and the identification of data collection methods and analytic procedures. What differentiates CPA from traditional policy analysis, is the way methods are used through the application of critical theoretical perspectives. The choice of theory, as discussed previously in this chapter and elsewhere in this book is significantly influenced if not determined by one's own positionality. As Young (1999) argued, "one cannot assume to be able to transcend one's own positionality, that one's social location has an epistemologically significant impact" on one's scholarship, including the theoretical perspectives and methods one chooses to employ (Young 1999, p. 691). In the following three subsections, we present several critical approaches to researching the work, membership, and influence of SBOEs. Although, we have sought to be expansive in the options we present, we recognize that our own epistemological positionalities and the accompanying interests, values, and perspectives circumscribe the options we outline.

4.1 A Critical Historical Analysis of SBOEs

The first study we suggest in exploring SBOEs is a critical historical analysis. Critical historical analysis, a mainstay of critical theorists, is employed to identify the historical roots of institutional and cultural factors, the interactions that brought them in existence and shaped them, as well as their changes over time. For SBOEs they offer the opportunity to examine why they were developed, what function(s) they were intended to serve, how those functions changed overtime, whether the functions they served reflected their purpose, and what factors shaped the development of SBOEs. Importantly, one wouldn't need to reach back to the very origins of SBOEs to conduct a critical historical analysis; on the contrary one could use critical historical approach to consider a contemporary change or development, such as the 1999 dissolution of the SBOE in Minnesota (Stout and Stevens 2002). Regardless, by contextualizing one's inquiry within the political, economic and social contexts during which a policy organization was imagined, developed and/or transformed, one can gain a deeper understanding of the organization and its purpose(s).

Many scholars who engage in critical historical discourse analysis have been inspired by the writings of Michel Foucault, whose work involved an attempt to understand how objects (e.g., beliefs, practices, policies) were constituted at any given time due to the intersection of discourses, institutions, and other forces (Kendall and Wickham 1998; Scheurich and McKenzie 2005). Although, Foucault did not suggest a definite set of methodological strategies, a number of scholars have used his work to craft methodological approaches, many of which involve the analysis and interpretation of texts within their historical contexts in order to gain insight into the constitution of specific subjects and objects (e.g., Ball 1994; Scheurich 1994).

However, the historical methodologies drawn from Foucault's work represent only a facet of critical approaches to historical analysis, just as they represent only a facet of Foucault's influence. Others draw from traditional critical theory, feminist theory, critical race perspectives, and neo-institutional perspectives. In each case, the selection of theoretical framework impacts the refinement of the research problem and questions and the methods used to investigate those questions (Diem et al. 2014; Diem and Young 2015; Young 1999). For example, Brewer (2014) examined historical factors that structured possibilities for educational equity. Whereas the majority of research within education considers issues of educational equity as currently operating, with little mention of preceding historical contexts and issues, Brewer's research utilized a critical historical approach to inform current research and discourse. Specifically, Brewer sought to understand the viability of a contemporary pairing of education and anti-poverty policy in schools by investigating the historical disintegration of the link between education and anti-poverty policy.

The perspective that a researcher adopts has significant epistemological and methodological implications. According to Fischer (2003), for example, critical discourse analysis operates under the assumption that actions, objects, and practices are socially constructed and are shaped by the social and political context of a historically specific time period. Another take on discourse analysis is exemplified by Fairclough (1992), who delineates a post-structural conception of discourse. According to Fairclough the analyst examines the text, the process by which the text is created, and the sociohistorical conditions under which it was created. Using Fairclough's approach to explore, for example, the establishment SBOEs or the expansion or contraction of SBOE authority would allow a researcher to scrutinize data sources in terms of contextual factors like power and conflict.

A number of principles are considered essential to discourse studies, including:

- Discourse should be studied in talk and text,
- Discourse should be studied as a constitutive part of its local and global, social, and cultural contexts,
- Discourse studies should focus on the analysis of ongoing informal and formal verbal dialogue,
- Discourse includes both the social and written forms of social practice in sociocultural contexts,
- Discourse studies should consider the ways social members interpret, orient to and categorize the properties of their social world,
- The influence of discourse should be understood from a linear and sequential perspective,
- Constitutive units of discourse may be functionally used, understood, or analyzed as elements of larger ones,

- Discourse analysis should theoretically decompose discursive layers of discourse while connecting relationships between various levels of discourse,
- Discourse analysis should search for meaning and functional implications,
- Discourse should be recognized as rule governed, though rule violation should also be examined,
- Discourse reveals the use of strategies to realize social goals, and
- The sociocultural representations embedded in language play a fundamental role in discourse (Van Dijk 1993).

According to Carpenter (2011), the addition of discourse analysis to a critical interpretative policy framework helps reframe the actions of political actors by providing an often-neglected understanding of how discourses interact with the practices of policy making. By examining textual material derived from the work of SBOEs (e.g., minutes, policies, etc.) as well as about SBOEs (e.g., news sources, governmental sources, etc.), a CPA scholar could explore a variety of questions concerning the role SBOEs were originally intended to serve, the arguments made in support of their development, the values and beliefs embedded in such intentions and arguments, the needs they were intended to address, the work in which they engaged, and the impact of their development (both in terms of their work as well as their mere existence). Furthermore, following Brewer's (2014) methods, one could use critical discourse analysis to explore the relationships between earlier SBOE developments and one or more current issues or developments.

The initial phases of this project could involve comparisons across states or examinations of SBOEs longitudinally. Such analytical work would require sources that allow one to examine state policy texts establishing SBOEs and any subsequent texts outlining changes to these policy organizations. Such work would also benefit from data sources that reveal the intentions and rhetoric that influenced the organization and its work, such as policy memos and reports, news articles, and other archival materials. A variety of available sources provide glimpses into such developments as well as the values and beliefs that influenced these policy making bodies as well as the language and symbolism that was used to communicate about SBOEs and their work. In chronological order, the following list includes sources that could serve as a starting place for a policy discourse analysis concerning SBOEs:

- Howerth (1913) – This report was produced prior to WWI report on behalf of the Department of Information and Social Welfare,
- Deffenbaugh and Keesecker (1940) – This report was generated between the two world wars on the status and legal powers of SBOEs and CSSOs for the US Office of Education,
- Keesecker (1950) – This is a post-WWII reprisal of a previous report, and provides an interesting opportunity to see how the same authors' discourse around the same topic transformed over time,
- CCSSO (1953) – This organizational report includes recommendations for SBOE structure and function and is an early example of the influence of professional organizations, later authors suggest that these recommendations influenced subsequent SBOE structural changes,

- Beach and Will (1955) – This report was developed for the US Office of Education on the structure of public education at the state level, steeped in language that reflect the Cold War era,
- Fuller and Pearson (1969a) – This CCSSO report details the histories of state education governance, with each entry written by a high ranking state education official, and
- Badarak (1990) – This report reflects the increasing role of outside influences on SBOEs and education policy, and
- McCarthy et al. (1993) – Like the Badarak (1990) report, this report captures the increasing role of outside influences on education policy.

This list, which captures the SBOE as a policy making entity from its early years through the 1990s is not exhaustive, but it provides an overview of the kinds of resources a CPA scholar would want to review, along with original policy texts, for a critical historical analysis. At a minimum, they would enable one to examine the text, the process by which the text was created, and the sociohistorical conditions under which it was created (Fairclough 1992). Depending on one's specific research questions, one could also supplement these sources with oral history interviews, state-specific historical documents, and media resources. Brewer's (2014) work, for example, involved the analysis of data collected through life history interviews and documents archived in the Carter Presidential Library, demonstrates the complexity of educational politics and policy. Projects of this nature not only provide a historical sense of policy entities such as SBOEs, but they also peal back a layer or more of taken-for-granted assumptions about how and why such entities emerged, why they emerged as they did at a particular time, and why they developed as they did and with what impacts.

4.2 A Critical Feminist Examination of SBOEs

The second study we outline makes use of a critical feminist framework to examine the individuals who serve on state boards of education. The focus of critical feminist theory (Marshall and Young 2013; Young and Marshall 2013) is power and patriarchy. It is employed to highlight power sources that control and benefit dominant groups, through discourse and, the generation, legitimation, and interpretation of policy choices. It enables the search for how our thinking is mediated by historically constituted power relations. It enables the search for the embedded "facts" and assumptions that were once constructed, in some historical context, and then perpetuated as aspects of reality. It enables us to identify how some groups have gained and maintained privilege (Young and Marshall 2013). Unlike what most consider traditional perspectives of analysis, critical feminist analysis acknowledges context, group values, and the contestable nature of problem definition, research findings and policy solutions (Blackmore 1997; Fischer 2003; Marshall 1999; Rochefort and Cobb 1994). Critical feminist analysis focuses on arenas of power and dominance, like boards, courts, and legislators as well as on powerful policy artifacts (e.g., curriculum guidelines) and critical feminists ask questions such as:

what issues are identified as important, how problems are identified and defined, what counts as knowledge, and how policy is shaped, implemented, and interpreted?

Through feminist research in education, we have learned much about how gender inequalities have been created and structured within our systems, policies, and practices (Bell 1988; Skrla and Young 2003). Feminist research has documented the persistent underrepresentation of women in high-paying and/or prestigious educational leadership and policy positions, it has charted the persistent failure of educational policy makers to address gender issues in their work, and it has demonstrated how the combination of gender and race intensify issues of inequity (Skrla and Young 2003). For SBOEs, the critical feminist framework offers the opportunity to explore the make up of state boards of education, how this has changed over time, and who boards actually represent as well as what communities are left with little or no representation. As Flax (1990) argued, feminist theory focuses on "how we think or, equally important, do not think about" gender issues and women (p. 40). Such questions open up further opportunities to explore the networks that influence board members and the relationship, if any, between those networks and the issues upon which board members focus.

By examining historical data on state boards of education (e.g., policies, state board records, NASBE reports), a CPA scholar would be able to explore a variety questions concerning the membership of SBOEs. For example, using Howerth (1913), Beach and Will (1955), and NASBE (2015b), one could examine trends in the requirements for SBOE membership. Such an examination would reveal a variety of requirements in terms of gender, race, religion, political party affiliation, and level of education as well as what kinds of factors (e.g., serving as a religious leader or public school teacher) made one ineligible for service on the state board. SBOE member requirements could be compared across states during these specific time periods, or one could take a specific state and examine requirements for membership over time. For example, one could begin with the Beach and Will's finding that in 1955 Hawaii limited women's appointments on the SBOE to no more than three of the fifteen members at any given time.

Requirements for SBOE members are typically codified in state statue, which would enable one to review published state codes over time. Then, using critical feminist theory, one could then explore what contextual factors appeared to be influencing requirements, whether such requirements were reflected in other public sector leadership positions, and what language was used to discuss such requirements. In examining the requirements for board participation one would also be identifying the discourses of exclusion that emerge. That is, in developing understanding and agreement around preferred candidates for SBOE positions, those influencing these policies also excluded other groups (Flax 1990; Young 1999, 2003). Choices about who is fit to govern and who is not, are based on beliefs and assumptions concerning gender, race, education, socio-economic status, age, etc. These assumptions, according to critical feminist theory, reflect dominant (i.e., White, middle-class, male) perspectives (Ferguson 1984; Marshall 1994; Young and Marshall 2013). It is worth noting, based on our review of SBOE materials, we found very few states with explicit requirements concerning gender or racial diversity. Exceptions include New Jersey which required at least three women be on the SBOE as early as the 1950s, and as of the McCarthy et al. 1993 report for ECS, only Tennessee required at least one member from a minority racial group, though NASBE's (2015b) report did not reconfirm Tennessee's requirement. The absence of gender and race as criteria could be interpreted in a variety of ways, including as another example of the discourse of exclusion (Young 2003).

In addition to examining the requirements, one could also look into the demographics of board members over time to determine how well they represented the state population. As Henig (2013) noted, who governs "is not important for its own sake. From the data available on SBOEs it is clear that the board lacks representativeness of the state's school population, however, the degree to which this is the case and the impact of the SBOEs lack of representation requires further exploration. It is important because it affects who has influence over what governments do and how they do it" (p. 119). It also influences what they care about, what they pay attention to, and what they work to achieve. Building on those findings, one could conduct a network analysis of one or more state boards to determine the types of communities, organizations, or individuals exerting influence on board members and their work. Few researchers have examined the networks of state board members, though McCarthy et al. (1993) did provide a state-by-state review of the relationships among the SBOE members, the state superintendent, governor, state legislature, and the electorate.

Subsequently, one would want to explore the work of state boards. Such analyses would be helpful not only to gain a sense of the work of individual boards across states or time periods, but they may provide insight into the influence of board members' networks. According to Young (2003), an analysis of SBOE work should explore not just what boards focused on but what they did not (i.e., the margins of their work and areas of silence). In her examination of the Iowa policy maker's deliberations concerning the leadership shortage, Young discovered three constructions of the leadership shortage, two of which were identified through what was explicitly included within policy discussions, while the third became evident "only when one examines the areas of silence in the policy discourse and the normalizations that made the emergence of this particular policy problem possible" (p. 267). Specifically, Young found that policy deliberations not only treated gender as a non-issue but also reinforced status quo beliefs about leadership and gender. Young's use of the critical-feminist framework highlighted the "incompleteness" of traditional policy analyses that take a neutral stance on issues of gender and other social categories (e.g., race, class, religion, level of education, ability).

Significantly, related to who serves on SBOEs is how they achieved their positions. By reviewing data from 12 primary and secondary sources, we were able to chart changes in how SBOE members were selected and by whom between 1913 and 2015 (NASBE 2012, 2015a, b; ECS 2006; McCarthy et al. 1993; Badarak 1990; CCSSO 1983; Harris 1973; Fuller and Pearson 1969a; Beach and Will 1955; Keesecker 1950; Deffenbaugh and Keesecker 1940; Howerth 1913). Figure 1, which

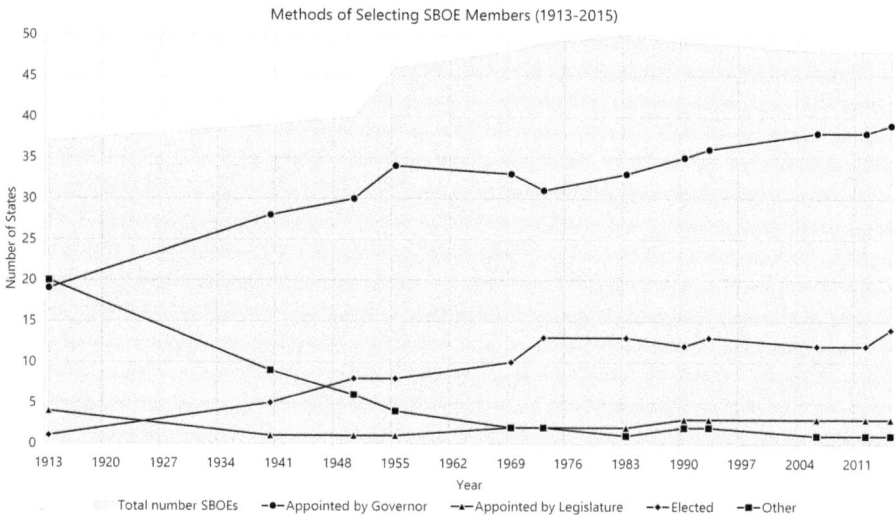

Fig. 1 The change in methods of selecting SBOE members between 1913 and 2015

captures these changes, shows how gubernatorial appointments have increased the most significantly over time. The grey area of Fig. 1 reflects the total number of SBOEs in the US during each specific time frame.

The rise in gubernatorial appointments, particularly compared to other methods for selecting state board members, raises important questions about how well state boards represent the broader state population, and could serve as a helpful way to cross reference findings concerning board demographics and members' networks. Furthermore, linking back to the critical historical analysis described in the previous section, one could also consider the changes in appointment as well as changes in the size of SBOEs (see Fig. 2) in terms of the politicization of the field of education (NASBE 2012, 2015b; ECS 2006; McCarthy et al. 1993; Badarak 1990; CCSSO 1983; Harris 1973; Fuller and Pearson 1969a; Beach and Will 1955; Keesecker 1950; Deffenbaugh and Keesecker 1940; Howerth 1913). Campbell and Mazzoni (1974), for example, observed the rise of governor involvement in education, with nine of the 12 state governors having included education in their 1970s campaign, marking the beginning of an increasing trend towards "education governors" (Henig 2013; Shober 2012).

Feminist critical policy analysis is concerned with the dimension of gender. However, a critical feminist examination of the membership of state boards of education and the ways in which board positions are typically filled is not only an examination of the strength and depth of the predominance of White, middle and upper class men in positions of power, it is foremost an examination of power, control, and dominance and the trail of inequities that such forces leave in their wake. Feminist research makes use of many of the same methodological

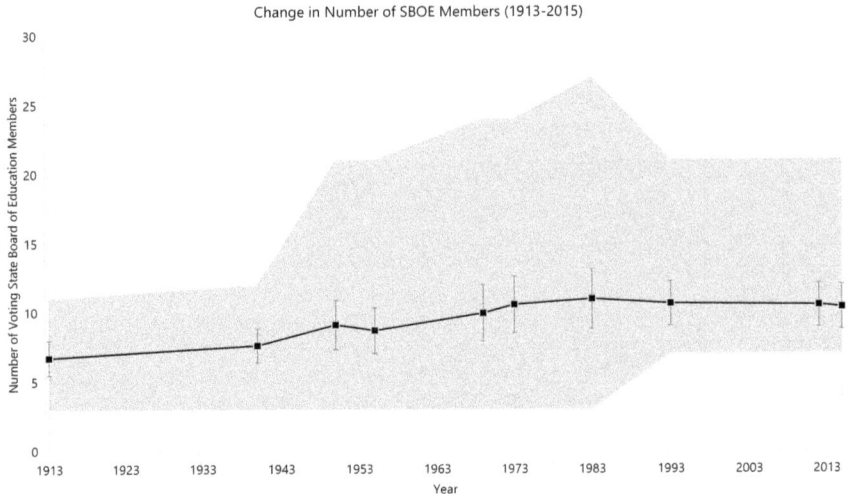

Fig. 2 Changes in the total number of voting SBOE members on SBOEs between 1913 and 2015. The *line* represents the average number of SBOE members, the bar reflects the standard deviation, and the *grey* area highlights the maximum and minimum numbers of SBOE members

tools as other frameworks (e.g., discourse analysis, interviews) in an effort to understand whose voices and perspectives are heard, what issues are identified as important, how some issues become defined as problems while others are ignored or considered of lesser importance, and how policy is developed. Finally, feminist critical policy analysis "advocates action that results in more equitable distribution of resources and opportunities for those who have been marginalized" (Grogan 2003, p. 18).

4.3 State Boards of Education as Policy Actors

The third study we outline makes use of a critical framework to examine SBOEs as policy actors. Thinking about SBOEs as policy actors, as Brewer does in his chapter, focuses attention not only on the power, authority, and policy making functions of state boards of education, but also on their actions and the discourses constructed through the performance(s) of their policy work. Examinations of SBOEs as policy actors, thus, offer the opportunity to explore what governing models have existed over time and across states and with what authority, what their specific policy roles and responsibilities are within the educational policy system, how they interact with other policy actors and networks, and to what end.

Of the three studies we have suggested, a focus on SBOEs as policy actors has received the most attention within the educational policy literature. The earliest robust study of SBOE governing models was Campbell and Mazzoni's (1974) research of 12 states. The study, which used comparative case methodology to analyze the data, and political systems and allocative theory as complementary theoretical lenses, found that although the intended purpose of SBOEs is education policymaking, they are limited in their influence on policymaking, in large part due to their reliance on state legislatures for access to monetary resources and on the CSSO for access to information. Only 28 % of the legislators Campbell and Mazzoni surveyed reported that SBOEs were important in forming education legislation, and the remainder reported that they were a minor influence (50 %) or not important at all (22 %).

Following the publication of Campbell and Mazzoni's study, we found no cross-state comparisons of SBOE influence; thus, it is unclear whether SBOEs continue to lack influence relative to other state educational policy making bodies or whether the level of influence is consistent across states. Furthermore, a critical analysis of SBOEs as policy actors would not rely solely on the perspectives of other policy workers in determining the power, influence, authority, and policy making functions of state boards. Rather, a critical policy scholar would investigate a variety of sources for insight into SBOEs as policy actors. Such investigations, however, can begin with more traditional literature, such as various studies focused on mapping the state educational governance models in which SBOEs operate.

The focus on education governance models continued in an Education Commission of the States (ECS) report by McCarthy et al. (1993). The study focused on organizational relationships and their change over time using surveys of state education policy makers, relevant state code, and reviews of education literature and news. The result is a detailed summary of the state level governance structures of all 50 states. The models suggested by McCarthy and her colleagues are similar to earlier reports (Badarak 1990; Sanchez and Hall 1987) and were repeated in NASBE and ECS reports in the years to follow. Figure 3 charts the four most commonly used education governance models from 1913 to 2014: (1) Governor appoints the SBOE, SBOE appoints the CSSO ($n = 13$); (2) SBOE is elected, SBOE appoints the CSSO ($n = 6$); (3) Governor appoints the SBOE, CSSO is elected ($n = 9$); (4) Governor appoints the SBOE and the CSSO ($n = 11$); and the other 12 states fall into one of nine other governance configurations (NASBE 2013a, 2014; ECS 2004, 2006, 2011; McCarthy et al. 1993; Badarak 1990; Sanchez and Hall 1987; CCSSO 1983; Harris 1973; Fuller and Pearson 1969a; Beach and Will 1955; Keesecker 1950; Deffenbaugh and Keesecker 1940; Howerth 1913). A majority of states ($n = 39$) now fall into these four governance models (NASBE 2014).

Analyses of the four SBOE governance models have suggested that some models were associated with higher SBOE influence, in particular, those SBOEs that were elected and/or who had the authority to appoint the CSSO were considered to have greater power and influence. As shown in Fig. 3, however, this is the least common model in existence today. The fourth model reflects the most powerful governor and

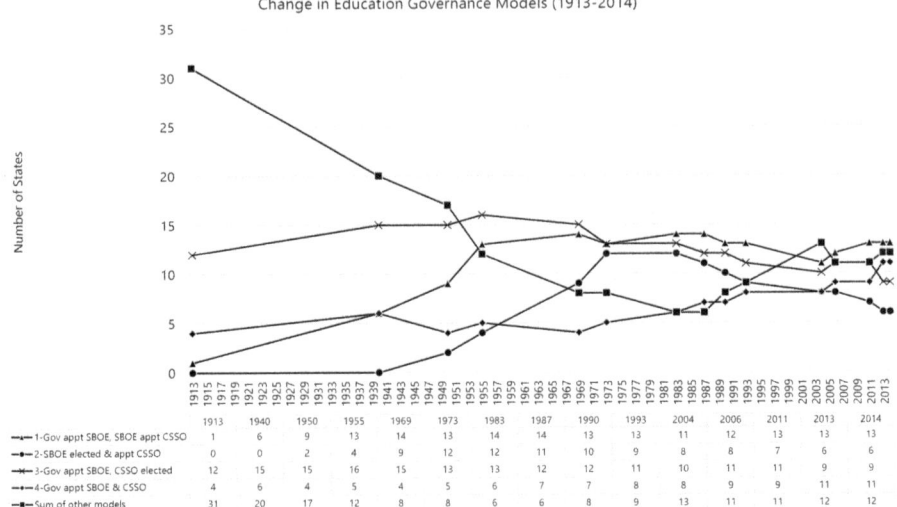

Fig. 3 Summary of data on the models of state education governance for all states with a SBOE from 1913 through 2014

weakest SBOE, and the second model reflects the weakest governor and strongest SBOE (Manna 2012). Debate over which governance model is best has existed as long as SBOEs have (Timar 1997), however, as Fuller and Pearson (1969b) suggested, "Lacking substantial evidence of which system is best for any given state or all states as a whole, much of the conflict has merely reflected opinions" (p. 78).

Little is known about how or why the above four models developed as they did, why elected boards grew in popularity until the 1990s and then stagnated and declined, or why governor appointed boards and CSSOs are now the most common. A critical analysis of these trends would consider the historical and political contexts in which these changes took place, searching for an understanding of the individual factors, trends and patterns impacting state board models. As such, comparisons could be made between SBOEs to other entities within the political system, entities with varying levels of power and influence. Using Hajer's perspective on institutional ambiguity, one could then explore how such policy entities interact in an effort to increase their influence. According to Hajer (2006),

> Established institutions often lack the powers to deliver the required or requested policy results on their own. They therefore have to interact in (1) multi-party, (2) polycentric (and often trans-national) and, almost by necessity, (3) inter-cultural networks of governance. (p. 43)

Within periods of institutional ambiguity, new policy alliances often emerge, alliances characterized by the phenomenon of multisignification (Hajer 2006), wherein a wide array of interests attempt to define the significance of what is necessary to solve policy issues, each operating from "a biased system of signification" (see Carpenter, chapter 10).

Furthermore, within an examination of the power and influence of the board vis-à-vis the power and influence of other educational policy entities, a critical scholar could explore their actions and products. Focusing on the actions of boards as well as language is important because, actions or "performances" convey meaning just as language does. In Carpenter's chapter, for example, he examines the performances associated with the US Department of Education's Listening & Learning Tour. He analyzes what is said (i.e., scripts), where it is said and with and to whom (i.e., staging and setting) to demonstrate how these performative aspects of the events legitimated the Title I SIG program of 2009 as a credible policy solution. In his study, Carpenter examined primary and secondary resources in order to gain a sense of the chronology of the policy events as well as the story lines and policy vocabularies that were used to promote the events and the Title I SIG program. Conducting such an analysis of SBOE work and events, could provide insight into rhetoric and reality of SBOE efforts.

There are several methodological approaches one could take in critically examining state boards as policy actors. One would involve the use of primary data collected through personal interviews and direct observation of board members, the individuals and groups who work with board members, and others that constitute the policy elite. Another option would involve analyzing published data sources. A variety of sources, including meeting minutes or recordings (when available), policy, and news sources, may be used to conduct these kinds of analyses. A summary of state governance information from NASBE (2015b), for example, reveals that the source of authority for 25 states is the state constitution, while the source of authority for the remaining states with SBOEs is from statute. If a researcher was interested in considering how sources of authority have changed over time, Keesecker (1950) and Howerth (1913) also provide this data. In contrast, Stout and Stevens (2002) report on how the SBOE in Minnesota came to be abolished in 1999. An interesting case that highlights how dynamics within political networks can change and how previously influential actors can be weakened and then eliminated.

Given the variation in SBOEs across the states, it may be difficult to comprehensively describe the role of SBOEs. According to NASBE (2016), however, there are four roles that are fairly common across state contexts. These include: (1) policymakers who are responsible for policies that promote educational quality, (2) advocates who are responsible for quality education for all students, (3) liaisons who seek to foster relationships and two-way communication between education and others, and (4) consensus builders who work to find common ground among the various parties that influence education policy. Using one or more critical frameworks, a CPA scholar could evaluate the validity of NASBE's framework and/or examine the implications of such roles for educational policy and the communities impacted by policy. For example, in a number of states, SBOEs are tasked with reviewing, editing, developing and/or approving curriculum standards. In states like Texas and Kansas, this work has been both controversial and strongly publicized, providing an opportunity to explore in depth the boards work and impact. Like O'Malley and Long did in their chapter, one could gather and analyze news media sources and policy documents, though interviews could also provide significant insight.

Another way to critically examine the SBOEs as policy actors would involve shifting from the consideration of the SBOE as a unitary policy actor among other unitary policy entities to viewing state boards as part of a policy network (Agranoff and Maguire 2001; Ball 2008; Ball and Junemann 2012; Bevir and Rhodes 2003; Rhodes 1997). The work of government has become increasingly complex, and in order to fulfill the many responsibilities, it depends upon a wide variety of official and unofficial policy actors.

> These new policy communities bring new kinds of actors into the policy process, validate new policy discourses and enable new forms of policy influence and enactment, and in some respects disable or disenfranchise or circumvent some of the established policy actors and agencies. (Ball 2008, p. 748)

As such, the policy goals of government are achieved through different means that depend on new modalities of power, agency, and social action. Tracing and representing the networks in which state boards operate could be considered over time, during a certain period of time or around a specific issue or set of issues. One could begin by tracing relationships among board members and between board members and those external to the board. Such information can be gathered through internet searches, the review of news sources, and interviews. One might interview, if possible, board members themselves or those close to them, as well as individuals identified as part of the network. According to Ball (2008), networks are indicative of "a new 'architecture of regulation' based on interlocking relationships between disparate sites in and beyond the state" (p. 761). In this new architecture policy is influenced and made piecemeal in a variety of spaces by a variety of actors and then welded together based on alliances and network goals. Important, network goals may not be the same as those publicly and formally communicated by governmental bodies. Thus, network analysis provide a particularly powerful strategy for interrogating SBOEs as policy actors.

5 Implications and Conclusion

> The research frame one uses dictates, to a large extent, the way one identifies and describes policy problems, the way one researches these problems, the policy options one considers, the approach one takes to policy implementation, and the approach taken for policy evaluation. (Young 1999, p. 681)

Although almost every state in the US has a state board, they have received relatively little attention within the educational policy literature. Their similarities and differences across the states make them interesting, contextually-dependent, policy making entities (Kysilko 2011; McCarthy et al. 1993; Manna 2012). SBOEs present a unique opportunity to examine a variety of policy questions, including how SBOEs have shaped the public education, their role as policy actors, the make-up of state boards, the representative nature of boards, how changes in SBOE selection have shifted the power dynamics in public education, and their role in policy networks.

"The profound shifts taking place in contemporary social life require a shift in our research traditions" (Young 1999, p. 705). Non-traditional framing of policy, policy entities, and policy actors facilitates the development of questions that are rarely asked when traditional perspectives are employed.

> In reconsidering questions that are not asked by the prevailing models of policy inquiry, a theoretically informed policy analysis strives to identify the grounds for contentions that arise from the theoretical assumptions, conceptual orientations, methodological commitments, disciplinary practices, and rhetorical approaches closely intertwined in policy disputes. (Fischer 2003, p. 14)

In this chapter, three approaches for framing research on SBOEs were outlined: a historical analysis, a critical feminist analysis and an examination of state boards as policy actors. Importantly, our intent in this chapter was not only to outline a number of approaches to the study of SBOEs but also to articulate how one can think about and plan critical policy analyses. In doing so, we attempted to explicate the connection between theory and research practices, to highlight issues, and suggest useful data sources. However, the approaches we have outlined are neither an exhaustive set of critical, qualitative approaches to critical educational policy analysis, nor is it an attempt to engage in an esoteric debate about how best to engage in policy analysis work. Indeed, there are a multitude of other possible choices as well as theoretical frameworks that could be utilized in doing so, including an analysis informed by one or more critical-race perspectives (Crenshaw et al. 1995) and a variety of other feminist perspectives (Ferguson 1984; Young and Marshall 2013). What we have provided in this chapter is a set of exemplars intended to be constructive to understanding CPA and the use of critical theoretical perspectives in educational policy research.

References

Agranoff, R., & Maguire, M. (2001). Big questions in Public Network Management Research. *Journal of Public Administration Research and Theory, 11*, 295–326.
Badarak, G. W. (1990). *Recapturing the policymaking function of state boards of education.* Charleston: Policy and Planning Center of the Appalachia Educational Laboratory.
Ball, S. J. (1994). *Education reform: A critical and post-structural approach.* Buckingham: Open University Press.
Ball, S. J. (2008). New philanthropy, new networks and new governance in education. *Political Studies, 56*, 747–765.
Ball, S. J., & Junemann, C. (2012). *Networks, new governance and education.* Bristol: Policy Press.
Bell, C. S. (1988). Organizational influences on women's experience in the superintendency. *Peabody Journal of Education, 65*(4), 31–59.
Bevir, M., & Rhodes, R. A. W. (2003). Searching for civil society: Changing patterns of governance in Britain. *Public Administration, 81*(1), 41–62.

Blackmore, J. (1997). Level playing field? Feminist observations on global/local articulations of the re-gendering and restructuring of educational work. *International Review of Education, 43*(5–6), 439–461.

Bowe, R., Gewirtz, S., & Ball, S. J. (1994). Captured by the discourse? Issues and concerns in researching 'parental choice'. *British Journal of Sociology of Education, 15*(1), 63–78.

Braun, A., Ball, S. J., Maguire, M., & Hoskins, K. (2011). Taking context seriously: Towards explaining policy enactments in the secondary school. *Discourse: Studies in the Cultural Politics of Education, 32*(4), 585–596.

Brewer, C. A. (2014). Historicizing in critical policy analysis: The production of cultural histories and microhistories. *International Journal of Qualitative Studies in Education, 27*(3), 273–288.

Burnette, D. (2016). *State EdWatch*. Education Week. Retrieved from http://blogs.edweek.org/edweek/state_edwatch/state-boards/?tagID=0&blogID=78&categoryID=681&rblog=0&page=1

Campbell, R. F., & Mazzoni, T. L. (1974). *State policy making for the public schools: A comparative analysis* (Bureau of Elementary and Secondary Education Grant OEG-0-73-0499). Ohio State University, Educational Governance Project. Retrieved from files.eric.ed.gov/fulltext/ED095666.pdf

Carpenter, B. W. (2011). *(Re) Framing the politics of educational discourse: An investigation of the Title I School Improvement Grant Program of 2009*. ProQuest LLC. 789 East Eisenhower Parkway, PO Box 1346, Ann Arbor, MI 48106.

Carpenter, B. W., Diem, S., & Young, M. D. (2014). The influence of values and policy vocabularies on understandings of leadership effectiveness. *International Journal of Qualitative Studies in Education, 27*(9), 1110–1113.

Council of Chief State School Officers. (1953). *Our system of education: A statement of some desirable policies, programs and administrative relationships in education*. Council of Chief State School Officers.

Council of Chief State School Officers. (1983). *Educational governance in the states: A status report on state boards of education, chief state school officers, and state education agencies*. Washington, DC: U.S. Dept. of Education. Retrieved from http://catalog.hathitrust.org/Record/003003501

Crenshaw, K., Gotanda, N., Peller, G., & Thomas, K. (1995). *Critical race theory: The key writings that formed the movement*. New York: The New Press.

deLeon, P., & Vogenback, D. M. (2007). The policy sciences at a crossroads. In F. Fischer, G. J. Miller, & M. S. Sidney (Eds.), *Handbook of public policy analysis: Theory, politics and methods* (pp. 3–14). Boca Raton: Taylor & Francis Group.

Denzin, N., & Lincoln, Y. (2005). *The SAGE handbook of qualitative research* (3rd ed.). Thousand Oaks: Sage.

Diem, S., & Young, M. D. (2015). Considering critical turns in research on educational policy. *International Journal of Educational Management, 29*(7), 838–850. doi:http://dx.doi.org/10.1108/IJEM-05-2015-0060

Diem, S., Young, M. D., Lee, P., Mansfield, K., & Welton, A. (2014). Understanding critical policy analysis. *International Journal of Qualitative Studies in Education, 27*(9), 1068–1090.

Fairclough, N. (1992). *Discourse and social change*. Cambridge: Polity Press.

Ferguson, K. E. (1984). *The feminist case against bttreaucracy*. Philadelphia: Temple University Press.

Fischer, F. (2003). *Reframing public policy: Discursive politics and deliberative practices*. New York: Oxford University Press.

Flax, J. (1990). *Thinking fragments: Psychoanalysis, feminism, and postmodernism in the contemporary West*. Berkeley: University of California Press.

Grogan, M. (2003). Laying the groundwork for a reconception of the superintendency from feminist postmodern perspectives. In M. D. Young & L. Skrla (Eds.), *Reconsidering feminist research in educational leadership* (pp. 9–34). Albany: SUNY Press.

Hajer, M. A. (2006). The living institutions of the EU: Analysing governance as performance. *Perspectives on European Politics and Society, 7*(1), 41–55.

Henig, J. R. (2013). *The end of exceptionalism in American education: The changing politics of school reform*. Cambridge, MA: Harvard Education Press.

Kendall, G., & Wickham, G. (1998). *Using Foucault's methods*. Thousand Oaks: Sage.

Klein, R. (2015, June 8). These biased ideas are presented as fact in Texas curriculum standards. *The Huffington Post*. Retrieved from http://www.huffingtonpost.com/2014/10/22/texas-social-studies-standards_n_6029224.html

Kysilko, D. (2011). State boards: A critical link to quality education. *Policy Update (NASBE), 18*.

Maguire, M. (2007). Gender and movement in social policy. In C. Skelton, B. Francis, & L. Smulyan (Eds.), *The sage handbook of gender and education* (pp. 109–124). London: Sage.

Manna, P. (2012). State education governance and policy: Dynamic challenges, diverse approaches, and new frontiers. *Peabody Journal of Education, 87*, 627–643. http://doi.org/10.1080/0161956X.2012.723508.

Mansfield, K. W., Welton, A. D., & Grogan, M. (2014). 'Truth or consequences': A feminist critical policy analysis of the STEM crisis. *International Journal of Qualitative Studies in Education, 27*(9), 1155–1182.

Marshall, C. (1994). *The new politics of race and gender: The 1992 yearbook of the Politics of Education Association*. Bristol: Falmer Press.

Marshall, C. (1997). Dismantling and reconstructing policy analysis. In C. Marshall (Ed.), *Feminist critical policy analysis: A perspective from primary and secondary schooling* (pp. 1–39). London: The Falmer Press.

Marshall, C. (1999). Researching the margins: Feminist critical policy analysis. *Educational Policy, 13*(1), 59–76.

Marshall, C., & Young, M. D. (2013). Policy inroads undermining women in education. *International Journal of Leadership in Education, 16*(2), 205–219. http://www.tandfonline.com/doi/abs/10.1080/13603124.2012.754056#preview.

McCarthy, M., Langdon, C., & Olson, J. (1993). State education governance structures (Research No. EG-93-1) (pp. 124). Denver: Education Commission of the States. Retrieved from http://files.eric.ed.gov/fulltext/ED369167.pdf

Mehta, H. (2016, February 13). Texas State Board of Education candidate is a creationist who thinks Obama was a "male prostitute." *Patheos*. Retrieved from: http://www.patheos.com/blogs/friendlyatheist/2016/02/13/texas-state-board-of-education-candidate-is-a-creationist-who-thinks-obama-was-a-male-prostitute/

Morrow, R. A., & Brown, D. D. (1994). *Critical theory and methodology*. Thousand Oaks: SAGE Publications.

National Association of State Boards of Education. (2016). *State boards of education* [Web page]. Retrieved from http://www.nasbe.org/about-us/state-boards-of-education/

Rhodes, R. A. W. (1997). *Understanding governance: Policy networks, governance, reflexivity and accountability*. Buckingham: Open University Press.

Rochefort, D. A., & Cobb, R. W. (Eds.). (1994). *The politics of problem definition: Shaping the policy agenda*. Lawrence: University of Kansas.

Scheurich, J. J. (1994). Policy archeology: A new policy studies methodology. *Journal of Educational Policy, 9*, 297–316.

Scheurich, J., & McKenzie, K. (2005). Foucault's methodologies: Archeaology and genealogy. In N. Denzing & Y. Lincoln (Eds.), *The handbook of qualitative research* (pp. 841–868). Thousand Oaks: Sage Publications.

Shober, A. F. (2012). Governors make the grade: Growing gubernatorial influence in state education policy. *Peabody Journal of Education, 87*, 559–575. http://doi.org/10.1080/0161956X.2012.723494.

Skrla, L., & Young, M. D. (2003). Introduction: Reconsidering Feminist Research in Educational Leadership. In M. D. Young & L. Skrla (Eds.), *Reconsidering feminist research in educational leadership* (pp. 1–6). Albany: SUNY Press.

Slevin, P. (2005, November 9). Kansas Education Board first to back' Intelligent Design. *The Washington Post*. Retrieved from http://www.washingtonpost.com/wp-dyn/content/article/2005/11/08/AR2005110801211.html

Stout, K. E., & Stevens, B. (2002). A state board's demise: The case of the failed diversity rule. *The State Education Standard, 3*, 14–19. National Association of State Boards of Education retrieved from http://www.nasbe.org/wp-content/uploads/Governance-The-Demise-of-Minnesota-state-board.pdf

Taylor, S. (1997). Critical policy analysis: Exploring contexts, text and consequences. *Discourse: Studies in the Cultural Politics of Education, 18*, 23–35.

Timar, T. B. (1997). The institutional role of state education departments: A historical perspective. *American Journal of Education, 105*, 231–260.

Winton, S., & Brewer, C. A. (2014). People for education: A critical policy analysis. *International Journal of Qualitative Studies in Education, 27*(9), 1091–1109.

Young, M. D. (1999). Multifocal educational policy research: Toward a method for enhancing traditional educational policy studies. *American Educational Research Journal, 36*(4), 677–714.

Young, M. D. (2003). The leadership crisis: Gender and the shortage of school administrators. In M. D. Young & L. Skrla (Eds.), *Reconsidering feminist research in educational leadership*. Albany: SUNY Press.

Young, M. D., & Marshall, C. (2013). Critical feminist theory. In B. Irby, G. Brown, R. Lara-Alecio, & S. Jackson (Eds.), *The handbook of educational theories* (pp. 975–984). Charlotte: Information Age Press.

Sayer, A. (1992). *Method in social science: A realist approach* (2nd ed.). London: Routledge.

Van Dijk, T. A. (1993). Principles of critical discourse analysis. *Discourse & Society, 4*, 249–283.

Weis, L., & Fine, M. (2004). *Working method: Research and social justice*. New York/London: Routledge.

Data Sources

Badarak, G. W. (1990). *Recapturing the policymaking function of state boards of education* (Policy Issues). Charleston: Appalachia Educational Lab, Policy and Planning Center. Retrieved from http://eric.ed.gov/?id=ED325947

Beach, F. F., & Will, R. F. (1955). *The State and education: The structure and control of public education at the State level* (Misc. No. 23). US Dept. of Health, Education, and Welfare, Office of Education.

Council of Chief State School Officers. (1953). *Our system of education: A statement of some desirable policies, programs and administrative relationships in education*. Washington, DC: Author.

Deffenbaugh, W. S., & Keesecker, W. S. (1940). *State boards of education and chief state school officers: Their status and legal powers* (Bulletin 1940, no. 6; Monograph no. 1). Washington, DC: United States Office of Education, Federal Security Agency.

Education Commission of the States. (2004, April). *Models of state education governance* (State Notes: Governance). Denver: Author.

Education Commission of the States. (2006, January). *Models of state education governance* (State Notes: Governance, State Boards/Chiefs/Agencies). Denver: Author.

Education Commission of the States. (2011, January). *Models of state education governance* (State Notes: Governance, State Boards/Chiefs/Agencies). Denver: Author.

Education Commission of the States. (2013, August). *State Education Governance Models* (State Notes: State Boards/Chiefs/Agencies). Denver: Author.

Fuller, E., & Pearson, J. B. (1969a). *Education in the states: Historical development and outlook*. Washington, DC: Council of Chief State School Officers.

Fuller, E., & Pearson, J. B. (1969b). *Education in the states: Nationwide development since 1900*. Washington, DC: Council of Chief State School Officers.

Harris, S. P. (1973). *State departments of education, state boards of education, and chief state school officers: Including reference to legally created statewide coordinating agencies for higher education* (DHEW Publication No. (OE) 73–07400). Washington, DC: US Department of Health, Education, and Welfare.

Howerth, I. W. (1913). *State boards of education* (Bulletin no. 1). Berkeley: Department of Information and Social Welfare, University of California Publications, University California Press.

Keesecker, W. S. (1950). *State boards of education and chief state school officers: Their status and legal powers* (Bulletin 1950, no. 12). Washington, DC: United States Office of Education, Federal Security Agency.

National Association of State Boards of Education. (2012, April). *State education governance: State-by-state chart of essential governance information*. Alexandria: Author. Retrieved from http://www.nasbe.org/

National Association of State Boards of Education. (2013a, March). *State education governance models*. Alexandria: Author. Retrieved from http://www.nasbe.org/

National Association of State Boards of Education. (2013b, March). *State education governance: State-by-state chart of essential governance information*. Alexandria: Author. Retrieved from http://www.nasbe.org/

National Association of State Boards of Education. (2014, July). *State education governance models*. Alexandria: Author. Retrieved from http://www.nasbe.org/

National Association of State Boards of Education. (2015a, August). *State education governance models*. Alexandria: Author. Retrieved from http://www.nasbe.org/

National Association of State Boards of Education. (2015b, January). *State education governance: State-by-state chart of essential governance information*. Alexandria: Author. Retrieved from http://www.nasbe.org/

Sanchez, R. L. V. T., & Hall, G. C. (1987). *Models for selecting chief state school officers* (Policy Memo series, no. 1). Bloomington: Indiana University, Consortium on Educational Policy Studies.

A Critical Policy Analysis of the Politics, Design, and Implementation of Student Assignment Policies

Sarah Diem

Abstract Legal rulings on school segregation have played critical roles in shaping the demographic make-up of public schools in ways that we continue to struggle with long after separate schools were declared unequal. School districts' efforts to racially diversify their schools are not only impacted by these rulings but the politics (local, state, federal) surrounding student assignment policies also influence their design and implementation. Pairing a critical policy analysis approach with a policy implementation framework, I provide a nuanced analysis of the complexities behind the development and implementation of three student assignment policies that use a number of factors in assigning students to schools in order to achieve racial and socioeconomic diversity, paying particular attention to how and why decisions are made, and the (un)intended consequences of the policy implementation process. By examining different student assignment policies in different contexts, we can begin to understand what types of policies may work best to achieve racial and socioeconomic diversity.

Keywords Desegregation • Policy design • Policy implementation • Critical policy analysis • Student assignment • Context • Diversity • Politics

> We come then to the question presented: Does segregation of children in public schools solely on the basis of race, even though the physical facilities and other "tangible" factors may be equal, deprive the children of the minority group of equal educational opportunities? We believe that it does. – Chief Justice Warren, *Brown v. Board of Education* (1954)

> We conclude that in the field of public education the doctrine of "separate but equal" has no place. Separate educational facilities are inherently unequal. – Chief Justice Warren, *Brown v. Board of Education* (1954)

> Despite the districts' assertion that they employed individual racial classifications in a way necessary to achieve their stated ends, the minimal effect these classifications have on student assignments suggests that other means would be effective. – Chief Justice Roberts, *Parents Involved in Community Schools v. Seattle School District No. 1* (2007)

S. Diem (✉)
Department of Educational Leadership and Policy Analysis, University of Missouri, 202 Hill Hall, Columbia, MO 65211, USA
e-mail: diems@missouri.edu

© Springer International Publishing Switzerland 2017
M.D. Young, S. Diem (eds.), *Critical Approaches to Education Policy Analysis*, Education, Equity, Economy 4, DOI 10.1007/978-3-319-39643-9_3

> The way to stop discrimination based on race is to stop discrimination based on race. –
> Chief Justice Roberts, *Parents Involved in Community Schools v. Seattle School District No. 1* (2007)

From *Brown v. Board of Education* (1954) to *Parents Involved in Community Schools v. Seattle School District No. 1* (2007), two separate decisions handed down over 50 years apart, the U.S. Supreme Court has played a significant role in the racial diversification of public schools. In its race-conscious approach, *Brown* outlawed racial segregation in public schools in order to provide equal educational opportunities for all students. While any type of meaningful segregation did not occur until well after *Brown*, and after the passage and enforcement of the Civil Right Act of 1964, the decision was clear in its intent to eradicate racially separate and unequal educational settings (Orfield and Lee 2007). Alternatively, in *Parents Involved*, the Court took a race-neutral approach toward racial diversity, forbidding school districts from taking individual students' race into account when implementing voluntary plans to racially diversify schools. The *Parents Involved* decision has left school districts in a quandary, as the options they have to pursue racial diversity in demographically changing school settings have been considerably limited (Wells and Frankenberg 2007). Indeed, legal rulings on school segregation have shaped the demographic make-up of public schools in ways that we continue to wrestle with over 60 years after *Brown*.

In this chapter, I examine three present-day school desegregation policies, which I refer to as student assignment policies, from the following districts: (1) Berkeley Unified School District (Berkeley, CA), (2) Jefferson County Public Schools (Louisville, KY), and (3) Omaha Public Schools (Omaha, NE). Each uses a different set of factors in assigning students to schools in order to achieve diversity. Utilizing a critical policy analysis (CPA) approach alongside a policy implementation framework, I pay particular attention to how the politics surrounding these policies (local, state, and federal) impacts their design and implementation. Critical policy analysts seek to interrogate the policy processes and roots, and provide a much more nuanced analysis of the various factors that can influence policy development and implementation (Diem et al. 2014b). Thus, a CPA approach was essential in my analysis as it assists in illustrating the complexities behind the development of the policies, how and why decisions were made, and the (un)intended consequences of the policy implementation process.

This chapter operates from the premise that pursuing racial diversity is still imperative, particularly given the current levels of segregation and unequal educational opportunity existent in public schools. I begin the chapter by providing an overview of desegregation in the U.S. in order to situate the current context of school desegregation. Next, I describe the framework I use in my CPA of the politics of policy development and implementation, and explain why this framework is suitable for exploring the relationship between design, implementation, and context of the student assignment policies under investigation. I then provide information on my methodological approach to this study and discuss the three policies under examination. I highlight key findings from my analysis and conclude the chapter by discussing the future of school desegregation in a politically and demographically changing context.

1 History of School Desegregation

When the history of school desegregation is discussed, the conversation often begins at *Brown v. Board of Education* (1954). However, 9 years prior to the historic ruling in *Brown*, another less famous decision on school desegregation was handed down in a California federal court, *Mendez v. Westminster* (1946), that ended de jure segregation in the state. The court held that the segregation of Mexican and Mexican American students into separate schools was unconstitutional as the equal protection of laws guaranteed that the public education system be open to all children regardless of their ancestry. The decision was appealed to the U.S. Court of Appeals for the Ninth Circuit where the ruling was affirmed.

Nearly a decade after the *Mendez* decision, the landmark *Brown v. Board of Education* (1954) case was argued in front of the U.S. Supreme Court where it was ruled that in the field of public education, the principle of "separate but equal" established in *Plessy v. Ferguson* (1896) has no place; separate school systems are fundamentally unequal. In *Brown v. Board of Education II* (1955), the Court attempted to place parameters around when school desegregation should be achieved, concluding that such plans be carried out with "all deliberate speed." The Court's vague attempt to address the timing of desegregation plans led to delays in implementation in many school districts, and in many cases, desegregation never occurred (Orfield and Eaton 1996).

Thirteen years after *Brown II*, the Court presided over its next desegregation case, *Green v. County School Board of New Kent County* (1968), which challenged the use of "freedom of choice" plans that had been implemented across many southern school districts. These plans gave students the option of choosing between Black and White schools, resulting in many Blacks choosing to attend White schools and no Whites choosing to attend Black schools. The Court ruled that such plans were not in compliance with the provisions set forth in *Brown II* and segregated dual systems must be dismantled "root and branch." The Court stated that desegregation must be achieved among a number of factors, known as the "green factors," including students, faculty, facilities, extracurricular activities, and transportation. The following year, the *Alexander v. Holmes County Board of Education* (1969) case took *Green* one step further with the Court declaring that desegregated school systems can be achieved immediately and "...operate now and hereafter only unitary schools."

In 1971, the Supreme Court ruled in *Swann v. Charlotte-Mecklenburg Board of Education* that school systems be fully integrated, arguing for the use of busing as a means to achieve desegregation (*Swann v. Charlotte-Mecklenburg Board of Education* 1971). The Court stated that assigning students to schools closest to their homes would not serve to eliminate racially separate school systems. At the time of the ruling, two-thirds of Black students in the Charlotte-Mecklenburg district were attending schools that were almost, if not entirely, Black. After the Court allowed mandatory busing as a way to combat racial segregation, the school district was lauded across the country for its desegregation success (Mickelson 2001; Orfield and Eaton 1996).

The next desegregation case heard by the Supreme Court occurred in 1973, when the Court decided for the first time on school segregation in a non-southern state and school district, and involved both Latino and Black students. In *Keyes v. School District No. 1, Denver, Colorado* (1973), the Court ruled that intentional segregation was occurring in a portion of the Denver, Colorado school system, which included gerrymandering attendance zones and constructing an elementary school in a racially isolated neighborhood. The Court ruled that since de jure segregation was occurring in this portion of the district, the entire school system was being affected and had to be desegregated (Horn and Kurlaender 2006).

Following the *Keyes* ruling, as the make-up of the Supreme Court shifted so, too, did its position on school desegregation. The *Milliken v. Bradley* (1974) decision would become the turning point in desegregation as the Court ruled against inter-district, city-suburban efforts that sought to desegregate racially isolated city schools in Detroit, Michigan. At the time of the case, the majority of Detroit residents were Black and any type of meaningful desegregation in the city was nearly impossible. Thus, a metropolitan plan was pursued that would bring White suburban students to the city and send Black students to the suburbs. The Court ruled against the metropolitan plan and stated that school districts were not held liable for desegregation between districts unless it could be proven that suburbs or the state were implementing racially segregated policies (Holme et al. 2016).

After the *Milliken* decision, school desegregation plans began to break down across the country, even in school districts where they voluntarily wanted to maintain such plans. *Riddick v. School Board of the City of Norfolk, Virginia* (1986) was the first federal court case to permit a school district, upon being declared unitary, to annul its desegregation plan and return to local control. Following the *Riddick* decision, a series of cases in the 1990s continued the Court's reversal of desegregation policy (Orfield and Eaton 1996). In 1991, the Supreme Court ruled in *Board of Education of Oklahoma City Public Schools v. Dowell* that the Oklahoma City school district's unitary status established in federal court released the district from its desegregation mandate. Thus, the school board's vote to return to segregated neighborhood schools was deemed legal (*Board of Education of Oklahoma City Public Schools v. Dowell* 1991). In *Freeman v. Pitts* (1992), the Supreme Court allowed a once-segregated system to end its student desegregation plan without ever having desegregated its faculty or provided students equal access to educational programs (Orfield and Eaton 1996). Three years later in *Missouri v. Jenkins* (1995), the Supreme Court ruled that equalization remedies that were used in the Kansas City, Missouri School District exceeded their authority and should be limited in time and extent without actually showing any correction of the educational harms of segregation (Orfield and Eaton 1996). Rulings of the Supreme Court in the 1990s restored local control back to school districts, many of which have returned to segregated schools by spending money on "separate but equal" alternatives (Dounay 1998; Orfield and Yun 1999; Reardon and Yun 2003).

In 2007, the Supreme Court handed down its first major decision on school desegregation in 12 years in the *Parents Involved in Community Schools v. Seattle School District No. 1* (2007) case. The Court struck down two voluntary desegregation plans (the case was ruled together with *Meredith v. Jefferson County Board of Education*) and stated that individual students may not be assigned or denied a school assignment on the basis of race in voluntary plans even if the intent is to achieve integrated schools (Orfield and Lee 2007). However, a majority of the Court also held that there are compelling reasons for school districts to seek integrated schools and that some other limited techniques are permissible. Indeed, the use of socioeconomic status to integrate schools has grown in popularity since the *Parents Involved* ruling. A recent student found that over 80 school districts are using socioeconomic status as a factor in student assignment as a means to attain socioeconomic and racial integration, which is over double the number of school districts that were utilizing such plans when the *Parents Involved* case was decided (Potter et al. 2016). Yet in reaching its conclusion in *Parents Involved*, the Court left it up to school districts whether to pursue desegregation efforts such as socioeconomic-based integration plans (Orfield and Lee 2007), which is alarming given the rise of economic and racial segregation in public schools.

2 Framework: Education Policy Implementation

I drew from the research on policy implementation to situate my analysis and contextualize it within the larger sphere of critical policy analysis. The policy implementation lens is a tool that enables one to examine the multiple stages of the policy process, including design and implementation. Viewing my study through a policy implementation lens allowed me to pay particular attention to the interactions among policy, people, and places, three dimensions that work together to help explain the conditions in which education policies get designed and implemented and meet the requirements of the policy (Honig 2006). It also focuses on the places or contexts that work to influence the design and implementation of a policy, which is key to my study as I am interested in the role of context and its place in the policy process.

Critical policy scholars tend to pay much of their "attention to the complex systems and environments in which policy is made and implemented" (Diem et al. 2014b, p. 1073) so they can better understand how policies have evolved over time and the role of context in such processes (Weaver-Hightower 2008). Pairing a critical policy analysis (CPA) approach with a policy implementation framework assists in illuminating the complexities behind the development of the policies, how and why decisions were made, and the (un)intended consequences of the policy implementation process, as well as the space between policy development and implementation (Ball 1998; Honig 2006; Malen et al. 2002). The policy implementation process no longer can be viewed in terms of one group of people working to shape and influence how a policy gets implemented. Policymakers and those individuals who implement the policy (local actors) play essential roles in co-constructing the design and implementation of policy (Datnow 2006). Moreover, Werts and Brewer (2015) argue that the perspectives and voices of local actors involved in the co-construction of policy, "those living out the policy" (p. 224), need to be put at the forefront when trying to understand how they make sense of and engage with policies, which is also a concern of scholars engaged in CPA work (Diem et al. 2014b).

Scholars who employ critical policy approaches in their research are also interested in looking at the root and development of policies so they can better understand how they emerge, change over time, and how they may be reinforcing dominant ideologies and cultures (Burke 2004; Chartier 1988; Green 1999). This is a critical factor in my study as I am interested in understanding the history behind the development of three present-day school desegregation policies so that I can gain a better grasp of the changes, conditions, and outcomes of the policies (Brewer 2008, 2014).

Research has also shown how policy implementation can be affected by relationships among people and their participation within diverse communities. For example, Hill (2006), in her study on the impact of language on implementation, talked about the concept of teachers belonging to different discourse communities, which has significantly shaped how they choose to respond to the demands placed on them through reform efforts. Moreover, Smylie and Evans (2006) discussed how social interactions and trusting relationships can promote and obstruct reform. Taken together, these studies have shown how people can be swayed one way or the other by almost anyone during the policy implementation process.

Politics can also play a major role in policy implementation as it works to shape the adoption and implementation of education policies (Malen 2006). The policy implementation process is reflective of the institutional and environmental forces around it, as well as the actors involved in the process. According to Malen (2006), "... opportunities to examine politics beyond the bureaucratic boundaries of public school systems are available," which speaks to the influence of the larger sociopolitical context in which policies operate. Malen goes on to specifically discuss desegregation stating, "The ongoing shifts in desegregation policy provide natural laboratories for tracing how the 'politics of policy nullification' may evolve over time, as well as across communities" (p. 102). Thus, it is crucial to examine the political context of policies in concert with the policy implementation process to gain a comprehensive understanding of why policies may fail or succeed in meeting their intended goals.

3 Methodology

In order to better understand the relationship between policy design, implementation, and context in three different student assignment policies examined in this study, I utilized qualitative case study methodology. This approach was appropriate for my study as it allowed me to gather rich and descriptive data that provides a thorough understanding of the processes around student assignment in each of the cases, and how individuals made meanings of these processes. It also helped me explore the role of context in shaping each of the plans and better understand how the present day iterations came to fruition (Merriam 1998). Moreover, the research design of my study is in line with educational leadership and policy scholars who engage in critical policy work as they place a heavy emphasis on the significance of context and have "a tendency to emphasize methods that enabled thick description and contextual grounding" (Diem and Young 2015, p. 846).

I chose to examine three distinct student assignment policies so I could compare and contrast how the plans' policy design, context, and implementation interact to produce particular outcomes. The Jefferson County Public Schools (JCPS) Student Assignment Plan, Omaha Public Schools (OPS) Student Assignment Plan, and Berkeley Unified School District (BUSD) Student Assignment Plan all use socioeconomic status via a structured and regulated choice plan to increase diversity and overall student achievement within their districts. However, each plan is unique in its design and implementation, due in large part to the context and locale of each school district. JCPS is a large countywide district that incorporates the city of Louisville and its surrounding suburbs in the student assignment policy. The district has a student population of just over 100,000, the majority of whom are White (46.9%), followed by Black (36.1%), a small but growing Latino population (9.4%), and Asian (3.6%). The district also has a high percentage of students (66.3%) receiving free or reduced price meals (JCPS 2015). OPS is a smaller, inner-city district, about half of the size of JCPS with a student population just under 52,000, the majority of whom are Latino (34.0%), followed by White (29.1%), Black (25.3%), multi-racial (5.3%), and Asian (5.2%). The majority of the students in OPS (74.3%) are receiving free or reduced price meals (OPS 2015). BUSD is the smallest of the districts I examined with a student population of about 9,400; 36.4% White, 24.5% Latino, 18.8% Black, 12% multiracial, and 7.3% Asian/Pacific Islander/Filipino (CDE 2015). The district also has a much lower percentage of students receiving free or reduced price meals (41%) compared to JCPS and OPS (BUSD 2013).

My data collection methods for this study included conducting a historical analysis of school desegregation in each of the cities and counties where the plans are located. I collected archival records and documents, including court cases, school board meeting materials, newspaper articles, district student assignment reports, and policy proposals, that helped me better understand the impact of school desegregation in each of these contexts. I also looked at demographic data including school level demographics in order to see how successful the school districts were in achieving their stated diversity goals prior to and after the implementation of their student assignment policies. Additionally, I looked at demographics from the U.S. Census and other datasets in order to learn more about the context in which the plans are situated. Lastly, I conducted 21 in-depth interviews in the fall of 2009 with key individuals involved in the design and implementation of the student assignment policies, which allowed me to learn more about the evolution of the plans and whether these individuals felt the plans were successfully achieving racial and socioeconomic diversity within their districts. Each interview was audio-recorded and I took extensive notes during my meetings with the stakeholders. I transcribed all of the interviews upon completion of my visit to each site. I then coded my data into themes that focused specifically on the politics of policy design and implementation in each of the districts and how context played a role in the design and implementation of the policies. Since my study involves multiple cases, data were collected and analyzed in two stages using within-case and cross-case analyses. The within-case analysis helped me decipher the details of each case so I could provide a deeper account of the complexities involved in the development and implementation of the districts' student assignment policies, question why certain policy options were chosen during these processes (Diem et al. 2014b), and then make comparisons among each of the cases in my cross-case analysis (Miles and Huberman 1994).

4 Findings

In this section I first present brief descriptions of each of the three student assignment policies under investigation in this study. I do this in order to provide contextual information regarding the development of the policies in each school district and illustrate where the policies currently stand in comparison to when they were initially conceived. Building off of the description of the three student assignment policies, I then present cross-case findings of the three policies examined, which provides additional insight regarding the role of the local sociopolitical and geographic contexts in these policies. The cross-case findings also demonstrate how bringing together a CPA approach with a policy implementation framework can provide a deeper understanding of the myriad of factors involved in the policy process.

4.1 Description of the Student Assignment Policies

4.1.1 Jefferson County Public Schools Student Assignment Plan

The Jefferson County Public Schools (JCPS) district was created through a 1974 court-ordered merger of the Louisville and Jefferson County school districts after segregation was found to be occurring in both districts (*Newberg Area Council, Inc. v. Board of Education of Jefferson County* 1974). After the court order was issued, a countywide desegregation plan was implemented in the new district that included the creation of clusters of schools that were either majority Black or White; students were bused within these schools in order to achieve racial balance. Busing continued throughout the county, even after the court's active supervision of the desegregation plan ended in 1978 ("Timeline," 2005). Interestingly, there is not a lot of agreement as to why this occurred. During the 1970s, Kentucky showed one of the largest declines in segregation, in large part because of the JCPS desegregation plan (Orfield and Eaton 1996).

Several JCPS schools were no longer meeting the mandatory racial balance guidelines set forth in the desegregation plan by the mid-1980s (*Parents Involved in Community Schools v. Seattle School District No. 1*, 2007). In 1984, the racial balance guidelines of the plan were revised to mirror shifting demographics in the county. The revised plan also allowed the bulk of students to attend schools in their residential area, which led to an estimated annual reassignment of 8,500 Black and 8,000 White students (*Parents Involved in Community Schools v. Seattle School District No. 1*, 2007). By the late 1980s, the district had achieved substantial progress in its desegregation plan and for the first time since its implementation, all of the JCPS schools were racially balanced (Cummings and Price 1997).

In 1992, a new iteration of the district's desegregation plan was adopted that included controlled school choice and replaced most of the busing throughout the district. The plan allowed students to apply to schools of their choice and they were given priority based on available space, racial guidelines, and in some cases admissions criteria. A few years after this version of the plan was implemented, it was revised to include the same racial guidelines (between 15 and 50% Black students at each school) for all students in the district (JCPS 2008).

In 2000, significant changes were made to the plan as a result of a lawsuit against the district and their use of racial guidelines (*Hampton v. Jefferson County Board of Education* 2000). The plaintiffs argued that African American students were being denied the opportunity to attend a magnet school in the district because of the racial balance policy and requested that the district's desegregation decree be lifted. The motion was eventually carried out and 25 years of court-ordered desegregation came to an end in JCPS. The district modified the plan to meet the court's requirements regarding student assignment to magnet schools, yet continued to implement a voluntary race-conscious plan that sought to achieve racial diversity in the district (*Parents Involved in Community Schools v. Seattle School District No. 1*, 2007).

In 2002, another lawsuit was filed against the district regarding the manner in which they were assigning students to schools. In this case, the plaintiff claimed that his sons were denied enrollment into a magnet school because they were White. Three additional plaintiffs would eventually join the case, including Crystal Meredith, who argued that her son was denied a transfer to a school closer to their home because in doing so the racial balance of the requested school would no longer be intact. Meredith claimed that by not allowing her son to transfer schools, the district was violating the Equal Protection Clause of the Fourteenth Amendment of the U.S. Constitution (*Meredith v. Jefferson County Board of Education* 2007). The case eventually made its way to the U.S. Supreme Court where it was argued alongside *Parents Involved* (2007). As a result of the ruling, the district could no longer use race as a sole factor in assigning or denying students to schools.

Since the *Parents Involved* (2007) ruling, JCPS has gone through a number of variations of its plan. The first plan post-*Parents Involved* included organizing the district into two geographic areas: Geographic Area A and Geographic Area B. The plan required elementary schools to have between 15 and 50% of their student population from Geographic Area A, which included neighborhoods with high minority students, low household income, and education levels that ranged from less than a high school diploma to some postsecondary education; Geographic Area B included the rest of Jefferson County (JCPS 2009). The implementation of the geography-based plan faced some hiccups during its first 2 years so the district decided to bring in experts to advise them on how to modify the plan so that it would be more effective (Diem et al. 2014; Diem and Young 2015). The school board adopted a revised version of the plan in 2012, which includes defining neighborhoods by census block group and categorizing them as 1, 2, or 3, rather than Geographic Area A or B. The district still uses race, income, and education in determining student assignment but parental choices would now be made within each of the 13 clusters they were assigned to that were established in the district (Diem et al. 2014).

Opponents to JCPS' plan have continued to challenge its legality since the *Parents Involved* (2007) ruling. In one case, plaintiffs claimed the new plan relied too heavily on race (the case was eventually dropped). A second case alleged that Kentucky state law provided children the right to attend a school closest to their home (the state ruled against the plaintiffs). Moreover, Republicans in the Kentucky legislature have tried to pass neighborhood school bills in two recent legislative sessions, both of which failed (McDermott et al. 2015).

4.1.2 Omaha Public Schools Student Assignment Plan

Omaha Public Schools (OPS) was not mandated to desegregate its schools until 1975, over 20 years after the *Brown* ruling. The federal court order was handed down as a part of a lawsuit, *U.S. and Nellie Mae Webb et al. v. School District of Omaha* (1975), which ruled that the district was intentionally creating and maintaining segregation throughout its schools. The district was ordered to be integrated, establish guidelines that work toward that end, and remain under court supervision during the process. The district operated under this court order until it was declared unitary in 1984 (OPS 1999).

At the time of the *Webb* case, the district had a student population of approximately 60,000, only 20% of whom were Black. Over 50% of these Black students attended schools with Black student populations of 80–100%, whereas 73% of White students attended schools with Black student populations of less than 5% (*U.S. and Nellie Mae Webb et al. v. School District of Omaha* 1975). Moreover, the city of Omaha was also intensely residentially segregated, which contributed directly to the number of segregated schools in the district.

As a result of the *Webb* ruling, the district experienced a mass exodus of White families to surrounding suburban school districts, losing approximately 16,000 White students from the 1975–1976 to the 1985–1986 school year. Moreover, an inter-district choice policy established by the Nebraska State Legislature in 1989 that allowed students to transfer between schools was also used as a mechanism by families to avoid desegregation. As option enrollment was increasingly being utilized and OPS was changing demographically, the need for a new student assignment became more urgent.

The process of developing a new student assignment plan began in 1996 when the OPS school board requested the superintendent and staff to examine the current status of desegregation in Omaha and submit proposals for a new plan. Over the next 2 years, the district, working alongside a newly created Desegregation Task Force made up of members of the community, was to come up with a plan guided by a number of key principles: ensuring equitable and integrative educational opportunities for all students, maximizing parental involvement and opportunities for students to participate and have access to extracurricular activities, providing choices that promote voluntary integration and reduce the mandatory assignment of students whenever possible, and ensuring continuous evaluation of the Student Assignment Plan (OPS 1999). The district eventually recommended the board implement a socioeconomic-based zone-controlled choice plan that sought to integrate schools to mirror the socioeconomic diversity of the district (socioeconomic status is determined by eligibility to participate in the federal free or reduced-price lunch program).

On February 23, 1999, the plan was approved by the board with the stipulation that a $254 million school bond must be passed by the city to renovate all OPS schools. There was a recognition that if the district was to end busing in the district and all students were to return to neighborhood schools, the schools in the Northeast portion of the city, home to predominately Black residents, would have to be updated and brought up to the same standards as those schools in the Western portion of the city (home to a predominately White population), according to an interviewee. The bond narrowly passed, paving the way for renovation and expansion efforts in old and overcrowded school buildings in the district (Goodsell et al. 1999). In the 1999–2000 school year, the district implemented its new student assignment plan.

The 1999 OPS Student Assignment Plan operated at every grade level. The elementary plan divided the school district into four zones; each zone represented a portion of the school district running east to west (OPS 2007). Low income and students of color tend to live in eastern portions of each zone while more affluent, White students tend to reside in the western portions thus the zones worked to capture a large swath of all student populations. Students could either attend the school in their home attendance area or they could choose from schools within their attendance zone. There were also two magnet schools in each attendance zone in which students can also apply (OPS 1999, 2007).

Ten years after the initial implementation of the OPS Student Assignment Plan, the district revised the plan to be better aligned with a new inter-district regional desegregation plan established in the Omaha metropolitan area. The Learning Community was created by the Nebraska State Legislature in 2007 and requires 11 school districts across Douglas and Sarpy counties (Omaha is located in Douglas County) to work together to increase socioeconomic diversity and academic achievement across all of the participating school districts (Holme and Diem 2015). In OPS, students are allowed to choose to attend a school within their home attendance area or apply to any of the schools in the district in which they are selected on a space-available basis. OPS students can also apply to schools within the 11 districts in the Learning Community with priority first going to siblings of students enrolled in schools and second to students who contribute to the socioeconomic diversity of the school (when space is available).

OPS monitors its student assignment plan regularly via various committees that review "student-school option patterns, academic achievement trends, equity of resource distribution, and staffing patterns, and when necessary, recommend modifications to the OPS school board to advance socioeconomic diversity" (OPS, n.d.). The district recently adopted a new student assignment plan for grades K-8 called the Partner Plan. The new plan will be implemented in the 2017–2018 school year and will include changes to the transportation eligibility requirements for elementary and middle schools (not high schools). Additionally, the new plan guarantees school choice to the neighborhood (home attendance area) in which the student resides, while placement in non-neighborhood schools will depend on space availability. The plan prioritizes school choice to neighborhoods first, followed by siblings of students attending the desired school, and lastly by schools outside of home attendance neighborhoods. The plan includes the creation of eight elementary and four middle school partner zones and does not consider socioeconomic status when determining transportation eligibility (OPS 2016).

4.1.3 Berkeley Unified School District Student Assignment Plan

Located across the bay from San Francisco, Berkeley is a very densely populated community still hovering around the same population level as the initial days of school desegregation; today the city has almost 113,000 residents (U.S. Census Bureau 2010). The city is only about 10.5 square miles yet it is the fourth largest city in Alameda County. Berkeley prides itself in being "a city with a small population and a big reputation," known for its academic achievement, progressive ideology, and ability to attract people from across the world (City of Berkeley 2010).

When it comes to its history of school desegregation, Berkeley is considered to most a rare and exceptional city. At the peak of the Civil Rights Movement, in September 1968 Berkeley became the first city in the country with a population over 100,000, including almost an even percentage of Black and White students, to voluntarily integrate its schools (BUSD 2004; Sullivan and Stewart 1969). According to Sullivan and Stewart (1969), the motivation for integrating Berkeley schools was straightforward: "The rationale for school integration is very simple. It is also very old and very obvious. 'Because it is the law,' we say. And 'Because it is right.'" (p. 8).

The district's 1968 desegregation plan included a two-way busing piece in which Black children in grades 4–6 were bused to the portion of the city that is predominately White (known as "the hills") and White students were bused to the portion of the city that is predominately Black (known as "the flats") (Sullivan and Stewart 1969; Wollenberg 2008). The plan sought to achieve a racial balance in each of its elementary schools of 50% White, 41% Black, and 9% other (Chavez and

Frankenberg 2009). Approximately 3500 of the 9000 elementary school children in the city were bused during this time (Sullivan and Stewart 1969).

BUSD's initial desegregation plan remained a district policy well through the 1990s before it was revised (Wollenberg 2008). The district was dealing with a number of complaints from Berkeley parents about the quality of some schools and students (predominately White students) were leaving the district after the third grade, the year they would have to be bused (Holtz 1989). In response to the growing concerns of Berkeley parents as well as the White flight occurring in the district, in 1992 the school board approved a $165 million bond that would be devoted to the reconstruction of schools. While voters approved the measure, there was still a growing sentiment that changes needed to be made to the plan to correct some of the key components that were provoking great dissatisfaction among parents (Wicinas 2009b).

In 1993, the school board voted to phase out the district's two-way mandatory busing plan and established a new controlled-choice within-zone student assignment system. The district was divided into three elementary zones—North, Central, and Southeast—each of which included portions of the hills and flats. Racial residential patterns were then determined in each zone through a mapping process of 445 planning areas, each about four to eight city blocks in size. The goal of the plan was to maintain a racial balance in each school that mirrored each geographic zone, plus/minus five percentage points (Wicinas 2009b). The plan allowed families to choose among three elementary schools within their zone, ranking their preferences, yet knowing that placement prioritized siblings and the ethnicity of individual students (Olszewski 1995; Wicinas 2009b).

During the initial implementation of the district's student assignment plan, Proposition 209 was passed in the state of California, which prohibited governmental institutions to consider race, among other factors, in public education, public employment, and public contracting. The district became concerned that its student assignment plan was vulnerable and could potentially face lawsuits, thus they began considering how their plan could hold up in court and still achieve racial integration (Wicinas 2009a). Then Superintendent Jack McLaughlin convened a citizen's advisory committee, the Student Assignment Advisory Committee (SAAC), comprised of administrators, principals, and parent representatives from each school, to work toward developing alternatives to the current student assignment plan. Specifically, the SAAC was directed by the school board to develop two proposals, including multiple factors to achieve integration; race was only to be included in one of the plans (Wicinas 2009a). The SAAC presented its proposal to the school board at the end of 2002, which included a plan that consisted of achieving diversity through income and parent education (BUSD 2002). The board elected not to implement the plan and chose to move forward with the existing race-conscious plan (Wicinas 2009a).

The following year, the Pacific Legal Foundation filed a suit against BUSD for its use of race in its student assignment policy, claiming it was a direct violation of Proposition 209 (*Avila v. Berkeley Unified School District* 2004). The Pacific

Legal Foundation had won a similar case 2 years earlier, forcing a school district to abandon their student transfer program that was based on race (Artz 2004a). As the lawsuit began, a group of three former SAAC members met regularly to strengthen the original plan proposed to incorporate the board (Wicinas 2009a). The final version of the student assignment plan was submitted to the BUSD school board on January 21, 2004. In the plan, elementary schools remained divided into the same three zones, parental choice was still used, sibling priority continued, and a student was still allowed to attend a school that had a needed language program. The new plan moved away from assigning children to schools by race and instead used demographic characteristics of the planning areas where students resided (Artz 2004b). The *Avila* lawsuit was dismissed in April 2004 after the court ruled in favor of BUSD.

The district's current student assignment plan uses parent education level, parent income level, and race and ethnicity to achieve integrated school settings. The plan also continues to use the 445 planning areas to devise a composite diversity map consisting of three categories (1, 2, & 3), taking into consideration the three diversity factors (parent education level, parent income level, and race and ethnicity). Category 1 consists of planning areas that have lower parental education and income levels, and a higher percentage of students of color, while planning areas in Category 3 have higher parental education and income levels and a lower percentage of students of color; those planning areas in Category 2 fall in the middle (BUSD 2004; also noted by an interviewee). The composite diversity categories are used to assign students proportionately to elementary schools with the goal of achieving socioeconomic and racial diversity reflective of the diversity within an elementary attendance zone in Categories 1, 2, and 3, within the range of 10 percentage points (BUSD 2004). It is important to note that the plan is implemented proportionally by zone, not the entire city.

The district faced another legal challenge with the Pacific Legal Foundation in 2006 over its student assignment plan but in April 2007, the challenges were dismissed with the judge ruling that race was one of many of factors considered in the plan and thus was not in violation of Proposition 209. The ruling was appealed but the earlier ruling was upheld based on the grounds that neighborhood demographics, not a student's individual race, was not a violation of Proposition 209 (*American Civil Rights Foundation v. Berkeley Unified School District* 2009).

4.2 Cross-Case Findings

The ways in which policies are designed and implemented are greatly influenced by the surrounding sociopolitical and geographic contexts. In turn, these contexts play a critical role in shaping the ways in which policies are supported as well as in their ultimate success. It is difficult to gain a complete understanding of education policy implementation without first recognizing the context in which the policy was realized (Dumas and Anyon 2006). As is the case in all of the policies analyzed in this study, the local sociopolitical and geographic contexts played fundamental roles in how the three distinct policies were shaped and adopted. In the subsections below, I highlight two important cross-case findings. The first focuses on how a district's diversity policy is designed can impact how it is received in the community. The second takes a macro-level perspective on the cases and notes how the current federal education policy context can influence how plans are shaped, focusing more on achievement at the expense of diversity.

4.2.1 Process and Design Affect Political Support

It was clear in the policies I studied that process and design affected political support: policies that bring more people to the table are more likely to receive buy-in as well as continued support. Critical policy scholars are often interested in examining the (im)balance of power during the policymaking process, who is or is not sitting at the table when policies are being decided, and whose voice is being received (Diem et al. 2014b). In all of the plans I analyzed in this study, there was a high level of community engagement throughout the design process of the policies. While my past experiences in the field of public policy have taught me the importance of engaging community members at all points during the policy process, this point was reaffirmed throughout this study as I talked to administrators, district level employees, and community members about the types of outreach that were provided during the creation of the integration plans. Community members in particular shared with me their desire to feel like they are part of a process that in turn plays a huge role in their children's lives and also holds the district accountable to the community. Administrators and district-level employees also recognized the need to involve parents and the greater community in the policy process and want the community to hold them accountable in meeting their stated goals and objectives. In the case of OPS, the engagement surrounding the student assignment plan continued during the time of my data collection through a Student Assignment Accountability Advisory Committee. The committee met monthly to examine the student assignment plan, making sure the district was meeting the promises it made to the community regarding the plan and provided recommendations to the school board on how to improve the plan. In JCPS, community forums were held throughout the county, briefings were held with constituents, and parents and members of the community were surveyed about the characteristics desired in a new student assignment plan. Gaining input from the public has been integral in JCPS's efforts of developing and redeveloping their student assignment plan. In BUSD, convening committees and task forces has always been the means in which to gain the public's trust and eventual buy-in of new or revised district policies; it's part of Berkeley's culture (Wicinas 2009a). Indeed, the Student Assignment Advisory Committee (SAAC) was comprised of parent representatives from each school in addition to principals and administrators, who would help facilitate the process of developing the district's student assignment plan. By providing the community a constant voice at the table when it comes to making changes to policies like student assignment, the process may allow for more inclusiveness and less unforeseen incidents from occurring.

4.2.2 Plans May Be Undermined by Narrow Accountability Systems

Diversity plans run a risk in the accountability age: accountability systems may undermine diversity plans. The success of diversity plans may be influenced by the increase in the use of test scores to evaluate school quality. Indeed, Orfield and Lee (2007) argue that "The basic educational policy model in the post-civil rights generation assumes that we can equalize schools without dealing with segregation through testing and accountability" (p. 7). Wells and Holme (2005) also assert that since the inception of statewide accountability systems, a "good" school is associated with higher test scores regardless of the school's other programs or achievements. Furthermore, schools that are more socioeconomically and racially diverse are more likely to have lower test scores as compared to majority White, affluent schools, which only adds to the perception set forth by statewide accountability systems that racially diverse schools are not as "good" as schools in more White, affluent communities (Wells and Holme 2005). In JCPS, the good versus bad school argument has clearly been an issue with their Student Assignment Plan as parents identify what schools are "good" for their children to attend. The idea that a school is defined as "good" or "bad" based on scores from a standardized assessment begs the question of what should be held accountable in schools. Wells and Holme (2005) suggested that schools should held accountable for not only test scores but for multiple other factors, such as diversity among students and teachers, teacher quality, curriculum, specialized programs such as drama or art, number of high school graduates, college acceptance rates, extracurricular programs, athletics, and so on. The recent reauthorization of No Child Left Behind in December 2015, now known as the Every Student Succeeds Act, has significantly narrowed the federal government's role in elementary and secondary education and provided more flexibility in how state's hold schools accountable. However, these changes may also have a direct impact on the future of integration plans and whether diversity is configured into states' policy provisions.

5 Conclusion

School desegregation policies were initially created to provide equal educational opportunities for all students. While *Brown* (1954) outlawed racial segregation in public schools, over 60 years after the landmark moment we are witnessing the unfulfilled promise of the decision as schools are undergoing resegregation and racial groups are becoming increasingly isolated and separated. Further, in contemporary legal and political environments that support race-neutral or color-blind approaches to addressing the continued racial disparities in education, school districts seeking to maintain racial diversity face a new challenge of trying to generate methods of student assignment while not being race-conscious.

There is no question that racial integration should continue to be an important and desired goal for our schools and society. Decades of social science research point to the educational, social, and economic benefits of racially diverse schools (e.g., Linn and Welner 2007; Mickelson 2008; Mickelson and Nkomo 2012), yet because of the current legal and political environment race-based plans are off the agenda in most public schools (Holley-Walker 2010; Ryan 2007). Making the goal of integration even more difficult, the current high-stakes accountability environment has effectively narrowed the focus of education to "achievement," which "limits the measures of schools, particularly in ways that desegregation is likely to bring about the most benefits for students" (Frankenberg et al. 2016, p. 21; Wells and Holme 2005). However, as was evident in the school districts I examined, community engagement can offer a venue where people can come together around the common goal of integration and determine a way to make sure their districts' methods of achieving integration works within this new legal environment *and* is helping students achieve academically.

The policies analyzed in this study illustrate some of the major successes and challenges each of the school districts faced as they designed and implemented their student assignment plans. By examining different student assignment policies in different contexts through a CPA lens, we can begin to understand what types of plans may work best to achieve racial and socioeconomic diversity, which is of great significance today particularly given the ongoing segregation occurring in our public schools.

References

Alexander v. Holmes County Board of Education, 396 U.S. 1218 (1969).
American Civil Rights Foundation v. Berkeley Unified School District, A121137 No. RG0692139 (Cal. Ct. of Appeal 1st District, March 17, 2009).
Artz. M. (2004a, January 16). BUSD asks for lawsuit dismissal.*The Berkeley Daily Planet*, News section.
Artz, M. (2004b, January 23). New school assignment plan debuts. *The Berkeley Daily Planet*, pp. 1
Avila v. Berkeley Unified School District, No. RG03-110397 (Cal. Super. Ct. April 6, 2004).
Ball, S. J. (1998). Big policies/small world: An introduction to international perspectives in education policy. *Comparative Education, 34*, 119–130.
Berkeley Unified School District. (2002). *Student Assignment Advisory Committee preliminary report to the board of education, December 17, 2002*. Berkeley: Author.
Berkeley Unified School District. (2004). *Berkeley Unified School District Student Assignment Plan/Policy*. Retrieved from http://www.berkeley.net/student-assignment-plan/
Berkeley Unified School District. (2013). *BUSD district profile sheet 2013*. Berkeley: Author.
Board of Education of Oklahoma City Public Schools v. Dowell, 498 U.S. 237 (1991).
Brewer, C. A. (2008). *Interpreting the policy past: The relationship between education and antipoverty policy during the Carter administration*. Unpublished doctoral dissertation, The University of Texas at Austin, Austin.
Brewer, C. A. (2014). Historicizing in critical policy analysis: The production of cultural Histories and microhistories. *International Journal of Qualitative Studies in Education, 27*(3), 273–288.
Brown v. Board of Education of Topeka, 347 U.S. 483 (1954).
Brown v. Board of Education of Topeka (II), 349 U.S. 294 (1955).
Burke, P. (2004). *What is cultural history?* Cambridge: Polity Press.

California Department of Education. (2015). *Enrollment by ethnicity for 2014–15, Berkeley Unified*. Retrieved from http://dq.cde.ca.gov

Chartier, R. (1988). *Cultural history: Between practices and representations* (L. G. Cochrane, Trans.). Cambridge: Polity Press.

Chavez, L., & Frankenberg, E. (2009). *Integration defended: Berkeley's unified strategy to maintain school diversity*. Berkeley/Los Angeles: University of California, Chief Justice Earl Warren Institute on Race, Ethnicity & Diversity, & University of California, Civil Rights Project/Proyecto DerechosCiviles.

City of Berkeley. (2010). *About Berkeley*. Retrieved from http://www.ci.berkeley.ca.us/

Cummings, S., & Price, M. (1997). Race relations and public policy in Louisville: Historical development of an urban underclass. *Journal of Black Studies, 27*(5), 615–649.

Datnow, A. (2006). Connections to the policy chain: The "co-construction" of implementation in comprehensive school reform. In M. I. Honig (Ed.), *New directions in education policy implementation: Confronting complexity* (pp. 105–124). Albany: State University of New York Press.

Diem, S., & Young, M. D. (2015). Considering critical turns in research on educational leadership and policy. *International Journal of Educational Management, 29*(7), 838–850.

Diem, S., Frankenberg, E., Cleary, C., & Ali, N. (2014a). The politics of maintaining diversity policies in demographically changing urban-suburban school districts. *American Journal of Education, 120*(3), 351–389.

Diem, S., Young, M. D., Welton, A., Mansfield, K. C., & Lee, P. L. (2014b). The intellectual landscape of critical policy analysis. *International Journal of Qualitative Studies in Education, 27*(9), 1068–1090.

Diem, S., Frankenberg, E., & Cleary, C. (2015). Factors that influence school board policymaking: The political context of student diversity in urban-suburban districts. *Educational Administration Quarterly, 51*(5), 712–752.

Dounay, J. (1998). *Desegregation policy across the nation: Practices and questions*. Denver: Education Commission of the States.

Dumas, M. J., & Anyon, J. (2006). Toward a critical approach to education policy implementation: Implications for the (battle)field. In M. I. Honig (Ed.), *New directions in education policy implementation: Confronting complexity* (pp. 149–168). Albany: State University of New York Press.

Frankenberg, E., Diem, S., & Cleary, C. (2016). School desegregation after *Parents Involved*: The complications of pursuing diversity in a high-stakes accountability era. *Journal of Urban Affairs*. DOI: 10.1111/juaf.12309

Freeman v. Pitts, 503 U.S. 467 (1992).

Goodsell, P., Matczak, M., & O'Connor, M. (1999, May 12). Voters end busing in Omaha bonds win by margin of 1,465 history of integration in Omaha schools. *Omaha World-Herald*. News section.

Green v. County School Board of New Kent County, 391 U.S. 430 (1968).

Green, A. (1999). *The houses of history: A critical reader in twentieth-century history and theory*. Manchester: Manchester University Press.

Hampton v. Jefferson County Board of Education, 102 F. Supp. 2d 358, 360 (W.D. Ky. 2000).

Hill, H. C. (2006). Language matters: How characteristics of language complicate policy implementation. In M. I. Honig (Ed.), *New directions in education policy implementation: Confronting complexity* (pp. 65–82). Albany: State University of New York Press.

Holley-Walker, D. (2010). After unitary status: Examining voluntary integration strategies for southern school districts. *North Carolina Law Review, 88*, 877–910.

Holme, J. J., & Diem, S. (2015). Regional governance in education: A case study of the metro area Learning Community in Omaha, Nebraska. *Peabody Journal of Education, 90*(1), 156–177.

Holme, J. J., Finnigan, K., & Diem, S. (2016). Challenging boundaries, changing fate? Metropolitan inequality and the legacy of Milliken. *Teachers College Record, 118*(3), 1–40.

Holtz, D. L. (1989, December 16). Berkeley hopes to woo Whites to city schools. *San Francisco Chronicle*.

Honig, M. (Ed.). (2006). *New directions in educational policy implementation: Confronting complexity.* New York: State University of New York Press.

Horn, C., & Kurlaender, M. (2006). *The end of Keyes: Resegregation trends and achievement in Denver Public Schools.* Cambridge: The Civil Rights Project at Harvard University.

Jefferson County Public Schools. (2008). *Agenda Item III, May 28, 2008 Board of Education meeting.* Louisville: Author.

Jefferson County Public Schools. (2009, October). *Governing urban schools in an era of change.* Presentation given at the CUBE 42nd annual conference, Austin.

Jefferson County Public Schools. (2015). *Elementary, middle, and high school data books.* Retrieved from http://www.jefferson.k12.ky.us/Departments/AcctResPlan/databook/index.html

Keyes v. School District No. 1, Denver, Colorado, 413 U.S. 189 (1973).

Linn, R., & Welner, K. (Eds.). (2007). *Race-conscious policies for assigning students to schools: Social science research and the Supreme Court cases.* Washington, DC: National Academy of Education.

Malen, B. (2006). Revisiting policy implementation as a political phenomenon: The case of reconstitution policies. In M. I. Honig (Ed.), *New directions in education policy implementation: Confronting complexity* (pp. 83–104). Albany: State University of New York Press.

Malen, B., Croninger, R., Muncey, D., & Redmond-Jones, D. (2002). Reconstituting schools: "Testing" the "theory of action". *Educational Evaluation and Policy Analysis, 24*(2),113–132.

McDermott, K. A., Frankenberg, E., & Diem, S. (2015). The "post-racial" politics of race: Changing student assignment policy in three school districts. *Educational Policy, 29*(3), 504–554.

Mendez v. Westminster School District, 64 F. Supp. 544 (S.D. CA 1946).

Meredith v. Jefferson County Board of Education, 551 U.S. 05–915 (2007).

Merriam, S. (1998). *Qualitative research and case study applications in education: Revised and expanded from case study research in education.* San Francisco: Jossey-Bass.

Mickelson, R. A. (2001). Subverting Swann: First- and second-generation segregation in the Charlotte-Mecklenburg Schools. *American Journal of Education, 38*(2), 215–252.

Mickelson, R. A. (2008). Twenty-first century social science research on school diversity and educational outcomes. *Ohio State Law Journal, 69,* 1173–1228.

Mickelson, R. A., & Nkomo, N. (2012). Integrated schooling, life course outcomes, and social cohesion in multiethnic democratic societies. *Review of Research in Education, 36*(1), 197–238.

Miles, M. B., & Huberman, A. M. (1994). Data management and analysis methods. In N. K. Denzin & Y. S. Lincoln (Eds.), *The SAGE handbook of qualitative research* (pp. 769–802). Thousand Oaks: Sage.

Milliken v. Bradley, 418 U.S. 717 (1974).

Missouri v. Jenkins, 115 S. Ct. 2038 (1995).

Newburg Area Council, Inc. v. Board of Education of Jefferson County, 510 F.2d 1358 (6th Cir. 1974).

Olszewski, L. (1995, March 18). School choice delivers in Berkeley: Most children get into the campuses parents had picked. *San Francisco Chronicle.*

Omaha Public Schools. (1999). *Omaha Public Schools student assignment plan.* Omaha: Author.

Omaha Public Schools. (2007). *Student Assignment Plan 2007–2008.* Omaha: Author.

Omaha Public Schools. (2015). *Assessments and statistics.* Retrieved from http://district.ops.org

Omaha Public Schools. (2016). *Transportation eligibility changes: 2017–2018.* Retried from http://sap.ops.org/

Omaha Public Schools. (n.d.). *Student assignment plan summary.* Omaha: Author.

Orfield, G., & Eaton, S. (1996). *Dismantling desegregation: The quiet reversal of Brown v. Board of Education.* New York: The New Press.

Orfield, G., & Lee, C. (2007). *Historic reversals, accelerating resegregation, and theneed for new integration strategies.* Los Angeles: University of California, The Civil Rights Project/Proyecto DerechosCiviles.

Orfield, G., & Yun, J. T. (1999). *Resegregation in American schools*. Cambridge, MA: The Civil Rights Project at Harvard University.

Parents Involved in Community Schools v. Seattle School District No. 1, 551 U.S. 05–908 (2007).

Plessy v. Ferguson, 163 U.S. 537 (1896).

Potter, H., Quick, K., & Davies, E. (2016). *A new wave of school integration: Districts and charters pursuing socioeconomic diversity*. New York: The Century Foundation.

Reardon, S. F., & Yun, J. T. (2003). Integrating neighborhoods, segregating schools: The retreat from school desegregation in the South, 1990–2000. *North Carolina Law Review, 81*(4), 1563–1596.

Riddick v. School Board of the City of Norfolk, Virginia, 784 F. 2nd 521 (4th Cir. 1986).

Ryan, J. (2007). The Supreme Court and voluntary integration. *Harvard Law Review, 121*(1), 131–157.

Smylie, M. A., & Evans, A. E. (2006). Social capital and the problem of implementation. In M. I. Honig (Ed.), *New directions in education policy implementation: Confronting complexity* (pp. 187–208). Albany: State University of New York Press.

Sullivan, N., & Stewart, E. S. (1969). *Now is the time: Integration in Berkeley schools*. Bloomington: Indiana University Press.

Swann v. Charlotte-Mecklenburg Board of Education, 402 U.S. 1 (1971).

Timeline: Desegregation in Jefferson County Public Schools. (2005, September 4). *The Courier-Journal*.

U.S. & Nellie Mae Webb et al. v. School District of Omaha, 521 F.2d 530 (8thCir.1975).

U.S. Census Bureau. (2010). *Berkeley city, California, 2010*. Retrieved from http://factfinder.census.gov

Weaver-Hightower, M. B. (2008). An ecology metaphor for educational policy analysis: A call to complexity. *Educational Researcher, 37*(3), 153–167.

Wells, A. S., & Frankenberg, E. (2007). The public schools and the challenge of the Supreme Court's integration decision. *Phi Delta Kappan, 89*(3), 178–188.

Wells, A. S., & Holme, J. J. (2005). No accountability for diversity: Standardized tests and the demise of racially mixed schools. In J. C. Boger & G. Orfield (Eds.), *School resegregation: Must the South turn back?* (pp. 187–211). Chapel Hill: The University of North Carolina Press.

Werts, A. B., & Brewer, C. A. (2015). Reframing the study of policy implementation: Lived experience as politics. *Educational Policy, 29*(1), 206–229.

Wicinas, B. (2009a). *Chronology: The fashioning of a race-blind integration plan in Berkeley Unified School District, 1999–2004*. Retrieved from http://friendofberkeley.com/busd/TimelineBerkeleyPlan2003.htm

Wicinas, B. (2009b). *The gestation of the 1993 integration plan, Berkeley Unified School District, 1989–1995*. Retrieved from http://friendofberkeley.com/busd/TimelineBerkeleyPlan1993.htm

Wollenberg, C. (2008). *Berkeley, a city in history*. Berkeley: University of California Press.

Public Educational Policy as Performance: A Queer Analysis

Michael P. O'Malley and Tanya A. Long

Abstract This critical policy analysis examines the publicly contested process through which one school district in Texas successfully enacted a queer inclusive policy. The purpose of this research is to illuminate dynamics of policy adoption in order to support development of equitable educational policies. Analysis focused on performativity of the body politic, with attention to how emergent transgressive discourses of queer equity in educational policy are taken up, enacted, and contested within the public sphere. Data sources were a sample of 74 print media articles from 2006 to 2014 reporting on the policy development and statewide struggle related to the district's 2012 adoption of domestic partner benefits. The analysis identified two key strategies used in the public sphere to impede policy adoption: (1) a patterned public representation of queer inclusive policy as hetero-exclusive; (2) a restratification of heteronormative social organization through disciplinary mechanisms. It also identified two strategies used by the district to facilitate adoption of this equity oriented policy: (1) socially transformative leadership through systematic engagement across differences; (2) building district social justice capacity. Implications identify strategies for managing equity oriented policy development within contested contexts, and also address the value of queer theory as an intellectual tool for critical policy analysis.

Keywords Critical policy analysis • Queer theory • Educational policy • Performativity

Educational communities and policy systems within the U.S. are located on rapidly shifting terrain in terms of inclusion and equity for queer persons in society. Sears' (1993) observation nearly one generation ago that queer persons in public schools have been relegated to the status of invisible minority remains steadfastly accurate in some contexts and decidedly interrupted in others. This current decade's acceleration of federal judicial rulings affirming legalization of "gay marriage" as

M.P. O'Malley (✉) • T.A. Long
Counseling, Leadership, Adult Education and School Psychology Department,
Texas State University, San Marcos, TX, USA
e-mail: mo20@txstate.edu

a matter of equal rights culminated in the U.S. Supreme Court's 2015 decision in *Obergefell v. Hodges* that affirmed the right of same-sex couples to marry in all U.S. states. The majority decision's reliance on the due process and equal protection clauses of the 14th Amendment to acknowledge a fundamental constitutional right for gay couples to participate in the social institution of marriage raises additional questions about school districts' legal responsibilities to ensure that differences involving sexual identity, gender identity, and gender expression do not lead to limitations in equity and access in regards to participation in the social institution of public education. Regardless of how and when recognition of these legal obligations unfolds, public school leaders already face an immediate ethical imperative to address what is currently known about limitations to educational and employment equity and access for queer persons. The underlying equal protection principle that guarantees access to the institution of marriage for queer persons carries logical implications for other state institutions oriented toward the common good, such as the public school. This is a remarkably significant and rapid shift in the U.S. policy landscape, and it is one for which educational leaders, policymakers, and the general field of educational leadership appear woefully underprepared.

The educational research base provides clear documentation that a disproportionate number of queer youth experience harassment and assault at school as well as elevated risk factors in comparison to their straight identifying peers (Himmelstein and Brückner 2010; Kosciw et al. 2012; Robinson and Espelage 2011, 2012). Principals themselves are cognizant of this reality, with only one third of surveyed secondary school principals reporting that lesbian, gay, and bisexual youth feel very safe at their school and one quarter of those same respondents reporting that transgender youth feel very safe at their school (GLSEN and Harris Interactive 2008). Despite this established field-wide knowledge, respondents to a survey of full time professors associated with principal preparation in University Council for Educational Administration (UCEA) member institutions indicated that, when preparing candidates for equitable leadership practice, sexual orientation and religion/belief are the least attended of eight identity constructs surveyed[1] (O'Malley and Capper 2015). In sum, principals report that a clear majority of queer youth do not feel very safe at school; the research documents that these youth experience elevated risk for harassment and assault *at school* as well as additional risk factors (such as cyber-bullying, victimization, suicidality, school absenteeism, and lower levels of school belongingness); and professors of educational leadership self-report that nonetheless preparation for equitable leadership for queer persons is among the least attended identity and diversity constructs within their programs. This

---

[1]For respondents who identified their principal preparation program as social justice oriented (n = 179), 48.6 % indicated that that their program gives high to moderate emphasis to leadership in relation to differences in sexual orientation and 45.1 % reported the same related to religion/belief. For respondents who reported that their principal preparation program is not characterized as social justice oriented (n = 39), 0.0 % indicated that that their program gives high to moderate emphasis to leadership in relation to differences in sexual orientation and 13.9 % reported the same related to religion/belief (see O'Malley and Capper 2015).

is particularly troubling given that survey respondents represented a minimum of 64.6 % of UCEA institutions (n = 53, with less than half of respondents identifying their institution) located across all U.S. Census Divisions (O'Malley and Capper 2015).

Within this context, it is fairly easy to project future moments in which public school leaders in many states will be scrambling to meet newly clarified legal obligations regarding equal and non-discriminatory access to public schools, inclusive of study and employment practices, for queer youth, families, and staff.[2] Such a scenario calls to mind the complications and confusion evident as many higher education institutions and school districts sought to respond to the U.S. Department of Education's 2014 *Questions and Answers on Title IX and Sexual Violence*. There is an obvious lack of leadership in waiting to reactively develop and implement queer inclusive policies in schools as a response to new legal mandates rather than proactively doing so at a systems level. Given the challenges of the present moment, developing adequate queer inclusive policies is a matter of ethical and equitable leadership practice, and must involve both developing protective policies aimed at establishing a minimally safe environment (anti-bullying, harassment, or discrimination) and extending these into inclusive policies that create an authentically equitable environment for queer youth, staff, and families in public educational settings (Goodman 2005; Koschoreck and Slattery 2010; O'Malley 2013). Inclusive policies for students, for example, might unequivocally address rights of same-sex students to attend school dances or proms together as dates, transgender students' access to athletic teams, queer students to equal self-expression in the classroom, and inclusive curricula representing queer histories and knowledge (O'Malley 2013). Arguably, a significant portion of local, state, and federal educational policies currently fail in this regard.

Against this policy background of a lack of coherent leadership from university-based principal preparation programs and many legislative assemblies, our inquiry focused on searching out meaningful leadership practices enacted at the school district level that might serve as guidance for both principal preparation programs and policy actors. Specifically, this critical policy analysis (Diem et al. 2014; Eppley 2009) focused on the publically contested process through which one school district in Texas successfully enacted a concrete queer inclusive policy. Our policy case utilized a queer theoretical framework to examine the process by which Pflugerville Independent School District (PfISD) became the first school district in Texas to adopt domestic partner benefits, inclusive of same sex couples, which occurred in 2012–2013 prior to the *Obergefell* decision. Through the lens of queer theory, our analysis engaged print media representations as a unit of analysis to identify normalizing assumptions inscribed within selected educational policies and map

---

[2]At publication, 35 states have no laws or regulations prohibiting discrimination against queer students; 20 states have no laws or policies prohibiting discrimination against queer employees. The Federal Equal Employment Opportunity Commission is now accepting complaints of gender identity discrimination in employment based on Title VII. (Human Rights Campaign, April 5, 2015).

the public process through which the district's queer inclusive school policy was negotiated within the contemporary Texas policy environment. Implications from this case analysis support adoption of additional queer inclusive and other equity oriented policies by school districts in complex and contested environments.

1 Conceptual Tools: A Queering of Critical Policy Analysis

Eppley (2009) describes Critical Policy Analysis (CPA) as overtly political work oriented toward justice. She defines its goal as analysis to "contextualize policy within its historical and political landscape, positioning policy as reflective of a group or individual's vision of an ideal society" (p. 1). Informed by this understanding, we conducted our particular analysis through a queer theoretical lens in order to make visible and problematize the socio-political constructions that frequently render the design of queer inclusive educational policy for K-12 schools a Sisyphean task. Queer theory is a systematic and disciplined framework for social inquiry that is less interested in mapping discrete definitional categories onto the bodies and desires of gendered and sexualized minorities than it is in troubling the implications of cultural production within heteronormative societies (O'Malley 2013). For critical policy scholars, taking up this critique of heteronormativity requires deliberative awareness of how normalizing circulations of power and privilege within the policy environment historically and most frequently presume that citizens implicated in any given educational policy are and will forever "be" heterosexual. As Lugg and Murphy (2014) explicate, for queer theory "homophobia is expected to be part of everyday life, no matter how enlightened the institution or particular individual might claim to be – even including queer people themselves" (p. 1186–1887). Warner (1993) crystallizes the import of heteronormativity by defining it as the assumption that "humanity and heterosexuality are synonymous" (p. xxiii). The historically located social imagining of schools and their communities as constituted by heterosexuals (Blount 2000; Lugg 2003) has the regulatory effect of making queer inclusive educational policies appear abnormal, which further provides the illusion of a threat calling for the mobilization of social actors and institutions in order to restratify heteronormative modes of social organization. Sedgwick (1990) argues that this presumption of heterosexuality and its attendant polarization of heterosexual and homosexual identities has been such a foundational organizing principle in contemporary Western societies that failure to interrogate it renders analysis of "virtually any aspect" of culture "damaged" (p. 1).[3] The influence of this organizing principle is evident even in the corpus of Critical Policy

---

[3]While heteronormativity is hardly constrained to Western societies, it is important for cultural inquirers to untangle the globalized regulatory and representational implications of European colonization. See, for example, Nina Asher's (2015) discussion of the introduction of anti-sodomy laws into India via Chapter XVI, Section 377 of the Indian Penal Code, which she also describes as "a gift from our kind colonizers" (personal communication, April 10, 2015).

Analysis scholarship, an analytical frame oriented toward uncovering structures of oppression within social, institutional, and professional configurations (Lugg and Murphy 2014). For example, our review of CPA scholarship published in primary U.S. educational leadership and policy journals between the years 2009 and 2014 noted minimal attention to queer issues and no discussion of the implications of structural heteronormativity for educational policy development. Following from Sedgwick (1990), this observably patterned trajectory within CPA renders this otherwise immensely valuable body of work simultaneously damaged.

Informed by a queer theoretical lens, then, our critical analysis foregrounds interrogation of heterosexuality as a frequently privileged and compulsory construct in educational policy development that depends on the "closet," understood as codes of knowing and not knowing, for its own "intimate representational needs [that the closet] serves in a way less extortionate to [itself]" (Sedgwick 1990, p. 69). The metaphor of the closet functions as an organizing discursive arrangement that nominally involves degrees of silence and visibility in regards to one's sexual and gendered difference from the presumed heterosexual norm. In a classic manifestation of Cartesian inherited dualistic thinking, one is either "in" or "out" of the closet. Of course, this metaphor works from the vantage point of the presumed heterosexual voyeur who enjoys the privilege of not having to describe oneself in relation to the regulating constraints of the closet. Heterosexuality is centered, presumed, and normative; while queer experience is a focal point for the panoptic gaze that either enforces closeting or permits levels of transgressive openness. The key to Sedgwick's thinking is that the discursive construction of heterosexuality as both normative and dominant depends on the closet. Put differently, the presumption of heterosexuality and its attendant privileging requires the oppositional imagining of a queered other who is "not us." Epistemologically, the closet serves the representation of heterosexuality not queerness.

Interrogation into the functioning of these codes of knowing and not knowing that constitute the discursive structure of the closet, and its attendant material effects in lives and social institutions, is particularly interesting in relation to the work of Critical Policy Analysis in education. Such work is located within a larger educational leadership and policy field that expresses clear trajectories of sympathy for creating welcoming and inclusive environments for queer persons while simultaneously failing to substantively incorporate such issues into the field's research agendas or principal preparation practices (see O'Malley and Capper 2015). Our review of the CPA literature in educational leadership over the most recent 5 years reflects a similar absence of queer issues from its scholarly agenda. In terms of knowing/not knowing, there appears to be in place in the field a complex coding system that allows the claiming of a queer ally status without actually incorporating queer related issues into teaching and research programs in substantive ways. This line of thinking frequently extends into even the simplest of strategies, as evident in the field's predominant commitment to subjugating research participants or graduate student candidates into the exclusionary gender categories of male and female despite extensive scientific knowledge regarding the biological and social complexity of gender (Fautso-Sterling 2000; Slattery 2013; Thurer 2005).

Such epistemological stances are particularly dangerous because they allow for "knowing" the importance of queer inclusion, and the attendant assuaging of liberal heterosexual guilt that this positionality provides, while "not knowing" how or even that such work ought to be taken up in educational research, policy, and practice.

2 Methods

Within this historical and theoretical context, our study examined the social reality of schooling as created through discursive processes, such as educational policy, and performativity – the continued bodily and structural repetition of those discursive arrangements via enactment within social institutions (Butler 1990; Gamson 2000). Our critical policy analysis, augmented by the poststructural investments of queer theory, focused specifically on performativity of the body politic, with attention to how emergent transgressive discourses of queer equity within educational policy have been taken up, enacted, and contested within the public sphere. Given our conceptual understanding of the general location of U.S. educational policy within a heteronormative matrix, we were particularly interested in the process through which one school district operating in a state with high opposition to LGBT equitable educational policy nonetheless successfully introduced one such inclusive policy. Print media representations were the primary data source for this analysis because we have been most interested in the performance of the body politic in relation to this issue, which is to say how a constellation of public actors and social institutions reacted to the district's interruption of the structural enactment of heteronormalized educational policy. These print media representations from major news outlets in the state provided a comprehensive, albeit partial, view of processes through which the body politic resinscribed and interrupted heteronormative performance. Because queer theory impels us to move beyond critique to advocacy and activism that alters material conditions, we took as our starting point the demonstrated leadership of the district staff and attended most directly to public intersections with other policy actors so as to inform further capacity building for systematically equitable policy enactment across a range of differences.

Data sources included a sample of 74 print media articles from 2006 to 2014 reporting on the development, implementation, and state-wide struggle over the 2012 adoption of domestic partner benefits (DPB) in the Pflugerville Independent School District in Central Texas. Pflugerville Independent School District (PfISD) was the first school district in Texas to adopt these benefits. Located in the Austin-Round Rock-San Marcos metropolitan area, just north of the Austin city limits, Pflugerville consists of nearly 46,936 residents with approximately 64.1 % identifying as White, 27.7 % as Hispanic or Latino, 15.5 % identify as African-American, 7.4 % identify as Asian, and .1 % identifying as Native Hawaiian/Pacific Islander (United States Census Bureau 2010). Overlapping a northwest section of the City of Austin, PfISD reported a 2014 total enrollment of 24,000 students within 3 high schools, 6 middle schools, 19 elementary schools, and 2 alternative campuses ("Pflugerville Texas Official Website," 2015). The print media sample was produced via a comprehensive search of online databases between the years 2006 and 2014 for the following five Texan newspapers: *San Antonio Express News*, the *Austin American Statesman*, *The Dallas Morning News*, the *Houston Chronicle*, and *Community Impact News*. The first four of these newspapers were selected for the sample in order to include a media perspective from each of the four largest metropolitan areas in Texas (Houston, San Antonio, Dallas and Austin). A news outlet's circulation within the state's larger metropolitan areas was identified as an indicator of the papers' visibility and influence. These four newspapers rank in the top five highest circulation of Texas daily newspapers, with the *Fort Worth Star-Telegram* excluded because the Dallas-Forth Worth metropolitan region is represented in the sample by a Dallas paper (Cision 2013). *Community Impact News* was included in the sample because it provides local news reports focused on the Austin metropolitan region, within which Pflugerville ISD is located. Search categories focused on PfISD and domestic partner benefits, Texas school districts and domestic partner benefits, and social justice and equity topics related to PfISD. Secondary sources included selected media representations from other outlets that were identified through a general search of significant themes emerging from the five print sources, and which were assessed as relevant to understanding public performativity of the body politic in regards to this case.

Data analysis for print sources was conducted in two iterative processes. The first stage used the media sample to construct a chronological narrative of the policy adoption process, tracking it through development to final approval. This narrative is a critical analytic work that forms a microhistory of this policy event, one that is shaped to "reveal patterns of long-term social interactions and domination, while showing how people on a smaller scale still disrupt and bend these social structures" (Brewer 2014, p. 274). Assembled from media reports of public events and re/actions, this microhistory aims less at probing the personal meaning making of individual policy actors than at mapping the constellation of public representation that both defined the policy conflict and illuminated contesting discourses and actions within the body politic. The second stage of analysis involved coding and categorizing methods to identify primary codes across the texts (Lieblich et al. 1998). Queer theory informed this analysis by focusing primary coding on mapping heteronormative assumptions, queer inclusive strategies, the interruption of heteronormative structures, and expression of social codes of knowing and not knowing in relation to queer persons and issues. From the primary codes, we developed a theme-based framework to further analyze the data. This framework focused analysis on (1) how queer inclusive educational policy was represented, (2) specific reactions or engagement in the public sphere in relation to this policy, and (3) strategies that supported the policy adoption through interruption of normalizing claims. The purpose of this analytical format was to display the case of queer inclusive policy implementation in a manner that both addresses this particularized experience and also allows implications to be drawn for other policy cases (Stake

2000). The following sections first use the news sources to create a case history of the policy adoption process and then discuss the analytical themes generated from that history.

3 Data Presentation: A Social Justice Microhistory

Pflugerville Independent School District's 2012 ratification of a DPB policy is best understood within the context of the district's visible arc of developing social justice and equity-oriented practice. Tracking back to 1996, for example, PfISD Personnel Director William Jennings was cited in an *Austin American Statesman* article regarding the import of an equity focus in increasing the percentage, rather than number, of minority educators in a growing area school district ("Striving for Diversity," 1996). Four years later, PfISD hired Rachel Warren as an Assistant Principal in Dessau Elementary School in 2000. In 2010, Warren became the Director of Secondary Staffing, and then the Director of Professional Learning. Warren became founder of the PfISD Diversity Steering Committee, a committee that helped to establish partnerships with Texas A&M University and various other organizations concerned with social justice issues. According to the PfISD website (n.d.), Warren helped to organize PfISD's 1st Annual Diversity Conference in 2006 in conjunction with her alma mater, the University of Texas at Austin. The conference agenda presented a thematic focus "for Equity and Social Justice in Education" ("Pflugerville Independent School District," n.d.). Warren was an integral player in establishing the Anti-Defamation League's (ADL) *No Place for Hate* program within the Pflugerville schools in 2009 ("Pflugerville Independent School District," n.d.). This program was designed by the ADL for "fighting hatred and encouraging diversity in schools K-12" ("Anti-Defamation League," 2015, para. 2). In October of 2010, *Community Impact News* reported that PfISD's Gay-Straight Alliance (GSA) was hosting the district's first Ally Night "as a way to support members of the Lesbian, Gay, Bisexual, Transgender (LGBT) community and work to create an inclusive and safe environment for all students" (LaFlure 2010, para. 1). According to this article, the efforts of the PfISD GSA were offered, in part, as a response to a 2009 student conducted survey where 37 % of the PfISD population in both the middle and high schools stated that they had been victims of discrimination. Initially, this survey sparked a gathering of approximately 50 students, staff and parents collectively concerned about the findings. LaFlure quoted Leslie Nguyen-Okwu, at the time a senior at Pflugerville High School and co-president of the GSA, as saying "It's something that many high schools are affected with, and we want to send a message that it's going to get better... No one deserves to be alone" (LaFlure 2010, para. 3). These actions document the development of a disposition within PfISD to openly discuss and promote diversity, inclusive of queer populations. We identify these actions as evidence of an evolving diversity profile of this school district that led to the DPB policy proposal in 2012. It is evident that

PfISD deliberatively sought to construct an expansive equity based infrastructure. In turn, such an infrastructure disposed the district toward publically and proactively taking up a broad range of justice issues. This is a marked contrast to reactive policy and practice approaches that begin to address particular equity issues when indicated by legislation, case law, public protest, or the public occurrence of negative or tragic events.

3.1 Domestic Partner Benefits in Pflugerville

When the *Austin-American Statesman* reported in October 2012 that PfISD was intending to adopt a domestic partner benefits program, it was hardly a step out of the district's social justice trajectory (Taboada 2012a). PfISD Superintendent Charles Dupre stated:

> We're going to advocate for equity and social justice and set expectations for valuing our employees. We went into this knowing with our eyes open that there'd be people who weren't supportive of the idea, but we'd been having hard discussions about social justice. You have to make decisions that are not popular but are in the best interest of the organization and the people of the organization (para. 3–4).

Information related to this particular report was also posted on a national blog website later that same month ("Education News," 2012). The new post entitled "Pflugerville School District is Gay Friendly" reported within the first few lines of the narrative that "Pflugerville school district will be the first in Central Texas — and probably the first in the state — to offer insurance benefits to same-sex and heterosexual domestic partners" ("Education News," 2012, para. 1). By late October, many news reports associated with the district's DPB policy characterized this policy as an LGBT platform issue, even though Superintendent Dupre repeatedly stated that the DPB policy was in the best interests of all PfISD employees (Vinson 2012). Later that October, the *Austin American Statesman* published an article entitled "Pflugerville Schools' Same-Sex Benefits Policy Draws a Crowd Thursday Night" (Taboada 2012b). According to this report, more than 150 attendees were present at the monthly PfISD school board meeting, a majority to oppose the decision by the board to adopt the DPB policy and calling for the board to rescind the decision. During this period of time, media accounts began to increase surrounding the topic of DPB policies in Pflugerville. In late October, statements about Pflugerville's policy initiative made by Donna Garner–a retired teacher from the state of Texas, a columnist, a conservative activist, and an active contributor to the *Education News* blog site ("Donna Garner," n.d., para. 1)–were published to the KGAB.com website:

> By setting up such a policy, PISD would draw LGBT teachers (and pedophiles) from all over the country who would want to come to Pflugerville for the same-sex insurance benefits. Obviously, where is the best place for homosexuals and pedophiles to recruit? They love being around vulnerable children and teens. This would in turn endanger the children of PISD and would also cost the taxpayers huge sums of money to provide insurance coverage

for the unhealthy LGBT employees. (How would the PISD taxpayers like the idea of paying for the transgender operations and medical procedures for their children's teachers? How would parents explain to their children that their teacher's name was Mr. Smith one day and Ms. Smith the next?). (Garner 2012, para. 4)

KGAB is an a.m. radio station broadcasting out of Wyoming. KGAB is also an affiliate of FOX Radio and, as part of regular programming, includes broadcasts of national shows such as The Rush Limbaugh Show and The Sean Hannity Show ("On Air," n.d., para. 2–3). By the end of October, the news of PfISD's proposal of DPB was beginning to reach national attention as information was being picked up by more nationally distributed news sources. Performances like the trope about "LGBT teachers (and pedophiles)" gaining access to the vulnerable children of Texas (Garner 2012, para. 4) were complemented by a request from then Senator Dan Patrick of Houston (currently the lieutenant governor of Texas) that Attorney General George Abbott (currently the governor of Texas) "issue an opinion on whether government entities that provide domestic partner insurance benefits are violating the state Constitution" (Baugh 2012, para. 1). Senator Patrick further requested that Abbott review all county and city governmental entities in Texas offering domestic partnership benefits, which included "at least three counties and five cities in Texas, including San Antonio, Fort Worth, El Paso, Dallas and Austin" (Baugh 2012, para. 2).

In November 2012, the *Austinist* published a web-based article entitled "Pflugerville ISD Backtracks on Same-Sex Partner Benefits" (Sandoval 2012). At that time, PfISD did not actually "backtrack" on the decision to offer DPB, but rather at the request of a small and "vocal minority" agreed to "review its decision" at a board meeting to be held in December 2012 (Sandoval 2012, para. 1). As *Community Impact News* reported, "several of the board members stated they were unaware of what they were approving when they voted Aug. 16 to allow the insurance coverage change as part of the district's overall budget plan" (Eichmiller 2012, para. 3). The *Houston Chronicle* drew a public correlation between Pflugerville's DPB policy and the actions taken by Senator Patrick in reporting Patrick's statement that "the question is, are they pushing the envelope to the edge or are they violating the law" (Hassan 2012, para. 3).

In December of 2012, the Pflugerville ISD Board of Trustees revisited the ratification of the DPB policy. Amidst a fairly strong political backlash and public controversy, the board voted to endorse the DPB policy by a 5:1 vote. The next day, local news media posted a range of headlines such as "Pflugerville ISD Votes to Violate Texas Constitution" (Walls 2012) and reports that "Trustees, before a crowd of 225 employees, parents and other residents, in a 5 to 1 vote, rejected a motion by Trustee Jimmy Don Havins to rescind the insurance benefits" (Taboada 2012c, para. 4). In February 2013, Board Trustee Carol Fletcher explained the reasoning behind the DPB policy ratification: "We did it because we believe in treating everyone equally. Our job is to take care of the Pflugerville family and that's how we see our employees: as family" ("Texas Association of School Boards," 2013, para. 4). During the 83rd Legislative Session of Texas in 2013, State Representative Drew Springer filed HB 1568 which proposed to cut 7.5 % funding for instructional facilities and debt payment to schools that adopted a DPB policy. By February

26, 2013 the bill had 27 coauthors and Springer had indicated that "Pflugerville ISD's decision conflicts with the Texas Constitution, citing the 2003 Defense of Marriage Act, which defined marriage in the constitution as a union between one man and one woman" (Kezar 2013, para. 4). As *United States v. Windsor* landed on the U.S. Supreme Court docket, Springer forged ahead stating that "our tax-dollars are for educating kids, not for enacting policies that attempt to get the state to recognize homosexual relationships ... to think Pflugerville has sued the state for more funding, while at the same time bankrolling a lifestyle most Texans do not agree with is quite disturbing to me" ("Daily Kos," 2013, para. 2).

The suit referenced by Springer was filed by a coalition of school districts that were challenging Texas' school financing mechanisms with the view that "districts must have substantially equal access to similar revenue per pupil at similar levels of tax effort" (Scharrer 2011, para. 3). A relevant clarity presented in the media regarding fiscal issues related to PfISD's initiative include an *HR Exchange* post in early February, reporting that "the district self-funds its health insurance plan and only pays for employee coverage. Employees pay insurance premiums for family members. The same rule applies to domestic partners" ("Texas Association of School Boards," 2013, para. 4). In addition, the district, the board, and Superintendent Dupre publically stated that the DPB policy was not a gay or straight issue but an issue of equal access. Although HB 1568 was voted out of committee, it did not make it to a House vote and was not signed into law ("Texas Legislature Online," 2013).

In March of 2013, the adjacent and significantly larger Austin Independent School District (AISD) adopted a DPB policy. The AISD DPB policy was projected to cost the district approximately $600,000 annually. This was distinct from PfISD's policy that, according to this report, had "'dependents' who pay into their partners' insurance plan, at no additional cost to the district or state" (Farmer 2013, para. 2). Nevertheless, AISD decided to go ahead with the DPB policy. Until this point, Abbott had not commented on DPB policies as Sen. Patrick had requested. In April 2013 Abbott made the statement that "the political subdivisions you ask about have not simply provided health benefits to the partners of their employees. Instead, they have elected to create a domestic partnership status that is similar to marriage" (as cited by Hoppe 2013, para. 2). This was an act considered by many within Texas political spheres to be in direct contradiction to state law. Abbott's generalized critique encompassed other Texas cities and counties that had previously established DPB policies prior to the PfISD case, as well – cities such as San Antonio – claiming that they were squandering taxpayer funds. Abbott's statements referenced a 2005 amendment to the Texas Constitution, supported by 76 % of voters, which defined marriage as a union between a man and a woman (Hoppe 2013; Kuffner 2013; Lindell 2013). In June 2013, after Abbott's statement, AISD rescinded their original offer of DPB; "the Austin school district will not offer health insurance benefits to domestic partners – for now, at least" (Taboada 2013, para. 1). Later in June 2013, *Community Impact News* reported the U.S. Supreme Court's June 26, 2013 ruling striking down a key aspect of the Defense of Marriage Act (DOMA) prohibiting federal recognition of same-sex marriages prompted AISD to revisit the notion of their inclusive DPB policy. According to AISD's Chief Human Capital Officer, "now that the Supreme Court rulings have been issued, and subject to extensive due diligence that must occur, it is possible that something may change over the next few months and allow the district to return to its original intent of offering domestic partnerships coverage" (Weldon 2013a, para. 1). Along with the DOMA ruling, in a separate court case concerning California's Proposition 8, the Supreme Court opened the field for the legalization of same-sex marriage and attendant benefits within the state of California, which "leaves other states to decide whether to allow same-sex marriages" (Weldon 2013a, para. 2). In August 2013, AISD reconstituted a DPB policy and began offering these benefits to both same-sex and heterosexual domestic partners (Weldon 2013b). Meanwhile, prior to the Supreme Court rulings, two PfISD board members who supported the DPB policy and who had been targeted for non-renewal were reelected to a new term in May 2013 (Austin American Statesman 2013).

4 Discussion

Our analysis in this case was less concerned with evaluating the impact of this specific policy than with the policy adoption process. We were focused on understanding the socio-political systems and contexts shaping equity-oriented policy development and adoption, and interested in the involvement of various stakeholder groups within this process. Contested equity policy development occurs within a politics of absence, a cultural location that imagines the "not yet" called for by justice work. This politics of absence invites the body politic to "approach monolithic and apparently immutable narratives ... to peer more closely, to lean in across their surprisingly permeable boundaries, to move in ways both thoughtful and energetic that fracture and break open self-supporting worldviews" (O'Malley 2009, p. 251). Our critical policy analysis identified five core themes related to a fracturing of a heteronormative educational policy structure that was elicited by the proposal of this DPB policy in PfISD. These include: patterned public representations of queer inclusive educational policy as hetero-exclusive, re-stratification of heteronormative social organization through disciplinary mechanisms, socially transformative leadership through systematic engagement across multiple and intersecting differences, and building district social justice capacity through structural efforts in professional development, hiring, and community engagement. Each of these themes are discussed in the following sub-sections.

4.1 Patterned Public Representation of Queer Inclusive Educational Policy as Hetero-Exclusive

Perhaps one of the most interesting findings in our analysis is the extent to which this queer inclusive policy was read by a significant component of the body politic as hetero-exclusive. Although Superintendent Dupre and the district were clear that DPB would include both heterosexually and LGBT identified persons, much of the media and legislative representation portrayed the policy as a specifically gay oriented policy. In a corollary to Warner's (1993) assertion that heteronormativity equates heterosexuality and humanity as synonymous, it appears that including queer persons in a policy is enough of a challenge to normative constraints to render policy portrayal as *homonormative*. Presenting this policy, which applied equally to both heterosexual and homosexual domestic partners, as "same-sex benefits" or "gay friendly," media representation fairly consistently identified the policy as LGBT oriented in headlines and news briefings. A similar representation is evident in particular legislative actions to block DPB implementation. Reflective of Sedgwick's (1990) concern about the centrality of the homo/heterosexual binary to social organization, these dynamics reveal a trajectory within the public sphere that codes gay inclusive policy as inapplicable to heterosexually identified persons. Identification of the policy's beneficiaries as exclusively or primarily comprised of a marginalized population facilitates a discursive process in which the policy can "more easily be slotted into a hierarchy or grid and then manipulated [and] dismissed" (St. Pierre 2000, p. 408).

4.2 Re-stratification of Heteronormative Social Organization Through Disciplinary Mechanisms

PfISD's adoption of DPB provided a substantive interruption of heterosexuality as a central principle of social organization in district and state level educational policy and practice (Sedgwick 1990). As the hetero-exclusive discourse noted above created an object for a collective straight gaze to ponder as ontologically separate and distinct from its own reality, disciplinary mechanisms rooted in this vantage point quickly emerged to re-stratify the "eruptive lines of flight" (de Zegher 2007, p. 17) evident in the district's policy initiative. Initial restraining efforts within the public sphere relied on a panoptic disciplinary mechanism (Foucault 1995), one which took up vocal protest, innuendo that the board had been misled, and overt linking of LGBT teachers with pedophilia in order to pressure the board and community into abandoning the policy. Masquerading as robust democratic engagement, such efforts work from and reassert a hegemonic construction of schools and schooling as heterosexual spaces. When panoptic discipline failed to reverse the initiative, which was instead reaffirmed in a 5:1 school board vote, more overt forms of punishment emerged. The clearest of these was HB 1568 which sought a 7.5 % reduction in state funding for instructional facilities and debt payment to school districts that adopted a DPB policy. While this sanction was nominally linked to DPB costs, PfISD self-funded its benefits and employees paid for family coverage. This escalated castigation would have had the effect of directly harming the district's instructional and fiscal operations in order to ensure that health benefits would not be afforded to a gay partner. Such efforts manifested within the body politic a material repetition of heteronormative discursive arrangement, a performativity that worded the schooling world as a "straight" reality (Butler 1990; St. Pierre 2000).

4.3 Socially Transformative Leadership Through Systematic Engagement Across Multiple and Intersecting Differences

Equal access and equity issues within the public institutions of marriage and schooling are democratic ideals at the crux of events as they unfolded in Pflugerville. Under Texas state law, private companies could adopt DPB policies but the state would not recognize any union other than those between heterosexual couples. PfISD demonstrated remarkable leadership in taking up a socially contested equity issue, in contrast to strong legislative and governmental opposition. By the fact of PfISD being the first Texas public school district to propose DPB, it is clear that the district operated from a unique vision distinct from the political norm in Texas. The question we took up in our analysis, and report out in this and the subsequent theme, is what dynamics generated this possibility. The reported history of PfISD in the sample of print media representations makes it clear that PfISD leadership was proactively engaged over extended time in advancing equity over multiple justice issues. The district had demonstrated substantive commitments to countering racism and anti-Semitism through its participation in *No Place for Hate*, advancing equitable representation of minority persons in the teaching force, engaging positively with the high school's Gay Straight Alliance, and hosting a public community forum to facilitate understanding across religious differences. PfISD's movement and unanticipated leadership on DPB policy in Texas is substantively linked to its ongoing culture and practice of advancing equity across multiple and interesting forms of difference. This initiative and its success were not achieved in isolation; rather the DPB policy work was part of a structured equitable educational policy initiative conducted via an intersectionality framework (Capper et al. 2006; O'Malley and Capper 2015). As such, it represents an alternate performativity within the body politic that challenges observed silences within educational leadership research and principal preparation practices, via a complicated strategy of organizing primarily by building alliances across difference rather than by identity (Brady 2006).

4.4 Building District Social Justice Capacity Through Structural Efforts in Professional Development, Hiring, and Community Engagement

The Pflugerville policy case can serve as a reflective lens for educational policy-making and leadership. There is a specific path that Pflugerville followed to arrive at the DPB policy that is precisely the opposite of a naïve attempt to act on a socially and politically contested equity issue in isolation. In contrast, PfISD's history demonstrates a deliberate practice of establishing structural supports to foster a climate of cultural awareness and equity. For example, the district systematically hired individuals with strong dedication to social justice and a deep understanding of the political shifts occurring both within Texas and the United States. It offered professional development at school and district levels to build capacity for social justice practice through its conferences and similar activities, and it publically engaged its community in learning related to equity across differences. This policy case, and PfISD's unique role as the first Texas school district to adopt LGBTQ inclusive domestic partner benefits, underscores the importance of systematic leadership to build structural capacity across the organization and its community to understand and engage equity issues.

5 Concluding Implications

Recalling that the metaphor of the closet demands interrogation of heterosexuality as a frequently privileged and compulsory construct in educational policy development (Pinar 1998; Sedgwick 1990), this analysis problematized the discursive arrangements and performative acts of a heteronormative perspective visible within this policy case. It further sought to understand how one school district successfully conceptualized and navigated adoption of a new equity policy. Critical Policy Analysis positioned our study to construct a historical narrative of this policy event that illuminated grids of hegemonic cultural production and emancipatory intervention (Brewer 2014), while applying queer theory as an analytic framework through which to interpret the data allowed us to focus on the intricacies through which normalization was resinscribed and resisted. Queer theory also gave us conceptual tools for refocusing analysis away from a study of "queerness," which in this case would have been a conceptual red herring, and onto the construction and interruption of constraining heteronormative discourses.

Our analysis leads to four recommendations for educational policy makers and district level leaders seeking to adopt a new equity oriented policy within a contested environment: (1) develop policy within an intersectionality framework that consistently addresses equity issues across multiple manifestations of difference, avoiding strategies that fragment marginalized populations from one another or from a consistently integrated equity practice; (2) precede policy proposal with systematic capacity building through leadership hiring and development, educator professional development, community engagement, and board communication; (3) publicly communicate that the policy serves multiple and intersecting constituencies, resisting external attempts to isolate the policy effect to only one marginalized population; and (4) anticipate an escalating disciplinary reaction, and be prepared to manage this through a transparent communication plan engaging multiple stakeholders. Taken as a whole, these recommendations form learning opportunities that relate to stakeholders as partners in equity work and create new possibilities to build as yet unrealized alliances across difference rather than by identity (Brady 2006). For educational policy scholars, we highlight the necessity of producing quality research that illuminates the experiences of LGBTIQ persons in schools and which supports policymakers and district leaders in advancing LGBTIQ equitable educational policy. It is time to end the extended silences within the educational leadership research community regarding LGBTIQ equity. Finally, we propose the value of queer theory as an intellectual tool for problematizing and interrupting normalizing assumptions inscribed in specific educational policies that have the material effect of fostering inequity across multiple manifestations of difference. Taking up queer theory as a resource for investigating equity issues not directly linked to LGBTIQ populations has the twinned benefit of expanding the intellectual and conceptual flexibility of our field and also legitimating "queer" associated topics, issues, insights, and theories as a pathway to knowledge within the field of educational leadership and policy. We invite our colleagues to join us in probing the possibilities that queer theory offers us in inquiry for a wide range of educational and social issues.

References

Anti-Defamation League. (2015). About [Website]. Retrieved from http://austin.adl.org/about/
Asher, N. (2015, April). *Queer, quotidian, and questioning in global times: Engaging hybrid identities and cultures in education*. Annual meeting of the American Educational Research Association, Division D: Measurement and research methodology, Section 3: Qualitative research methods, Chicago, IL.
Austin American Statesman. (2013, May 12). Incumbents retain their seats. Retrieved from http://nl.newsbank.com/nl-search/we/Archives?p_product=AASB&p_theme=aasb&p_action=search&p_maxdocs=200&s_hidethis=no&p_field_label-0=Author&p_field_label-1=title&p_bool_label-1=AND&s_dispstring=Pflugerville%20same%20sex%20AND%20date(all)&p_field_advanced-0=&p_text_advanced-0=(Pflugerville%20same%20sex)&xcal_numdocs=40&p_perpage=20&p_sort=YMD_date:D&xcal_useweights=no
Baugh, J. (2012, November 2). Houston senator questioning domestic partner benefits. *San Antonio Express News*. Retrieved from http://www.mysanantonio.com/default/article/Houston-senator-questioning-domestic-partner-4004826.php
Blount, J. M. (2000). Spinsters, bachelors, and other gender transgressors in school employment, 1850–1990. *Review of Educational Research, 70*(1), 83–101.
Brady, J. F. (2006). Public pedagogy and educational leadership: Politically engaged scholarly communities and possibilities for critical engagement. *Journal of Curriculum and Pedagogy, 3*(1), 57–60.
Brewer, C. A. (2014). Historicizing in critical policy analysis: The production of cultural histories and microhistories. *International Journal of Qualitative Studies in Education, 27*(3), 273–288.
Butler, J. (1990). *Gender trouble*. New York: Routledge.
Capper, C. A., Theoharis, G., & Sebastian, J. (2006). Toward a framework for preparing leaders for social justice. *Journal of Educational Administration, 44*(3), 209–224.
Cision. (2013). *Top 10 Texas daily newspapers*. Retrieved from http://www.cision.com/us/2013/05/top-10-texas-daily-newspapers/

Daily Kos. (2013, February 21). *TX bill would cut funding for school districts that offer domestic partner benefits* [Blog post]. Retrieved from http://www.dailykos.com/story/2013/02/21/1188823/-TX-bill-would-cut-funding-for-school-districts-that-offer-domestic-partner-benefits

de Zegher, C. (2007). Julie Mehretu's eruptive lines of flight as ethos of revolution. In C. de Zegher (Ed.), *Julie Mehretu drawings* (pp. 17–33). New York: Rizzoli International Publications, Inc.

Diem, S., Young, M. D., Welton, A. D., Mansfield, K. C., & Lee, P. L. (2014). The intellectual landscape of critical policy analysis. *International Journal of Qualitative Studies in Education, 27*(9), 1068–1090.

Donna Garner. (n.d.). Retrieved February 20, 2016, from http://eagnews.org/author/donna-garner/

Education News. (2012, October 8). *Pflugerville school district is gay-friendly* [Blog post]. Retrieved from http://www.educationviews.org/pflugerville-school-district-is-gay-friendly/

Eichmiller, J. P. (2012, November 16). Pflugerville ISD to reopen domestic partners insurance debate. *Community Impact News*. Retrieved from http://impactnews.com/austin-metro/round-rock-pflugerville-hutto/pflugerville-isd-to-reopen-domestic-partners-insurance-debate/

Eppley, K. (2009). Rural schools and the highly qualified teacher provision of No Child Left Behind: A critical policy analysis. *Journal of Research in Rural Education, 24*(4), 1–11.

Farmer, L. (2013, April 10). Lawmakers propose cutting funds to schools with same-sex partner benefits. *The Texas Observer*. Retrieved from http://www.texasobserver.org/districts-same-sex-benefits-threatened/

Fautso-Sterling, A. (2000). *Sexing the body: Gender politics and the construction of sexuality*. New York: Basic Books.

Foucault, M. (1995). *Discipline and punishment*. New York: Vintage Books.

Gamson, J. (2000). Lesbians, gays, straights, and the media. *GLQ: A Journal of Lesbian & Gay Studies, 6*(3), 451–454.

Garner, D. (2012, October 9). *Pflugerville ISD decision would put children in danger* [Blog post]. Retrieved from http://kgab.com/pflugerville-isd-decision-would-put-children-in-danger/

GLSEN & Harris Interactive. (2008). *The principal's perspective: School safety, bullying and harassment: A survey of public school principals*. New York: GLSEN.

Goodman, J. M. (2005). Homophobia prevention and intervention in elementary schools: A principal's responsibility. *Journal of Gay & Lesbian Issues in Education, 3*(1), 111–116.

Hassan, A. (2012, November 2). Sen. Patrick questions legality of domestic partnership benefits. *The Houston Chronicle*. Retrieved from http://www.chron.com/default/article/Sen-Patrick-questions-legality-of-domestic-4004790.php

Himmelstein, K. E. W., & Brückner, H. (2010). Criminal-justice and school sanctions against nonheterosexual youth: A national longitudinal study. *Pediatrics, 127*(1), 49–57.

Hoppe, C. (2013, April 29). AG says governments can't give benefits to domestic partnerships. *The Dallas Morning News Trailblazer's Blog* [Blog spot]. Retrieved from http://trailblazersblog.dallasnews.com/2013/04/attorney-general-says-no-to-domestic-partner-benefits.html/

Human Rights Campaign. (n.d.). Retrieved April 5, 2015, from www.hrc.org

Kezar, K. (2013, February 26). Proposed bill could reduce funds for Pflugerville ISD based on domestic partner benefits. *Community Impact News*. Retrieved from http://impactnews.com/austin-metro/round-rock-pflugerville-hutto/proposed-bill-could-cut-funding-for-pflugerville-isd-based-on-domestic-partner-benefits/

Koschoreck, J. W., & Slattery, P. (2010). Meeting all students' needs: Transforming the unjust normativity of heterosexism. In C. Marshall & M. Oliva (Eds.), *Leadership for social justice: Making revolutions in education* (2nd ed., pp. 156–174). Boston: Pearson.

Kosciw, J. G., Greytak, E. A., Bartkiewicz, M. J., Boesen, M. J., & Palmer, N. A. (2012). *2011 National School Climate Survey: The experiences of lesbian, gay, bisexual and transgender youth in our nation's schools*. New York: GLSEN.

Kuffner, C. (2013, May 1). Abbott opines on domestic partner benefits. *Kuff's World* [Blog spot]. Retrieved from http://blog.chron.com/kuffsworld/2013/05/abbott-opines-on-domestic-partner-benefits/

LaFlure, R. (2010, October 22). Pflugerville students hold ally night to combat bullying. *Community Impact News*. Retrieved from http://impactnews.com/austin-metro/round-rock-pflugerville-hutto/pflugerville-students-hold-ally-night-to-combat-bullying/

Lieblich, A., Tuval-Mashiach, R., & Zilber, T. (1998). *Narrative research: Reading, analysis, and interpretation*. Thousand Oakes: Sage.

Lindell, C. (2013, April 29). Domestic partner benefits violate same-sex ban, attorney general rules. *The Austin-American Statesman*. Retrieved from http://www.mystatesman.com/news/news/domestic-partner-benefits-violate-same-sex-ban-att/nXbr3/

Lugg, C. A. (2003). Our straitlaced administrators: The law, lesbian, gay, bisexual, and transgendered educational administrators, and the assimilationist imperative. *Journal of School Leadership, 3*(2), 51–86.

Lugg, C. A., & Murphy, J. P. (2014). Thinking whimsically: Queering the study of educational policy-making and politics. *International Journal of Qualitative Studies in Education, 27*(9), 1183–1204.

O'Malley, M. P. (2009). Pedagogies of absence: Education beyond an ethos of standardization. *Childhood Education, 85*(4), 250–252.

O'Malley, M. P. (2013). Creating inclusive schools for LGBTIQ youth, staff, and families: Equitable educational leadership and research practice. In L. C. Tillman & J. J. Scheurich (Eds.), *Handbook of research on educational leadership for equity and diversity* (pp. 355–379). New York: Routledge.

O'Malley, M. P., & Capper, C. A. (2015). A measure of the quality of educational leadership programs for social justice: Integrating LGBTIQ identities into principal preparation. *Educational Administration Quarterly, 51*(2), 290–330.

On Air. (n.d.). Retrieved February 20, 2016, from http://kgab.com/shows/monday/

Pflugerville Independent School District. (n.d.). Retrieved from http://www.pfisd.net/site/default.aspx?PageID=1

Pflugerville Texas Official Website. (2015). Retrieved from http://www.pflugervilletx.gov/

Pinar, W. F. (Ed.). (1998). *Queer theory in education*. Mahwah: Erlbaum.

Robinson, J. P., & Espelage, D. (2011). Inequities in educational and psychological outcomes between LGBTQ and straight students in middle and high school. *Educational Researcher, 40*(7), 315–330.

Robinson, J. P., & Espelage, D. (2012). Bullying explains only part of LGBTQ heterosexual risk disparities: Implications for policy and practice. *Educational Researcher, 41*(8), 309–319.

Sandoval, T. (2012, November 30). Pflugerville ISD backtracks on same-sex partner benefits. *Austinist* [Blog spot]. Retrieved from http://austinist.com/2012/11/30/plugerville_isd_back_tracks_on_same.php

Scharrer, G. (2011, October 11). Lawsuit challenges Texas public school funding. *The Houston Chronicle*. Retrieved from http://www.chron.com/default/article/Lawsuit-challenges-Texas-public-school-funding-2212906.php

Sears, J. T. (1993). Responding to the sexual diversity of faculty and students: Sexual praxis and the critically reflective administrator. In C. A. Capper (Ed.), *Educational administration in a pluralistic society* (pp. 110–172). Albany: State University of New York.

Sedgwick, E. K. (1990). *Epistemology of the closet*. Berkeley: University of California Press.

Slattery, P. (2013). *Curriculum development in the postmodern era*. New York: Routledge.

St. Pierre, E. A. (2000). Poststructural feminism in education: An overview. *Qualitative Studies in Education, 13*(5), 477–515.

Stake, R. (2000). Case studies. In N. K. Denzin & Y. S. Lincoln (Eds.), *Handbook of qualitative research* (2nd ed., pp. 435–454). Thousand Oaks: Sage Publications, Inc.

Striving for diversity. *Austin-American Statesman*. (1996, April 29). Retrieved from http://nl.newsbank.com/nl-search/we/Archives?p_product=AASB&p_theme=aasb&p_action=search&p_maxdocs=200&s_hidethis=no&p_field_label-0=Author&p_field_label-1=title&p_bool_label-1=AND&s_dispstring=Pflugerville%20ISD%20diversity%20AND%20date(all)&p_field_advanced-0=&p_text_advanced-0=(Pflugerville%20ISD%20diversity)&xcal_numdocs=40&p_perpage=20&p_sort=YMD_date:D&xcal_useweights=no

Taboada, M. B. (2012a, October 7). Pflugerville ISD to offer benefits for domestic partners. *Austin-American Statesman*. Retrieved from http://www.statesman.com/news/news/local/pflugerville-district-first-in-texas-to-offer-bene/nSWRX/

Taboada, M. B. (2012b, October 18). Pflugerville schools same-sex benefits policy draws a crowd Thursday night. *Austin-American Statesman*. Retrieved from http://www.statesman.com/news/news/pflugerville-schools-same-sex-benefits-policy-draw/nShCy/

Taboada, M. B. (2012c, December 13). Pflugerville school board votes to keep benefits for domestic partners. *Austin-American Statesman*. Retrieved from http://www.statesman.com/news/news/pflugerville-school-board-votes-to-keep-benefits-f/nTWbr/

Taboada, M. B. (2013, June 29). AISD balks at same-sex benefits. *Austin-American Statesman*. Retrieved from http://nl.newsbank.com/nl-search/we/Archives?p_product=AASB&p_theme=aasb&p_action=search&p_maxdocs=200&s_hidethis=no&p_field_label-0=Author&p_field_label-1=title&p_bool_label-S=AND&s_dispstring=Pflugerville%20same%20sex%20AND%20date(all)&p_field_advanced-0=&p_text_advanced-0=(Pflugerville%20same%20sex)&xcal_numdocs=40&p_perpage=20&p_sort=YMD_date:D&xcal_useweights=no

Texas Association of School Boards. (2013, February). Pflugerville ISD the first in Texas to offer domestic partner benefits. *HR Exchange* [Blog spot]. Retrieved from https://www.tasb.org/Services/HR-Services/Hrexchange/2013/February-2013/A-Domestic-Partners.aspx

Texas Legislature Online. (2013, February 20). *HB 1568* [Government report]. Retrieved from http://www.legis.state.tx.us/BillLookup/BillStages.aspx?LegSess=83R&Bill=HB1568

Thurer, S. L. (2005). *The end of gender: A psychological autopsy*. New York: Routledge.

United States Census Bureau. (2010). *Pflugerville (city) QuickFacts from the US Census Bureau* [Government Report]. Retrieved from http://quickfacts.census.gov/qfd/states/48/4857176.html

Vinson, J. (2012, October 10). Pflugerville to provide benefits for same-sex partnerships. *The Daily Texan*. Retrieved from http://www.dailytexanonline.com/news/2012/10/10/pflugerville-to-provide-benefits-for-same-sex-partnerships

Walls, D. (2012, December 14). Pflugerville ISD votes to violate Texas constitution. *Texas Values Blog* [Blog spot]. Retrieved from http://txvalues.org/2012/12/14/pflugerville-isd-votes-to-violate-texas-constitution/

Warner, M. (1993). *Fear of a queer planet: Queer politics and social theory*. Minneapolis: University of Minnesota Press.

Weldon, K. (2013a, June 28). Austin ISD insurance not covering domestic partnerships; district might revisit. *Community Impact News*. Retrieved from http://impactnews.com/austin-metro/southwest-austin/austin-isd-revisits-domestic-partnership-insurance-coverage/

Weldon, K. (2013b, August 21). Austin ISD to offer employee insurance benefits to same-sex partners. *Community Impact News*. Retrieved from http://impactnews.com/austin-metro/southwest-austin/austin-isd-to-offer-employee-insurance-benefits-to-same-sex-/

The Politics of Student Voice: Conceptualizing a Model for Critical Analysis

Anjalé D. Welton, Tiffany O. Harris, Karla Altamirano, and Tierra Williams

Abstract For 2 years we worked with a high school class focused on social justice education where students conducted their own research in order to develop policy solutions for issues of injustice that mattered most to them. This class helped initiate school level interest in how student voice can be integral to school improvement and policy processes. However, we observed how the full potential of students' voice in school policy was not realized due, primarily, to the politics of power. For our study we use critical policy analysis (CPA) as a method to reveal the politics of student voice as it pertains to power and school policy. We also conduct a CPA of our work with the social justice class to develop a conceptual framework for understanding the politics of student voice in schools. Finally, this chapter is different from traditional co-authored papers in that we seek to honor the politics of student voice by including two students, as co-authors and a legitimate source of knowledge, one that is often times overlooked or dismissed.

Keywords Student voice • Youth activism • Social justice education • Power • School policy • Politics

Within the context of K-12 schools student voice is primarily defined as students having some role in school-based initiatives such as school reform and improvement planning, as well as changes in classroom curriculum and instruction (Mitra 2006). Yes, promoting student voice is a democratic ideal, however, when school personnel call on students' opinions and participation to resolve school reform issues they must consider the contradictions in doing this work (Rudduck and Fielding 2006).

A.D. Welton (✉) • T.O. Harris
Department of Education Policy, Organization and Leadership, University of Illinois, Champaign, IL, USA
e-mail: ajwelton@illinois.edu

K. Altamirano
Parkland College, Champaign, IL, USA

T. Williams
Southern Illinois University, Carbondale, IL, USA

© Springer International Publishing Switzerland 2017
M.D. Young, S. Diem (eds.), *Critical Approaches to Education Policy Analysis*,
Education, Equity, Economy 4, DOI 10.1007/978-3-319-39643-9_5

There is cause for concern that students' perspectives are often consulted only if their insight helps satisfy state standards or raise school achievement (Robinson & Taylor 1997).

On the one hand, student voice and participation encourages students' connectedness and engagement in school, developing their leadership skills. On the other hand, when student voice is used to fulfill the pressures of school reform it only serves the "competitive demands of a stratified society" (Rudduck and Fielding 2006, p. 224). Unfortunately, in the U.S. context of top down, mandated federal and state level educational reforms, the voices and activism of students is largely inhibited (Mitra et al. 2014). For example, administering a school climate survey to students may satisfy the requirements of certain reforms, such as the requirement that school turnaround processes solicit students' opinions, but it gives students little power in determining school policy. Instead, students should be empowered to take action on controversial issues that matter, not become products of neoliberal reform objectives that reproduce learning and discourage students from developing their own ideas (Rudduck and Fielding 2006).

At a rudimentary level, student voice involves youth sharing their sentiments regarding school problems and possible solutions. However, we argue that simply "letting" students "have a say" in school reform is not enough to give them some authority over their own learning, let alone enabling them to have an impact on systemic changes school-wide. Instead, student voice should foster young people's capacity to take the lead in addressing issues that are the most meaningful to them.

For 2 years we had the privilege of working together in a spring semester high school class focused on social justice education. Students wrestled with social justice topics that even teachers and administrators, as we observed in several faculty meetings, were largely resistant to openly addressing. During the first half of the semester, students learned key concepts of social justice education specific to issues of power, privilege, gender, sexuality, and race. While during the second half of the semester, students engaged in youth participatory action research (YPAR) to develop solutions for issues that mattered most to them.

This class helped initiate school and district level interest in how social justice education and student voice can be integral to school improvement. Still, there were politics involved in fully supporting students' voices and activism school-wide and even in the class itself. Indeed, the students did impact the school and community wide conversation on social justice, they were able to alter some school regulations based on their research findings, and they facilitated professional development for teachers, university students and professors about social justice issues. Nevertheless, we observed how and acknowledged that the full potential of students' voice in school policy was not realized due, primarily, to the politics of power (see Bautista et al. 2013; Bertrand 2014).

Accordingly, we use this chapter as a platform to reflect on lessons learned from our experiences and search for ways to ensure that student voice is not just a novelty that is adorned, but is a normalized practice in educational policy and the quest for social justice. To accomplish this we use critical policy analysis (CPA) as a method to reveal the politics of student voice as it pertains to power and school policy. More specifically, we conduct a CPA of our work with the social justice class to develop a conceptual framework for understanding the politics of student voice in schools. Furthermore, this chapter is different from traditional co-authored papers in that we seek to honor the politics of student voice by including two students, Tierra and Karla, as co-authors and a legitimate source of knowledge, one that is oftentimes overlooked or dismissed.

For the purposes of this chapter, it is important to clarify how we operationalize "student," "youth" and the semantics of the terms when linked to the concept "voice." Scholars and practitioners for pragmatic purposes use the term "voice" as a "shorthand," yet the word has a number of meanings (Cook-Sather 2007; Robinson and Taylor 2007, p. 6). Literally, voice means speech, tone, inflection, verve, or accent, but voice can also be interpreted as the particular meaning or perspective the speaker conveys (Robinson and Taylor 2007). Voice also means speaking up on an issue (Hirschman 1970). Tierra asserts, "voice is something powerful, annunciated, for example the phrase of your opinion." Whereas, Karla equates voice to action, emphasizing that "voice is an interpretation of how you put feelings and actions into words."

While student voice typically refers to the impact students have on K-12 or postsecondary institutions, we recognize that throughout history students have also played a role in transforming institutions beyond schools, initiating some of the most significant social movements. Also, the social construct *youth* has taken on different meanings throughout different times in history (Kellner 2014). As a result, we recognize that in the field of education *youth voice* and *student voice* are used interchangeably and we consult from research that uses both concepts.

In our chapter, we first review literature on various models of student voice, making the distinction between student voice and youth activism. We then provide an overview of critical theoretical perspectives of youth that help consider how power can be captured in our conceptual framework. Next, to further inform our framework we examine the role power played in how students from the social justice (SJ) class aimed to articulate their voice on school and community injustices and impact the culture, policies, and practices of the school. Finally, we use our experiences with the research to provide recommendations for authentically engaging in student voice efforts, while still being open about the politics involved in doing the work.

1 Research Background

First, in this chapter we use CPA as a method to challenge the power hierarchies and spoken and unspoken traditions of authorship in academic scholarship, by collaborating with two students as co-authors; as it would be remiss in this study to critique the politics of student voice without actually giving students a voice in the methodological and analytical processes of doing so. Karla is a graduate of CHS and currently enrolled as a freshman at a local community college and Tierra is an expected graduating senior at CHS. There are several value-laden assumptions about who constitutes as an academic; therefore, we feel it necessary to explain that *we* mean co-authorship *with* students. In fact, co-author Karla, described how the "we" throughout this chapter is easily perceived as (comes across as) solely Dr. Welton and Tiffany. Karla suggested that all authors be clearly introduced before the first we. We, all four authors, believe that this chapter is an initial attempt towards actually incorporating student voice into discussions about school policies.

The first two authors of this chapter were already working as researchers with Carter High administration in restructuring the school's improvement processes to include more equity-oriented approaches. We realized the most authentic way to make equity the foci of Carter High's school improvement initiatives would be via student voice. Thus, we approached Ms. Collins, the teacher, about working with the SJ class in some capacity. We decided to organically determine the impact of the collaboration between the research team and the class along the way, whether it was supporting the high school students in their own research, working with students to impact school policy, or educating others about social justice issues through professional development. We were involved in conducting research in some capacity from January 2013 to December 2014, and observed the class specifically during the spring 2013 and 2014 semesters. All members of the core research team identified as a person of color, which consisted of one university professor (Black female) and three doctoral students (one Black female, one Black male, and one Asian American female). Also all the research team members were former teachers in urban school districts. Furthermore, we want to be transparent that the collaborative nature of the project meant that the researchers at times had a role and participated in the SJ class dialogue, and in the future we plan to write about the methodological complexity of this participatory process.

Borrowing from qualitative case study approaches, the class and the high school context in which it was situated served as a critical case or "bounded system," of which there are few examples in the research on student voice in high school classrooms with a diverse set of student identities (Stake 1978, p. 7). During the two spring semesters the class was held, the research team consistently conducted classroom observations 4 days out of every week. We conducted approximately 200 hours of classroom observations, writing detailed field notes that captured the classroom activities and dialogue. As participant observers we took "part in the daily activities, rituals, interactions, and events" in those engaged in the SJ class in order to learn "the explicit and tacit aspects" of the class (DeWalt and DeWalt 2011, p. 260). In addition to participatory observational field notes of the classroom, we also reviewed and consulted the teacher on the development of the class syllabus and lesson plans, as well as curricular and instructional artifacts. We examined artifacts such as student work products and any curricular materials in the form of graphic organizers used to help students synthesize their learning, readings and any handouts or presentation slides that Ms. Collins used to articulate concepts. In addition to class curricular and instructional materials we also included materials from various student-led lessons, presentations and professional development workshops. We then conducted two reflective and informal interviews with Ms. Collins, the teacher, to provide additional context to the larger case study. Lastly, as a final data source the two student co-authors of this chapter engaged in journaling as well as follow up meetings with the first two authors to discuss a series of reflective questions pertaining to the role of student voice in the SJ class and school-wide. The student co-authors reflected on their descriptions of the context (school and classroom), definitions and examples of student voice, and the extent to which they truly had a voice in school and in the classroom.

Secondly, we use CPA as a method to re-examine the abovementioned data. While CPA is a critical perspective with a number of utilities, for this chapter we relied specifically on CPA's focus on power. Diem, Young, Welton, Mansfield, and Lee (2014) conducted oral history interviews of self-identified critical policy scholars. One key research question the authors aimed to understand was how their participants "do" critical policy scholarship and why it is important (p. 1074). The scholars interviewed identified that one purpose of CPA is to study the role of power and voice in the policy process by asking questions such as, *Who may or may not be represented*? and *Who is privileged in making decisions and why?* Other questions considered were, *How does one social group's accumulation and domination of power results in another group's losses*? Scholars used CPA to uncover what voices are not heard in the policy process, and indeed, it is only fitting that we similarly use CPA in our research to understand the relative power of students' voices in the SJ class, as well as the level of influence students have on school-wide policy concerns that they deem are important to their educational experiences and opportunities. That is, we used CPA as method to consider "how did student voice influence the school culture, policy and decision making?"

Finally, we also use CPA as a method to develop an emerging conceptual framework for the politics of student voice. For the purposes of this chapter, we view a conceptual framework as a visual representation of a system of concepts, assumptions, expectations, beliefs, and theories and the relationship between them (Miles and Huberman 1994). Subsequently, in order to inform our conceptual frame, we examine how power is considered in the existing research literature on student and youth voice as well as our research with the SJ class.

2   Various Models of Student Voice in Schools

There are varying degrees of student voice in K-12 schooling. Michael Fielding (2001), whose work is commonly referenced in student voice scholarship, proposes the following continuum for student involvement in school improvement. The lowest level consists of teachers simply viewing *students as data sources for* gathering performance information such as exams or student attitudinal surveys. The subsequent level, *students as active respondents* is still teacher led, however, teachers do acquire students' input and feedback. Next, are *students as co-researchers*, where teachers collaborate with students to develop pedagogy, and conduct research to develop action plans for school improvement. Though collaboration is valued, as a caveat this level involves students' voices merely to support school initiatives that are adult led. Finally, the optimal level of involvement is *students as researchers* where the dialogue and activities for school improvement are student initiated and led. Similarly, Mitra (2005), proposes student voice proceeds in a pyramid with *being heard* at the base, next *collaborating with adults*, and *building capacity for leadership* at the apex. *Being heard* involves school personnel merely listening to students share their school related concerns. Next, students can *collaborate with adults* by collecting data that leads to solutions to address school problems. Finally, *building capacity for leadership* is the ideal form of student voice, but unfortunately the least achieved. At this level, students have a leadership role in making school policy decisions and are viewed as "capable public actors rather than clients of school-based services" (Kirshner and Pozzoboni 2011, p. 1636).

Instead of proposing progressing levels, Lodge (2005) suggests students' involvement in school improvement can be situated along a matrix of two dimensions—passive or active involvement. Passive forms only see *students as sources of information* or use student input for *quality control* purposes. Unfortunately, active student voice can be deceivingly misused as *compliance and control* when student input merely serves institutional/adult agendas. Whereas open, honest, and engaged *dialogue* is an approach to active student voice that acknowledges that youth can be active participants in their own learning. Kennedy and Datnow (2011) adapted Lodge's matrix in order to craft a three-tiered typology of student engagement in data-driven decision-making (DDDM). *Tier 1, students' active, dialogic involvement in DDDM*, is the highest level of the typology, and one example of this is student initiated and designed surveys that inform school improvement. *Tier 2* involves *using data to assess student engagement* in learning such as administrators conducting classroom "walk-throughs" to observe how students are participating in the instruction. Tier 3, *engaging students in data analysis and reflection*, students are not directly involved in reform but are at least asked to discuss data used to drive the reform. For example, students could be asked to reflect upon their own achievement data. While these various models are useful for conceptualizing student voice in K-12 settings, one critique would be that they are used to primarily examine students' involvement in school reform and improvement, which delimits other ways students can be involved in school transformation and display leadership.

While we appreciate the aforementioned literature that outlines the role of student voice in schools, each of these models do not explicitly/necessarily rely on students' opinions. Here, we choose to intentionally highlight the definitions of student voice based on Karla's and Tierra's perspectives as co-authors. Tierra explains student voice as "allowing youth to have an opinion to be supported by adults. If we way say something we feel like they can shut us down at any moment so we should be able to have the opportunity. We can teach adults. They have something to learn from us." Tierra explained further that, "Instead of the teacher trying to prove that they are right, the teacher understands that the student can be right also and learn from the student themselves. The adults always tell us that we should view things from different perspectives and they should be willing to do that themselves." Karla describes student voice as "interpretation of how you put feelings and actions into words. Most people who want to make a change show it with their actions."

3 Distinguishing Student *Voice* from *Activism*

It is one thing for students to have a "voice," but simply "being heard" is not enough to invoke the type of change school communities need to achieve their context specific equity-oriented goals (see Mitra 2005, 2006). As demonstrated by history, young people have the courage to not just simply have a "voice" but also take "action" even when there are social and political conditions impeding their social justice efforts. There is historical evidence that young people are the spark for and are often on the front lines of social justice agendas in their communities.

It is important to distinguish student *voice* from youth *activism*. According to Karla an "activist's voice brings together people with the same ideas; not simply standing on a pedestal talking to people. Also, action involves marches, talking to the community, promoting other people to follow your beliefs, transmitting ideas to people who don't have the same vocabulary."

Similarly Mitra et al. (2014) define youth activism as "young people taking collective action to challenge injustices that they experience in their schools or neighborhoods" (Mitra et al. 2014, p. 294). Although often dismissed, young people are key actors for ushering in social transformation over time (Costanza-Chock 2012), and youth activism is vital to understanding our global and national social movement history. The various roles that youth have played include both historical and contemporary examples that range from participation in the Civil Rights Movement, the Anti-War Movement, series of various feminism waves, environmental justice, the Occupy Movement, and immigration rights campaigns. Many of these organizing efforts are accompanied by the respective media of the time, "used to create, circulate, and amplify movement voice and stories" (Costanza-Chock 2012, p. 1). Youth activism has sustained through the years despite several challenges associated with perceptions about youth, how young people are represented in the media, and stricter public and educational policies.

Historical Examples Young people were at the forefront of mobilizing efforts during twentieth century social movements. For example, in 1951, 16-year-old Barbara Johns of Farmville, Virginia, organized a student walkout in protest of her overcrowded, segregated Moton High, and thus demanded a new school. This walkout helped to lay the groundwork for the National Association for the Advancement of Colored People (NAACP) involvement in incorporating the *Davis v. County School Board of Prince Edward County* case as one of the five combined cases collectively leading up to the *Brown v. Board Education* (1954) decision (Ajunwa 2011). Likewise, a student organization, *Advocating Rights for Mexican American Students* (ARMAS) in Houston, Texas, planned a walkout on September 16, 1969 to end discriminatory practices and argued for culturally relevant curriculum (Ajunwa 2011). More broadly, student voice and youth activism in the Civil Rights Movement included 15-year-old Claude Colvin being arrested for not giving up her seat on a Montgomery bus to a white person 9 months before Rosa Parks; Diane Nash playing a crucial role in strategizing for the Freedom Rides; and the Student Non-Violent Coordinating Committee's (SNCC) multifaceted approach of sit-ins, voter registration, and larger societal issues focused on feminism, white liberalism, and anti-war efforts (Costanza-Chock 2012).

More Contemporary Examples There are a number of contemporary examples of student voice initiating social movements and transforming policy. In February 2000, the *Youth Force Coalition* protested against zero tolerance policies in San Francisco Bay Area schools and the California Juvenile Justice Crime Bill, demanding more equitable opportunities (Ginwright et al. 2005). The *Books Not Bars* coalition, in 2001, attended a meeting of the California Board of Corrections "armed with statistics, reports, and financial forecasts" these "young people persuasively presented the board with a sound rationale and prompted it to deny funding. In a 10–2 vote, the board rejected Alameda County's $2.3 million funding request to build the prison" (Ginwright et al. 2005, p. 35). Furthermore, the October 2001 *Schools Not Jails* campaign consisted of student activism calling for more equitable funding to lower-income communities of color, a statewide review of standardized test effectiveness, and advocated for ethnic/women/queer studies courses to be offered in schools (Ginwright et al. 2005). Similarly, youth researchers participating in the *Edúcate* project support undocumented students by providing information about Utah's in-state tuition policy HB 144, updates on educational reports, and scholarship information (Quijada Cerecer et al. 2013).

Finally, the current #BlackLivesMatter movement, which was precipitated by the countless violence (both physical and symbolic) on young Black bodies across the U.S., continues to gain groundbreaking traction in demanding nationwide institutional and policy changes to eradicate systemic racism and white supremacy. All of these examples illustrate the influential role that youth activism has contributed to the policy decision-making process.

4 Leaning on Critical Theoretical Perspectives of Youth

While there are a number of critical theoretical perspectives that can be applied to a broad set of contexts in which youth engage, schools have political distinctions that warrant a framework to understand how students employ their voice within the institutional circumstances of schooling. Similarly, Kellner (2014) calls for

> a critical theory of youth that articulates positive, negative, and ambiguous aspects in their current situation. A critical theory delineates some of the defining features of the condition of contemporary youth to indicate the ways that they are encountering the challenges facing them, and to suggest how these might best be engaged. (p. 2)

Therefore, we aim to fulfill Kellner's appeal by using our research and experiences from the high school social justice class to develop a framework that teases out the politics of student voice in school policy processes. Although research specific to student voice in schools centers on increasing student involvement in school reform (Mitra 2006; Kennedy and Datnow 2011; Lodge 2005), scholars express concern that the contextual nuances and power dynamics that envelop student voice are minimally considered in the existing research (Rodríguez and Brown 2009; Mansfield 2014; Mansfield, Welton, and Halx 2012). Accordingly, our conceptual framing will help elucidate what is missing from student voice scholarship—the examination of *context* and how this matters to the *power* dynamics, or the politics of student voice.

Given the limitations in student voice research and to assist in the development of our framework on the politics of student voice, we turned to the field of *youth studies* where scholars have made more explicit attempts to craft critical theoretical perspectives on power as it pertains to *youth*.

There is a wide array of academic disciplines that make up the field of youth studies including cultural studies, ethnic studies, global studies, and much more. Traditionally, most research about youth has been studied through the context of schooling and developmental psychology. However, the field of youth studies seeks to complicate youth as a social construction by unpacking the following: (1) universal category of development; (2) as a category of modernity; (3) historical, cultural, social, and political emergence; (4) institutions and social structures that separate, create youth and age, and (5) youth as a metaphor for society (Ben-Amos 1995; Cote 2014; Enright et al. 1987; Kwon 2013; Sukarieh and Tannock 2014).

In our search we settled on the following three critical theoretical perspectives to examine their treatment of *context* and *power*: critical youth studies (CYS), social justice youth policy and/or development (SJYP/D),[1] and youth participatory action research (YPAR) (see Table 1). We define *context* as the sociopolitical circumstances and conditions in which student voice is enacted (see Milner 2012; Nieto and Bode 2009; Rodríguez and Brown 2009). Therefore, quite simply *power* is the capacity to do, act or "can-ness" (Holloway 2002, p. 28). Malen and Cochran (2008) emphasize that power from a "radical" or "critical" perspective is not always a direct/overt influence but is more often an "opaque 'third face'" form of "power relations" that "shape aspirations and define interests" through more subtle "processes of socialization/indoctrination" (p. 4). Also, it is important to understand how policies represent and are equivalent to power and knowledge (Childers 2014). Hence, in our conceptual framing we distinguish how an individual student or group's capacity to have voice in school political processes typically fluctuates from either having the *power to* versus other forces having the *power over* their voices (Holloway 2002, p. 28).

---

[1]The scholars who designed the frameworks social justice youth policy and social justice development use similar principles to define each framework. Therefore, we merged these two frameworks in our overview of various critical theoretical perspectives on youth.

Table 1 Critical theoretical perspectives on youth

Critical perspectives on youth	Key concepts	Context	Power
Critical youth studies (CYS)	Criticism of adult-centered institutions; prolematizes how youths' behaviors are policed by adults; criticizes institutional and individual discourses that characterizes certain youth (based on race, class, gender, and sexuality) as deviant and deficit; youth have power to critique, analyze, & research their social context & resist repressive state & ideological institutions; sees *youth* as action/agentic & a socially, culturally constructed, performative category, & identity; the study of *youth* as political; examines how agencies of power work & effect youth	Youths' global & social contexts;	Institutional = criticizes oppressive institutionalized discourses & agencies of power that effect youth
Ibrahim and Steinberg (2014) and Quijada Cerecer et al. (2013)		State & ideological institutions	Micropolitical = youth identities are agentic complex, changing, & performative
Social justice youth policy or development (SJYP/D)	Recognizes institutional & structural barriers to youth's democratic participation; moves from a deficit, *problem-driven* to a *possibility-driven* perspective of youth; youths' collective ability to effect social change, i.e. community-based social capital, in schools & communities; principles are youth (1) analyze power within relationships, (2) make identity central, (3) promote systemic change, (4) encourage collective action, (5) embrace youth culture	Schools &/or communities	Institutional = critiques policies & institutions that aim to control & contain youth
Ginwright and James (2002) and Ginwright et al. (2005)			Micropolitical = community social capital, collective community level attributes & efforts to effect change; alter social conditions through non-institutional means
Youth participatory action research (YPAR)	Youth are experts on their own educational experiences; knowledge that is student-centered & action oriented; youth actively research, make decisions, identify problems, collect & analyze data, & provide recommendations for school reform, improvement & transformation; youth are active participants rather than products of school reform	Schools &/or communities; situated in social contexts in which youth live & learn	Institutional = youth have influence over official/validated knowledge
Bautista et al. (2013), Irizarry (2009, 2011) and Rodríguez and Brown (2009)			Micropolitical = power with, relationship building, collaboration, co-create, co-research, shared, bottom-up problem solving approach

Next, we compared and contrasted the critical theoretical perspectives' execution of context and power. In terms of *context*, two of the critical perspectives (YPAR and SJYP/D) centered on schools and/or communities as the unit of analysis. However, CYS broadly considers youths' global and social contexts in juxtaposition to state and ideological institutional contexts (Quijada Cerecer et al. 2013). Likewise, according to YPAR context is the day-to-day reality of youth or the "social contexts in which... youth live and learn" (Rodríguez and Brown 2009, p. 25). For *power* we noticed variations in the discussion of the level, *institutional* or *micropolitical*, each critical perspective situates its focus. Suitably, we offer two derivatives for the concept institutional: institutional power and institutionalization.

Institutional power is the way in which one group is in the position to impose and control ideologies and political rules (Sensoy and DiAngelo 2012). Eventually, a dominant group's ideologies and rules become normalized, and this *institutionalization* is the process in which norms, beliefs, and behaviors become routine, shared, and established through a public institution, and in the case of our research school-wide (Larson and Ovando 2001). As such, policy doesn't necessarily become institutionalized by law or authorized force, but instead is developed and reinforced by our informal networks, practices, memory, and lived experiences (Childers 2014).

Lastly, *micropolitics* are politics at the interpersonal or micro level, and consist of "arenas of struggle... where conflict, competition, cooperation, compromise, and co-optation co-exist" (Malen and Cochran 2008, p. 4). This interpretation of "policies as practices of power" acknowledges that policy occurs on the ground, hence micropolitical (Childers 2014, p. 77). We examined how the three critical theoretical perspectives on youth considered both institutional and micropolitical forms of power.

In reference to *institutional*, two of the perspectives, CYS and SJYP/D, aim to critique institutional power over and oppression of youth and policies and practices that attempt to control youth. CYS critiques adult-centered institutions and state sponsored and ideological forms of institutional power and oppression based on race, social class, gender, sexual identity, ability, language, and nationalism. Similarly, YPAR aims to change what institutions count as knowledge, and that youth should have the power and influence over what is considered legitimized knowledge.

Additionally, for *micropolitical* power all three of the perspectives use terms synonymous with sharing power such as community, collective, collaborative, relationship building, and co-create/co-research. Accordingly, when there is an equitable interpersonal exchange of power, even more power is gained. Finally, YPAR advocates for more bottom-up forms of micropolitical power, which is distinctive from institutional power that is unfortunately top-down. Accordingly, in alignment with CPA these critical theoretical perspectives highlight the role that power plays in policymaking, yet underscoring how youth are important to this process.

5 Analyzing Our Research to Conceptualize a Framework

Subsequently, we consider how *context* and the two concepts of *power*, institutional and micropolitical, are apparent in our research on student voice in the social justice class and school-wide. As articulated in Fig. 1, in the following sections we delineate in detail a conceptual framework for the critical analysis of student voice that examines: (1) the *context* in which student voice must operate, and the (2) the *institutional* and *micropolitics* that consists of either the *power over* students' voices or students' *power to* use their voice. According to CPA, context matters and influences how politics of power unfold in the policy process (Taylor 1997). Therefore, from a CPA perspective our conceptual framework allows us to locate how the context shaped the power dynamics involved when students attempted to have a voice in changing school-wide culture, policies, and practices to be more socially just. In the subsequent sections, we use the conceptual framework to first examine how the school-wide and classroom level context of this study affected students' power to have voice in changing school culture and policies, and how this in turn influenced students' power to address social injustices at the institutional and micropolitical levels.

5.1 Understanding the Context for Student Voice

The first component of our framework is that the sociopolitical context must be considered when initiating student voice efforts. Indeed, schools do not function in a vacuum. Leaders, both adults and students, must consider how their decision-making and the daily operations of the school are never politically neutral, but are undeniably influenced by larger structures and ideologies endemic to society

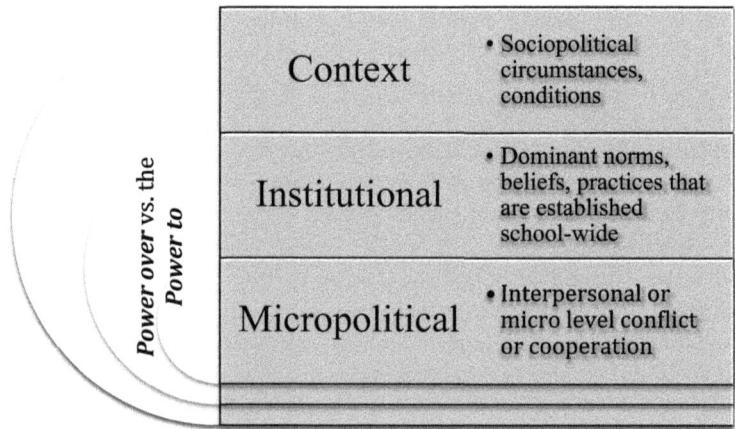

Fig. 1 A critical analysis of the politics of student voice: a conceptual frame

(Milner 2012; Nieto and Bode 2009). Yet unfortunately, if school leaders adopt a context-neutral mindset, according to Milner (2012), they fail to "recognize deep-rooted and ingrained realities embedded" in their school (p. 708). Therefore, it is critical that school leaders understand how context "situates and mediates the play of power" in schools (Malen and Cochran 2008, p. 4) when involving student voice in school reform and improvement. Context matters to student voice, and the sociopolitical conditions in which the social justice class operated in some ways had political ramifications for how students were able to have the *power to* have voice in school improvement.

School-Wide Context There were distinct differences in how the adult leadership considered context between year one and two that we were involved with the research. In year one the adult leadership facilitated more context-conscious school improvement efforts school-wide and for the social justice class specifically. For example, the former principal was publicly known in the community for spearheading social justice initiatives, some of which included a school-wide Social Justice Committee, social justice as a strand in the school improvement plan, and of course the social justice education class elective. The interim principal in year one of our research, Mr. Lawson, paid attention to this historical context previously established by the former administration, and decided to build upon the former principal's efforts. One way to accomplish this was by engaging teachers in PD that encouraged them to revisit their conceptualization of equity and social justice. However, the resistance received from some teachers during the PDs, especially considering the school's notoriety for promoting social justice initiatives, surprised Mr. Lawson. There was some pushback from teacher leaders who believed that because they had "good intentions" and "cared about students" they saw themselves absolved of school-wide issues of equity and social justice, especially race. Furthermore, some teacher leaders expressed to the interim principal that they were offended by him as well as the university research team's efforts to engage them in discussions about racism, deficit thinking, and white privilege, and vocalized that they were beyond such conversations. Later, in our discussions on the politics of student voice we will demonstrate how this contextual contention—adult leaders' inconsistent support of social justice initiatives—complicated student voice efforts in the social justice class.

In addition to the impact of context on faculty, Mr. Lawson was also acutely aware of how the disparate opportunity structures within the school impacted students. Unfortunately, schools inevitably reflect societal injustices, and Carter High similarly mirrors the institutionalized inequities present in the surrounding community. Students are socially and academically segregated across racial, linguistic, and socioeconomic lines. According to Ms. Collins, the SJ Class teacher, more specifically, "homogenously White, affluent, native English speaking students comprise honors/AP preparatory courses and predominantly black, low SES students constitute college prep courses." Thus, Mr. Lawson, adopted "an intentional and conscious approach to recruit students" for the SJ class by "intersecting racial, linguistic, and socioeconomic backgrounds that reflected our entire student and family demographics."

However, the adult leadership in year two took a more context-neutral stance, which was particularly colorblind. Mr. Nash, the new principal in year two of our study, was also new to the district. He previously spent most of his career working as a school administrator in a predominately white and rural school community context that was considerably different from CHS. With little experience in working with such a diverse student body he had a considerable task of learning about and understanding the context specific needs of the CHS community. Nonetheless, he primarily adopted policies and procedures he was familiar with from his previous school. Moreover, his leadership generally adopted the philosophy of "it's not about race, but about poverty."

Yet to Mr. Nash's credit, early on in his first year he did make an attempt to meet with students from the SJ class to discuss their recommendations based on their previous research. The university research team also shared with the new principal a report focusing on culturally responsive school improvement that summarized the research team's role/relationship, preliminary research findings and recommendations, and a glossary of related terms. However, it was hard for him to address all students' and research team's recommendations as he was faced with other competing school reform and improvement priorities. Some of these competing priorities included the state and district adoption of the federal Race to the Top grant, newly state mandated principal and teacher evaluation processes, as well as the roll out of the Common Core state standards and new assessments attached to these standards. Also, since he was transitioning into his position in a new district, he did not have the opportunity to facilitate recruiting students as Mr. Lawson did, and this had some effect on the tenor and tone of the class.

Finally, Carter High has a predominantly White faculty (92 %), a faculty whose population unfortunately does not match the racially, culturally, and linguistically diverse student population. CHS is composed of approximately 1,200 students from 9th through 12th grade, a diverse population of students (according to district reported data) who are 40 % White, 40 % Black, 10 % Latina/o, 5 % Asian, and 5 % multiracial. Thus, CHS is transitioning to becoming a majority "minority" school. CHS is the only high school in its district and its student and faculty demographics represent that of the district-at-large. Even though the high school student body is extremely racially diverse, the town in which the school is situated is predominately white (58 %), with Black (17 %) and Asian (16 %) proportionally close in representation, and Latino (5 %), Native American (.2 %), and Pacific Islanders (.04 %) least represented, respectively.[2] For this reason, students of color felt that their identity was not represented in their classes because of pervasive whiteness.

Classroom Context Carter High is a traditional comprehensive public high school and the SJ class is just one of many elective course options that students can choose from. Students in the SJ class engaged in scholarly debates and decon-

---

[2]Demographic data was retrieved from the county website, but is not cited for purposes of maintaining the anonymity of the research site.

structed articles on topics such as "why is colorblindness the new racism?" spent time defining terms such as "intersectionality" and "heterosexism," and discussed how heteronormativity plays out in their high school. Ms. Collins found the intentionally diverse student composition to be a "hugely important" instructional, social and cross-cultural tool in which to discuss issues of social justice especially considering there was a broad representation of student identities based on race, class, gender, sexuality, (dis)ability, language, citizenship, and nationality in the class. This purposeful diversity in enrollment brought students together who might not have had interactions with each other prior to the class. Also, since the first 2 weeks of the class was focused on "why identity matters," students began to appreciate the different perspectives their collective identities brought to the table and formed initial relationships that enabled them to engage in social justice topics. When describing the context of the SJ class Tierra explained,

> The way I was raised we don't talk about it, like sexuality or society. The only thing we talked about was race because I was Black. It sparked my interests and made me learn more. I was never nervous, I was excited. To hear another Black person who was raised differently, or to hear another kid's perspective who is Caucasian or Hispanic was important, because I know my life and related stories, and it is important to learn how my experiences are different from other people's experiences..

Alhough this class was a rare intentionally diverse space in a school setting for important discussions about social injustices, as we describe in the second component of our conceptual framework, the class was not absolved or divorced from the politics of power and privilege.

The teacher, Ms. Collins, shared with students in the class that she identifies as a White, "culturally Jewish" female. Additionally, she wanted to be transparent about her privilege as a straight, cisgender, English speaking, American citizen. Ms. Collins is dually certified in English and Social Studies and minored in Women and Gender Studies as an undergraduate. At the time of data collection, she taught primarily English Language Arts courses at CHS and served as the high school's Social Justice Committee Chair, a committee of teachers, administrators, and parents which as mentioned earlier, was a strategic initiative in the school improvement plan. In the first year of data collection for this study, Ms. Collins was in her second year both in her teaching career and at CHS.

The first half of the semester students engaged in key topics on social justice, while the second half they conducted their own youth participatory action research (YPAR). In year one of our research students in the class voted and selected the following topics as important related to the overarching issue of *institutionalized racism* at CHS: (1) Teacher and student relationships, (2) lack of faculty diversity (92 % White faculty; 60 % students of color), (3) underrepresentation of students of color in advanced courses (4) disproportionate dress code enforcement on females of color, and (5) overrepresentation of students of color being disciplined. In year two the class took a more intersectional approach to studying how institutionalized racism, classism, sexism, and heterosexism work to generate inequities in the school. In year two their YPAR topics consisted of the following: (1) college and career pathways, (2) curriculum and instruction, (3) district funding, and (4) school rules and policies.

5.2 Recognizing the Politics of Student Voice

The second facet of our framework is disclosing the politics, or the role that power plays in student voice. Giroux (1986) argues that the concept of power would need to be "redefined" in the daily experiences, and most importantly in the classroom pedagogy and student voice (p. 49). He suggest that power be redefined as:

> a concrete set of practices that produces social norms through which different experiences and modes of subjectivities are constructed. Power, in this sense, includes but goes beyond the call for institutional change or for the distribution of political and economic resources; it also signifies a level of conflict and struggle that plays itself out around the exchange of discourse and the lived experiences that such discourse produces, mediates, and legitimates." (p. 49).

Yet unfortunately, dominant school culture favors the "privileged voices of white middle and upper classes" (Giroux 1986, p. 65). Consequently, students' voices can also be entangled in power relations that exclude certain students and prefers voices that align with dominant ideologies and power structures. Likewise, Karla, student co-author, found that even in the SJ class inequitable power structures were evident. She witnessed how in the class "white students benefited the most because of their privilege" and connected this observation to one of the class readings of Peggy McIntosh's (1989) essay *White Privilege: Unpacking the Invisible Knapsack*. Also, in hindsight Karla remembers that first year she was in the SJ class "50 percent of the white students were open listening," however, the other half "were stuck in their mindsets." Therefore, as Karla suggest, the reality is that there are still politics of power involved in student voice.

To further operationalize the concept power we turn to Holloway's (2002) work on revolutionary politics using his distinction of power as the *power to* versus the *power over*. According to Holloway, the *power to* is not an individual effort but indeed social, as "it is when the social flow of doing is fractured that power-to is transformed into its opposite, power-over" (p. 28). Hence, *power over* is when those deemed powerful position themselves as the primary doers, placing those assumed/perceived without this same power and privilege as invisible and voiceless. Holloway argues the *power to*, a positive form of power, can easily become the exploitative *power over* when our "capacity-to-do" turns into our "incapacity-to-do... the incapacity to realize our own projects, our own dreams," and where "the vast majority of doers are converted into the done-to, their activity transformed into passivity, their subjectivity into objectivity" (p. 29). In the following sections we highlight how both adults and even students at times either exhibited the *power to* or the *power over* students' voices school-wide and the social justice class specifically.

Also, within these two dichotomies we distinguish whether and how the power was *institutional* or *micropolitical*.

Power To Students' *power to* have voice and engage in activism was more so *micropolitical* as their ability to facilitate change primarily occurred at the class or micro/site-level (see Bertrand 2014). Many of these micropolitical conflicts were racialized, but necessary for learning. For example in the first year of our work with the class, one of the YPAR groups researched whether there is disproportionate dress code enforcement on females of color. The racial tension amongst this group of all females (three Black and three White) was readily apparent in their mutual silence and avoidant body language. As a result, they initially struggled to work together on their research. The Black female students in the group were able to share their lived experiences with racism and how administrators unfairly disciplined them because of how they dressed. Conversely, since White female students were privileged in not having the same firsthand experiences with racism, they were unwilling to see (i.e. colorblind) how racial inequities in dress code enforcement was even an issue.

Consequently, white students' privilege prevented them from seeing race as an issue, i.e. colorblindness, which became a source of conflict. Yet eventually, Jade, one of the Black students in the group, during a heated debate took a courageous risk, because for women of color the personal is political, pushing Kelly to recognize her white privilege by telling her, "that's because your privileged!" Once held accountable for facing her white privilege, Kelly responded, "You're right. I am privileged." Ultimately, Jade's micropolitical activism and vulnerability in sharing her experiences with racial oppression was not only transformative to her white peers' learning, but also important to cross-racial relationship building in the class. In the end, by facing the racial micropolitics head on the students were then able to learn to work together.

Yet, conflict was not the only form of micropolitics. At times, shared power and cooperation between teacher and students in the social justice class also served as a micropolitical endeavor that made students feel as if they indeed had impact on the instructional and curricular design of the classroom. As such, this level of student involvement in designing the class permitted students to take ownership of their learning. Students who previously took the social justice class had the option to enroll a second time as a weighted credit (similar to advanced or honors). Eventually, these 7 students were trademarked as the "Social Justice II students" to distinguish their leadership role.

The Social Justice II students had additional responsibilities such as designing lesson plans and teaching segments of each unit to the class. Karla, ascertained her role as a Social Justice II leader was important because "maybe students felt more comfortable talking to other students [versus the teacher] instead of feeling like they are not heard by adults." Moreover, she could tell that her peers "were surprised that Social Justice II leaders knew as much as they did" and for many of the students in the class "it was their first time they adapted to using the [social justice] vocabulary to express their ideas."

Social Justice II students also provided professional development (PD) for teachers at the high school and at district-wide teacher in-service days. A couple of students were invited by the superintendent to speak on issues of colorblindness at a teacher in-service. These PDs either generally centered on how teachers can integrate social justice education and YPAR in their curriculum and instruction, or focused on specific social justice topics pertaining to race/and or gender and sexuality. Additionally, Ms. Collins frequently solicited Social Justice II students' suggestions on curricular ideas and resources for the class, especially social media recommendations such as You Tube videos, TED talks, blogs, and relevant feeds on social networking sites. Also, one of the students recommended and took the lead on designing a website that catalogued the class's work (curricular materials, presentations, and research) online.

Even still, most of the class instruction was teacher directed. However, the emerging co-teaching efforts set precedence for the possibilities of integrating student voice to promote learning. Positioning students as co-teachers is micropolitical in that it fosters a reciprocal power dynamic between teacher and students that, in turn, affirms students' ways of seeing and legitimizes their expertise as useful to the class. Furthermore, we would argue that *students as co-teachers* is "subtle" micropolitical activism in that it challenges the status quo while staying under the radar. (Marshall and Anderson 2009, p. 11). Ideally, ongoing co-teaching efforts would yield pedagogical effectiveness to the point that norms about what constitutes good teaching changes to more student initiated and co-led and less teacher directed. Hence, with time students teaching at the micro-level could lead to institutional changes transforming school-wide norms and beliefs about teaching and learning.

Furthermore, although adults primarily held control over high school institutional structures and decisions, students were beginning to cultivate institutional power and recognition outside the formal school space. For instance, on several occasions the social justice class was invited to the local university to speak about their work. Student representatives from the class, as well as Ms. Collins, were keynote speakers at a university sponsored PD for an audience of 80 teachers from area school districts. The keynote addressed how the integration of student voice in curriculum and instruction is important to developing a more culturally responsive teaching practice. Math and science teachers in the audience were especially interested in any insights students had on how they could use YPAR to support student learning. Building upon their keynote address, the class also presented preliminary results from their YPAR projects at a graduate student organized workshop on how critical educators can "re-imagine education for youth in and beyond the classroom."

Several students from the class were also guest instructors for courses at the local university. About eight students from the class volunteered to guest teach in an undergraduate level course on social foundations of education. One would think that high school students of color would be intimidated by teaching a lecture of approximately 120 mostly white college students, but students appeared confident and were rather poignant in articulating the rewards and challenges of engaging in social justice pedagogy and research in their school community. The high school students began the lecture asking, "What does social justice mean to you?" Unfortunately, there was general silence from the audience and in response the high school students decided to "cold call" on people to garner participation. Considering this level of silence, it was ironic that later on in the presentation one of the high school students brought up how "white guilt" can be problematic if it manifests into resistance to engaging in social justice discussions. In general, the SJ class presenters were all surprised that college level students, especially teacher education majors, had limited experience with and exposure to social justice topics.

A university professor also approached the SJ Class for assistance because she was concerned her educational leadership doctoral students were vocal on issues of race, gender, and poverty, but were relatively silent on discussions related to LGBT youth and families. A few Social Justice II students volunteered their time to teach a lesson that catered to the needs of future school administrators. The guest instructors assessed doctoral students' knowledge of key terminology related to gender and sexuality. They also emphasized how sexuality, gender identity and expression are fluid, not rigid. The students modeled this by sharing with the class how their identity and expression has changed at various points in time. Witnessing the savvy of these high school student instructors helped the doctoral students/future school administrators see firsthand how they could commission students to lead discussions amongst their staff on difficult social justice topics. Ongoing invites from the community to teach and present helped students in the SJ class realize they indeed had institutional expertise on issues of social justice to offer.

Finally, Tierra found that the SJ class gave her tools and the power to critically examine inequitable power hierarchies that exist between different student groups and even between teachers and students in her other classes. According to Tierra,

> Because social justice class was at the end of the day I would be able to go home and reflect on it with my mom and my sister and say "today in class we," and we would talk about it and I would come back tomorrow and it would be stuck in my head and I would be more observant of things. And it allowed me to notice teachers and the asymmetrical power relationships between teachers and students. That is what we talked about and that is what it allowed me to do, and so I loved that part about it.

Power Over Unfortunately, today, many of our social institutions (family, school, and legal) are structured as adult centered to provide discipline, protection for and over young people (Quijada Cerecer et al. 2013). This institutional ideology views teenagers, (generally accepted as) those persons 13–19 years old, as not fully cognitively developed and therefore not capable of serious decision-making and ultimately in need of adult supervision (Quijada Cerecer et al. 2013). Education and social science research is also a major producer of the cultural deprivation narrative that is more so directed towards youth of color (Ginwright et al. 2005). This research narrative can reduce young people of color's "complex interactions with their environment to simple manifestations of maladaptive behavior" and does not accurately depict how education has shifted from a system with "its primary role of supporting youth" to one that largely facilitates "punishment and control of young people" (Ginwright, Cammarota, and Noguera 2005, p. 28).

Unfortunately, the multiple ways in which youth positively defy these negative depictions and engage in activism in their schools and communities is often ignored by policy and research discourse (Ginwright et al. 2005). Steinberg (2014) would argue that is because we have yet to have an active conversation about why we perceive youth as a problem. Thus, schools and curricula are designed "to keep students in" exercising *power over* students' voices (Steinberg 2014, p. 428), and ultimately as Karla explained school then feels like a "prison." Regrettably, this deficit outlook towards students positions them as subjects of schooling instead of engaged and invested participants in their own learning.

Undeniably, there were contradictions between the empowerment students gained in the SJ class, and the institutional power students felt adults held over them in all other aspects of their schooling. According to Karla, in the SJ class students had the freedom to conduct their own research and were recognized for the various research presentations and talks they gave in other institutional settings. Yet, the high school at-large did not feel like a place students would want to come and learn. Instead, the school felt like a place where students were judged everyday for doing something, and whatever students did was not good enough. During Karla's senior year counselors and deans would tell her that in a couple of months she would be out in the real world, but in school they would treat students like kids and monitor students in every single way they could. She described how adults would control student movement throughout the school by giving students very few hall pass privileges a semester, and although the hall monitors knew most students of color by name, they would still target and prejudge them specifically as if they were up to no good.

Along the same vein, adults' deficit perceptions of students were due in part to their fear of youth (see Steinberg, p. 428). Adults' resistance could stem from their trepidation (and guilt) over exposing how they may play a role in generating the very social injustices that students in the SJ class were using YPAR to uncover. As described earlier, students were operating within a context in which the faculty was generally suspicious of the term social justice and related initiatives, and as a result some adults directed this apprehension towards the SJ class. One example of adult resistance occurred in year one of our research. Students requested teachers' support their YPAR projects by either participating in an interview or help administer student surveys. Several teachers failed to respond to students' requests via email, and one academic department emailed Ms. Collins directly "that the teachers in their department would not be participating in the Social Justice Class's research." Some teachers even refused to allow their students to attend the SJ class' end of the year research presentation. It was evident, that adults at times in order to preserve the status quo used their institutional power to thwart students' voices and activism in social justice inititiaves and subsequent policy changes.

Karla acknowledged the SJ class did have some impact on school level policy changes. She agreed that "students in the class got attention, whether it was good or bad, they still got attention. This attention made administrators acknowledge that students do have voices that are not taken too seriously too often." For example, it was recommended by the YPAR group studying the inequitable enforcement of dress code on girls of color that demographic data is collected on who receives infractions. In response, the deans of discipline followed through with this request changing policies and practices for how disciplinary data was collected and reported.

Although the class encouraged adults to acknowledge that students can powerfully speak about social injustices, administration still did not always take students' policy recommendations seriously. In year two of our research the school rules and structures group revisited the progress made on the dress code policy. Administration relaxed the restrictions on the length of girls' shorts by a couple of inches and felt that this resolved the students' policy concerns. However, students in this particular YPAR group felt the amended dress code policy placed the blame on young women by forcing them to change, but did little to address the hypersexualization or sexual harassment of young women in the overall school culture. To students the administration's resolution was simply a quick fix that failed to link the root of the problem to the "rape culture" that may be pervasive in the school and society at-large.

Therefore, students generally felt that school adults in general, but administration specifically, did not take their recommendations for policy changes seriously. There was no real administrative movement on student recommendations, and what little action from adults that did occur was a safer, superficial, neutral approach. Students recalled instances where administration called their research "cute", diminishing and delegitimizing students' efforts. During our second year of research there was an emotional class discussion when students expressed how they were tired of adults in school not taking their work seriously. The class came to a consensus that they were not going to craft research presentations based on adult expectations, but instead "do the work for themselves." As a result, some YPAR groups challenged adult academic norms, by taking a more creative, art-based approach to their research presentations.

Adults' questioning was not just directed towards students, but also the teacher. Some faculty questioned the academic legitimacy of the course asking the teacher "How can you test or evaluate the students about social justice, especially if the content isn't based on any district or state standardized curriculum?" and "Social justice isn't a certifiable subject area, so is the teacher qualified to instruct the course?" This level of questioning indirectly impacted student voice as it placed unwarranted stress on the teacher. Ms. Collins felt exhausted and alone in her quest to address social injustices. Her vulnerability was due in part to a school-wide context in which adults, for the most part, had ceased to engage in critical dialogue about social justice. In some ways, limiting social justice education to a single class pardons other faculty from responsibility to address equity and social justice head on.

However, it was not just adults who exhibited institutional power over students; there were also power struggles, or micropolitics, amongst students in the class. For example, students were contradictory in their concerns for one type of racism, colorblindness. Students of color primarily identified how they were personally impacted by colorblindness. Several students of color mentioned how their White teachers were mostly colorblind, or culturally unresponsive, because they use their dominant ideologies to structure the classroom and "teach what they think they are."

Nonetheless, some students, even students of color, let societal dominant ideologies shape their perceptions of what counts as racism. After a class viewing of a documentary about the removal of the local university's Native American mascot, some students were colorblind and dismissed how the mascot was racist. Even though students were able to identify their personal experiences with racial stereotypes, when a stereotype was directed towards Native Americans specifically, many students (both students of color and White students) could only see how the removal of the mascot hurt them personally. As one White student explained "going to college games and chanting with [the mascot] was what my parents and grandparents grew up with and did together...they didn't think about how eliminating the [college] mascot would hurt our town!" Thus, students did not employ the same social justice mindset when the issue threatened what they viewed as their personal rights/property.

Micropolitics also occurred between the teacher and students. Although equal power relations between teacher and students are ideal, Ms. Collins at times had to use her power over to address white students' privileged resistance. One class requirement was that students maintain a journal for personal reflection. Ms. Collins used the journal as another method in which to communicate with students. After the class conflict over the Native American mascot, one White female student expressed that Ms. Collins made her feel uncomfortable during the discussion about the mascot. She wrote in her journal to Ms. Collins that, "I just don't want you to think I'm racist, and I'm really afraid you do." Ms. Collins continued the journal correspondence to challenge the students' reluctance to see her white privilege.

Plus, in year one of our research we observed similar racial divisions during the process of selecting the class YPAR topics. The majority of the white students voted on topics not about race, but instead favored *safer*, not as risky topics like the nutritional value of the school lunch, supporting classmates with disabilities, and gender inequities. However, according to Karla "they [white students] did not realize the class was about talking about uncomfortable issues," and instead "they tried to avoid talking about it." Ultimately the class consented to research issues that explicitly addressed race, but still there was some opposition to the decision. Once the class agreed to research racism, a few White female students approached Ms. Collins after class and expressed they did not want to participate in the research. Ms. Collins felt this group of White students used their voice as privileged resistance to addressing racism. She encouraged the class to be critically aware of how their resistance impacts how they choose their research teams because "we do not want to further [racially] divide ourselves."

6 Recommendations for a Critical Analysis of Student Voice

Even radical educators who value student voice can get caught in the throws of institutionalized structures and practices that subject students to "ideological and economic subordination" instead of positioning them for "possibility" and "empowerment" (Giroux 1986, p. 49). In order for students to truly have a voice in school improvement, all stakeholders involved (administrators, teachers, families, community members, among others) must admit that there are hierarchies of power that can get in the way of students' efforts. We used our research with the social justice class to reveal the hierarchies of power that occurred when involving student voice in changing school culture, policies, and practices.

From our study we found that within the boundaries of schooling adults primarily held the institutional *power over* students, whereas students' *power to* have voice was more so micropolitical. Yet, students in the social justice class gained affirmation and notoriety in other institutional settings, given their power to have a say in policy decisions within the school was quite limited. Our research suggests that despite the institutional limitations of schooling, students will find a way to have voice in policy. Ultimately, the spaces for youth to emanate their voice have no boundaries. Youth continue to innovate and challenge the norms for the locale of activism to influence policy, especially now that technology, the internet, and social networking platforms such as Twitter, Instagram, Snap Chat, Vine, and Tumblr mean youth can instantaneously have impact on a global scale (see Middaugh and Kirshner 2015).

Furthermore, the co-teaching that emerged between teachers and student leaders in the SJ class can only lead to institutional level changes in teaching practices if the supportive conditions exist in which to do so. Despite Ms. Collins's attempt to collaborate with student leaders to develop innovative pedagogies, the SJ class cannot disconnect from and must operate within pervasive whiteness. The predominately white teacher teaching force questioned the pedagogical practices in the SJ class, and it is difficult for white teachers like Ms. Collins who aim to be critically conscious of their white privilege, to support student voice when they operate within school-wide structures of whiteness. It is easy to become complacent, and eventually disempowered, within these institutional circumstances. It was evident that the adults at Carter High were hesitant to give youth the *power to* lead on school improvement and policy related matters. Steinberg (2014) suggest that,

> Incanting the term, youth leadership, most educators and parents speak out of both sides of their mouths, giving the term, and taking the power...no one seems to want kids to lead, to make responsible decisions, and to eventually replace a stagnant status quo. (p. 429)

Eventually, the continued questioning from adults left students with only one decision—to do the social justice work for themselves.

For this reason, in addition to steps one and two, considering the *context* and *politics*, of our emerging framework on student voice, we also suggest a step three and four, *learning* and *changing* (Fig. 2). Adult and student leaders must be willing

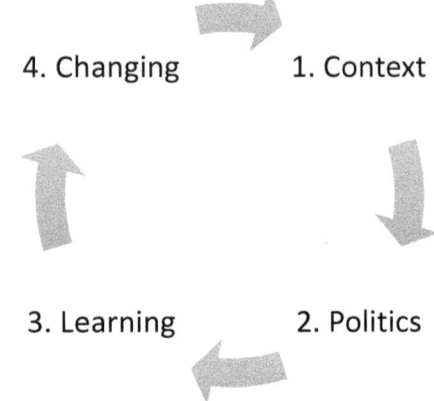

Fig. 2 The critical analysis of student voice as praxis

to *learn* from their experiences with the politics of student voice, and in response *change* institutional norms and practices in the policy process. We have yet to witness this type of praxis come full circle in our work with Carter High and the SJ class, but we hope overtime we can use our expertise in the field of student voice to help all stakeholders involved commit to this transformative approach to school improvement and the policy process.

We argue that youth voice in school improvement has the potential to be one of the most authentic, democratic forms of engaging in public policy, in the true sense of the word *public*. When students have a voice in school policy they can be the architects of their own educational trajectories. Students are able to provide unique perspectives and often able to approach issues of social justice that adults are afraid or unwilling to discuss (Mitra 2006; Welton et al. 2015). Thus, students are able to model for adults how to engage in advocacy that encourages school communities to take an honest look at equity issues (Mitra 2006). However, students are not able to realize the full capacity of their voice in school policy processes if there are power structures impeding their capacity for change. The students in our study did not allow larger institutional constraints to keep them from doing the policy work on the ground and found ways beyond formal school spaces to speak to policy issues that they care about. Ultimately, the students were doing critical policy work by challenging dominant school norms for what it means to be involved in the policy process—that policy work in schools is just for adults.

As such, school personnel should be cautious of whether the reasons for and methods in which they engage student voice in school reform are reproductive and further alienate students from school policy decisions. In this current policy environment, more stakeholders than ever vie for the attention of policymakers and want to insert their opinion and influence on the direction of educational reform (Conner et al. 2013). Students' and parents' voices are the least heard and attended to in policy matters (Conner et al. 2013). Alienating students and their lived experiences from the policy and school reform processes is ill advised, because students are an "untapped source" and have creative ideas and recommendations for school improvement (Smith et al. 2005, p. 28).

As Tierra, high school student co-author, concludes, student voice will always be very important for the student versus teacher relationship. Regrettably, students are forced to sit in class and take on lectures and notes without even opening their mouths sometimes. However, allowing students to teach others and sometimes the teacher as well, closes the asymmetrical gap between the teacher-student. In the SJ class we used student voice heavily to get our points across to classmates. Doing this work allowed people with not much knowledge on one subject to be able to open up without being shut down or intimidated by an authorized figure. As an activist we have the right to say what we want. We fear shut out from teachers just as much as they fear the honest opinion and the option for democracy in a classroom.

References

Ajunwa, K. (2011). *It's our school: Youth activism as educational reform, 1951–1979*. Doctoral Dissertation. Retrieved from Proquest. (UMI 3474827).
Bautista, M. A., Bertrand, M., Morrell, E., Scorza, D., & Matthews, C. (2013). Participatory action research and city youth: Methodological insights from the council of youth research. *Teachers College Record, 115*(10), 1–23.
Ben-Amos, I. (1995). Adolescence as a cultural invention: Philipe Aries and the sociology of youth. *History of the Human Sciences, 8*(2), 69–89.
Bertrand, M. (2014). Reciprocal dialogue between educational decision makers and students of color. Opportunities and obstacles. *Educational Administration Quarterly, 50*(5), 812–843.
Childers, S. M. (2014). Promiscuous methodology: Breaching the limits of theory and practice for a social science we can live with. In R. N. Brown, R. Carducci, & C. R. Kuby (Eds.), *Disrupting qualitative inquiry: Possibilities and tensions in educational research* (pp. 71–78). New York: Peter Lang.
Conner, J., Zaino, K., & Scarola, E. (2013). "Very powerful voices": The influence of youth organizing on educational policy in Philadelphia. *Educational Policy, 27*(3), 560–588.
Cook-Sather, A. (2007). Resisting the impositional potential of student voice work: Lessons for liberatrory educational research from poststructuralist feminist critiques of critical pedagogy. *Discourse: Studies in the Cultural Politics of Education, 28*(3), 389–403.
Costanza-Chock, S. (2012, December 17). *Youth and social movements: Key lessons for allies.* Kinder & Braver World Project: Research Series, Berkman Center for Internet and Society at Harvard.
Cote, J. E. (2014). Towards a new political economy of youth. *Journal of Youth Studies, 17*(4), 527–543.
DeWalt, K. M., & DeWalt, B. R. (2011). *Participant observation: A guide for fieldworkers.* Lanham: Rowman AltaMira.
Diem, S., Young, M. D., Welton, A., Mansfield, K., & Lee, P. (2014). The intellectual landscape of critical policy analysis. *International Journal of Qualitative Studies in Education, 27*(9), 1068–1090.
Enright, R., Levy, V., Harris, D., & Lapsley, D. (1987). Do economic conditions influence how theorists view adolescents? *Journal of Youth Adolescents, 16*, 541–559.
Fielding, M. (2001). Students as radical agents of change. *Journal of Educational Change, 2*, 123–141.

Ginwright, S., & James, T. (2002). From assets to agents of social change: Social justice, organizing, and youth development. *New Directions for Youth Development, 96*, 27–46.

Ginwright, S., Cammarota, J., & Noguera, P. (2005). Youth, social justice, and communities: Toward a theory of urban youth policy. *Social Justice, 32*(3), 24–40.

Giroux, H. (1986). Radical pedagogy and the politics of student voice. *Interchange, 17*(1), 48–69.

Hirschman, A. O. (1970). *Exit, voice, loyalty.* Cambridge, MA: Harvard University Press.

Holloway, J. (2002). *Change the world without taking power. The meaning of revolution today.* London: Pluto Press.

Ibrahim, A., & Steinberg, S. R. (2014). *Critical youth studies reader.* New York: Peter Lang.

Irizarry, J. G. (2009). Reinvigorating multicultural education through youth participatory action research. *Multicultural Perspectives, 11*(4), 194–199.

Irizarry, J. G. (2011). *The Latinization of U.S. schools: Successful teaching & learning in shifting cultural contexts.* Boulder: Paradigm Publishing.

Kellner, D. (2014). Toward a critical theory of youth. In A. Ibrahim & S. R. Steinber (Eds.), *Critical youth studies reader* (pp. 2–14). New York: Peter Lang.

Kennedy, B. L., & Datnow, A. (2011). Student involvement and data-driven decision making: Developing a new typology. *Youth and Society, 43*(4), 1246–1271.

Kirshner, B., & Pozzoboni, K. M. (2011). Student interpretations of a school closure: Implications for student voice in equity-based school reform. *Teachers College Record, 113*(8), 1633–1667.

Kwon, S. A. (2013). *Uncivil youth: Race, activism, and affirmative governmentality.* Durham: Duke University.

Larson, C. L., & Ovando, C. J. (2001). *The color of bureaucracy: The politics of equity in multicultural school communities.* Belmont: Wadsworth Press.

Lodge, C. (2005). From hearing voices to engaging in dialogue: Problematising student participation in school improvement. *Journal of Educational Change, 6*, 125–146.

Malen, B., & Cochran, M. V. (2008). Beyond pluralistic patterns of power: Research on the micropolitics of schools. In B. S. Cooper, J. G. Cibulka, & L. D. Fusarelli (Eds.), *Handbook of education politics and policy* (pp. 148–178). New York: Taylor and Francis.

Mansfield, K. C. (2014). How listening to student voices informs and strengthens social justice research and practice. *Educational Administration Quarterly, 50*(3), 392–430.

Mansfield, K. C., Welton, A., & Halx, M. D. (2012). Listening to student voice: Toward a more inclusive theory for research and practice. In C. Boske & S. Diem (Eds.), *Global leadership for social justice: Taking it from research to practice.* Charlotte: Information Age Publishing.

Marshall, C., & Anderson, A. L. (Eds.). (2009). *Activist educators: Breaking past limits.* New York: Routledge.

McIntosh, P. (1989). White privilege: Unpacking the invisible knapsack. *Peace and Freedom, 49*(4). Retrieved from http://www.library.wisc.edu/EDVRC/docs/public/pdfs/LIReadings/InvisibleKnapsack.pdf

Middaugh, E., & Kirshner, B. (2015). *#youthaction. Becoming political in a digital age.* Charlotte: Information Age Publishing.

Miles, M. B., & Huberman, M. (1994). *Qualitative data analysis. An expanded sourcebook* (2nd ed.). Thousand Oaks: Sage Publications.

Milner, H. R. (2012). Beyond a test score: Explaining opportunity gaps in educational practice. *Journal of Black Studies, 43*, 693–718.

Mitra, D. L. (2005). Adults advising youth: Leading while getting out of the way. *Educational Administration Quarterly, 41*, 520–553.

Mitra, D. L. (2006). Student voice or empowerment? Examining the role of school-based youth-] adult partnerships as an avenue toward focusing n social justice. *International Electronic Journal for Leadership in Learning, 10*, 222. http://www.acs.ucalgary.ca/~iejll/.

Mitra, D., Serriere, S., & Kirshner, B. (2014). Youth participation in US Contexts: Student voice without a national mandate. *Children & Society, 28*(4), 292–304.

Nieto, S., & Bode, P. (2009). *Affirming diversity: The sociopolitical context of multicultural education.* New York: Pearson/Allyn and Bacon.

Quijada Cerecer, D. A., Cahill, C., & Bradley, M. (2013). Toward a critical youth policy praxis: Critical youth studies and participatory action research. *Theory Into Practice, 52*(3), 216–223.

Robinson, C., & Taylor, C. (2007). Theorizing student voice: Values and perspectives. *Improving Schools, 10*(1), 5–17.

Rodríguez, L., & Brown, T. M. (2009). From voice to agency: Guiding principles for participatory action research with youth. *New Directions for Youth Development, 123*, 19–34.

Rudduck, J., & Fielding, M. (2006). Student voice and the perils of popularity. *Educational Review, 58*(2), 219–231.

Sensoy, O., & DiAngelo, R. J. (2012). *Is everyone really equal?: An introduction to key concepts in social justice education*. New York: Teachers College Press.

Smith, P., Petraila, J., & Hewitt, K. (2005). Tuned in: Listening to student voice. *Principal Leadership: High School Edition, 6*(3), 28–33.

Stake, R. E. (1978). The case study method in social inquiry. *Educational Researcher, 7*(2), 5–8.

Steinberg, S. R. (2014). Redefining the notion of youth. Contextualizing the possible for transformative youth leadership. In A. Ibrahim & S. R. Steinber (Eds.), *Critical youth studies reader* (pp. 426–433). New York: Peter Lang.

Sukarieh, M., & Tannock, S. (2014). *Youth rising?: The politics of youth in the global economy*. New York: Routledge.

Taylor, S. (1997). Critical policy analysis: Exploring contexts, text, and consequences. *Discourse: Studies in the Cultural Politics of Education, 18*(1), 23–35.

Welton, A. D., Harris, T. O., La Londe, P. G., & Moyer, R. T. (2015). Social justice education in a diverse classroom: Examining high school discussions about race, power, and privilege. *Equity and Excellence in Education, 48*(4), 549–570.

When Parents Behave Badly: A Critical Policy Analysis of Parent Involvement in Schools

Erica Fernández and Gerardo R. López

Abstract The discourse surrounding parental involvement has long been a topic of discussion among educational scholars. However, over the last three decades, legislators, policymakers, and political bodies have begun to take interest in the parental involvement arena. Utilizing a Critical Policy Analysis, this chapter focuses on the power dynamics of parental involvement in schools, and how the role, function, and meaning of involvement are not only prescribed for parents, but well-delimited within school spaces occupied by marginalized parents. In order to capture the power dynamics of parental involvement in schools, we provide a case study of parental involvement—based on our current and previous research—which details the various ways in which parents are positioned in Latin@ impacted schools, while also showcasing how they are treated by school personnel when parents transgress their expected roles. We then interrogate how and why involvement has become a taken-for-granted idea within education's discourse (Weaver-Hightower 2008).

Keywords Parental engagement • Critical policy analysis • Parent organizing • Latin@ parental engagement • Parent positionality • Iimmigration legislation

The discourse surrounding parental involvement has been a topic of discussion among educational scholars for quite some time. Over the past three decades, however, interest in parental involvement matters has intensified among legislators, policymakers, and political bodies that have collectively taken an interest in the subject. But, what exactly is parental involvement? Who gets to define it? Which forms of involvement are privileged in both policy and practice? Questions such as these highlight how power and authority emerge when trying to determine and define parental involvement. But why is parental involvement such a key

---

E. Fernández (✉)
Department of Educational Leadership, Neag School of Education, University of Connecticut, 249 Glenbrook Road, Unit 3093, Storrs, CT 06269, USA
e-mail: erica.fernandez@uconn.edu

G.R. López
Department of Educational Leadership and Policy, College of Education, The University of Utah, 1721 Campus Center Drive RM 2220, Salt Lake City, UT 84112, USA

© Springer International Publishing Switzerland 2017
M.D. Young, S. Diem (eds.), *Critical Approaches to Education Policy Analysis*, Education, Equity, Economy 4, DOI 10.1007/978-3-319-39643-9_6

issue within education's discourse—particularly in the present day? Has parental involvement always been an issue of political importance? Did we always think about parental involvement the way we do now? These questions frame this chapter and lead us to examine critical questions surrounding the troubling dimensions of parental involvement. Our aim is to partially answer these larger questions by centering a narrative of Latin@ parent organizing in an urban school in the Midwest.

Throughout this chapter we will be using elements of Critical Policy Analysis (CPA): an analytic and methodological tool that helps us make sense of the world around us, while interrogating the problematic nature of oppressive systems and structures that reproduce inequalities in society (Atwood and López 2014; Brewer 2014; Marshall 1999; Prunty 1985). CPA focuses on the politics of the everyday and what is normally take for granted with/in the world—including the very structures that organize our daily lives (e.g., legal, educational, political, societal, etc.). Its aim is to highlight the multiple ways in which these structures reproduce and reify inequities in society (Marshall 1985; Prunty 1985). In this regard, CPA does pay attention to the formal/governmental "policies" that emerge from the policy arena, but it also pays close attention to the informal, invisible and "discursive" policies that profoundly shape how we experience and come to know the world around us (Atwood and López 2014; Weaver-Hightower 2008). It posits that social inequalities are not naturally occurring phenomena, but are an intentional by-product of the structures and discourses that shape our world.

In effect, CPA suggests that we are constantly immersed in a world of "policy." For all intents and purposes, policy is "reality" as we have come to know it (Ball 1994). By interrogating what we take for granted on an everyday basis, CPA aims to expose those very systems and structures that shape and structure our world (Marshall 1985). As such, CPA asks us to pay close attention to broader issues of knowledge, power and truth. It fully recognizes that certain understandings of/about the world are readily accepted as universal "truths" while other perspectives are marginalized and are rendered invisible altogether (Delgado 1989; Prunty 1985; Solórzano and Yosso 2001). CPA not only aims to "expose the sources of domination, repression, and exploitation" (Prunty 1985, p. 136) that allow particular truths to flourish, but also to seek ways to reform those systems in order to work towards a more equitable and just society. Without a doubt, CPA is expressly political (Prunty 1985); it does not shy away from a profound commitment to social justice.

1 Why Is CPA Necessary in Understanding Parent Involvement?

What we are attempting to do in this chapter is take a critical look at issues of parental involvement by interrogating its function and purpose as a "disciplinary" exercise of power, as well as an unquestioned policy construct in today's educational discourse. To be certain, parental involvement is an everyday/routine phenomenon that is simply taken-for-granted in most schools. School leaders and teachers expect a certain degree of involvement from parents, researchers study better ways to get parents involved, and school reformers and policy makers try to improve schools by setting up systems and policy levers that institutionalize parental involvement as a central component of schooling (Hill and Tyson 2009; Honig et al. 2001). In effect, as an educational community, we not only expect parents to be "involved" in school matters, but demand that their involvement be central to the schooling process. Parental involvement is simply a normal and expected part of the everyday activities in school.

However, when one looks at the research literature, it overwhelmingly suggests that Parents of Color are not involved in the same rate as their White middle-class counterparts (Chavkin 1993; Lee and Bowen 2006; Trotman 2001). This apparent lack of involvement, has not only perplexed the research community, but the practitioner community as well, who constantly search for new and different ways to engage parents and families (Epstein 1995; Horvat and Baugh 2015; Khalifa et al. 2015). In contrast to some of these scholars, we take the position that the "problem" of involvement has very little to do with marginalized parents (who seem uninvolved) or with schools (who seem unable to involve these parents). Rather, we posit that the problem of involvement is a discursive one where very specific/discrete understandings of involvement are recognized and privileged in school settings while other forms of involvement have been marginalized, rendered invisible, or discouraged altogether (López 2001; Young 1999).

In other words, how we define the terrain of legitimate parental involvement actions—as well as the policy and practical structures that privilege particular involvement forms over others—is an important first step in understanding the problem of (under)involvement (Olivos 2009). In this regard, CPA is important in helping us understand the various ways in which particular forms of involvement become privileged and entrenched in schools, and how such practices render certain populations as "uninvolved" in the educational lives of their children (Young 1999).

Moreover, we also believe that the ways in which parental involvement has been operationalized and practiced in schools is a relatively recent phenomenon. This is not to suggest that we believe parental involvement is unimportant or trivial, but rather, that its universality as a pressing area of concern within the field of education is neither time-honored nor established. As an educational community, we tend to take parental involvement for granted, often assuming that the practice of engaging parents and communities in particular ways has always been along-established practice and policy concern within education. We believe that CPA can helps us better understand when parental involvement became inscribed in policy (as well as practice) and why it has become such a taken-for-granted notion within the educational community.

As such, CPA helps us to better locate the historiography and contemporary usage of parental involvement as a policy construct, while shedding light on how it shapes and structures current schooling practices. Moreover, it allows us to better understand when parent involvement became a dominant policy concern, while providing some insights as to why it's such a universal construct within education at this particular point in time. We feel it is critically important to raise such questions about these particular practices rather than simply take them for granted.

With this in mind, this chapter utilizes CPA as an analytical tool in order to push our thinking on the topic of parental involvement while providing us with new possibilities for insight and understanding in this particular area. It should be stated that CPA is not simply an alternative way of "doing" policy analysis. Rather it is a different way of thinking about the role and nature of policy; fully recognizing that the policies that shape and structure our everyday/lived world are not neutral, objective, or value-free (Diem et al. 2014). As such, CPA is not a typical or traditional policy analysis where researchers make policy decisions or recommendations based on an established protocol. Instead, CPA aims to critically interrogate the world around us and shed light on the visible and invisible structures, discourses, and systems that shape our world (Atwood and López 2014; Prunty 1985).

Given this understanding, we use CPA in this chapter to trouble the terrain of parental involvement—both the types of practices and actions that are privileged in the literature as well as in the field (i.e., the "what" of involvement), and the expressed rationale for inscribing involvement within education's discourse (i.e., the "why" of involvement). We posit that involvement is discursively regulated and controlled by schools and their agents for particular purposes, and that various school actors (administrators, teachers, researchers, policy makers, etc.) frown upon any deviation from this involvement "script." We contextualize this assertion through an example from a real world case study, showcasing how a group of Latin@ parents organized around particular issues of importance to them, but were increasingly marginalized by the school administration for their grassroots efforts. We then problematize the case study by interrogating the "why" of parental involvement. Lastly, we conclude with some insights surrounding the utility of CPA as a vehicle to understand the discursive nature of parental involvement and how it is used in schools as a mechanism of power and control.

2 Interrogating the "What" of Parental Involvement

The literature surrounding the multiple factors affecting educational outcomes often suggests that a strong relationship exists between parental involvement and high levels of educational success (Jeynes 2014; LaRocque et al. 2011; Núñez et al. 2015). Moreover, educators, practitioners, and policy-makers have certainly touted parental involvement as an important area of study within the educational arena (López 2001).

The different ways in which parents can, and ought to be "involved" was made popular by Joyce Epstein, whose famous typology was popularized in the 1980s (Epstein and Becker 1982; Epstein and Dauber 1989; Epstein 1995). Epstein and her colleagues argued that involvement centered around a specific set of practices and activities within the home as well as in the school. These activities typically included things like participation in parent-teacher associations (PTA), parent-teacher conferences, volunteering, chaperoning field trips, fundraising, as well a host of home-based activities and actions (e.g., turning off the television, supervising homework, reading to a child, etc.). Although Epstein insists that her typology was never intended to be prescriptive (Epstein 1995), it quickly became a top choice for researchers, policymakers and practitioners who were looking for a handy way to think about involvement and operationalize its practices. As a result, Epstein's typology has become a dominant trope in the parental involvement research literature (López 2001). Critics argue that Epstein's typology is far too rigid, and perpetuates a singular view of parental involvement that privileges certain parental activities while ignoring others, reaffirming what deCarvalho (2001) describes as a "romanticized view of family/school relationships" (p. 2).

Indeed, the discourse surrounding parental involvement has recently undergone a shift that has problematized the structures and ideologies that perpetuate a homogenized and simplified understanding of parental involvement. Prior to the effort of critical scholars (e.g., deCarvalho 2001; Hong 2011; López 2001; López and López 2010; Olivos 2004, 2006, 2009; Young 1999) the discourse surrounding parental involvement used to focus on the energies of parents within the schooling space or having parents do school-related "acts" within the home. Such a limited view of parental involvement resulted in what Olivos (2006) described as a, "...diluted...laundry list of activities that 'experts' feel good parents (ought to) 'do' to blindly support the schools' agendas" (p. 13). Not only does the laundry list includes only those parental actions taking place within the traditional schooling space, but such activities symbolize and reflect White middle-class forms of involvement (Young 1999). In other words, the "laundry list" of idealized involvement activities was created within a system that effectively excluded the actions and involvement forms of historically marginalized parents.

Attempting to include the voices and experiences of parents of color, scholars such as López (2001), thus began to expand the spatial boundaries that restricted the discourse of parental involvement. López (2001) describes traditional parental involvement as actions that are "...transparent [and] relegate[ed]...to a scripted role to be performed" around school-centered activities (p. 417). Notwithstanding, scholars such as Pérez-Carreón et al. (2005) are currently challenging the school-centric view of involvement described by López. For example, Pérez-Carreón and his colleagues (2005) note that, "...parental involvement or engagement needs to be understood through parents' *presence* in their children's schooling, regardless of whether that presence is in a formal school space or in more personal, informal spaces, including spaces created by the parents themselves" (p. 466). This expansive lens of parental engagement has helped to examine and acknowledge the various parental involvement actions of Latin@ parents that often stand outside traditional/discursive configurations as noteworthy and beneficial (Atwood and López 2014; Weaver-Hightower 2008).

More recently, studies exploring Latin@ parental agency found Latin@ parents to be active decision-makers in the educational lives of their children (Carreon et al.

2005; McClain 2010). This set of research studies finds that Latin@ parents often manifest their involvement in more discrete ways: i.e., strategically selecting the schools that their children attend and/or the curriculum that best suits their children's needs/interests (i.e., dual immersion, bilingual, etc.). In effect, Latin@ parents are deeply informed and involved—always aware of their power as decision-makers within the educational sphere. McClain (2010) suggests that Latin@ parental agency in the schooling of their children has "illuminate[d] parents as grassroots educational decision makers, negotiating the borderlands between parents and schools" (p. 3078). The boundary that previously confined Latin@ parental engagement has thus expanded even further, suggesting that Latin@ parents are now actively accessing their power through decision-making efforts within the schooling space.

In recent years, Latin@ parents have been joining forces in order to advocate for change within schools. As a result, schools are being transformed into places where Latin@ parents can organize, acquire knowledge, become critical, and advocate for change. Studies focusing on the empowerment and agency of Latin@ parent collectives have found schools to be both supportive and resistant to the efforts of Latin@ parent groups (Cline and Necochea 2001; DeGaetano 2007; Olivos 2004, 2006, 2009; Jasis and Ordóñez-Jasis 2004; Ramirez 2003; Shah 2009). For example, Olivos (2004) found that schools support for parental activism was withdrawn once parents began to advocate for change. In other words, Latin@ parents were not considered a threat by schools and administrators when they were performing their expected involvement "script." However, once parents began to acquire the political consciousness "necessary to grasp how the school system implicitly (and explicitly) works" and began advocating for change, the support of the school administration magically diminished.

Despite the resistance and fears of schools, Latin@ parents have continued to push for change. Studies have found that Latin@ parent groups have been able to successfully restructure schools and, in some cases, advocate for the removal of school level administrators that were excessively combative and resistant to Latin@ student populations (DeGaetano 2007; Jasis and Ordóñez-Jasis 2004; Olivos 2004; Ramirez 2003). More powerful still, have been the efforts of Latin@ parent groups to actively forge and maintain effective partnerships with schools (DeGaetano 2007; Jasis and Ordóñez-Jasis 2004). And yet, results from the aforementioned studies reveal that when parents enacted their agency and power to create change, school administrators became resistant. We believe that the resistances to such grassroots efforts can be partially found in what administrators believe are acceptable forms of involvement actions. In other words, when parents violate the unspoken terms of their involvement agreement, school administrators begin to withdraw their support for their involvement. This suggests that the terms, expectations, and norms of involvement are not only discursively bound, but are controlled by school officials who have deemed certain forms of involvement more acceptable than others.

The narrative below provides more insight into this particular disciplinary practice while highlighting the ways in which parental activism was discouraged, regulated, and managed by school administrators. The events in this particular account were taken from a research study that was conducted by the first author a few years ago. Although the events are real, the names of the school site and research participants are pseudonyms.

2.1 Behind Closed Doors: How One School Regulates Parental Involvement

Franklin Elementary is an urban elementary school in the Midwest located in a district struggling with declining enrollments and student under performance. During the 2013–2014 school year, Franklin had an enrollment of 610 students. Ninety-two percent of students at the school qualified for free or reduced lunch. Of the total student population, 54 % were Black, 39 % were Latin@, 4 % were of Mixed Race origin, and 2 % were White. In addition, 33 % of the students at the school were designated English Language Learners. At the time of the study, the school had yet to make Adequate Yearly Progress (AYP), and in 2010, it was designated as a "Turnaround Status" school. This new classification resulted in the hiring of a new principal and many new teachers (51 % of teachers were new to the school). The school was placed on a strict improvement plan by the state, with the understanding that it would close or reconstitute the school if improvement was not achieved within a given timeframe.

Unfortunately, Franklin failed to demonstrate student growth or improvement. During the 2012–2013 and 2013–2014 academic years, Franklin Elementary garnered a grade of an "F" – the lowest grade given to schools by the state. While the repercussions of this designation are unknown (at least at the time of writing this chapter), Franklin Elementary was turned into a Full Service Community School (FSCS) with the assistance of a federal grant and the support of a local university. As a FSCS, Franklin was able to involve and incorporate partnerships with multiple organizations in order to bring social, health, and human services to families in the school community into its daily operations.

Unlike two other schools in the district that were also transformed into FSCSs, Franklin Elementary also served as the ELL "feeder" school for the surrounding community. This meant that any student living within the surrounding community who needed ELL services was assigned and bussed to Franklin Elementary. Additionally, the surrounding community included an increasing number of Spanish-speaking families, most immigrating from Mexico. According to the most current data from the United States Census Bureau website, it is estimated that over the previous 10 years, the Latin@ population in the city more than doubled, comprising approximately 10 % of the city's population.

Additionally, during the 2010–2011 state legislative session, the state legislature and county governments passed measures targeting undocumented immigrants. The anti-immigration legislation authorized law enforcement officials to question and/or arrest individuals based on their assumed immigration status. To complicate things, state-issued identification cards were no longer issued to undocumented individuals. This had a deleterious impact on an already-vulnerable population.

To make matters worse, counties across the state adopted the Secure Communities Program: a partnership between local law enforcement agencies, the Federal Bureau of Investigation (FBI), and Immigration Customs Enforcement (ICE). This partnership allowed local and federal agencies to share documents (such as fingerprint files) – making it easier for local law enforcement agencies to hold individuals based on their immigration status, thus also making it easier for individuals picked up by police to get transferred to ICE detention.

Passage of the anti-immigration legislation and the establishment of Secure Communities created a hostile and threatening climate for Latin@ immigrants and their families. Simple everyday acts that were previously taken for granted (i.e., parents dropping off children at school, driving to the grocery store, etc.) threatened to separate families. This resulted in many Latin@ families living in the shadows, hiding their immigration status from any agency (including schools) as well as individuals that posed a threat to their well being.

Within the shadows, however, have emerged spaces of hope, dreams, and more importantly, action. Schools, which were often perceived as unwelcoming, marginalizing, cold, and harsh were transformed through parental action into spaces where families, in this case Latin@ families, felt welcomed, appreciated, and acknowledged – particularly as active agents and decision-makers in the daily educational lives of their children. Specifically, in Franklin Elementary, the community room was transformed by Latin@ parents. What once served as a meeting space for community partners became a hub for Spanish-speaking Latin@ immigrant parents. Unfortunately, school administrators failed to acknowledge the time and work spent by Latin@ parents creating and cultivating a welcoming space for Latin@ families as authentic acts of parental engagement. For instance (and as will be discussed later in the chapter), several Franklin school staff (including Mrs. Palmer, the principal) often referred to the parent group as a "social group" – delegitimizing the parent organizing that was taking place within the school. By failing to acknowledge these acts as authentic acts of parental engagement, school administrators further marginalized Latin@ parents while also evading their concerns.

2.1.1 *"Es Como Si Fuera Un Odio/*It's Like a Hatred"

As noted in the previous section, during the timeframe in which data for the above case was collected, Latin@ families in this region were dealing with the threats and consequences that came with the recently passed immigration policies – deportation and the separation of families. Reflecting on the current state of Latin@s in the U.S., Eva, a Franklin parent, noted:

[Es] como si fuera un odio. Es algo como un refundió que tienen hacia los hispanos. Ustedes la raza latina ellos no la trata de una manera, de gracias de la mano de obra de ellos.	It's like a hatred. It's as if they want to recast the Hispanics. They don't treat Latinos in a manner that thanks them for their labor.

As evidenced by Eva's statement, anti-immigration policies created a space where Latin@ families not only felt unwelcome and unappreciated, but their very livelihood was threatened. Eva suggested that this "*odio*/hatred" relegated Latin@s to that of a group of people that must be recast. This feeling of being pushed to the margins of society was also felt by other Latin@ families in schools. Flora, a Latina mother, stated, "In the first place, there are many families that say they are fearful of sending their kids to schools. Why? Because of all this of the immigration. The topic of immigration is like a panic." It was this panic surrounding immigration reform that sparked Latin@ parent organizing at Franklin Elementary.

During the Fall of 2010, in an effort to engage targeted groups of parents/guardians, the parent advocates at Franklin Elementary developed and held a series of "study circles" – meetings in which groups convened to learn about, discuss and develop action around issues related to families and students. Miguel, the bilingual parent advocate at Franklin, was charged with convening a study circle with a group of Latin@, Spanish speaking parents.

Three study-circles were held in the community room and brought together parents—mostly mothers—who discussed challenges they faced in common such as fear of deportation and separation of the family. The study circles provided a setting where parents could share experiences, offer examples and suggestions, and identify common barriers for Spanish-speaking immigrant families. In the de-briefing notes, Miguel described the moment when parents realized their ability to support one another. He wrote, "They [Latin@ immigrant parents] saw that they have the answers to the problems and have proposed to keep meeting after the circles." From these study circles emerged a Latin@ parent group, *Padres Unidos*/United Parents who organized around issues related to anti-immigration reform. However, as will be described in the subsequent sections of this chapter, the community room has remained closed and unacknowledged by school administrators. Yet, despite the lack of administrative acknowledgment and support, Latin@ immigrant parents continued to organize behind closed doors, particularly around issues of importance to them.

2.2 Emerging from the Space

With the formation of *Padres Unidos*, the participants of the study circles had a new focus and awareness. They recognized that they had concerns that extended beyond the walls of the school. However, they also acknowledged that they possessed knowledge and skills that they could use to help empower and uplift other community members. As a collective, *Padres Unidos* decided to begin taking steps to transform Franklin Elementary into a welcoming space for Latin@ families. Through their initial organizing efforts, *Padres Unidos* decided to construct and display something that honored their heritage and traditions – building an altar for *Día de los Muertos*, as well as bring awareness to the group's formation through a door-knocking campaign.

Franklin Elementary had never experienced anything like this – a parent-initiated, parent-lead, and parent-organized group. Interestingly, school representatives perceived the altar as a "small" gesture from parents within the school. However, parents understood this to be a "loud" message of solidarity and affirmation. Simply put, parents were tired of being ignored and feeling unwelcome within the school and sought to take a stand against the racism that targeted the increasing Latin@ community in the school and surrounding area. After the alter had been constructed, parents from *Padres Unidos* felt a sense of cultural pride and accomplishment that only propelled their momentum and creative energy.

As such, *Padres Unidos* used the third (and last) study circle to establish a tentative plan for the future of the group. De-briefing meeting notes indicate that members decided to meet on a weekly basis and focus meetings around issues that Latin@ immigrant families, parents, and students faced. These issues ranged from bullying to transportation to the unique struggles and challenges facing immigrant populations (immigration reform, know your rights training, etc.). *Padres Unidos* sought to conduct workshops that focused on disseminating specific knowledge to others, with the hope that this would ultimately lead towards transformative change within the school and broader community.

With momentum in the group rising, members of *Padres Unidos* felt that it would be a good time to bring awareness to the group. In order to do this, members of *Padres Unidos* decided to begin a door-knocking campaign that took place during two consecutive Saturdays in the spring of 2011. Because Franklin was the ESL feeder school for many districts, the door-knocking campaign took members to different segments of the city. Parents met at Franklin Elementary early in the morning in order to divide the addresses of Latin@ families that attended the school. Members were then given their materials for the day – identification badges, folders that included information about the group (including a list of weekly meeting topics and visitors), and a short survey that was to be administered by the members of *Padres Unidos* to the targeted families. The parents then divided into small groups and with their children in tow proceeded to knock on doors, bringing attention to not only the group but to Franklin Elementary.

Through the door-knocking campaign and the construction of an altar for *Día de los Muertos*, *Padres Unidos* made Franklin Elementary a more welcoming place for Latin@ immigrant families in the community. However the efforts made by *Padres Unidos* remained at the margins of a school administrators' agenda. In other words, because the group's concerns centered predominately around immigration legislation their actions and push for reform within the school were continuously being evaded or ignored by school officials; because according to school officials immigration reform fell outside of the school's purview.

2.3 Diverging Perceptions

Padres Unidos faced many obstacles, challenges, and hurdles during their first 2 years as an organized parent group at Franklin Elementary. During the 2011–2012 academic school year Mrs. Palmer was appointed principal at Franklin. Almost immediately, she made it clear that she was under extreme pressure to "turn the school around." This was further expressed during a school task force when she shared with the group that, "Central office expects me to do in one year what research indicates takes five to seven years." As such, it became clear that Mrs. Palmer knew the pressures she faced, and was strategic in zeroing in on the topic of student achievement. As a result, anything beyond the purview of her focus was put on the backburner, or in the case of the concerns of *Padres Unidos* completely ignored altogether.

For instance, during a parent leadership training, two members of *Padres Unidos*, raised a concern facing immigrant parents to Mrs. Palmer. Although Latin@ immigrant parents expressed interest in volunteering at the school, district policies required that all parent volunteers be fingerprinted and have a criminal background check. However, because of the anti-immigration legislation in the state, immigrant parents feared that if they got fingerprinted they could face deportation. This was a risk they were unwilling to take. Principal Palmer, responded to the parents' concern by noting that immigration concerns were outside the school's responsibility and "the school could not get involved in those matters." As a result of Mrs. Palmer's evasiveness, many of the parents of *Padres Unidos* did not feel as though the school and school leaders recognized the group as a legitimate parent group. Miguel explains:

> Mrs. Palmer knows that there is a meeting every Wednesday at night. She doesn't know what is going on in the meetings. I don't even think she knows that we are teaching parents [how to use] computers. [...] It's been because the relationship has been, "Let them do what they need to do in the community room. As long as they don't go over 8:30, and as long as they don't have kids running around in the hallway..." Which has been a really good freedom for us because then we can really talk about anything but it hasn't [...], given an acknowledgment from the school about the commitment that the parents have to being engaged and coming and wanting to learn and wanting to be involved.

As Miguel suggested, during Mrs. Palmer's tenure, *Padres Unidos* were seen within the school but school leaders did not consider them a formally recognized group. In other words, the work of *Padres Unidos*, including the altar they constructed and their door-knocking campaign, remained ambiguous, a fact that both benefited and hindered their efforts. However, by evading immigration concerns Mrs. Palmer positioned the Latin@ immigrant families at her school as second class citizens. As a result of Mrs. Palmer's decision to evade the topic of immigration, she dismissed the seriousness of the fear and worry that it created among the families and community surrounding her school.

As noted by members of *Padres Unidos*, immigrant families who experienced the traumatic consequences of immigration reform developed a fear and distrust of governmental agencies/agents, including schools. Mrs. Palmer's response to immigration issues being beyond the scope and capacity of the school's responsibility only further perpetuated these anxieties and fears, marginalizing Latin@ immigrant families and their concerns. Sadly, Mrs. Palmer only maintained the status-quo of school/family relationships rather than engaging with families. Miguel describes the relationship between *Padres Unidos* and the school as follows:

Well, I think [the school]… is just kind of like, "We'll have translators for you guys but that's as far as we are going to go." You know. Changing curriculum or being open to culture coming in, something that presents a different perspective in life, like the celebration of the day of the dead, um that starts kind of threatening people. […] So I think it's kind of like "We'll just put you in this corner, we'll give you your space but stay real quiet over there. And then if we see people starting to make too much trouble then we are not going to accept that."

Miguel's impression of the family-school relationship that was established between *Padres Unidos* and the school in many ways reflected the prevailing images of parental engagement. The dominant image in the literature of an "involved" parent is one who is constantly participating in approved school-centered activities – volunteering at the school, attending school-sponsored events, helping their children with homework, etc. The diverging views of *Padres Unidos* and Mrs. Palmer regarding their involvement only highlights the tensions that emerge when parents and school personnel have diverging understandings of involvement.

In the next section, we will focus on why issues of involvement have become more streamlined in recent years while interrogating why and how involvement became closely aligned with the school reform movement. In the example above, the school principal was given a specific set of marching orders: she was tasked to turn the school around and focused her energies on improving student academic outcomes—almost at the expense of everything else. As a result, the principal—feeling the pressure by the state—clearly chose to let the parent organization do their own thing. Adding insult to injury, the alienated parents felt further rejection from the principal when they approached her about their concerns surrounding the fingerprinting policy. Rather than figure out creative ways to get the parent organization back into the fold, the principal felt that immigration concerns were simply not the purview of the school. Sadly, the principal was so caught up in trying to remedy the student performance issue, that she lost a key constituent that could have helped her do just that.

3 Interrogating the "Why" of Parental Involvement

Principal Palmer's actions can be better understood when one looks at the ways in which parental involvement has been articulated and inscribed within educational policy. We believe that educational policy not only informs what parental involvement ought to "look like" in schools, but in doing so, it delimits the range of acceptable involvement practices. In other words, policies not only shape our impressions of expected parental actions and practices, but also provide visible signposts that determine and shape how schools ought to be working with parents on a day-to-day basis. Nowhere is this more evident than in federal educational policy and legislation.

Before 1983 little, if any, federal attention was given to issues of parental involvement. In fact, it was not until the publication of *A Nation at Risk* when parental involvement began to take shape at a federal level. Although the National Commission on Excellence in Education (1983) was tasked with providing a report on the quality of education in America, the report went beyond its Commission by providing a set of "practical recommendations" (p. 1) that presumably would fix the shabby state of American schools and set the nation on a corrective path.

Some of these recommendations addressed parents and students directly, under the guise that "the success of our recommendations does not fall to the schools and colleges alone" (p. 34). More importantly, *A Nation at Risk* did not mince words, arguing that "more important" than the role of faculty members, administrators, and policymakers, was the role of parents and students in the school reform effort:

> As surely as you are your child's first and most influential teacher, your child's ideas about education and its significance begin with you. You must be a living example of what you expect your children to honor and to emulate. Moreover, you bear a responsibility to participate actively in your child's education. You should encourage more diligent study and discourage satisfaction with mediocrity and the attitude that says "let it slide"; monitor your child's study; encourage good study habits; encourage your child to take more demanding rather than less demanding courses; nurture your child's curiosity, creativity, and confidence; and be an active participant in the work of the schools. Above all, exhibit a commitment to continued learning in your own life. Finally, help your children understand that excellence in education cannot be achieved without intellectual and moral integrity coupled with hard work and commitment. Children will look to their parents and teachers as models of such virtues (p. 35).

With this brief statement, the Commission single-handedly named parental involvement as a focus of concern while formally introducing parental involvement into the national conversation surrounding school reform. More importantly, the Commission not only suggested that parental involvement was a key factor in school reform efforts, but identified the specific ways in which parents could be "involved" in their children's educational lives. It is these types of directives that shape and influence how we come to know and understand the expected roles of parents in schools.

The topic of parental involvement would again take national stage in 1991 under President George H. W. Bush's *America 2000: An Education Strategy*. Under *America 2000*, parental "choice" policy levers were formally introduced into the policy arena, paving the way for bolder ideas involving testing, accountability, vouchers/certificates, and the power of parents to use choice as a vehicle to foster educational reform and change: "It's time parents were free to choose the schools that their children attend. This approach will create the competitive climate that stimulates excellence in our private and parochial schools as well" (Bush 1991). In effect, *America 2000* encouraged parents to vote with their feet in order to force schools to be more accountable to children as well as to hold schools accountable for precious taxpayer dollars. In addition to choice, parental involvement was also articulated in very specific ways, providing guidance and direction for how parents were expected to be involved in the educational process:

> Q: What can parents do to help?
> A: A thousand things. They are the keys to their children's education, and there is no part of the AMERICA 2000 Strategy in which they do not have an important role. As for what

they can do *today*—they could read a story to their children, check to see that tonight's homework is done, thank their child's teacher, talk with their teachers and principals about how things are going in school, and set some examples for their children of virtuous, self-disciplined and generous behavior. (America 2000, 1991, p. 34)

In contrast to the policy prescriptions outlined in President Reagan's *A Nation at Risk*, President Bush's *America 2000 Strategy* shifted the scope of parental involvement beyond the role of passive supporter in the home to one of active involvement in both the school and home fronts. Parents were no longer expected to simply encourage their children, but to be more hands-on and proactive in the schooling process: i.e., engaging in specific/discrete "involvement" activities in the home on the one hand, while promoting a culture of choice and market competition on the other.

In 1994, President Clinton included parental involvement as part of his *Goals 2000: Educate America Act:* "By the year 2000, every school will promote partnerships that will increase parental involvement and participation in promoting the social, emotional, and academic growth of children" (*Goals* 2000, Goal 8). Although the initial legislation left the terrain of parental involvement undefined, the *Goals 2000 Policy Guidance Manual* (1996) made it clear that:

Children do best when parents are enabled to play four key roles in their children's learning: teachers (helping children at home), supporters (contributing their skills to the school), advocates (helping children receive fair treatment), and decision makers (participating in joint problem-solving with the school at every level).

The manual then went on to note that parents were expected to be involved in these four roles at all levels of education, including the state level ("State plan must be developed in consultation with parents, as well as with LEAs, teachers, pupil services personnel, administrators and other staff.") as well as the local level ("An LEA must develop jointly with, agree upon with, and distribute to parents of participating children a written parent involvement policy that is incorporated into the LEA's plan."). The *Goals 2000 Policy Guidance Manual* (1996) further stated that schools not only needed to have a written parental involvement policy, but that such policy would need to detail how the LEA would formally involve parents in all levels of school improvement.

While President Clinton's *Goals 2000* had a short shelf-life as a federal education legislation, it certainly had a long-lasting impact in profoundly shaping the discourse on parent involvement. If *A Nation at Risk* was a plea for parents to be more involved in the home front and *America 2000* was meant to encourage more meaningful partnerships between home and school, Clinton's *Goals 2000* was a clarion call for parents to have a more formal seat at the table in both state and local education matters. The policy shift from its previous policy predecessors was certainly evident: parent involvement had become thoroughly inscribed in federal education policy.

While President George W. Bush's *No Child Left Behind Act* of 2001 effectively brought a formal end to President Clinton's *Goals 2000*, it is important to note that many of the parental involvement provisions under *Goals 2000*, were simply incorporated and folded into *NCLB* (in many instances, the language of the parental involvement policy remained virtually unchanged). However, unlike its policy predecessor, *NCLB* now tied Title I monies to its parental involvement initiatives, meaning that districts and schools, needed to demonstrate how they were meeting the spirit of the law and involving parents in meaningful ways. According to *NCLB*, Section 1118 of Title I:

> A local educational agency may receive funds under this part only if such agency implements programs, activities, and procedures for the involvement of parents in programs assisted under this part consistent with this section. Such programs, activities, and procedures shall be planned and implemented with meaningful consultation with parents of participating children.

While LEA's were still responsible for co-developing a written parental involvement policy in consultation with parents under *NCLB*, their responsibilities for ensuring that parents were involved in meaningful ways and in every realm of the educational process grew exponentially. Under *NCLB*, local education agencies were now tasked with the following:

1. Setting aside moneys to co-develop and implement their parental involvement programs,
2. To have an annual meeting where parents are informed of the LEA's parent involvement policy and provided an opportunity to participate along with routes for successful collaboration,
3. To inform parents of the educational progress of their children and extend to parents the opportunity to formulate curricular and pedagogical suggestions for improvement,
4. To develop a school-parent "compact" that explicitly focuses on student achievement and which details how parents will be responsible for supporting their children's academic success,
5. To build capacity for meaningful involvement at the school, including routes for parent education, the development of professional development training materials, and other assistance (e.g., transportation, meals, daycare, etc.) that aim to improve and facilitate parental involvement at the school,
6. To ensure that specific target populations such as ELL parents, parents with special needs, migrant parents, etc. are not left behind or placed at a disadvantage, and
7. To collaborate with state and regional Parent Information Resource Centers on delivering services to parents at the school.

Indeed, parental involvement under *NCLB* was quite a logistical and organizational undertaking. Under *NCLB*, parental involvement became a laundry list of very specific requirements that needed to be met. If schools and/or districts fell short of these requirements, education agencies ran the risk of being sanctioned. Therefore, in order to meet both the language and spirit of the new law, particularly with respect to "meaningful" involvement practices, schools increasingly began to work with state, regional, and national organizations such as The National Network of Partnership Schools at Johns Hopkins University (Epstein 2005) to identify activities and approaches for parent involvement.

The National Network of Partnership Schools (NNPS), under the direction of Joyce Epstein, was an important player in disseminating practical information to schools and states surrounding parental involvement policies and practices during this time (Epstein 2004). The Network boasted an impressive roster of about 1000 schools, districts, and states, that received training and guidance in research based practices for involvement:

> Schools in NNPS begin with an Action Team for Partnerships (ATP), a committee of the school improvement team. The ATP uses six types of involvement—parenting, communicating, volunteering, learning at home, decision making, and collaborating with the community—to ensure that parents have many different ways to become involved at home, at school, and in the community (Epstein 2004, p. 14).

To be certain, Epstein's 6-part typology was comprehensive, and provided schools with multiple entry points for parental involvement. In fact, Epstein and her collaborators (Epstein et al. 2002) identified very specific practices under each of type of involvement, for schools, districts, and states to consider. As a result, Epstein's typology became the "go-to" framework for states and LEA's to fulfill the parental involvement requirements for meaningful involvement under *NCLB*, and rapidly became a staple in the parent involvement discourse.

When one looks at the progression of parent involvement within the federal policy making arena since the publication of *A Nation of Risk*, we can see that involvement became more and more "inscribed" in educational policy with each successive federal law. Moreover, as the policy stakes got higher, parent involvement became increasingly honed and formalized under the threat of sanctions. Given the regulatory functions of *NCLB*, the work done by the National Network of Partnership Schools provided a key policy "link" to help operationalize parental involvement practices via Epstein's 6-part typology of involvement at the state and local levels.

Parent involvement is now at the point where only those practices and actions that correspond to Epstein's typology are recognized and privileged in schools (Howard and Reynolds 2008; López 2001). In other words, parent involvement has become homogenous and uniform across public school settings. It has now reached a point of discursivity: where parental involvement is so common, and so universally understood that it needs no definition or description (Olivos 2009). We simply take involvement as for granted and as a universal given. As educators, administrators, policy makers, researchers and scholars, we implicitly "know" what parental involvement is, what it looks like, and what it *supposed* to look like in a school setting. Parents who behave badly are those who do not subscribe to our pre-existing understandings of involvement, or whose involvement forms stand outside discursive configurations. However, as we've discussed in this chapter, our very understandings of "involvement" did not occur naturally. Rather, there were very specific policy levers and institutional players that "naturalized" certain forms of involvement practices over others.

4 Implications of Using Critical Policy Analysis

Critical Policy Analysis reminds us that policies are both visible and invisible; simultaneously textual and discursive (Weaver-Hightower 2008; Young 1999). In other words, the politics of the everyday–what we experience, know, witness, and take for granted on a "day-to-day" basis—is not objective or neutral, but discursively formed (Atwood and López 2014; Weaver-Hightower 2008). They are powerful ideological constructs that shape and influence our understanding of the world. CPA reminds us that our job, as critical policy scholars, is to interrogate the world around us in order to better understand the various structures, discourses, and systems that shape our world and give it life. It also calls for us to recognize how these dicourses contribute to inequitable ourtcomes in order to rethink what we take for granted and radically transform our world.

In this chapter, we have examined how issues of parental involvement are not only informed by federal education policies, but are reinforced by local policy actors who seemingly take particular forms of involvement for granted. We have applied the tenets of CPA in order to better understand what constitutes the terrain of acceptable parental involvement behaviors and why school officials continue to privilege a very narrow set of parental practices and actions in their everyday work. Moreover, our case study highlights the ways in which this process unfolds at the building level and how parental actions that stand outside traditional/discurvive configurations are not only invalidated but are rarely recognized as legitimate forms of involvement.

Indeed, we have demonstrated that involvement is not only discurvely situated, but that school agents rely on this discursive script to make decisions about "appropriate" parental actions in schools. This is not to suggest that school personnel (and other educational actors) are acting out of spite or ill-will, but that they rarely question their own understandings of involvement and do not take the time to understand the various systems that inform their world views about these matters. As critical educators and scholars, it is important that we raise fundamental questions about our own taken-for-granted assumptions and shed light on the discourses that shape our world and our understanding of phenomena within it. CPA not only challenges us to see the world differently, but to take critical action to change our practices so that we don't continue to perpetuate inequities in our profession as well as in our daily lives.

References

America. (2000). *An education strategy*. Washington, DC: U.S. Department of Education.

Atwood, E., & López, G. R. (2014). Let's be critically honest: Towards a messier counter story in critical race theory. *International Journal of Qualitative Studies in Education, 27*(9), 1134–1154.

Ball, S. J. (1994). *Education reform: A critical and post-structural approach*. Buckingham: Open University Press.

Brewer, C. A. (2014). Historicizing in critical policy analysis: The production of cultural histories and micro histories. *International Journal of Qualitative Studies in Education, 27*, 273–288.

Bush, G. H. W. (1991, April). *Remarks by the President at presentation of national education strategy.* Washington, DC: White House.

Carreon, G. P., Drake, C., & Barton, A. C. (2005). The importance of presence: Immigrant parents' school engagement experiences. *American Educational Research Journal, 42*(3), 465–498.

Chavkin, N. F. (1993). *Families and schools in a pluralistic society.* Albany: State University of New York Press.

Cline, Z., & Necochea, J. (2001). ¡ Basta Ya! Latino parents fighting entrenched racism. *Bilingual Research Journal, 25*(1–2), 89–114.

deCarvalho, M. E. (2001). *Rethinking family-school relations: A critique of parental involvement in schooling.* Mahwah: L. Erlbaum Associates.

DeGaetano, Y. (2007). The role of culture in engaging Latino parents' involvement in School. *Urban Education, 42*(2), 145–162.

Delgado, R. (1989). Storytelling for oppositionists and others: A plea for narrative. *Michigan Law Review, 87*, 2411–2441.

Diem, S., Young, M. D., Welton, A. D., Mansfield, K. C., & Lee, P. L. (2014). The intellectual landscape of critical policy analysis. *International Journal of Qualitative Studies in Education, 27*(9), 1068–1090.

Epstein, J. L. (1995). School/family/community partnerships: Caring for the children we share. *Phi Delta Kappan, 76*(9), 701.

Epstein, J. L. (2004). Meeting NCLB requirements for family involvement. *Middle Ground, 8*(1), 14–17.

Epstein, J. L. (2005). Attainable goals? The spirit and letter of the *No Child Left Behind Act* on parental involvement. *Sociology of Education, 78*(2), 179–182.

Epstein, J. L., & Becker, H. J. (1982). Teachers' reported practices of parent involvement: Problems and possibilities. *The Elementary School Journal, 83*(2), 103–113.

Epstein, J. L., & Dauber, S. L. (1989). *Teacher attitudes and practices of parent involvement in inner-city elementary and middle schools* (Report no. 32). Baltimore: Center for Research on Elementary and Middle Schools.

Epstein, J. L., Sanders, M. G., Simon, B. S., Salinas, K. C., Jansorn, N. R., & Van Voorhis, F. L. (2002). *School, family, and community partnerships: Your handbook for action* (2nd ed.). Thousand Oaks: Corwin Press.

Goals 2000: Educate America Act. Retrieved from https://www.govtrack.us/congress/bills/103/hr1804

Hill, N. E., & Tyson, D. F. (2009). Parental involvement in middle school: A meta-analytic assessment of the strategies that promote achievement. *Developmental Psychology, 45*(3), 740–763.

Hong, S. (2011). *A cord of three strands: A new approach to parent engagement in schools.* Cambridge, MA: Harvard Education Press.

Honig, M., Kahne, J., & McLaughlin, M. (2001). School-community connections: Strengthening opportunity to learn and opportunity to teach. In V. Richardson (Ed.), *Handbook of research on teaching* (4th ed., pp. 998–1028). Washington, DC: American Educational Research Association.

Horvat, E. M., & Baugh, D. E. (2015). Not all parents make the grade in today's schools. *Phi Delta Kappan, 96*(7), 8–13.

Howard, T. C., & Reynolds, R. (2008). Examining parent involvement in reversing the underachievement of African American students in middle-class schools. *Educational Foundations, 22*(1), 79–98.

Jasis, P., & Ordóñez-Jasis, R. (2004). Convivencia to empowerment: Latino parent organizing at La Familia. *High School Journal, 88*(2), 32–42.

Jeynes, W. (Ed.). (2014). *Family factors and the educational success of children.* New York: Routledge.

Khalifa, M., Arnold, N. W., & Newcomb, W. (2015). Understand and advocate for communities first. *Phi Delta Kappan, 96*(7), 20–25.

LaRocque, M., Kleiman, I., & Darling, S. M. (2011). Parental involvement: The missing link in school achievement. *Preventing School Failure, 55*(3), 115–122.

Lee, J. S., & Bowen, N. K. (2006). Parent involvement, cultural capital, and the achievement gap among elementary school children. *American Educational Research Journal, 43*(2), 193–218.

López, G. R. (2001). The value of hard work: Lessons on parent involvement from an (im)migrant household. *Harvard Educational Review, 71*(3), 416–437.

López, M. P., & López, G. R. (2010). *Persistent inequality: Contemporary realities in the education of undocumented Latina/o students*. New York: Routledge.

Marshall, C. (1985). Facing fundamental dilemmas in education systems. *Education and Urban Society, 18*(1), 131–134.

Marshall, C. (1999). Researching the margins: Feminist critical policy analysis. *Educational Policy, 13*(1), 59–76.

McClain, M. (2010). Parental agency in educational decision making: A Mexican American experience. *Teachers College Record, 112*(12), 3074–3101.

National Commission on Excellence in Education. (1983). *A nation at risk: The imperative for educational reform: A report to the nation and the Secretary of Education, United States Department of Education*. Washington, DC: The Commission.

No Child Left Behind Act of 2001, P.L. 107–110, 20 U.S.C. § 6319 (2002).

Núñez, J. C., Suárez, N., Rosário, P., Vallejo, G., Valle, A., & Epstein, J. L. (2015). Relationships between perceived parental involvement in homework, student homework behaviors, and academic achievement: Differences among elementary, junior high, and high school students. *Metacognition and Learning, 10*(3), 375–406

Olivos, E. M. (2004). Tensions, contradictions, and resistance: An activist's reflection of the struggles of Latino parents in the public school system. *High School Journal, 87*(4), 25–35.

Olivos, E. M. (2006). *The power of parents: A critical perspective of bicultural parent involvement in public schools*. New York: Peter Lang Publishing Inc.

Olivos, E. M. (2009). Collaboration with Latino families: A critical perspective of home-school interactions. *Intervention in School & Clinic, 45*(2), 109–115.

Pérez-Carreón, G., Drake, C., & Barton, A. C. (2005). The importance of presence: Immigrant parents' school engagement experiences. *American Educational Research Journal, 42*(3), 465–498.

Policy Guidance for Title I, Part A: Improving Basic Programs Operated by Local Educational Agencies. (1996).Available: https://www2.ed.gov/legislation/ESEA/Title_I/parinv.html

Prunty, J. J. (1985). Signposts for a critical educational policy analysis. *Australian Journal of Education, 29*(4), 133–140.

Ramirez, F. (2003). Dismay and disappointment: Parental involvement of Latino immigrant parents. *The Urban Review, 35*(2), 93–110.

Shah, P. (2009). Motivating participation: The symbolic effects of Latino representation on parent school involvement. *Social Science Quarterly, 90*(1), 212–230.

Solórzano, D. G., & Yosso, T. J. (2001). Critical race and LatCrit theory and method: Counter-storytelling Chicana and Chicano graduate school experiences. *International Journal of Qualitative Studies in Education, 14*(4), 471–495.

Trotman, M. F. (2001). Involving the African American parent: Recommendations to increase the level of parent involvement within African American families. *Journal of Negro Education, 70*(4), 275–285.

U.S. Department of Education. (1991). *America 2000: An education strategy*. Washington, DC: U.S. Department of Education.

Weaver-Hightower, M. B. (2008). An ecology metaphor for educational policy analysis: A call to complexity. *Educational Researcher, 37*(3), 153–167.

Young, M. D. (1999). Multifocal educational policy research: Toward a method for enhancing traditional educational policy studies. *American Educational Research Journal, 36*(4), 677–714.

A Feminist Critical Policy Analysis of Patriarchy in Leadership

Catherine Marshall, Mark Johnson, and Torrie Edwards

Abstract This chapter examines patriarchal assumptions of leadership in superintendencies in American public education. Using feminist critical policy analysis as a guiding framework, we first present historical trends of sex segregation in education, noting that while teaching has historically been feminized, higher positions in leadership are most often occupied by White, heterosexual men. We note shifts: as women have recently begun to fill more principal positions, this has been accompanied by a solidification of men's dominance of the superintendency. We unpack the historical cultural assumptions of gender embedded in influential cultural texts, including the Bible and political discourse. These texts provide important insight into the prevailing underrepresentation of women in higher leadership positions they depict women as naturally subservient and in need of men's protection. Thus, biblical and political speech reinforce and perpetuate traditional gendering of educational leadership. We conclude with a call for further integration of feminist theory and practice into educational leadership.

Keywords Educational and political leadership and women • Feminist critical policy analysis • Cultural discourse • Superintendent

1 Introduction

White men continue to occupy the vast majority of superintendency positions in the United States. This chapter seeks to understand why this is the case. We use feminist critical policy analysis (hereinafter called FCPA) as an approach for exploring cultural discourses that subtly undermine women's chances to strive and thrive in top positions. We begin by outlining the startling statistics on women's positions, past and present, in education. We then search for explanations for male dominance, thus demonstrating the power of FCPA frameworks to uncover cultural arrangements that underlie persistent patterns in educational leadership. Our analysis focuses specifically on political and cultural messages that frame

---

C. Marshall (✉) • M. Johnson • T. Edwards
School of Education, University of North Carolina, Chapel Hill, NC, USA
e-mail: Marshall@email.unc.edu

policy documents. We argue that cultural assumptions persist in structural norms and policies-in-practice, which continue to undermine women's power, pay, status, and influence over decision-making. But we end with an optimistic vision for the future. Based on feminist literatures, we explore the potentialities of a "new imaginary" (Fairclough and Fairclough 2012), in which women are proportionally represented in top positions.

2 Historical Trends of Sex Segregation in Education

2.1 Teachers

At the start of the nineteenth century, the vast majority of America's teachers were men (Rury 2005). Things rapidly changed, however, with the spread of common schooling in the mid-1800s. By 1900, most teachers in American schools were women. The feminization of education was, in part, related to local districts capitalizing on the fact that women could be hired for less money than men (Apple 1985; Blount 1998; Rury 2005).

Well-established patriarchal norms and culturally accepted beliefs about gender roles served to advance the notion that teaching was "women's work." As described by Young and Marshall (2012), Strober (1984), "Advocates of women as teachers, such as Catherine Beecher, Mary Lyon, Zilpah Grant, Horace Mann and Henry Barnard, argued that not only were women the ideal teachers of young children (because of their patient and nurturing qualities) but that teaching was ideal preparation for motherhood" (p. 19).

At the beginning of the 1900s, 70 % of American teachers were women. This percentage continued to rise through to the 1920s and remained relatively consistent for the rest of the century.[1] According to National Center for Education Statistics (1993), approximately 66 % of America's teachers were women by 1980 (see Fig. 1). Then, starting in the 1980s, the percentage of female teachers began to rise again. By 2012, the percentage of women teachers in the United States was approaching 80 %. Teaching has been a feminized occupation for more than 150 years and, based on recent trends, it appears to again be increasingly so (see Fig. 2).

---

[1]Blount's historical analysis traces these as some of the reasons for that temporary decline: (1) the avoidance of hiring women who marry and become pregnant; (2) subtle homophobia—fears of "old maids"; and (3) belief that men deserved and needed jobs more than women (in the wake of the Great Depression and World War), coupled with the narrative that women work only for bits of spending money, rather than for necessity.

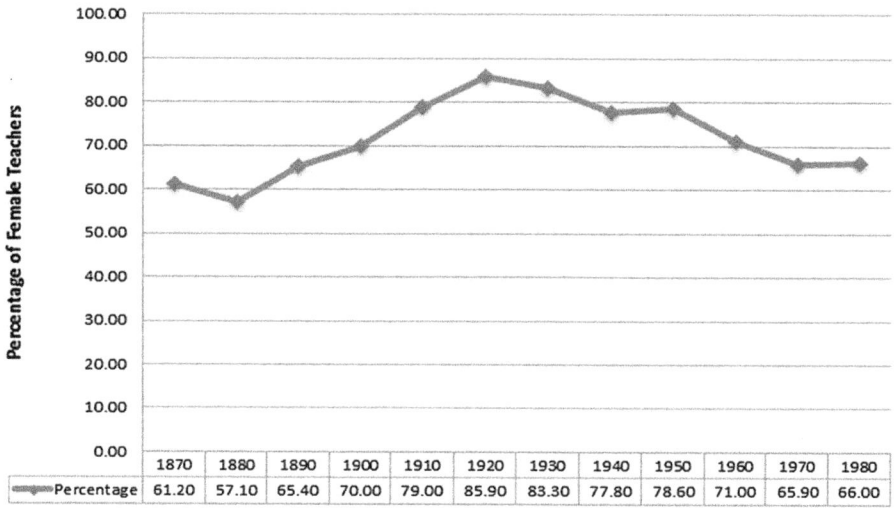

Fig. 1 Percentage of female teachers in the United States' public elementary and secondary schools. Selected years, 1869–1870 through 1979–1980. Data obtained from the National Center for Education Statistics (1993) – *120 Year of American Education: A Statistical Portrait*

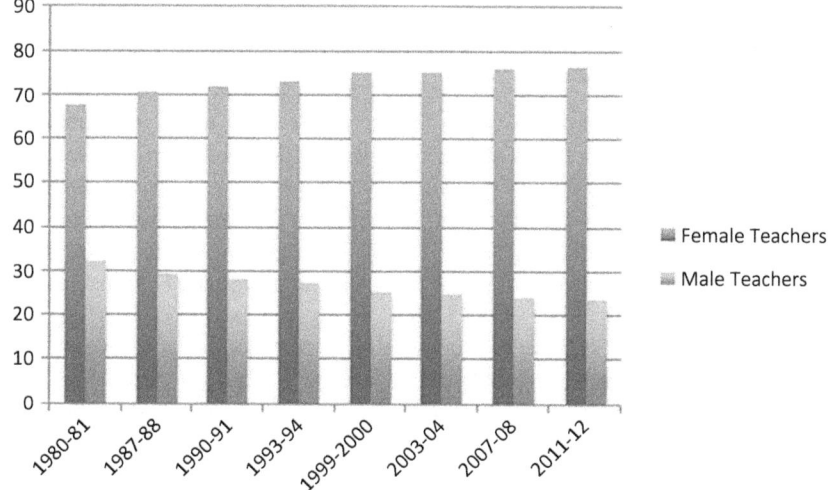

Fig. 2 Percentage distribution of teachers in the United States' public elementary and secondary schools, by sex. Selected years, 1987–1988 through 2011–2012. Data obtained from the National Center for Education Statistics (2012) – *Digest of Education Statistics*; and the National Center for Education Statistics (1993) *120 Year of American Education: A Statistical Portrait*

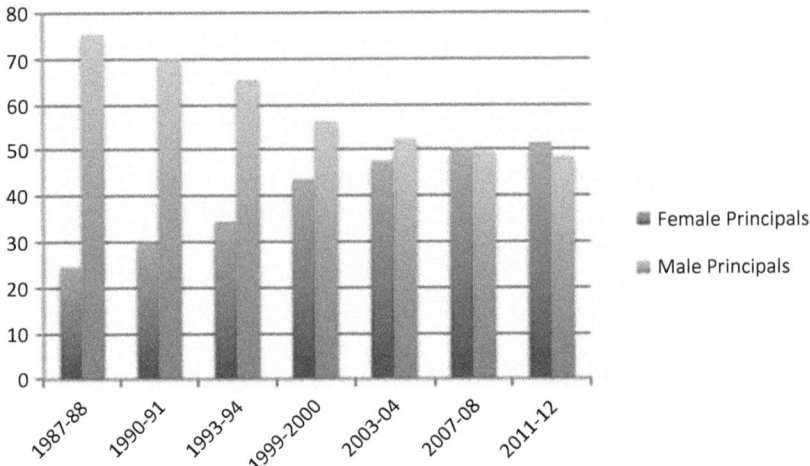

Fig. 3 Percentage distribution of principals in the United States' public elementary and secondary schools, by sex. Selected years, 1987–1988 through 2011–2012. Data obtained from the National Center for Education Statistics (2012) – *Digest of Education Statistics*; National Center for Education Statistics (1987–1988 and 1990–1991) – *Schools and Staffing Survey*

2.2 School Principals

For over a century, despite occupying the vast majority of the nation's classrooms, women teachers have disproportionately been managed by male principals (Marshall and Young 2013). More than half of all school leaders in the United States were women in 1910 (Shen 2005). At that time, women principals were concentrated mostly in rural districts and elementary schools, while men were predominantly leaders in urban districts and high schools. Nevertheless, from the 1920s through to the 1970s, the percentage of women school leaders plummeted. As late as 1988, only one fourth of all principals in the United States were women.

As shown in Fig. 3, significant shifts have occurred during the past quarter century. By the end of the first decade of the twenty-first century, women occupied a marginally higher percentage of school principalship positions than men. This shift happened, however, just as principals' jobs were increasingly being defined as "instructional leaders."

2.3 Superintendents

According to Blount (1998), 8.94 % of all superintendents in the United States were women in 1910. This percentage had slightly increased to 10.98 % by 1930, but subsequently fell to 3.38 % by 1971. Figure 4 shows the percentage of female

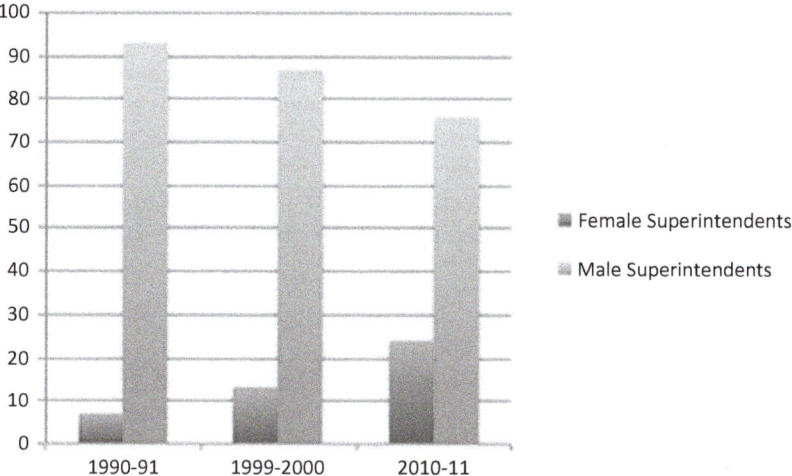

Fig. 4 Percentage distribution of superintendents in the United States' public school districts, by sex. Selected years, 1990–1991 through 2010–2011. Data obtained from Shakeshaft (1990); Glass (2000); and Kowalski et al. (2011)

and male public school superintendents from 1990 to 2011. Although the total percentage of women has increased over this time period, there still remains a much higher concentration of men in the role of superintendent.

Despite teaching being a deeply feminized profession, the superintendency remains male-dominated. How does one make sense of these trends?

3 Previous Research on Women in Leadership

3.1 Women as "Experiments" in Top Educational Leadership

In a report published in 1873 by the Commissioner of Education, women superintendents were described as being "a novel experiment that should be watched closely" (Blount 1998, p. 172). Almost 150 years later, their continued underrepresentation suggests that women superintendents are still regarded as tokens and vulnerable outsiders. Why is this?

3.2 Women on the Career Path to Top Leadership Positions

Research has shown that women's experiences as leaders are different from men's. Robinson (2013) found that women administrators leave the profession due to family demands and frustrations with attaining goals. Similarly, Grogan and Brunner (2005) described how women with less-than-supportive spouses, and/or with small children, seldom attain or remain serving in superintendent positions. One study revealed that 52 % of women superintendents versus 8 % of men were married (Olsen 2006). Further, research has shown that women experience different types of stress than men in leadership positions, including the sense that they have to prove themselves as being managerial, more masculine and rational, and to "counteract inappropriate or hostile assumptions about women managers" (Deem and Ozga 2005, p. 35).

3.3 Women Move Up Slower and Are Undermined

Sensing hostile assumptions, and often being surrounded by colleagues who are White males, women may not push their ideas or "show off" their competence in ways that get the attention of superiors, as is often necessary for upward career mobility. Even when women slowly gain access to management in education, they sometimes feel that they must have male sponsorship and worry that they will endure penalties for any assertive and challenging behavior, never mind any outward show of challenging men, whether they be school board members, parents, local business leaders, or male colleagues. This performance as role models in schools can perpetuate stereotypes that prevent girls from assertive behavior, exercising agency, or aspiring to leadership.

3.4 Selection Processes

Studying gatekeepers and the superintendent search and selection practices, Tallerico (2000) highlighted elements of the hiring process that provide narrow definitions of "quality, stereotyping, and the role of 'good Chemistry'" during job interviews. A few tidbits shown in these selection processes include: (1) preference for a military background and/or a business mentality, and the assumption that typically White male career paths are great preparation for the job; (2) routines for simplifying the search process, such as spreadsheets with "traditional" leadership qualities highlighted; and (3) cultural norms leading to questions about "just-how-tough-can-she-be," or "the-district-isn't-ready-for-a-woman." As one board search consultant described in Tallerico's case study stated, "It's almost axiomatic that we're going to hire a [married] male" (p. 33). According to Tallerico, consultants and board members also expressed anti-affirmative action sentiments, believing that issues of sexism were no longer a factor. Further, those men charged with making hiring decisions were described as being inclined to "go with the gut" in evaluating candidates, with a strong preference for people most like themselves.

In order to be hired, women school leaders must learn to talk, walk, and assert values that make them appear more like men. As Sawicki (1991) says, "dominant discourse assumes that all knowledge is masculinist... and that women's only alternatives are to speak in a masculine voice, construct a new language, or be silent" (p. 1).

4 Theoretical Framework

Feminist Critical Policy Analysis (FCPA) connects critical policy analysis with feminism to examine how policies buttress patriarchal power structures that institutionalize male dominance (Marshall and Young 2013). As described by Young and Marshall (2012), Critical Feminists focus on power and patriarchy prevalent in the cultural arrangements that repress and silence women and girls. FCPA homes in on structures and policies that powerfully reinforce those cultural arrangements in order to:

1. Expose how hegemonic power sources maintain a discourse that advances the interests of dominant groups, usually White males, shedding light on areas that have been blind to women's realities; and
2. Highlight arenas of power and dominance, including powerful policy artifacts, like curriculum guidelines and unobtrusive policies-in-practice, which reify White male hegemony.

One key approach in FCPA is discourse analysis, which enables the examination of "opaque as well as transparent structural relationships of dominance, discrimination, power and control as manifested in language" (Wodak and Meyer 2009, p. 10). According to FCPA, the discourse contained within policy documents can be deconstructed in order to uncover how patriarchal power structures are often enshrined in day-to-day practices and unstated assumptions.

5 Methodological Search for Explanations

FCPA guided our purposeful sampling of cultural discourse. We specifically chose to focus on Biblical texts and political speeches because of their power to shape deep assumptions about gender roles, as well as about leadership qualities. We ventured, therefore, far afield from the already-explored descriptions of women and men in education leadership careers – a well-documented area of research. Since more than five decades of research have not resulted in education policy attention, we sought alternative critical methodology and broader explanations by looking at wider societal contexts.

5.1 FCPA Applied to Research on Women in School Superintendencies

As described in an earlier section of this chapter, teaching has long been considered "women's work." Though historical studies and statistical reports can help frame our understanding of patriarchal dominance, they do not go far enough for FCPA purposes. FCPA is an assertive search for injustices and exclusions, with the aim of improving society. Research findings, Title IX, EEOC policies and declaring "The Year of the Woman" have not yet cleared the path for women ascending the superintendency. To borrow an understatement from the website of The Clinton Foundation's *No Ceilings* initiative (2015), "We are not there yet." The practices perpetuating such wrongs and exclusions persist, in spite of previous policy interventions.

5.2 Cultural Messages Persisting in the Demarcation of Women's and Men's Roles

From a feminist perspective, value-embedded assumptions about women are reified in dominant discourses. Identifying such assumptions is therefore essential for dismantling patriarchal conceptions of leadership. In the following section we identify several sources for the perspectives that function to preserve patriarchal assumptions and that deter female leadership. For example:

1. Women aren't leaders (the management perspective);
2. Women's work is less valuable (the economic perspective);
3. Women were created to serve men (the biblical perspective);
4. Women need protecting (the political perspective).

5.3 The Management Perspective: Women Aren't Leaders

The superintendency was created by men with political power and strong ties to corporate interests. Accordingly, the role of superintendent has come to imitate that of the male-dominated world of CEOs in the private sector (Blount 1998; Murphy 1990; Smith 1980). Moreover, much like the private sector, traditional patriarchal assumptions about gender roles have played an essential role in justifying and perpetuating inequitable access of women to school leadership positions. For instance, because of their supposed lack of strength, women were at one time considered to be incapable of disciplining children and maintaining order in the schools (Shakeshaft 1999).

As teaching became increasingly feminized, there was a push to give men more authority, promoting them quickly from teaching to administration. Historical and feminist research has shown that the feminization of the profession also coincided with a shift toward standardization and the stripping away of professional autonomy, resulting in a more prescribed curriculum, fixed wages, and heightened levels of male supervision (McFadden and Smith 2004; Strober and Tyack 1980; Richardson and Hatcher 1983). Reflecting trends that have prevailed across familial settings and private industry, men working in educational leadership have long been given the authority to manage women. In the words of Blount (1998), "The male educators who remained had to assert their masculine qualities somehow, thus many became administrators to control the labors of women just as fathers and husbands long had done in the home" (p. 37). Such conceptions of educational leadership as a masculine quality resulted in the exclusion of women.

5.4 Perspectives from Economics and Workplace Literatures: Women's Work Is Less Valuable

What other underlying assumptions exist about women as leaders in the workplace? How can we understand the gendered hierarchy in schools, where superintendents who are predominantly male manage the women who do most of the teaching? Fine (2010) says, "cultural realities and beliefs about females and males – represented in existing inequalities; in commercials, in conversations; in the minds, expectations, or behavior of others; or primed in our minds by the environment—alter our self-perception, interests and behavior" (p. 95). The rare persons who break out of these realities still live in environments where people are uncomfortable with them. Workplace literatures label this as a hostile environment. Cultural dynamics can lead to expectations that, when women lead a group, it must be an unimportant group.

Economists have attributed sex segregation and wage differentials to the "rational, utility-maximizing behavior of men and women within households and labor markets" (Bielby 2014, p. 865). According to this perspective, occupational segregation originates with the household division of labor:

> Women prefer, get stuck with, or have a competitive advantage caring for children and the home. Because of that, they invest less in market human capital. For example, intermittent labor-force participation leads to less work experience and thus to lower productivity and flatter age-earning profiles. Women rationally *choose* occupations that are easier to leave and reenter, where skills do not atrophy, and so on. (Bielby 2014, p. 865)

Bielby (2014) argues that traditional gender-role ideologies are what "sustain women's disadvantages in both workplace and family dynamics" (p. 874). From a feminist perspective, however, it is the impact of patriarchal societal norms and discrimination that both influence and limit the choices of women in the labor market.

Significant progress toward gender equality has been made since the 1960s, with increases in women's employment, greater access to birth control, women's college graduation rates surpassing that of men, a greater number of women entering into political office, and with gender discrimination in both education and employment being made illegal. And yet, "there has been little cultural or institutional change in the devaluation of traditionally female activities and jobs. As a result, women have had more incentive than men to move into gender-nontraditional activities and positions" (England 2010, p. 150; 2014). Despite an apparent shift toward increased access to upward mobility and gender equality, the continued devaluation of "women's work," combined with deeply entrenched cultural conceptions of gender norms that are often based on beliefs regarding gender essentialism, has rendered changes in the workforce composition of certain occupations uneven. This argument is supported by the data on the percentages of women and men working in the education system. An increase in the percentage of women principals has not coincided with a greater numbers of men entering the teaching profession. Instead, the opposite is true.

Perspectives from workplace theory and economics offer certain insights into the gendered assumptions of educational leadership, yet they still leave us, given our FCPA intentions, searching for perspectives that can help us understand why and how these cultural messages prevail. What is undergirding the continuation of underlying policy-as-practice that impedes women's ascent?

In order to unpack these questions we examine powerful cultural texts for clues. In doing so, we use a FCPA lens to explore Biblical and political perspectives, which argue:

- Women were created to serve and support men; leaders are male protectors of women and the family (the Biblical perspective);
- Men more easily fit in the leadership images of manager, controller, organizer, protector, warrior, and savior (the political perspective).

5.5 The Biblical Perspective: Women Were Created to Serve Men

Policies-in-practice are reinforced by organized religion and family life. Bible scriptures have long been used by conservative Christian organizations to corroborate the natural order of a benign patriarchal power structure (Brown and Bohn 1989; Lerner 1986). For example, theological framings of patriarchy and gender roles may be found in texts written by The Council on Biblical Manhood and Womanhood

(CBMW). Established in 1987, CBMW is an evangelical Christian organization that promotes the theory of complementarianism. In a foundational CBMW book titled *Recovering Biblical Manhood and Womanhood: A Response to Evangelical Feminism,* Piper and Grudem (1991) describe how, "If one word must be used to describe our position, we prefer the term complementarian, since it suggests both equality and beneficial differences between men and women" (p. 11). This text identifies several Biblical passages that support this notion of natural and interdependent differences between men and women.

> When the Bible teaches that men and women fulfill different roles in relation to each other, charging man with a unique leadership role, it bases this differentiation not on temporary cultural norms but on permanent facts of creation. This is seen in 1 Corinthians 11:3–16 (especially vv. 8–9, 14); Ephesians 5:21–33 (especially vv. 31–32); and 1 Timothy 2:11–14 (especially vv. 13–14). (Piper and Grudem 1991, p. 28)

Let's look at two of the Biblical passages pinpointed by Piper and Grudem (1991):

> 21 Submit to one another out of reverence for Christ. 22 Wives, submit yourselves to your own husbands as you do to the Lord. 23 For the husband is the head of the wife as Christ is the head of the church, his body, of which he is the Savior. 24 Now as the church submits to Christ, so also wives should submit to their husbands in everything. (Ephesians 5:21–24)
>
> 11 A woman should learn in quietness and full submission. 12 I do not permit a woman to teach or to assume authority over a man; she must be quiet. 13 For Adam was formed first, then Eve. 14 And Adam was not the one deceived; it was the woman who was deceived and became a sinner. (1 Timothy: 2:11–14)

The CBMW definitions of masculinity and femininity expound the belief that a man's role is to lead and protect, while a woman's role is to follow and nurture:

> AT THE HEART OF MATURE FEMININITY IS A FREEING DISPOSITION TO AFFIRM, RECEIVE AND NURTURE STRENGTH AND LEADERSHIP FROM WORTHY MEN IN WAYS APPROPRIATE TO A WOMAN'S DIFFERING RELATIONSHIPS. (Piper and Grudem 1991, p. 29)

Readers may protest that connecting the Bible to the issues of the promotion of women into school leadership is far-fetched. However, Christian values constantly re-emerge in political campaign rhetoric, in school district policies (especially in the rural South), and in subtle messages about women as educational and governmental leaders, and as President.

5.6 The Political Perspective: Women Need Protecting

Policies-in-practice may also be buttressed as they are reinforced in political discourse. Although there has been an increase in the percentage of women at the highest levels of American politics in recent decades (Marshall et al. 2015; Marshall and Young 2013), and despite frequent claims made about the end of patriarchy (Rosin 2012), gender stereotypes and discrimination continue to limit and deter female political leadership.

At the time of writing this chapter, <u>none</u> of the 44 Presidents of the United States have been a woman. Examples of sexism in politics are rife, including a well-publicized incident that occurred in 2007, where Hillary Clinton was heckled during a presidential campaign rally by two male audience members who repeatedly shouted "Iron my shirt." Elsewhere, also during Clinton's first run for president, conservative radio talk show host Rush Limbaugh made the comment that, "men aging makes them look more authoritative, accomplished, distinguished. Sadly, it's not that way for women.... Will Americans want to watch a woman get older before their eyes on a daily basis?" (Wheaton 2008). More recently, Donald Trump's 2016 presidential campaign has provided a case study of the use of gender stereotypes in political discourse. Notable examples include Trump touting his own masculinity (including the size of his hands) while seeking to emasculate his male opponents (e.g. referring to Marco Rubio as "little Marco"). Moreover, Trump suggested Hillary Clinton was "unqualified" to be president, and that she lacked strength and stamina. Another example of sexism in Trump's political discourse was when he asked, "if Hillary can't take care of Bill's needs, then how can Americans expect her to take care of the country's needs?" (Dittmar 2016).

Patriarchy is far from dead. The majority America's political and economic institutions are still led by men. Women candidates for political office in 2016 still have to worry that they will not be seen as tough Commander-in-Chief material. Though Democratic candidate Bernie Sanders and Republican candidate Donald Trump may be ideologically opposed, they share something in common: they can get away with behavior and discourse that Hillary Clinton never could present. While they bang their fists on their podium, present disheveled appearances, and shout, literally, about their platforms, Hillary Clinton has had to remain calm, cool, and collected. Although she has been met with criticism for being detached, should she campaign in the same ways as Sanders and Trump, she would be vilified. Sanders and Trump have been lauded by their respective followers for their passionate care for America, yet Hillary Clinton would likely be criticized for being overly emotional, unprofessional, and unqualified.

The fact that the gender composition of the 114th Congress (80 % male) was lauded as being the most diverse in history is illustrative of the equality blind spot that still existed in 2015. Themes promulgated by the Christian Right (men = protective leaders/women = nurturing subordinates) are also routinely espoused in political discourse. An example of how masculinity is tied to the protection of women includes the extent to which the defense of women has been used as a validation for military intervention (Bush 2011; United States Department of State 2001).

Dominant understandings of leadership based on stereotypes about masculinity serve to frame conceptions about the types of qualities or characteristics that should be embodied by the President of the United States of America (Barber 1992). According to Daughton (1994), "the president is the national patriarch: the paradagmatic American Man" (p. 114). Daughton's analysis of political discourse led her to the formulation of the characteristics associated with American masculinity, which included being a strong and competent fatherly leader, a decisive guardian of moral values, and a provider.

The fact that the Presidency entails responsibility for the command and control of the nation's military means that, despite not being required to lead on the battlefield, or even to have had any previous military service experience, physical strength continues to be associated with necessary presidential qualities. This expectation may be traced back as far as George Washington who was a tall, imposing presence with a temper, and who commanded respect and obedience from the Continental Army (Goethals 2005). More recently, the cowboy diplomacy of Reagan and Bush II has been founded on imagery and rhetoric designed to emphasize their powerful role as the Commander in Chief. In an article published in *Psychology Today*, Murray (2012) suggests that, "The preference for physically formidable leaders may help explain the nearly universal advantage that men, who throughout human history have been larger and stronger, hold over women in the acquisition of executive leadership power." As previously mentioned, being the President of the United States of America (or for that matter the superintendent of a school district) does not require direct involvement in combat, thus this justification for patriarchal prejudice is founded on a false logic.

Political discourse is littered with examples of American masculinity, often harkening back to the dialogue used in action movies. Such tough-guy discourses defines leadership as patriarchal dominance and, due to cultural expectations based on traditional gender roles, serves to exclude women:

> We're going to meet and deliberate and discuss – but there's no question about it, this act will not stand; we will find those who did it; we will smoke them out of their holes; we will get them running and we'll bring them to justice. We will not only deal with those who dare attack America, we will deal with those who harbor them and feed them and house them. (G. W. Bush 2001).

There are also examples of presidential discourse that blend the themes of both gender and religion. In his famous "Evil Empire Speech," President Reagan pushed for increased spending on nuclear weapons in order to protect America from the threat of communism. As part of this address, Reagan provided an anecdote about a "little girl," whose Christian values were threatened by the evil, atheist, Soviet government.

Conceptions of leadership are powerfully constructed as a combative, strong and competent fatherly leader, a decisive guardian of moral values, and a provider who will create orderly strategies to solve challenges and thus allay fears. Cultural embedded messages within Biblical and political texts perpetuate these frames and carry them over into assumptions about qualifications for top leadership in school districts. Not only are these messages conveyed to schoolchildren who learn to revere George Washington, but they also permeate school boards and superintendent search committees who evaluate the qualities for top educational leaders.

We have identified examples of cultural assumptions deeply embedded in powerful discourses. But cultural biases are not changed by policy fiats. Our review of the demographics in educational hierarchies and the research on women's access to top leadership, displayed so far in this chapter, leave us, still, with too few policy solutions. The persistent patterns of gendered hierarchies defy equal opportunity and fairness policy prescriptions.

But beyond the quest for simple fairness in the workplace, how can FCPA offer insight for a better, more just view of schools and society that demonstrates equality for women and wider ways of assessing leadership priorities? Would the creation of different definitions of top school leadership designate a preference for women? Beyond that, what insights would be accentuated if feminist voices and values were promoted?

6 Women in Top Leadership and Feminism's Insights Still Matter

We have demonstrated the continuing challenge of creating equal access and voice for women in the superintendency, and we have demonstrated the use of FCPA in our analysis. This last section now provides answers to why women's leadership and feminist values offer ways to alter assumptions about structures and goals for education.

6.1 Why Women's Leadership Matters

Strong arguments have been made that children see adults "like them" as they construct their social identities. School leaders who are women, who are people of color, and who are from a range of religious and sexual orientations, exercising power, authority, competence, and exhibiting pride send important messages and lend wider possibilities in curriculum and priorities in schools. The argument stops here. For females, the policy focus (and the funding) is focused on STEM careers, leaving gender role stereotypes unchallenged. Women exit the superintendency quietly, having had multiple career lessons within institutional silences and subtle prohibitions of speech regarding women's unequal position in society (Beekly 1994; Marshall 1993; Skrla 2003).

6.2 Women and Feminist Leadership Matter

As role models for girls in schools, women leaders must be able to thrive, rather than to quaver in superintendencies if we are to overcome stereotypes that prevent girls from exercising agency. This is not just about "add women and stir," which frames women as vulnerable tokens, ignoring their lack of social capital and the existence of institutionalized patriarchal power structures (Anucha et al. 2006; Lin et al. 2001), but rather this is about reframing gender and leadership altogether.

Education policy choices could benefit from the insights of feminist theory, and the values, concerns, and issues of women and girls. Feminism has supported women's ability to "talk back... in a spirited critique" (Devault 1999, p. 27), but how can their voices be heard if they are not in top leadership positions? School leaders who emphasize women's and girls' needs would focus on: unequal access and representation; sexism's widespread detrimental effects; the paucity of illustrations and problems showing competent women and girls in math and science texts; the unequal representation of strong women in power in policy arenas and school leadership; teenage pregnancy; and teachers' differential attention to boys and girls in classroom interactions. But it goes deeper once we analyze dominant discourses.

Discourse signifies ways of knowing and ways in which individual people make sense of their world, including their position in it, their expected roles and productive functions, and how they interact with others in society. It is important to acknowledge which discourses and frames dominate and the types of behaviors and positions that are valued above others. Discourse helps to create beliefs about leaders and leadership, as well as about how these behaviors and images align with concentrations of power in social structures (Allan et al. 2006). As normative behaviors of leadership have for so long required a masculine ethos, those who do not embrace these discursive identities are thus quickly relegated to lower positions.

Feminist frameworks offer alternative values and stances that move education toward much expanded definitions of the "important issues." In arenas that extend from the family to the Senate, cultural assumptions of patriarchy and gender essentialism have ensured that White male voices take precedence when policy choices must be made. It is primarily men who have the final word on issues ranging from disciplining the children in schools and the home, to legislative budget priorities, and questioning whether competition and job preparation are the be-all-and-end-all of curricular and extracurricular policies. Men still control the conversation surrounding the question of whether equity should be viewed as essential, rather than a luxury, and whether society ought to give much more than lip service to diversity and equal access. Men in top leadership still control the allocation of resources for equity enforcement. Consequently, feminist theory pushes back against the traditionally male-dominated search and selection of superintendents. Challenging the idea that gender gaps in placement exist because of some essential group characteristic, feminist theorists resist the supposedly objective concept of merit that is often invoked in these gatekeeping processes.

To supplement their arguments that resist an essentialist, hierarchical ordering of gender, race, and class, feminists have pushed for enriched cultural understandings and persistent re-framing of dominant valuations around "women's ways." The feminist focus on "women's ways" of valuing, knowing, meaning-making, living, and working, serves to elicit women's voices and values that have previously been excluded or devalued. Thus, the focus has largely been on how women's leadership operates differently from the managerial, unattached style associated with men's leadership. It operates instead through collaboration, interaction, and joint meaning making (Allan et al. 2006; Clifton 2012; Gordon et al. 2010; Noddings 1982). Noddings (1988) wrote of the feminine ethic of care as the center of women's experiences, explaining that an ethic of care diverges from Kantian ethics of moral objectivity and instead calls for one to act on a sense of love or a natural inclination to help others. Noddings (1988) contrasts her relational actor with Kant's "lonely and heroic ethical agent" in the "age of individualism" (p. 219). Hence, feminism points to the need for curricula to encompass skill-building for parenting, caring, nurturing, appreciation of the whole person (not just a child's achievement or an adult's productivity), affective development, acknowledgement of emotion, and for valuing the professions that do this kind of work (e.g. counseling, nursing, teaching, mothering). Relatedly, feminists critique bureaucracy, hierarchical management, control, and instead emphasize relationships, community and collaboration; they push back against stereotype-infused ideas about what is worth studying, charting the advantages from envisioning curricula that prepare all children for prospective child rearing and home management as well as for non-stereotypically male-female career choices.

While critiquing stereotype-driven school policy choices, feminist frameworks also demand that schools acknowledge diversity in its student populations. Third wave feminism focuses on deconstructing the dominant discourse on gender and advocates for recognition of the diversity of the female population. This perspective brings to the forefront previously blurred, yet very important, intersectional details like race, socioeconomics, and immigration status, which contribute largely to the individual female experience and ways of knowing (Mann and Huffman 2005; Menges and Exum 1983; Sowards and Renegar 2004). Today's feminism incorporates the many ways that women experience the world, encounter and deal with various oppressions and discrimination, and generally different realities and ways of knowing (Sowards and Renegar 2004). In this way, feminism recognizes integral elements of a person's identity, like sexuality, and how identity and relational development are crucial aspects of schooling.

Feminism does not just consider social roles and development, but also the ways in which gendered assumptions drive funding. Feminism can lay bare the gendered assumptions of what is and is not given money and attention. Feminism can widen the complex understandings of social life and thus construct a view of schooling that is committed to creating community, collaboration, and caring for children and families. Feminism can work to eliminate the policy-in-practice that reifies patriarchy and that continues societal assumptions that women and girls are to be controlled, as are people who are *not* white, heterosexual, Christian, and/or dominating males.

We lose possibilities for meaningful school leadership when policy discourses subtly discredit wider views and voices. Assumptions that toughness, physical strength and maintaining a competitive edge are quite outdated and inappropriate for school leadership. For school communities, facilitative and collaborative relationships are more appropriate, giving priority to teachers' insights in decision-making, setting up collaborative learning environments, and eliminating the hierarchical, competition-driven modes of behaviors.

6.3 Re-framing and Implications for Schooling

Women's voices, priorities, competencies, and values are tremendously useful to expanding more inclusive, family-oriented, nurturing, and collaborative schooling practices. In this chapter, we used FCPA to lay bare assumptions of gender essentialism and patriarchy; we offered possible analytic alternatives from critiques of deeply-held cultural beliefs. This use of FCPA not only demonstrates how biblical and political speeches reinforce patriarchal hegemony, but it also shows indications of ways re-frame current policies-in-practice.

In their career preparation, educators need at least to know the demographics of the profession, (as shown above) and also their professional history (including feisty women leaders who were once taking leadership positions in the 1920s – most have never heard of Ella Flagg Young). If reoriented with a feminist lens, educators would ponder how curricula could be more whole-child oriented and designed to emphasize community and collaboration rather competition and hierarchical structuring. Further, feminist insights would help educators critique history as a record made by the people in dominant positions of authority, who valorize and venerate military and political leaders. Such a critique can embolden educators to refuse school systems' reproduction of gendered hierarchies and the tendency for schools' failures to address needs of families of color, LGBT, girls and women those with differences in religion, immigrant status or language barriers and those who are impoverished to be written off and sanitized with a glib assertion that these groups are somehow deficient or unworthy.

The undercurrents of institutionalized patriarchy are sometimes flagrant, but more often they are subtle, and subtle bias against women's leadership is seldom useable in lawsuits or grievances. Policies redressing this bias are merely blunt policy instruments that leave institutionalized masculinist definitions of leadership firmly in place. Perhaps this stems from cultural fears that women's and persons of color's ascension to school leadership will prove detrimental to white male privilege?

The reframing and feminist insights we highlight can offer alternatives, rationales, and directions, to steer well-intended policy makers to question their assumptions and to look at wider contexts in the search to identify strategies to elicit the silenced voices and the discredited. A more just education system and society can be imagined with inclusion of the suppressed voices, and the alternative insights and values that supports a wider range of leadership models and that instills feminist values in the children who will lead our future. And, following our analysis of the superintendency, FCPA should provide alternatives for continuing challenges and puzzles. Clearly, a feminist analysis similar to ours can be done on wider cultural discourse, such as in discourses regarding gender issues in top leadership in business and in the discourse and debates in Congressional and Presidential platforms, for example. FCPA should also be used to unravel such issues as: adolescent pregnancy; of girls' seemingly complacent with their status as cheerleaders for boys' team sports; of brilliant women dropping out of special programs for STEM careers; of college women keeping quiet about fraternity dynamics that treat them as sexual harassment targets; and of schools of education and public policy, with no required courses on gender issues.

References

Allan, E. J., Gordon, S. P., & Iverson, S. V. (2006). Re/thinking practices of power: The discursive framing of leadership in The Chronicle of Higher Education. *The Review of Higher Education, 30*, 41–68. doi:10.1353/rhe.2006.0045.

Anucha, U., Dlamina, S., Yan, M. C., & Smylie, L. (2006). *Social capital and the welfare of immigrant women: A multi-level study of four ethnic communities in Windsor*. Ottawa: Status of Women Canada.

Apple, M. (1985). Teaching and "women's work": A comparative historical and ideological analysis. *The Teachers College Record, 86*(3), 455–473.

Barber, J. D. (1992). *The presidential character: Predicting performance in the White House*. Englewood Cliffs: Prentice-Hall.

Beekley, C. X. (1994). *Women who exit the public school superintendency: Four case studies*. Abstract from OVID file: Dissertation Abstracts Item: AAC9500864.

Bielby, W. T. (2014). The structure and process of sex segregation. In D. B. Grusky (Ed.), *Social stratification: Class, race, and gender in sociological perspective* (4th ed., pp. 865–875). Boulder: Westview Press.

Blackmore, J. (1993). 'In the shadow of men': The historical construction of educational administration as a 'Masculinist enterprise. In J. Blackmore & J. Kenway (Eds.), *Gender matters in educational administration and policy*. London: The Falmer Press.

Blount, J. M. (1998). *Destined to rule the schools: Women and the superintendency, 1873–1995*. Albany: State University of New York Press.

Blount, J. M. (1999). Manliness and the gendered construction of school administration in the USA. *International Journal of Leadership in Education, 2*(2), 55–68.

Brown, J. C., & Bohn, C. R. (Eds.). (1989). *Christianity, patriarchy, and abuse: A feminist critique*. Cleveland: Pilgrim Press.

Brunner, C. C. (Ed.). (1999). *Sacred dreams: Women and the superintendency*. Albany: SUNY Press.

Bush, G. W. (2001, September 15). Remarks in a meeting with the National Security Team and an exchange with reporters at Camp David, Maryland. *The American Presidency Project*. Retrieved from http://www.presidency.ucsb.edu/ws/?pid=63199

Bush, G. W. (2011, March 31). For George W. Bush, empowering women in Afghanistan lays a 'foundation for a lasting peace.' *On the Record* [Television Broadcast]. http://www.foxnews.com/on-air/on-the-record/transcript/george-w-bush-empowering-women-afghanistan-lays-039foundation-lasting-peace039

Clifton, J. (2012). A discursive approach to leadership: Doing assessments and managing organizational meanings. *Journal of Business Communication, 49*(2), 148–168.

Clinton Foundation. (2015). *We're not there yet: No Ceilings*. Retrieved from http://notthere.noceilings.org/

Daughton, S. M. (1994). Women's issues, women's place: Gender-related problems in presidential campaigns. *Communication Quarterly, 42*(2), 106–119.

Deem, R., & Ozga, J. (2005). Women managing for diversity in a postmodern world. In C. Marshall (Ed.), *Feminist critical policy analysis: A perspective from post-secondary education II* (2nd ed., pp. 23–37). Washington, DC: The Falmer Press.

DeVault, M. (1999). *Liberating method: Feminism and social research*. Philadelphia: Temple University Press.

Dittmar, K. (2016, May 27). *How one Trump event symbolizes the gender strategy of his campaign*. Presidential Gender Watch. Retrieved from http://presidentialgenderwatch.org/trump-gender-strategy/#more-8648

England, P. (2010). The gender revolution uneven and stalled. *Gender & Society, 24*(2), 149–166.

England, P. (2014). Devaluation and pay of comparable male and female occupations. In D. B. Grusky (Ed.), *Social stratification: Class, race, and gender in sociological perspective* (4th ed., pp. 919–923). Boulder: Westview Press.

Fairclough, I., & Fairclough, N. (2012). *Political discourse analysis: A method for advanced students*. Oxon: Routledge.

Fine, C. (2010). *Delusions of gender: How our minds, society, and neurosexism create difference*. New York: W. W. Norton & Company.

Gee, J. P., & Handforth, M. (Eds.). (2014). *The Routledge handbook of discourse analysis*. New York: Routledge.

Glass, T. E. (2000). Where are all the women superintendents? *American Association of School Administrators, 57*(6), 28–32.

Goethals, G. R. (2005). Presidential leadership. *Annual Review of Psychology, 56*, 545–570.

Gordon, S., Iverson, S. V., & Allan, E. J. (2010). The discursive framing of women leaders in higher education. In E. J. Allan, S. V. D. Iverson, & R. Ropers-Huilman (Eds.), *Reconstructing policy in higher education: Feminist poststructural perspectives*. New York: Routledge.

Grogan, M. (1999). Equity/equality issues of gender, race, and class. *Educational Administration Quarterly, 35*(4), 518–536.

Grogan, M., & Brunner, C. (2005). Women leading systems. *School Administrator, 62*(2), 46–50.

Grogan, M., & Shakeshaft, C. (2011). *Women and educational leadership*. San Francisco: Jossey-Bass.

Kowalski, T. J., McCord, R. S., Petersen, G. J., Young, I. P., & Ellerson, N. M. (2011). *American school superintendent; 2010 decennial study*. Lanham: Rowman & Littlefield Education.

Lee, V. E., Smith, J. B., & Cioci, M. (1993). Teachers and principals: Gender-related perceptions of leadership and power in secondary schools. *Educational Evaluation and Policy Analysis, 15*(2), 153–180.

Lerner, G. (1986). *The creation of patriarchy*. New York: Oxford University Press.

Limbaugh, R. H. (2007, December 17). *Does our looks-obsessed culture want to stare at an aging woman?* Retrieved from http://www.rushlimbaugh.com/daily/2007/12/17/does_our_looks_obsessed_culture_want_to_stare_at_an_aging_woman6

Limbaugh, R. H. (2015, January 30). *Pick the best people regardless of gender, race or ethnicity*. Retrieved from http://www.rushlimbaugh.com/daily/2015/01/30/pick_the_best_people_regardless_of_gender_race_or_ethnicity

Lin, N., Cook, K. S., & Burt, R. S. (Eds.). (2001). *Social capital: Theory and research*. New York: Transaction Publishers.

Mann, S. A., & Huffman, D. J. (2005). The decentering of second wave feminism and the rise of the third wave*. *Science & Society, 69*(1), 56–91.

Marshall, C. (1993). Politics of Denial: Gender and race issues in educational administration. In C. Marshall (Ed.), *The new politics of race and gender*. London: The Falmer Press.

Marshall, C., & Young, M. D. (2013). Policy inroads undermining women in education. *International Journal of Leadership in Education, 16*(2), 205–219. http://www.tandfonline.com/doi/abs/10.1080/13603124.2012.754056#preview

Marshall, C., Andre-Bechely, L., & Midkiff, B. (2015). Binders of women and the blinders of men: Feminism and the politics of education. In B. S. Cooper, J. G. Cibulka, & L. D. Fusarelli (Eds.), *Handbook of education politics and policy*. New York: Routledge.

McFadden, A. H., & Smith, P. (2004). *The social construction of educational leadership: Southern Appalachian ceilings*. New York: Peter Lang Publishing, Inc.

Menges, R. J., & Exum, W. H. (1983). Barriers to the progress of women and minority faculty. *The Journal of Higher Education, 54*, 123–144. doi:10.2307/1981567.

Murphy, M. (1990). *Blackboard unions: The AFT and the NEA, 1900–1980*. Ithaca: Cornell University Press.

Murray, G. (2012, September 30). When do we prefer male over female leaders?: Some important situations point us away from female leadership. *Psychology Today*. Retrieved from https://www.psychologytoday.com/blog/caveman-politics/201209/when-do-we-prefer-male-over-female-leaders

Noddings, N. (1982). *The challenge to care in schools: An alternative approach in education*. New York: Teachers College Press.

Noddings, N. (1988). An ethic of caring and its implications for instructional arrangements. *American Journal of Education, 96*, 215–230. doi:10.2307/1085252.

Olsen, J. (2006) Women Superintendents in Iowa: Where is the Momentum? Reflections on a national Malaise. *The forum on public policy*.

Piper, J., & Grudem, W. (1991). *Recovering biblical manhood and womanhood: A response to evangelical feminism*. Wheaton: Crossway Books.

Richardson, J. G., & Hatcher, B. W. (1983). The feminization of public school teaching 1870–1920. *Work and Occupations, 10*(1), 81–99.

Robinson, K. (2013) *The career path of the female superintendent: Why she leaves*. Doctoral dissertation. Retrieved from Virginia Commonwealth University Theses and Dissertations. (Paper 2960)

Rosin, H. (2012). *The end of men: And the rise of women*. New York: Penguin.

Rury, J. L. (2005). *Education and social change: Themes in the history of American schooling* (2nd ed.). Mahwah: Lawrence Erlbaum Associates.

Sawicki, J. (1991). *Disciplining foucault: Feminism, power and the body*. New York: Routledge.

Shakeshaft, C. (1990). *Women in educational administration*. Newbury Park: Sage Publications.

Shakeshaft, C. (1999). The struggle to create a more gender-inclusive profession. In J. Murphy & K. Seashore Louis (Eds.), *Handbook of research on educational administration* (2nd ed., pp. 99–118). Thousand Oaks: Sage.

Shen, J. (Ed.). (2005). *School principals*. New York: Peter Lang.

Skrla, L. (2003). Mourning silence: Women superintendents (and the researcher) rethink speaking up and speaking out. In M. D. Young & L. Skrla (Eds.), *Reconsidering feminist research in educational leadership*. Albany: State University of New York Press.

Smith, J. K. (1980). Progressive school administration: Ella Flagg Young and the Chicago schools, 1905–1915. *Journal of the Illinois State Historical Society, 73*(1), 27–44.

Sowards, S. K., & Renegar, V. R. (2004). The rhetorical functions of consciousness-raising in third wave feminism. *Communication Studies, 55*(4), 535–552.

Strober, M. (1984). *Segregation by gender in public school teaching: Toward a general theory of occupational segregation in the labor market*. Unpublished manuscript, Stanford University.

Strober, M. H., & Tyack, D. (1980). Why do women teach and men manage? A report on research on schools. *Signs, 5*(3), 494–503.

Tallerico, M. (2000). Gaining access to the superintendency: Headhunting, gender, and color. *Educational Administration Quarterly, 36*(1), 18–43.

United States Department of State. (2001, November 11). *Report on the Taliban's war against women*. Retrieved from http://www.state.gov/j/drl/rls/c4804.htm

Wheaton, S. (2008, January 7). Iron my shirt. The New York Times. Retrieved from http://thecaucus.blogs.nytimes.com/2008/01/07/iron-my-shirt/?_r=0

Wodak, R., & Meyer, M. (Eds.). (2009). *Methods for critical discourse analysis* (2nd ed.). Thousand Oaks: Sage.

Young, M. D., & Marshall, C. (2012). Critical feminist theory. In *The handbook of educational theories* (pp. 959–969). Charlotte: Information Age Pub., c2013.

Part II
Emphasis on Theory

> One does not go into the field to "see"–one goes to "look" for various sorts of patterns and themes. Theory–acknowledged or not–dictates what kinds of patterns one finds. And *any explanation, no matter how small, involves a theory waiting to be explicated.* When we "understand" or try to explain an observed event or recorded interviews, we are calling on theories, large or small (Anyon 2009, p. 4).

Theory carries a point of view. We call on theories in order to explain and thematize data we have collected, and strengthen our approaches to research (Anyon 2009). While the conceptualization of knowledge is typically not given much weight in methodology books (Danermark et al. 2002), critical policy scholars intentionally bring to the forefront how their perspectives and ways of knowing directly impact and inform the ways in which they conduct research. For critical policy scholars, theory cannot be separated from research as it is at the heart of helping us explain social phenomenon.

Integrating theory into CPA, the chapters in this part of the book demonstrate the need to center theory in the research process as it impacts how we think about problems, the questions we seek to ask about the issues, and the methods we employ to create new knowledge (Diem and Young 2015). Theory should challenge us to think in new ways and expand our ways of knowing by employing different lenses to examine problems. We believe the chapters in this part of the book offer such a challenge and push us to expand our way of making sense of the data presented in new and thought-provoking ways.

The first chapter in this section by Gill, Nesbitt and Parker, uses Critical Race Theory to center racial perspectives on policies effecting the education of African American students. Specifically, in their research they use counter-narratives to interrogate policy texts and policy discourse, examining texts for evidence of color and context-blindness. Similarly, in the twelfth and final chapter of the volume, "Policy Studies Debt: A Feminist Call to Expand Policy Studies Theory," Pillow utilizes a Women of Color (WOC) feminist epistemology as an "identity additive model" to challenge the policy debt existent in education. In the chapter, she highlights four characteristics of a WOC feminist epistemology and then discusses how these tenets can be applied to rethink how policy studies are analyzed to address our policy debt.

In the Chap. 9, Whiteman, Maxcy and Scribner use an institutionally-structured micropolitical critical policy framework to examine how institutional talk constructs administrative logics, marginalization as well as agency. Specifically, they applied the framework to data collected for three ethnographic studies and focused their analysis on policy enactments and the relationship between institutionally contingent language and micropolitical negotiations within schools.

Moving from the institution to the state, in Chap. 10, "Ontario's Fourth 'R': A Critical Democratic Analysis of Ontario's Fund-'R'aising Policy," Milani & Winton apply a critical policy framework to Ontario's fundraising policy. In their research they use a critical democratic lens, which is informed by a set of values (social justice, equity, inclusion, diversity, participation and participatory decision-making processes, knowledge inquiry and critical mindedness, community, dialogue, creativity, free and reasoned choices, citizen engagement and involvement, empowerment, and the redistribution of power) deemed critical to the public good. Using a critical democratic lens, the authors examined the conception of democracy advocated by the Ontario Ministry of Education's fundraising policy as well as by other policy actors in the province.

Chapter 11, "Examining the Theater of 'Listening' & 'Learning'," takes the reader to a federal level to examine the Obama/Duncan Administration's "Listening & Learning" tour. In this chapter, Carpenter explicates and applies the key tenets of Hajer's (2003, 2005, 2006) argumentative discourse analysis to the performance of politics enacted during the tour, specifically focusing the analysis on policy texts, tour-related news and internet resources, and official USDOE statements about the tour, and uses this analysis to delineate the relationships between the tour and the development of the Title I School Improvement Grant of 2009.

Finally, in Chap. 12, "Utilizing Michel de Certeau in Critical Policy Analysis," Brewer and Werts illustrate how Michel de Certeau's concept of consumption in the everyday can be used as an analytical tool for critical policy analysis in education. Building off of the notion of policy enactment, Brewer and Werts assert that understanding the consumption of the everyday allows educators to better understand their simultaneous roles as active democratic subjects and governed subjects, and find possibilities for radical forms of democracy through policy in ways that are neither normed or apart from their daily practices.

Education policy can significantly impact children's lives, teachers' working conditions, and the viability of communities. Thus, the implications for the critical analysis of educational policy, policy actors, and policy conditions can be substantial. The purpose of critical policy analysis is not to classify educational policy as either good or bad, useful or not, etc. Rather, it is to provide insight into the elements of policy that are often overlooked, left unquestioned, and how policies may impact different communities or structures in unintended ways, or contain elements that undermine the very values it intends to support. Theory plays a significant role in fostering these and other questions that should be asked in the process of analyzing educational policy.

References

Anyon, J. (2009). Introduction: Critical social theory, educational research, and intellectual agency. In J. Anyon (Ed.), *Theory and educational research: Toward critical social explanation*. New York: Routledge.

Danermark, B., Ekstrom, M., Jakobsen, L., & Karlsson, J. C. (2002). *Explaining society: Critical realism in the social sciences*. New York: Routledge.

Diem, S., & Young, M. D. (2015). Considering critical turns in research on educational leadership and policy. *International Journal of Educational Management, 29*(7), 838–850.

Silent Covenants in the Neoliberal Era: Critical Race Counternarratives on African American Advocacy Leadership in Schools

Chandra Gill, LaTasha L. Cain Nesbitt, and Laurence Parker

Abstract The intent of this chapter is to present a critical race policy perspective on advocacy leadership exemplified by a group of African American teachers, parents and community members in one Midwestern community and their adjacent school districts. For the most part, the African Americans in this particular community believed in the promise of desegregation and equal educational opportunity would be achieved in due time. However, faith and trust in that promise has slowly eroded over subsequent generations of African American families whose children who have gone to these schools, and a desegregation plan that moved away from equal educational opportunity toward a neoliberal agenda for school improvement though measures of accountability. Our project's significance stems from the interview data conducted with these advocates, and using critical race theory as a methodological lens to present critical race policy counternarratives about what these African American community activists have done to advocate for the educational well-being of African American students in this particular community. The African American voices inside this particular school district point to ways school leadership can be more broadly defined through the actions of teachers, parents and community leaders. They acted as advocates for African American student equity and seek to hold the school district accountable against the failed desegregation and neoliberal agenda that in reality seeks to work against the very students these policies support to leave no child behind.

Keywords Critical race theory & policy • Neoliberalism • African American education and Advocacy leadership

---

C. Gill (✉)
Blackacademically Speaking, P.O. Box 803468, Chicago, IL 60680, USA
e-mail: blackacademicallyspeaking@gmail.com

L.L.C. Nesbitt
Department of Educational Policy Organization and Leadership, College of Education, University of Illinois at Urbana-Champaign, Champaign, IL, USA

L. Parker
Department of Educational Leadership and Policy, College of Education, University of Utah, Salt Lake City, UT, USA

1 Introduction

The progress on equal educational opportunity has fallen victim to neoliberal priorities around choice and accountability. This political trend has proclaimed the importance of market-place and the choice of African American parents as consumers to assert their rights to obtain effective and equitable educational opportunities for their children (Pedroni 2007). Furthermore, there has been increasing political pressure placed on teachers, administrators and schools to be "held accountable" by standardized test results for student achievement, particularly of African American, Latino-Latina and other racial and language minority students (Hursh 2007; Viteritti 2012). This neoliberal policy agenda has dominated the political discourse around public schooling, at the expense of equal educational opportunity legal mandates under desegregation. The U.S. Supreme Court, the U.S. Congress and the general public has shown a color-blind "we've done enough" attitude on school desegregation (Tushnet 1996). This sentiment fits into the neoliberal policy discourse that the new way to solve the problems of education is through an emphasis on African American students and family choice. What this means is that the politics of the new public education agenda puts equality of educational opportunity in the hands of students and parents through choice options of private schools or charter schools. But the downside of this type of school choice is that neighborhood schools in African American communities face closure due to low achievement test scores, changing neighborhood demographics and white upper middle class families who are reluctant to send their children to majority African American or Latino schools in urban settings (Ladson-Billings 2004). The neoliberal agenda has also trumped legal concern about school desegregation that shaped and defined equal educational opportunity for generations of people of color, particularly African Americans.

The purpose of this chapter is to provide readers with counternarratives taken from one particular community in the U.S. Midwest that challenges this commonly expressed opinion about how to address racism in the current neoliberal/post-school desegregation era. We present the critical race counternarratives as critical policy analysis data that speaks back to the official policy narratives of continual progress of racial equality, from desegregation to school choice as the "solution" to solve equity and provide quality education for all students. This critical approach is in line with the central theme of this book which focuses on critical policy analysis. As articulated by Diem et al. (2014), the central approaches that are taken in critical policy analysis in education address the difference between official policy rhetoric juxtaposed against the implementation reality of how the policy impacts local communities. In conjunction with this critical perspective, critical policy analysis incorporates research that focuses on how non-dominant groups resist processes of domination and oppression and use activist and advocacy methods to change the deleterious impact of the policies. It is in this way that the counternarratives presented in this chapter using critical race theory should be viewed. These counternarratives can be viewed as "messy" or un-focused; but as

Atwood and Lopez (2014) powerfully point out, oftentimes in critical race theory, counternarratives and counterstories are complex and layered and do not and should not have to ask for permission from a policy audience to be legitimized. Rather, they posit that this form of evidence is documentation of how racial discrimination and its effects, both macro and micro, result in a generation of racial struggle and resistance to both overt and more "race neutral" policy discrimination against African Americans, Latino/Latina, Tribal Nation groups, Asian/Pacific Islanders, in combination with their intersectionalities (e.g., gender, sexual identity, social class status, language, religion/ethnic nationality). The critical race counternarratives we present in this chapter are representative of some of the perspectives of African Americans who were subjected to the well-intentioned policy orientation of equal educational opportunity through voluntary desegregation; but as the neoliberal agenda for schools came into the national, state and local policy landscape, the counernarratives you will read paint a portrait of African Americans who had to face more complexities around racial discrimination, and had to engage in different levels of resistance and racial activism for themselves and their children. The interviews in this chapter should be viewed in light of building on previous work done in critical race theory and critical policy analysis to document the myriad ways in which education policy (both in the U.S. and UK) has been conceptualized, developed and implemented (Gillborn 2008). This analysis puts whiteness in the most powerful position of racist ordering so that despite the rhetoric of addressing achievement for all and fixing the achievement gap through more testing or school choice and accountability; there is actually a wider gap of life-chances based on overt and structural racism that exists between the rich and the poor and groups of color and white wealthy elites (Tuck and Gorlewski 2016).

While not generalizable for all education equity policy and desegregation research, in our study, we found that some African American advocates truly believed in the spirit of voluntary desegregation in this Midwestern community and that the promise of equal educational opportunity would be delivered by their school districts. These individuals and their families placed their faith and trust in the promise of school desegregation. The African American community did believe and trust in the policy direction of equal educational opportunity in the 1960s. However, that has slowly eroded over time for subsequent generations of African American families and children who have gone to these schools. The African Americans in this particular community also noted that while laws like NCLB have created a climate of accountability for schools and teachers and administrators, the same problems of racial neglect and discrimination continue in the schools that their children attend.

Our chapter profiles the perspectives of African American community leaders, concerned citizens, teachers, and school-community leaders as they worked in advocacy leadership roles for African American students. In this chapter, we present counternarratives of African Americans who engaged students and through their advocacy leadership challenged racism in this particular school system (Anderson 2009). The voices of these African Americans were not representative of the formal leadership roles played by superintendents, principals, or teacher leadership teams.

Rather, these voices represent a particular form of advocacy leadership of critical race policy counternarratives that speak-back to official policy directives in order to fight racial subordination. These African Americans exemplify a type of advocacy leadership and critical race educational policy counternarrative that holds schools accountable for African American student failure, and they do what they can to ensure that this does not happen.

Our study seeks to build on the findings of Morris (2008) and the perspective of African American counternarratives regarding school desegregation. While school desegregation was intended to provide equal opportunity, the counter-perspective was that it harmed existing African American leadership, cultural, and spiritual forces that fostered learning within a segregated context based on race and social class and an education for democratic citizenship. Using Solórzano and Yosso's (2002) framework of critical race methodology in educational research, we sought out reflective counternarratives of different generations of African American citizens and leaders who were involved in the movement to desegregate schools in this mid-western community during the early-mid 1960s through 2010. The interview data we present in this chapter serves as a critical race policy analysis and seeks to carve out a space to challenge the ways in which official policy that purports to leave no children behind has actually left out African American children and families. We argue that it is important to critically analyze policy and see what is left out and who is not brought into the policy discussion (Rizvi and Taylor 2009; Pillow 2004). We argue that it is important under critical policy analysis to theorize racial ordering, discrimination and white supremacy and how it is imagined and operationalized in education policy (for more on this see works on settler colonialism in education policy by Tuck and Gorlewski 2016).

In the first part of the chapter, we briefly review the major consensus points that ground critical race theory and then link them to critical policy analysis. Then in the second part of our chapter, we highlight our research design for this study, most notably the use of critical race methodology to interpret the critical policy analysis counternarratives of the African American respondents. Part three provides readers with a summary description of the social and political context of the Midwestern community in which we conducted the study and the particulars of race and social class segregation in this Midwestern university town. Given this context, we present our findings in part four and interweave the counternarratives that describe how and why these African American leaders in this particular community engaged in advocacy leadership for the educational interest of African American students. In the final part of this chapter, the African American leadership counternarratives are connected to the broader work of advocacy leadership to counteract the neo-liberal policy agenda and progressive African American leadership for change in schools.

2 Part 1: Critical Race Theory in Connection to Critical Policy Analysis

According to Carbado and Roithmayer (2014), there are many points of currently established empirical arguments that represent critical race theory's commitments and claims on which there is general consensus and documented research evidence on the following findings:

1) Racial inequality is structurally built into the social and economic landscape of the U.S. political economy;

2) Through work documented in social psychology, racial microaggressions and racial battle fatigue, racism exists at both the conscious and subconscious levels. The elimination of intentional racism would not eliminate racial inequality;

3) Racism intersects with other forms of difference and identity that lead to discrimination (e.g., social class bias, homophobia, disability, etc.) and these inequities, both legal and political, and social change and shifts are based on historical and current social contexts;

4) Our racial past exerts contemporary effects on present contexts of race and racism;

5) Racial change sometimes happens when the interests of white elites converge with the interests of the racially disempowered, which is known as interest convergence;

6) Race is a social construction on whose meanings and effects are contingent and change over time;

7) The concept of color-blindness in law and social policy and the argument for race neutral practices often serve to undermine the interests of people of color;

8) Immigration laws that restrict certain groups (i.e., Muslims from the Middle-East, Mexicans, Pacific Islanders) perpetuate the view that certain racialized groups are and always will be foreigners and will be subject to racial political rhetorical and very real discrimination at key points in U.S. national and international policy discourse;

9) Racial stereotypes are ubiquitous in society and limit the opportunities of people of color. They also result in increased racial conflict and tension with law enforcement, school authorities, health care, environmental hazards in communities, and other public policy decisions based on efficiency and technocratic concerns; and

10) The success of various policy initiatives often depends on if the perceived beneficiaries are people of color (Carbado and Roithmayr 2014, pgs. 150–151).

We see the neoliberal racial agenda is one whereby these empirical arguments under critical race theory can be used to critique the current context of neoliberalism in national policy and education policy. For example, racism is a private action, and the state is no longer responsible as a governmental agency to combat or regulate discriminatory policy or practice (Goldberg 2012). Social-services, for which the state is responsible, are administered in a way that is race neutral in intent, but its effects are to re-enforce patterns of paternalism and control grounded in implicit racial assumptions about African Americans (Soss et al. 2011). Increased measures of security and surveillance happen under the neoliberal agenda, and the rhetoric of color-blindness in everyday race relations masks the problems of structural racism that has resulted in housing gentrification in urban areas, the loss of well-paying jobs for minority youth and young adults, poor health care, and the control and regulation of the poor (Wacquant 2009). With the privatization of services under neoliberalism, so, too, is racism considered more of a private matter best settled by market choice and private consumer interests. Equal educational opportunity in general and desegregation, once an issue taken on by the federal courts, states and districts across the country, is quickly becoming a private issue as well as cities close neighborhood public schools from efficiency traditional education policy projections, in favor of market-based charter schools or private school choice options that are in conjunction with socioeconomic neighborhood displacement of the poor and working class in favor of wealthier and predominantly white singles and families (Lipman 2002, 2011).

Given this backdrop, we saw the utility of combining critical race theory with critical policy analysis because it points to an emerging trend of critical race theory's traditional reliance on counterstories and counternarrative, with other more critical social science methodologies that examine racial bias or racial microaggressions. This is important in order to provide more useful analytical tools for legal scholars to analyze the impact of law and race, and for social scientists and education researchers to want to examine factors of structural racism, racial capitalism and the social psychology of racism (Carbado and Roithmayr 2014). The combining of critical race theory and critical policy analysis fits into this larger research agenda in that it provides a policy road-map that focuses on five major concerns: (1) attention to the difference between policy public relations symbolic rhetoric versus policy reality; (2) the origins of policy development and what it focuses on and how it changes over time; (3) the distribution of power and who wins and who is shut out of the policy process and access to policy resources; (4) the effect of policy implementation on overall structural inequality; and (5) the reaction and response of non-dominant groups to the deleterious impact of the policies and what acts of self-determination they take to change the policy discourse or actions (Diem et al. 2014). Therefore, we utilized critical race theory with critical policy analysis to critique how traditional policy views race as checklist of performance and how it ignores the unconscious bias of ways that racial subordination and white supremacy are being enacted in policy (Tuck and Grolewski 2016). More importantly, for the purpose of our specific work, we utilized this combined framework to illustrate the power of messy counterstories and counternarratives that Atwood and López (2014) argue are actually central to understanding the effects of overt and institutional racism and these stories are indeed legitimate forms of evidence of racial discrimination.

The intent of this research project was to ask questions of generations of African American leaders in this particular community how they felt about school desegregation and what symbolic meaning it had for them over time. We wanted to hear their counternarratives about whether desegregation had a positive impact on African American student achievement as the school district agenda changed toward a neoliberal emphasis on accountability. For our study, CRT methodology was utilized to examine desegregation and African American parent counternarratives (Howard 2008). Ladson Billings (1998) and Solórzano and Yosso (2002) argued for critical race methodology as an analytical framework to conduct research about the realistic racial results of commonly accepted school policies (e.g., curriculum and instruction, school resources), and their impact on students of color. A critical race methodology: (1) places race and its intersectionality with other forms of discrimination (e.g., social class, gender, language/national origin) at the center of research; (2) uses race in research to challenge the dominant scientific norms of objectivity and neutrality; (3) has the research connected with social justice concerns and potential praxis with on-going efforts in communities; (4) makes experiential knowledge central to the study by linking this knowledge to other critical research and interpretive perspectives on race and racism; and (5) places importance of transdisciplinary perspectives that are based in other fields (e.g., ethnic studies, women's studies, African American studies, Chicano/a-Latino/a studies, history, sociology) to enhance understanding on the effects of racism and other forms of discrimination on persons of color.

3 Part 2: Research Design & Methodology

Given the aforementioned rationale for using critical race methodology to frame the research of our study, we felt it was important to also utilize the qualitative methods associated with critical race policy analysis as "a means to discover and/or question the complexity, subjectivity and equity of policy, as well as to illuminate intended and unintended consequences of the policy implementation process" (Diem et al. 2014, p. 1083). As pointed out by Diem et al. (2014), individuals employing critical policy analysis more often use qualitative methods in order to better capture the full complexity of policy contexts over time. It is for these reasons that we found both methodological frameworks useful to conduct this qualitative analysis that sought to examine racial equity, concepts of white supremacy and school desegregation and discrimination and how these African Americans sought to negate the racial discrimination. We utilized news accounts from the original desegregation efforts, and subsequent efforts by the district to achieve racial equity; equity and racial achievement audits conducted by the school districts during the 1998–1999 academic years, federal desegregation court records, and interviews from African American community leaders. Secondary sources through law review articles, books and articles on the history of education policy in this community were also a key part of the data for the purpose of collecting information and providing historical and current political perspectives. We also used the secondary data as reflective documents that allowed participants to speak about critical incidents that had an impact on the way they saw racial school desegregation and racial progress. Using critical race methodology and critical policy analysis as the frameworks for content analysis purposes, our research questions focused on understanding African American ideas about schooling in this particular local community:

1. What was the motivational or driving goal or belief you had about desegregation in the initial period and how has this changed?
2. How have African American students in the schools actually obtained their education? Describe how you have helped in this goal by being an advocacy leader?
3. Has there been progress and where do you see the schools headed for in terms of racial equity as the schools emphasize accountability more than desegregation equity?

In this way, we hoped to see if there were recurring racial patterns and educational themes surrounding desegregation and racism and how these issues were addressed by these African American leaders in this particular community. Using parts Solorzano and Yosso's (2002) critical race methodology as our guide to the interviews, we used the three aforementioned questions as a guide to ask semi-sturctured questions in group interviews about the past desegregation efforts. We also used more open-ended questions with the African American leaders that asked them to reconstruct events and emotions regarding the discrimination they faced and were trying to address through their activist work at the time. For the purpose of this research, it was important for us to capture the counternarratives of what these particiapnts were saying about the individual and systemic racism they faced and tried to combat. Our goal was to capture why they felt in particular ways about policy enactments that took place at the macro-level in schools that had an effect on them or their children or the students they worked with. What emerged from our questions were a series of counternarratives that described what they did as involved African Americans who sought to counteract the racial injustice they saw being done to African American children. Whenever possible, we attempted to corroborate this knowledge of narrative data with descriptive statistics gleaned from primary and secondary documents. In essence, these interviews took on the form of oral histories in that they were not as highly structured as formal interviews (Denny 1978). Rather, what was most important was the unfolding of the counternarratives that yielded insights into the perceptions of a racial reality that school desegregation was supposed to achieve but did not through the lived experience racial discrimination that these African Americans faced over time (Alemán 2007; Dixson and Rousseau 2006; Duncan 2002; Gillborn 2005; Solórzano and Yosso 2002; Yosso 2006).

The research interview data was comprised from two sources.[1] In the spring of 2002 we conducted a focus-group video-taped interview (of about 3 h) with the original six African American community leaders who were involved with the initial negotiations with the mid-western school district where the study took place. This interview was the first time they had all gathered together since the late 1950s-early 1960s to critically reflect on what they did as parents and community leaders, why they did what they did, and to look back and speak to the pros/cons of what they were trying to achieve. We also had two follow-up shorter informal interviews with most of these leaders (one passed away in 2008) through 2010, where they told us about current issues facing the school district and African American student achievement, and how they felt about their grandchildren or (other young children they knew) attending these same schools now and the all-African American schools they attended in the pre-desegregation era in this Midwestern town.

As members of the African American community in this Midwestern town during the period from 2002 to 2010, we developed ties to many African American parents, church leaders, students, professionals, etc. We attended religious gatherings, participated and led African American student achievement initiatives and went

---

[1] The names used in this study as we presented the interviews are pseudonyms.

to some of the school community equity meetings during this time period. Our familiarity and knowledge of this particular community led us to develop a sense of "cultural intuition" (Delgado Bernal 1998) which guided our efforts to seek out and select eight participants to interview (on average 2 h/two sessions) who had a direct stake and critical historical and current insights into the effects of desegregation also interviewed. These participants were also selected in part because of their informal leadership roles in the schools and racial sincerity and validation by most African Americans in this community. Jackson Jr.'s (2005) ethnographic profiles of African Americans in Harlem and parts of Brooklyn offer a methodological definition of racial sincerity as one where the individuals have an internal belief structure that has agency and interacts with others and within a social context. Racial sincerity with these African Americans implies that the counternarratives they tell reveal to us "how these people think and feel their identities into a palpable everyday existence" that is more than just identity politics or authenticity (Jackson 2005, p. 11). Some of these participants were teachers in the district, or they sent their children to schools in the district or were involved in some aspect of African American community leadership. Some of them also had family historical ties to the desegregation efforts in that they had generations of family members who went through desegregation in this community in the 1970s and 1980s, as well insights through students who they knew of who were attending the schools in this district at the time of this study. Finally, when we read and re-read the data and started to use critical race theory as a methodology to examine patterns of racism from the counternarratives, what we found was that the participants had a different way in which they defined success; which was that it connected to cultural and racial validation. Furthermore, another consistent pattern of the data which emerged as a theme was that the leaders put time and work into challenging racially biased assumptions that emerged through policy actions and everyday occurrences. This was done to set a different and more racially supportive climate and culture for African American youth in this community.

4 Part 3: Brief Context: The Town Divided by University Avenue and Race

The Midwestern area in which this study took place was comprised of two adjacent towns with a combined population of about 1,500,000. While the towns had two separate school districts, they did share the similar histories by African Americans in both communities as to the shortcomings in overcoming racism and the problem of improving African American student achievement. For example, in both districts in which this study took place, 85 % of its teaching force was comprised of White European Americans in contrast to a 10 % African Americans in the teaching ranks. These figures mirror the communities where this study was situated as well. Amidst a major research university and a majority white populace, the makeup of this community included majority white students in all of its schools as well as a majority of white school board members, teachers, and administrators, which historically were known to favor its white students and parents around issues of segregation. The districts made some changes in response to voluntary desegregation efforts and/or consent decrees regarding racial sensitivity to tracking issues and gifted education. However, with the passage of NCLB, the mandates of increasing the use of testing to hold schools and teachers accountable, highlighting racial disparities, and using data to attempt to benchmark achievement goals, the data still showed evidence of persistently low levels of African American student achievement in key areas such as reading, and math where the schools failed up to approximately 35 % of its African American students who did not meet grade level on state standardized testing as of 2010.

With the university situated alongside a local hospital, they served as the main employers in this community, and there had been relatively steady economic growth between 1998 and 2008. The main thoroughfare divides the campus-town area from the majority African American neighborhoods, and is affectionately referenced as the "north end" by its residents. Due to a segregated housing past, African Americans were red-lined to this section of the town.

One of the districts in this study became the first in the state to institute a voluntary desegregation plan in 1966. In doing so, racial tension grew and resulted in many African American students being treated as and feeling unwelcomed:

> Black students have reported at meetings and discussions of their problems that they felt teachers discriminate against them by not expecting as much from them as from white students and by not challenging them with realistic tasks. Students also suspect teachers misunderstand them and the difficulties which are caused by poverty. (League of Women Voters 1968, p. 7)

Inclusive of the report furnished by the League of Women Voters (LWV) in 1968, was a characterized problem for these African American students that showed the high attrition rates in high school:

> While the drop-out rate for the school as a whole is 17 % to 20 %, for Black students it is about 50 %. This is a marked improvement since the early 1960s when the Negro drop-out rate was closer to 90 %. Several factors have contributed to this increase in the number of Negroes who graduate. Most frequently mentioned are the development of special education and vocational education programs and increased motivation on the part of Black students who are beginning to feel that they can find jobs after graduation without discrimination on the part of the employers. The percentage of Black students who graduate with honors is minimal. Ten to 15 % of Negro students, as compared with 58 % of Whites, are college-bound. (LWV 1968, pp. 7–8)

The staggering aspect of this historical backdrop is the parallel drawn alongside the many challenges for the districts. Each of the two districts represented in this study constantly grappled with racial disparities in such areas as suspensions, expulsions and drop-out rates. In addition, a 1998 Equity Audit conducted by one of the districts in this study found that similar problems lingered some 30 years after the League of Women Voters' initial study. For example, of the 1458 students enrolled in weighted academic classes as of 1996–1997, African American students were significantly under-represented, accounting for just 8.1 % (Equity Audit 1998). In contrast, they were significantly over-represented in special education programs. Understanding that "the School District does not group students by ability," having the "representation in gifted and upper level programs...to be determined by the individual's skill or knowledge level accompanied by a combination of counselor recommendation and parental input," many questioned the fairness component in this process; a process that debatably stratifies its students (Equity Audit 1998, pp. 40–41).

5 Part 4: Findings on Success (?), Students and Care, and Cultural Climate

In the sections that follow, the interviews paint a picture of lost hopes, dreams unfulfilled and educational debts that still need to be paid to generations of African American students in this Mid-western town. This is due to the implementation of acts harmful to African American students, and the failure of accountability policies under neoliberalism which have also contributed to the racial hostility and antagonism that has been a part of this community historically. The sub-sections highlight findings from the interviews regarding how the schools defined success versus the African American advocacy leaders, the views around perceptions of care and trust for the education of African American youth in this community, and racial/cultural climate that helped or hindered school achievement and racial/cultural validation in spite of the discrimination.

5.1 SUCCESS, Says Who?

The first significant aspect of the counternarrative to desegregation success in the district was the notable resistance to an African American adult mentoring presence in the schools. In a group interview conducted with African American activists who originally lobbied this district to engage in voluntary desegregation in the early 1960s, the group sentiment was one of hope and optimism regarding the quality of the education their children would obtain in a desegregated school, particularly in terms of access to resources. However, over a period of a generation, the perspective of these activists turned pessimistic at the notion of equal educational opportunity. For example one interviewee said, "We really believed in the ideal of equal educational opportunity, some did not back us, but we believed in it and trusted the school district leadership to do right for our kids, but pretty soon we learned they did not and we had to watch them constantly" (Focus group interview, personal communication, June 16, 2002). Another said, "I was in the school every day, I knew that I could come in any door and watch what those teachers and principals were doing to our kids and it wasn't until they got tired of me that they made me go through security and would tell the teachers I was on my way to the classroom" (Focus group interview, personal communication, June 16, 2002). When we asked about the school administration, all agreed they were indifferent or even hostile to African American parents as exemplified by this quote from one of the church leader's wives and a community activist:

> When we got in his office he said "You people had 5 minutes to make our case and then he would say Adios! He had the nerve to shake his index finger at me. My husband who was a minister was trying to calm me down but if he had come any closer to me I would have bit his finger off, that racist! (Focus group interview, personal communication, June 16, 2002).

These former activists and parents described a slow but steady decline of a concern about equity and racial justice in the schools in this community and they voiced concern about their grandchildren who were now attending the same school they tried to change. This sentiment was once again voiced at a school board meeting in the spring of 2010 when some members of the board lamented the fact that the school district had not met AYP standards under NCLB for its African American students. One of the authors attended this meeting and saw one of the former activists in the audience. After the meeting, this activist voiced continued frustration with the comment, "some things just don't change" in reference to the same conversations and concerns voiced in previous school board meetings decade after decade, yet nothing proactive was being done by the district to positively alter conditions for African American students (African American school leader at school board meeting, personal communication March, 2, 2010).

A similar theme of historical racism that continued from the early period of desegregation in the early 1960s emerged from the interview with Daniel (the names used throughout this chapter are pseudonyms) who grew up in the town and remembered how he was treated in the early desegregation period:

> As a child, I began to see that teachers favored other children and were not necessarily fair with me, and so the longer I stayed in the school system the more detached I became from it... I found it was negative, once I got to Junior High school listening to White people talk in derogatory terms about people from the North end as if we were some kind of aliens (Daniel interview, personal communication, February 22, 2006).

He went on to describe specific race-based issues he recalls as a young man growing up and attending these schools. Here he references his 6th grade teacher:

> By the time 6th grade came along, that woman just destroyed any kind of love for education that I had... I have no positive recollections of that woman... and it's interesting that I don't even remember her name (Daniel interview, personal communication, February 22, 2006).

As witnessed here, various social forces aided in perpetual notions of inferiority attached to African American students and families and community leaders. White supremacy in educational leadership and policy was at work in terms of resisting African American community leader's roles as change agents for social justice (Gillborn 2005). The collective actions on behalf of this community centered on proper schooling for African American children. What we found in the interviews was a consistent pattern of racial realism based on the efforts by these African

Americans themselves to counteract the slow unfulfilled real promise of *Brown*. Bell (2004) articulated this concept by stating that the liberal push for civil rights in the 1960s did not solve the seemingly permanent underclass status of many African Americans in the United States and real racial reform and equity in public schools. To be sure, some incremental structural changes came about and opened some doors of opportunity for members of the African American middle class. But for the most part, Bell argued that structural racism in the form of low job prospects, poor housing, and educational systems has hindered many African Americans to achieve middle class status, and those who have achieved it find that they still must deal with various forms of unconscious racism (Lawrence 1987). Therefore, Bell called on society to acknowledge the "silent covenant" maintaining white supremacy in terms of power, privilege and material resources and property rights. Racial realism would be a better way for African Americans to look realistically at the objectives of racial progress and it can potentially spur visionary strategies to achieve racial social justice through the efforts by African Americans themselves to improve education for their children (Bell 2004, p. 191). The interviews expressed by those who went through the history of desegregation process in this mid-western town experienced a type of racial realism through their reflective counternarratives.

One of the ways in which racial realism fostered African American strategic visions of progress came from an interview with Judith.[2] Judith served as the Community Service Liaison for the school district. A middle-aged woman with two children in schools in the district, she also saw herself as an advocate for African American children in the area and continually insisted on leveling the playing field for all students. Earning a Master's degree from an Ivy League institution, Judith firmly believed that all children can and should be educated:

> Making sure that those kids have every opportunity...equal opportunity to education, ...you have some students who are not the A students who are not even college potential students, but those kids have potential to do something other than listen to somebody tell them that they won't make it (Judith interview, personal communication, February 22, 2006).

Valarie, a middle-aged woman and director of a Freedom School (summer) initiative in one of the districts, believed that the school administrators, teachers, etc. have all contributed to the "intellectual neglect" of African American students. Her desire to witness academic progress, achievement and love for one's self for African American students was the driving force for her external work and development of such an initiative:

> We did the inventory and the results showed me that Black boys did not like being Black... so if there's no self-worth then why work hard in school? It was powerful and heart-wrenching and the older they got the worse it got...so if in 3rd grade they're already saying being Black is bad and we're not infusing them with anything opposite of that and

---

[2]We used pseudonyms in this study to replace real names. Also we did not use the name of the school district named in the League of Women Voters Report and the Equity Audit listed in the references.

we know the schools aren't then how do some kids make it and some kids don't... we know that they're not going to get it from the schools... those that do get a good dosage of it somewhere else... (Valarie interview, personal communication, February 20, 2006).

While the ideology of this school district was rooted in white supremacy within the desegregated district, and failure being linked to perception pathology of African American students, the community leaders realized this aspect of racial realism and focused efforts to advocate for the pedagogical importance and cultural sensitivity of African American students. The efforts of these teachers mirrored the critical race achievement ideology that sought to push for student learning in spite of racism (Carter 2008). These community leaders and teachers saw their role in the school district as advocates for the students and families because the promises of educational success after school desegregation and the No Child Left Behind agenda never really materialized for them.

5.2 Students Don't Care How Much You Know ...

Realizing the value of caring was another key theme that emerged from the interviews as an important issue that marked what desegregation was supposed to do, versus what it did not deliver on for African American students. From the early period of desegregation in this Midwestern community, there was a commonly held belief of a lack of care concerning the welfare and well-being of African American students.

Jameka exemplified this aspect of care in her comments about race in the district. She spent the majority of her academic career in the local town. As a (then) doctoral student at the university and Assistant Director of the African-American Culture Program, she argued wholeheartedly that African American students were capable of learning, and systemically were doomed in the two districts due to teachers not having a vested interest in African American student success:

> I believe that a large part of the reason why kids don't think that college is for them, is because they have a university in their town who wants nothing to do with them and kids are smarter than we think they are and in their mind if they don't want anything to do with them, that means they don't want them, Period! (Jameka interview, personal communication, February 28, 2006).

This position of caring extends beyond the classroom as outlined by Alice, who was at the time (2002–2006) the community outreach coordinator in the district and challenged the district on test score data around African American student failure and what this meant:

> These children wanna know I can joke with you and you understand, but they know where to draw the line, they want to know that there's somebody there who cares and they know when you don't... as adults we need to work harder, it's our job to make sure that these kids are comfortable (Alice interview, personal communication, March 3, 2006).

The historical importance of caring relationships as factors of success was felt more in the all-African American schools in this community, among teachers and parents, and also that of teachers and students. The African American schools offered a sense of community, and with that expectation for academic excellence was the standard. Those who we interviewed in this study shared and believed in this philosophical perspective, insisting that this was couched first in teachers caring for their overall student populace. In reflecting on his academic experience as a student in this area, Daniel, had few positive memories, but holds on to those few:

> There was some bright spots... my band instructor took an interest in me and that carried over into high school when that band instructor took an interest in me as well and that's how I began to blossom as a person and as an individual, because somebody saw some talent and encouraged me in it (Daniel interview, personal communication, February 22, 2006).

The role of caring teachers of the past, played a role in shaping the next generation of African American teachers in the district despite desegregation, as illustrated by our interview with Darrell who served as the one of the few only African American teachers in the middle-school for the school district. In receiving his degree from the local university in special education, Darrell decided to stay in the area to help facilitate change for young African American men. At the time, serving as the special education teacher alongside external roles as mentor and tutor, he believed that his personal experience as a young man in an eventual all white district could have been detrimental. However, when he had a particular teacher in high school that cared enough to push him beyond lower track, he insisted on doing the same for his own students:

> I'm trying to grab other brothers directly under my wing (so they can) learn how to follow things that are not negative. My fraternity has their own mentorship program... every Monday we mentor the younger brothers... we go out for those students that look like they need that additional help, that positive role model in the community... outside of school... we ask, what you need is a tutor, or just a friend... as an educator, for me mentoring doesn't stop (Darrell interview, personal communication, February 25, 2006).

Theresa, a special education teacher, felt the need for relationships nurture that put African American children at the forefront acknowledged the importance of their lives outside the classroom. The one major component for all programs she oversaw was:

> All (of my) programs are relationship based, that's who we are as a people... students don't care what degree you have, if they don't believe you like them, you have no credibility with them and our kids act that out every day, and white folk can't understand that... the janitor as opposed to the white psychologist could probably do a better job (Theresa interview, personal communication, February 25, 2006).

In sum, the theme of real caring came out in these interviews. In spite of the race neutrality of accountability policy and school desegregation directives to provide equal educational opportunity, the African Americans counternarratives paint a portrait of neglect that they had to then fulfill for the benefit of African American students in these schools. For us, we viewed this as an example of what critical race theory through the messy counternarratives and critical policy analysis showed us with regard to policy rhetoric vis-a-vis the lived reality of discrimination and how these African American leaders sought to counter-act these effects on African American youth.

5.3 A Climate That Is Culturally Conducive

Taking into account the theme of African American student success, there was important recognition of creating environments that were culturally sensitive and friendly for African American students. This was a prevailing area of discussion within the web of discourse centered on African American students achievement due to some positive results rendered. In this Midwestern school setting, the same approach had been utilized with attempts to foster some form of alternative educational experience for African American students. In her role as Freedom School director, Valarie spoke to those "few" on the frontline tackling the issues relative to African American students:

> We're frustrated...some get involved and try to change the system...some of us gave up; people like me create alternative options. Why are we trying to change systems? I did that work for a while and now I am frustrated with that...my thing is I gotta save the babies now, so I create my own, which is why freedom school came about, which is why Project, etc. came about...you don't want my kids in your building, fine, I'll create a space for them to come to and I'll show you that Black boys that have BD [Behavior Disorder] labels will finish high school. (Valarie interview, personal communication, February 25, 2006)

With another of her initiatives (Project, etc.), Valarie voiced a critical perspective on the high discipline rates among African American males characteristic of the accountability movement:

> Black boys were being expelled and suspended from school...we adopted a philosophy called "wrap-around" that suggested you look at a child's entire life, not just school...but what's happening in their 24-hour day and build 24-hour supports.... "Wrap-around," a Native-American philosophy is the way you grow a tree, when it's young you wrap its trunk and when it grows up(ward) it stands tall (Valarie interview, personal communication, February 25, 2006).

With Valarie's work, she conducted assessments such as Motivation to Read in an attempt to garner evidence on the state of African American students in the district. In doing so, the findings:

> yielded less than 20% results for our Black children...so then, my theory was, you can't make anyone learn something they don't want to learn or that they don't have an interest in learning...you wanna know why Black kids don't do well on their reading scores, they're not interested in what you're providing them to read...my job isn't to teach them to read...(but)...to send them back to you more motivated to read....a lil' more motivated to do well, because that's the expectation of them being Black (Valarie interview personal communication, February 25, 2006).

For Alice, the aforementioned realities concerning African American students prompted her summer Sankofa program. Her adoption of this label was due to the type of program she desired as an alternative. Sankofa's meaning has a communal angle with historical meaning suggesting that we must go back and reclaim our past so we can move forward; so we understand why and how we came to be who we are today. For Alice a summer program with cultural relevance for African American students was essential considering what they received during the school year:

Silent Covenants in the Neoliberal Era 171

> In today's society, when I take a look at the folks who have a true commitment to seeing that our children are going from point A to point B in achieving, I find so many mixed feelings and so few people that have that commitment and investment when it comes to African-American students, ... we might need to look at designing some other systems as opposed to just letting it float on, because we are floating on with these same teachers who we know year after year are destroying these kids.... (Alice interview, personal communication, March 3, 2006).

Denice's also had issues with the teachers of the school district. Centered on the naiveté of the teachers or best described as convenient ignorance and arrogance, she believed the following to be true despite the rhetoric of NCLB:

> If I had a room of White teachers right now and asked the question, do you think that there is a racial problem in the school district? Nobody would probably say that there is ... if I took it further and asked if race matters in the classroom, with a White teacher and an all-Black class, nobody would probably think that it does. Do you see anything that you use the word race in? It's going to be "No" to that group of people, because when we start to talk about the terms race, racist, that's not a word they wanna be defined as and if we trickle it down to the classroom, that's pointing to them because they are the teacher. (Denice interview, personal communication, March 3, 2006).

She elaborated further in the discussion of her white teacher colleagues denial of their racism by insisting that, "if asked any of the above questions, their response of 'I'm not racist' is the typical response from White teacher" (Denice interview, personal communication, March 3, 2006).

> We should say, I didn't call you one, but what I am saying is that you have a classroom full of Black kids and none of them are achieving, none of them are succeeding, and none of these parents seem to be able to communicate with you. As a matter of fact half of your parents say that when they try to talk to you, you always seem to blow them off.... (Denice interview, personal communication, March 3, 2006).

The prevalence of racism on behalf of the teachers was often overshadowed by color-blind language disguising itself as multi-cultural, diversity, and progressivism. "No one wants to be singled out as a racist because that implies that they are a bad person ... and they are not going to accept that" (Denice interview, personal communication, March 3, 2006).

From a CRT perspective what was apparent was that structural/ institutional racism alongside color-blindness and racial backlash contributed immensely to the problems within schools, from lack of resources, to uncaring teachers who have mis-taught generations of African American students in this setting, to educational leadership racial neglect (Brooks 2012). The interview data reflect the conceptual framework of CRT highlighted by Howard (2008) where he posited that schools basically "do not care" about the education of African American students from desegregation promises of equal educational opportunity to the accountability of NCLB. The counternarratives by these African American leaders and advocates support the critical race ethnographic findings of Vaught (2011) which documented a prevailing culture of white supremacy that normalized racial failure and power over African American and Latino youth. Through this all however, these counternarratives painted a portrait of racial empowerment at work with subsequent generations of African American teachers and community/school leaders attempting to create a critical race achievement ideology by any means necessary for success of African American students to break the "silent covenant" in this Midwestern town (Bell 2004; Carter 2008).

6 Conclusion: Put Race Discrimination Behind Us or Take Counternarratives as Evidence of On-Going Policy Issues?

In this neoliberal era, we are seeing what Goldberg (2012) predicted; namely that the state (legislatures, courts, executive branches of governments at the local, state and federal levels) would abandon involvement in addressing racial equity and social justice. For example, in a motion approved by the U.S. District Court of the central district of Illinois Peoria Division (August 24, 2009), the Champaign Unit 4 consent decree was officially terminated. In the opinion and order U.S. District Judge Joe Billy McDade, the school district has made good faith efforts to put equal educational opportunity at the center of its school reform efforts and:

> In a representative democracy, elected officials are held responsible for fidelity to their public trust at the ballot box, and elected school boards and the educational policies they espouse are subject to the same public accountability. The plaintiffs class, like all other interested citizenry, must invest time and involvement in the monitoring and helping the school district stay the course in advancing these goals of the consent decree.... The skepticism expressed by some at the public hearing is based on long memories of past transgressions rather than the past seven years of transformative progress toward a race neutral educational environment... with this mind-set, the parties and community can put the distant past behind us and look forward to the continuation of a new beginning where the educational needs of children of color are equally served by the school district (Johnson v. Board of Champaign Unit Sch. Dist. # 4, 2009, pgs. 16–17).

Despite the "desire" to amend a past legacy of racism by emphasizing steady progress through test score accountability, the counternarratives here reveal a perceived reality of racial realism ahead for some African American students, families and communities nationally.

The neoliberal policy agenda has trumpeted the new ways that desegregation is changing for the better in terms of the focus on accountability, or the success of charter schools and market forces as the new way to improve equal educational opportunity by empowering families of color as educational consumers who exercise choice for the best education for their children. However, our findings as demonstrated in these counternarratives of African American advocacy leaders who lived through the empty promises indicate they have actively worked in various ways to meet the spirit of the needs of the students to create a different learning culture based on love and caring of students of color (Scheurich 1998; Rodriquez 2008).

The utility of critical race theory and critical policy analysis points to the consequences of ignoring the racial reality of discrimination through seemingly neutral education policy outcomes. In our study, we found it useful to utilize critical race theory and critical policy analysis because one of the major implications is that we as a society should openly address the issue of racial trust/mistrust between school leaders and teachers and African American families that has been illustrated in these counternarratives. We posit that the major tenets of critical race theory that we highlighted at the start of this chapter have been aimed to examine patterns of racism and racial discrimination in institutions and policy actions. What we tried to show in this chapter is that the counternarratives of the African American leaders pointed to evidence of overt racial hostility to more subtle forms of historical racial neglect that the leaders had to address through an emphasis on racial and cultural validation. Critical policy analysis combined with critical race theory we feel is a powerful potential tool that can be used to address the legal and political wrongs of racial discrimination in policy and practice; because in a very real sense perception is reality, and whether judges, school officials, or teachers agree with this or not, it cannot be ignored and should be remedied and the debt finally repaid.

References

Alemán, E. A., Jr. (2007). Situating Texas school finance policy in a CRT framework: How "substantially equal" yields racial inequality. *Educational Administration Quarterly, 43*(5), 525–558.
Anderson, G. (2009). *Advocacy leadership*. New York: Routledge.
Atwood, E., & Lopez, G. R. (2014). Let's be critically honest: Toward a messier counterstory in critical race theory. *International Journal of Qualitative Studies in Education, 27*(9), 1134–1154.
Bell, D. A. (2004). *Silent covenants: Brown v. Board of education and the unfulfilled hopes for racial reform*. New York: Oxford Press.
Brooks, J. S. (2012). *Black school-white school: Racism and educational (mis) leadership*. New York: Teachers College Press.
Carbado, D. W., & Roithmayr, D. (2014). Critical race theory meets social science. *Annual Review of Law and Social Science, 10*, 149–167.
Carter, D. J. (2008). Achievement as resistance: The development of a critical race achievement ideology among black achievers. *Harvard Educational Review, 78*(3), 466–498.
Delgado Bernal, D. (1998). Using a Chicana feminist epistemology in educational research. *Harvard Educational Review, 68*(4), 555–582.
Denny, T. (1978, May). *Storytelling and educational understanding*. Address delivered at national meeting of International Reading Association, Houston.
Diem, S., Young, M. D., Welton, A. J., Mansfield, K. C., & Lee, P. L. (2014). The intellectual landscape of critical policy analysis. *International Journal of Qualitative Studies in Education, 27*(9), 1068–1090.
Dixson, A. D., & Rousseau, C. K. (2006). And we are still not saved: CRT in education ten years later. In A. D. Dixon & C. K. Rousseau (Eds.), *Critical race theory in education: All god's children got a song* (pp. 31–54). New York: Routledge.
Duncan, G. A. (2002). Beyond love: A critical race ethnography of the schooling of adolescent males. *Equity & Excellence in Education, 35*(2), 131–143.
Equity Audit. (1998).
Gillborn, D. (2005). Education policy as an act of white supremacy: Whiteness, critical race theory and education reform. *Journal of Education Policy, 20*(4), 485–505.
Gillborn, D. (2008). *Racism and education: Coincidence or conspiracy*. New York: Routledge.

Goldberg, D. T. (2012). *The threat of race: Reflections on racial neoliberalism*. Malden: Wiley-Blackwell.
Guba, E. G., & Lincoln, Y. S. (1981). *Effective evaluation*. San Francisco: Jossey-Bass.
Howard, T. C. (2008). Who really cares? The disenfranchisement of African American males in preK-12 schools: A critical race theory perspective. *Teachers College Record, 110*(5), 954–985.
Hursh, D. (2007). Assessing no child left behind and the rise of neoliberal education policies. *American Educational Research Journal, 44*(5), 493–518.
Jackson, J. L., Jr. (2005). *Real black: Adventures in racial sincerity*. Durham: Duke University Press.
Johnson, et. al., vs. Board of Champaign Unit School District #4, case no. 00-CV-1349 (August 24, 2009).
Ladson-Billings, G. (1998). Just what is critical race theory and what is it doing in a nice field like education. *International Journal of Qualitative Studies in Education, 11*(1), 7–24.
Ladson-Billings, G. (2004). Landing on the wrong note: The price we paid for Brown. *Educational Resarhcer, 33*(7), 3–13.
Lawrence, C. R., III. (1987). The id, the ego and equal protection: Reckoning with unconscious racism. *Stanford Law Review, 39*(2), 317–388.
League of Women Voters report (1968).
Lipman, P. (2002). Making the global city, making inequality: The political economy and cultural politics of Chicago school policy. *American Educational Research Journal, 39*(2), 370–422.
Lipman, P. (2011). *The new political economy of urban education: Neoliberalism, race, and the right to the city*. New York: Routledge.
Morris, J. E. (2008). Research. Ideology, and the Brown decision: Counter-narratives to the historical and contemporary representation of Black schooling. *Teachers College Record, 110*(4), 713–732.
Pedroni, T. C. (2007). *Market movements: African American involvement in school voucher reform*. New York: Routledge.
Pillow, W. S. (2004). *Unfit subjects: Educational policy and the teen mother*. New York: Routledge.
Rizvi, F., & Lingard, B. (2009). *Globalizing education policy*. London: Routledge.
Rodriguez, L. F. (2008). "Teachers know you can do more": Understanding how school cultures of success affect urban high school students. *Educational Policy, 22*(5), 758–780.
Scheurich, J. J. (1998). Highly successful and loving, public elementary schools populated mainly by low-SES children of color: Core beliefs and cultural characteristics. *Urban Education, 33*(4), 451–491.
Soloranzo, D. G., & Yosso, T. J. (2002). Critical race methodology: Counter-storytelling as an analytical framework for education research. *Qualitative Inquiry, 8*(1), 23–44.
Soss, J., Fording, R. C., & Schram, S. F. (2011). *Disciplining the poor: Neoliberal paternalism and the persistent power of race*. Chicago: University of Chicago Press.
Tuck, E., & Gorlewski, J. (2016). Racist ordering, settler colonialism, and edTPA: A participatory policy analysis. *Educational Policy, 30*(1), 197–217.
Tushnet, M. V. (1996). The 'we've done enough theory of school desegregation. *Howard Law Journal, 39*(3), 767–780.
Vaught, S. E. (2011). *Racism, public schooling and the entrenchment of white supremacy: A critical race ethnography*. Albany: SUNY Press.
Viteritti, J. P. (2012). The federal role in school reform: Obama's "race to the top". *Notre Dame Law Review, 87*(5), 2087–2120.
Wacquant, L. (2009). *Punishing the poor: The neoliberal government of social insecurity*. Durham: Duke University Press.
Yosso, T. J. (2006). *Critical race counterstories along the Chicana/Chicano educational pipeline*. New York: Routledge.

Policy Enactments and Critical Policy Analysis: How Institutional Talk Constructs Administrative Logics, Marginalization, and Agency

Rodney S. Whiteman, Brendan D. Maxcy, Erica Fernández, and Samantha M. Paredes Scribner

Abstract In this chapter, we move toward a framework for Critical Policy Analysis (CPA) grounded in linguistic foundations constructing and maintaining institutional logics. The framework is built on the Institutional Logics Perspective (Thornton et al, The institutional logics perspective: a new approach to culture, structure, and process. Oxford University Press, Oxford, 2012), and Searle's (Making the social world: the structure of human civilization. Oxford University Press, Oxford, 1995; The construction of social reality. Free Press, New York, 2009) linguistic theory of social institutions. The chapter first provides a general overview of the framework, and then further illustrates it in a discussion of three cases in which actors exert their agency by resisting marginalizing professional logics of school administration. We hope to show ways in which the linguistic foundations of institutional logics play a role in policy enactments and the micropolitical struggles between school administrators and members of school communities.

Keywords Micropolitics • Critical policy analysis • Policy enactment • The institutional logics perspective • Linguistic analysis • Organizational communication • Institutional messages • School leadership • School-community relations

In this chapter, we move toward a framework for Critical Policy Analysis (CPA) grounded in linguistic foundations constructing and maintaining institutional logics. We do this by first providing a general overview of the framework and then further

---

R.S. Whiteman (✉)
Department of Educational Leadership and Policy Studies, Indiana University, Bloomington, IN, USA
e-mail: whiteman@indiana.edu

B.D. Maxcy • S.M.P. Scribner
Department of Educational Leadership and Policy Studies, Indiana University—Purdue University Indianapolis, Indianapolis, IN, USA

E. Fernández
Department of Educational Leadership, Neag School of Education, University of Connecticut, 249 Glenbrook Road, Unit 3093, Storrs, CT 06269, USA

© Springer International Publishing Switzerland 2017
M.D. Young, S. Diem (eds.), *Critical Approaches to Education Policy Analysis*, Education, Equity, Economy 4, DOI 10.1007/978-3-319-39643-9_9

illustrating it in a discussion of three cases in which actors exert their agency by resisting marginalizing professional logics of school administration. We hope to show ways in which the linguistic foundations of institutional logics play a role in the micropolitical struggles between school administrators and members of school communities.

Scholars have long recognized the role that institutions—both formal and informal—play in shaping the actions and interactions of individuals and groups. Because institutions influence actors "by structuring or shaping the political and social interpretations of the problems they have to deal with and by limiting the choice of policy solutions that might be implemented" (Fischer and Gottweis 2012a, p. 17), we believe institutional theory can inform frameworks for CPA. As Fischer and Gottweis suggested, institutions influence actors' interests, and communicative practices within institutions make political action possible. Thus institutions allow analysts to connect policy, communicative practice, and politics. Such an approach can be fruitful when considering how institutions structure interactions between school administrators and historically marginalized communities. This approach can also reveal ways in which actors in these communities claim strategic agency and power in dynamic, unpredictable social settings (Thornton et al. 2012).

We propose an institutionally structured micropolitical orientation to critical policy analysis. Specifically, the focus of our analysis is micropolitical negotiation of policy enactments, particularly within the negotiation of institutional language. In this framework, we conceptualize schools as formal organizations (Bidwell 1965) embedded in a network of social institutions (DiMaggio and Powell 1983; Friedland and Alford 1991; Meyer and Rowan 1977; Thornton et al. 2012). Formal organizations like schools are not static; they are dynamic and always becoming through processes and language of organizing, the logics of which are drawn from the institutional environment (Bacharach and Mundell 1993). Consequently, organizations can be understood as patterns of practice and meaning making that are constantly negotiated (Bacharach and Mundell 1993; Czarniawska 2008). This introduces an inherently political dimension to the practice of schooling.

Additionally, we incorporate the linguistic turn in policy analysis (see Fischer 2003; Fischer and Forester 1993b; Fischer and Gottweis 2012b) by examining the linguistic foundations shaping the logics of social institutions. John Searle's social ontology (1995, 2009) includes a theory of institutional formation based on a set of statuses, rights and obligations, and determination of social facts that provide rationality for human action. By integrating Searle's social ontology into a discussion of institutional logics and logics of action, we hope to illumine linguistic mechanisms at play when school administrators struggle politically with parent and community groups hoping to advance their interests.

Our perspective on CPA assumes that policy transcends laws, regulations, rules, or procedures. We agree with Diem and her colleagues (2014) that policy analysis can move beyond technical-rational analysis of policy formation, implementation, and the measurable outcomes of implementation (see also Fischer 2003). In our view policies are complex, negotiated social practices in which policy formation and implementation are enacted into social arenas (Ball et al. 2012; Levinson and Sutton 2001). In other words,

> policy-making is a constant discursive struggle over the criteria of social classification, the boundaries of problem categories, the intersubjective interpretation of common experiences, the conceptual framing of problems, and the definitions of ideas that guide the ways people create the shared meanings which motivate them to act (Fischer and Forester 1993a, pp. 2–3).

The negotiations Fischer and Forester described suggest that policy enactments have political dimensions, as interests are negotiated among organizational actors (Levinson and Sutton 2001; Thorius and Maxcy 2014). Introducing a discursive component suggests the negotiation of interests is communicative. Following the linguistic turn, CPA can be an examination of micropolitical discursive struggles in which the language of organizational actors is examined and policy analysts interpret the intentionality and meaning of practice and communicative acts (Fischer and Forester 1993a; Levinson et al. 2009). This can be done with the understanding that language is contingent upon social institutions connecting macro-level systems to micro-level practices (Fischer and Forester 1993a; Habermas 1988; Thornton et al. 2012).

1 Institutions, Logics, and Language

Schools are influenced by the social environment in which they are embedded (Meyer and Rowan 1977). That environment comprises a network of interwoven institutional orders, such as religion, the professions, corporations, etc. (Friedland and Alford 1991) that are threaded through social organizations. Each institutional order has its own logics: symbolic and practical content such as meanings, metaphors, bases of legitimacy and power, and logics of action (Bacharach and Mundell 1993; Friedland and Alford 1991; Thornton et al. 2012). This strand of institutional theory is called the institutional logics perspective.

Institutional orders are differentiated because individuals using the logics and language of those orders have a shared understanding of what symbols mean and how they can be applied to inform rational action (Searle 1995, 2009). Because meaning varies between institutional orders, the language within an institutional order has its own idiosyncratic semantic content (Thornton et al. 2012). Methodologically, by interpreting and thematizing institution-specific meanings, we can begin to understand how actors linguistically construct institutional facts, assign social functions, and confer rights and obligations on individuals. In other words, we can understand how individuals are discursively positioned (Harré and Lagenhove 1999) within institutional logics, how actors accept or resist that discursive positioning, and what may be constructed as factual and by whom (Edelman 1977).

This suggests a framework for CPA that can be coarsely summarized as an investigation into the relationship between institutionally contingent language and micropolitical negotiations within schools. We are suggesting an approach extending the Institutional Logics Perspective to determine who has the power to define facts within a social situation, and how those facts are used to advance interests in policy enactments and practices (Thorius and Maxcy 2014). To illustrate the potential of such a framework, we turn to three ethnographic studies that highlight collective action by parents in historically marginalized communities. These parents attempt to engage school administrators in order to advance their own interests, which administrators see at odds with the schools' interests.

The first study is Nguyễn and Maxcy's (2010) investigation into how Vietnamese immigrant and refugee parents resist school officials' decision making processes at a Texas elementary school. The second is Larson's (1997) study of racial turmoil as Black parents protest policy enactments in a Midwestern suburban high school. The third is Fernández and Scribner's (2015) study of Latin@[1] parents' struggle for legitimate participation at a Midwestern elementary full-service community school. In each study, these distinctly different marginalized groups struggle to assert their rights vis-à-vis school administrators. Given the array of space, time, schools, and communities, these studies suggest an historic, durable, and institutionalized tension between parents and professionals regarding the rights to determine the terms of schooling.

Thus these studies were selected because they provide rich accounts of contested relationships between school administrators and parents, and because they suggest a consistent logic of school administration that recreates the marginalization parents in these cases are trying to resist. As we will discuss, this logic of school administration is an example of the professions as an institutional order. As an application of CPA, we show how the language of this particular institutional order positions historically marginalized students and parents in certain ways by (a) defining their status, (b) establishing their rights and obligations, and (c) determining school administrators' construction of social facts. These components (status, rights/obligations, social facts) are based on John Searle's (1995, 2009) social ontology, which is a linguistic theory of social institutions. As a further development and illustration of the framework, we will discuss components of the three cases using this Searlian theory and the language and concepts associated with that theory.

2 Illustration of the Framework

We now turn to three cases, discussed through the conceptual lens described above. Again, these ethnographies were selected because they provide rich descriptions of conflict between school administrators and historically marginalized parents. In all three cases parents are asserting collective interests, and in doing so find themselves at odds with the institutionalized logics and language of school administration. The discussion suggests an approach to CPA that highlights the importance of how

---

[1] We adopt Fernández and Scribner's use of the term "Latin@." This term rejects the Americanized "Latino," which privileges the masculine form of the Spanish word.

language informs institutional logics, including logics and rationales that make social facts and legitimate action possible (Bacharach and Mundell 1993; Searle 2009) in policy formation and enactment.

2.1 Professional Logics: The Interplay of Status Functions, Constitutive Rules and Collective Intentionality

The *professions*, one of the institutional orders comprising society (Friedland and Alford 1991; Thornton et al. 2012), relies on the expertise defined by its membership to identify problems and control the work in their purviews (Abbott 1988). As a profession, school administration can be characterized by institutionalized values of efficiency, safety, control (order), and reliance on university training (Rury 2013; Tyack 1974; Tyack and Hansot 1982). In this section, we focus on the concept of professional logics and associated status functions and constitutive rules that shape collective action. To illustrate these, we draw on a case in which a school district, parents, and community members discussed the future of a Vietnamese Language and Culture Program (VLCP), housed at Pecan Springs Elementary School. In this case, professional values seemed to shape school officials' practice, based both on the belief that a community meeting must be tightly controlled to facilitate information dissemination and also on narrow definitions of leadership (Nguyễn and Maxcy 2010).

The VLCP was established in 1983 to support Vietnamese refugee children (Nguyễn and Maxcy 2010). The program, which had grown from a handful of students to more than 200, provided a variety of linguistic, social, and cultural supports for students and the broader community. At the time of the study, between 2004 and 2006, the school faced increasing pressures from state accountability policies and also from enrollments which put the school well over capacity. The principal, concerned about the enrollment of students outside the attendance zone—including large numbers of Vietnamese students transferring because of the VLCP—enacted a new practice of exiting students from bilingual services after they passed the language proficiency standards *without consulting parents*. As the parents argued, and the administrators eventually conceded, the failure to inform parents in their native language and the failure to actively secure parent approval for exiting students were breeches of the state's education code. For our purposes, the dynamics of the interactions between school and district officials and community members that followed illustrates the ways institutions condition the collective action of participants.

Status Functions Responding to parent concerns regarding this change and the implications for the VLCP and students and community it served, school district officials convened a meeting to discuss the future of the program. Vietnamese parents members assumed the meeting was to get their input on servicing English Language Learners (Nguyễn and Maxcy 2010). However, it became clear that the district officials viewed the meeting differently. For district officials, the meeting appeared to function to inform parents about decisions that had already been made.

The school officials' professional logic was evidenced in the ways in which they tried to control the meeting. For instance, school officials deflected Vietnamese community members' attempts to participate through

> (a) deflection and relocation of accountability at lower and higher levels (campus and state); (b) drawing clear delineations of who may and may not participate; (c) defining the issue (what is and is not on the table); (d) appeals to civility; and (e) appeals to expertise (Nguyễn and Maxcy 2010, p. 197).

Indeed, these tactics were evident from the meeting's onset, in which the principal explained "the purpose of the meeting and the process by which it would proceed... [and] the agenda, ground rules, and timeframe for the meeting" (p. 197).

Suggestive of the latter, one particular community activist played a key role in the meeting dynamics. During the meeting, the organizer frequently challenged school officials on the exclusionary processes by which decisions were reached. At one point, a school official put the community advocate "in her place":

> First of all, I want to say thank you because you're not from [the school district], but you're here and I appreciate that. And I'm really interested to hear what kind of Vietnamese program [your school] has. So I'd love to talk to you (Nguyễn and Maxcy 2010, p. 198).

Through this exchange school officials discursively positioned the community organizer as an outsider (Nguyễn and Maxcy 2010). This "outsider" status is not insignificant, particularly within a school administrator's professional logic. The application of outsider status is what Searle (2009) would call a *status function*. A status function is a shared recognition of a person's or object's status, and how that status allows that person or object to function in social situations. By explicitly relegating the community organizer to outsider status, the administrator signaled his status to the other school officials. From the officials' professional logic, this was significant, as it messaged that they need only concern themselves with their own constituency and that outsiders, while "welcomed," had no real standing in the proceedings.

School officials frequently reframed the meeting and defined it in their own terms (Nguyễn and Maxcy 2010). "As the meeting proceeded, it was clear that school and district officials presumed the process of placing and exiting students for bilingual education was not up for discussion" (p. 196). This was clear because (a) the principal established the rules by which the meeting would be conducted (p. 195); (b) school officials "were interested in redirecting conversation toward the objectives they'd brought to the meeting" (p. 197); and (c) conversations were "again reframed along what is within and without bounds" (p. 198).

Constitutive Rules One way to interpret school officials' actions within their professional logic is to consider the *constitutive rules* making such a meeting possible. Constitutive rules set parameters within which a social interaction is made defineable and understandable, thus making a social phenomenon possible (Searle 2009). In this case, a network of status functions (e.g., school official as meeting convener, non-constituent as outsider) defined whether or not this event counted as a meeting. It is clear that from school officials' perspective, a meeting with the Vietnamese community was one which follows the pre-determined meeting agenda (Nguyễn and Maxcy 2010, p. 195), follows their definition of good public conduct and civility (p. 198), and solicits input only from constituents. Anything else would not be a legitimate meeting, would threaten how school officials are discursively and materially positioned by their professional logic and state law (p. 198), and threaten the expertise professions confer upon themselves and zealously protect (Abbott 1988). As we take up next, status and constitutive rules condition the collective efforts of the groups involved, broadly, school officials and members of the Vietnamese community.

Collective Intentionality Searle's social ontology depends upon a concept called *collective intentionality* (2009). Collective intentionality is a shared recognition of status function; status functions are dependent upon collective imposition and recognition of a status. This shared recognition is like a social heuristic that eases the burden of constantly negotiating the status functions of objects. While it is not necessary for an actor and her interlocutor to agree on, or for the interlocutor to approve of the status function, it is necessary that there is shared recognition. For example, the community organizer could only be effectively given the "outsider" status if other school officials shared the same intentionality toward both outsider status and the organizer. The status was implied in the bilingual education director's language ("because you're not from [this school district]"), and she assumed this sent the appropriate signal that, by the constitutive rules of a community meeting, the outsider did not belong.

Yet, collective intentionality is contingent upon the inhabitants of a social institution. Time and time again Vietnamese parents made clear they did not share the same intentions as school administrators (Nguyễn and Maxcy 2010). Vietnamese parents members were "eager to know more about what seemed an ambiguous and exclusionary process" (p. 196), raising questions of power dynamics and exclusionary practices (p. 197). It is clear that the conflict in this situation was taking place at the level of meaning. School officials assumed a network of status functions and constitutive rules; community members were actively resisting school officials' use of institutionally contingent, linguistically constituted status functions. To them, this simply was not a community meeting, at least not a meeting as they understood it. In the following section, we further take up the role that language and power play in conditioning conflict and collective action within institutions.

2.2 *Professional Language: Deontic Power and Establishing Institutional Facts*

Turning to the interplay of language and institutions, we discuss Colleen Larson's (1997) study of school-community conflict, "Is the Land of Oz an Alien Nation?"

In this study, Larson examined the fallout of a Black student protest at Jefferson Heights High School (JHHS) during an integrated high school talent show. Black students tore through a paper American flag, wadded up the pieces and threw them to the audience, and waved an African National Congress flag, greatly upsetting White students and parents in the audience. The principal and assistant principals were left to deal with the aftermath. Their responses were bureaucratic, which tended to exacerbate the unrest and catalyzed Black parent and community protests. Again, a complete analysis of Larson's study is not appropriate here, but we do want to point out ways in which a lens of linguistically constructed institutional logics may add depth and nuance to the discussion.

Deontic Power At JHHS, Black students and parents members articulated ways in which they did not have the same schooling experience as White students within the same school (Larson 1997). This difference could be explained by the status function the White community placed on phenotype and appearance. The declaration of "Blackness" applies a status function to members of the school community, which results in prohibitions on where some students, parents/caregivers, and teachers can go and what they can do. The rights, obligations, permissions, and prohibitions associated with status functions are called *deontic power* (Searle 2009).

To see how deontic power operates, consider this quotation from Larson's study:

> We have hired only three Black teachers at this high school. Twenty-three percent of this student body is Black. But the Black teachers who apply for jobs here are never quite good enough to be hired by the administrators. It seems they got to be superstars and look a certain way. But *you* know, and *I* know that all those White teachers ain't superstars—they don't look so good, and they get hired. I'd just like Black teachers to have the right to be average too (Larson 1997, pp. 332–333 emphasis in the original).

From this Black parent's perspective, Black and White teachers had different rights and responsibilities (deontic powers) based on the status function associated with phenotype. White teachers had the right to be hired, the right to be average or fallible, and the right to not be a "superstar." Black teachers had an obligation to be "superstars" in order to be considered for the right to be hired. This example also highlights ways in which meaning, language, logics, and social institutions are racially biased.

Early in the protests, members of the Jefferson Heights Black community tried to operate within the dominant administrative logic in order to affect change. As members of the school community, they were assigned status that granted certain rights (deontic powers). They had to right to air grievances to principals, the superintendent, and school board members. Larson explained that Black parents and community leaders attempted to work within the system (the dominant logic). However, the administrators assigned themselves status as protectors of order, and they thus had the right (deontic power) to maintain order in the school. This right was made material through policy. Within their logic, the Black students violated policy at the talent show and disrupted order and safety, and thus they deemed themselves to have responded legitimately. Administrators dismissed Black community complaints on the grounds of that logic, and they did not or could not acknowledge the underlying complaint of racial disparities. Thus Black parents acting within the system structured by a racialized administrative logic were neutralized by that very system.

Yet status functions are not static. Status functions and their associated deontic powers can shift as actors make meaning in social situations and interactions. At JHHS, Black parents and other community members were dismissed with an administrative logic that gave them the right to individually air grievances, but did not give them the right to bring about change. Larson (1997) showed how parents were viewed differently when they organized a sit-in, an action purposely designed to disrupt the dominant logic.

Drawing on Edelman's (1977) theory of political language, Larson explained that school administrators "typically view individual or group resistance to system policies and practices as inappropriate and potentially dangerous" (p. 335). Once resistance to an organization's dominant logic emerges, those in positions of power assign new meaning to resisting actors. JHHS administrators no longer viewed Black parents as participants within the system that could be dispatched through neutral application of policy; the parents were now adversaries. This new status introduced a new set of meanings (status functions and deontic powers) into the situation.

It should also be noted the Black community was asserting its own agency, claiming its own status function, and thus claiming its own deontic powers through acts of resistance. Drawing on a completely different institutional logic, one that might be described as a community logic (Thornton et al. 2012), they were asserting their rights to full membership of the school community. And to them, full membership meant visibility, legitimate consideration of their claims, and the right to not be dismissed by technocratic application of policy.

However, school administrators responded to this assertion by discursively positioning members of the Black community as outsiders and adversaries. These administrators did not have a language to allow them to accommodate the Black communities' needs or even understand what the problem was (Larson 1997). Like in the case of the VLCP in Pecan Springs, a marginalized community asserting its rights resulted in further attempts to control and exclude that community. Once members of the Black community called administrators' language and logic into question, the socially constructed facts of the situation changed. The construction of facts within an institutional logic is discussed below.

Institutional Facts On the topic of social facts, Larson (1997) cited Edelman (1977) when she wrote "the 'facts' in any conflict rest on the presuppositions of those defining them" (p. 331). We suggest that Searle's (2009) social ontology can draw attention to institutionally contingent linguistic mechanisms defining facts and shaping presuppositions.

White school officials viewed the Black student protests with an "impersonal, neutral, and bureaucratic" logic indicative of their profession (Larson 1997, p. 323). These administrators seemed to be operating under a different set of facts than the Black protesters, who complained administrators were unwilling or unable to see the situation from the Black protesters' perspective. We might understand these facts within an institutional order as *institutional facts*.

Institutional facts exist when a set of constitutive rules are satisfied (Searle 2009). Searle's formulation is "We make it the case by declaration that for any x that satisfies condition p, x has the status Y and performs the function F in context C" (p. 99). In other words, within the logic of an institution, such as school administration, any time a set of conditions is satisfied by a person or object, facts begin to emerge. Thus it is an institutional fact that students who disrupt a talent show with political speech are rule-breakers, and as rule-breakers they are subject to a corpus of prescribed sanctions (suspension, expulsion, etc.). Indeed, knowing that they likely could not sanction students based on their political speech, the JHHS school administrators took this technical, "rule-breaker" approach (Larson 1997).

Acceptance of an institutional structure precludes the necessity of accepting institutional facts (Searle 2009). If one accepts the logic of school administration, particularly the espoused color-blind logic at JHHS (Larson 1997), then conflict is merely epistemic (Searle 2009). Did students break the rules, or not? Note, however, that social facts are contingent upon the institutional logics and cultures which define them (Bates 1987; Thornton et al. 2012).

Identifying a clash of institutional facts from opposing institutional logics can be a productive way of understanding micropolitical conflict. Larson (1997) cited Perrow (1970), who claimed that during conflict, facts are reconstructed intentionally by actors omitting or overemphasizing details. This may be true, but we also want to point out ways in which language can shape facts, and how "facts" can shift when a situation is experienced and interpreted from different institutional logics. Furthermore, positioning people in relation to each other and the capacity to exert power is implicit in the construction of institutional facts, and the construction of resulting obligations and authority (deontic powers) to act.

Prior to busing and forced integration, it seems as though much of the Jefferson Heights community accepted the institutional structure created from the logic of school administration. It wasn't until the Black community began to openly question facts as the school administrators created them that the dominant institutional structure, complete with its language and logics, was made explicit.

For example, Larson (1997) uncovered the dominant collective application of status and obligations yielding institutional facts about what it meant to be Black at JHHS. During a "Speak Out" in which school administrators allowed a public airing of racial grievances by Black and White communities, the Black community claimed that the school's discipline system was responding to a fear of Black students, particularly Black males. In this (and other) White-dominated schools, it became an institutional "fact" that Black males are dangerous and should be feared. Thus, when enough Black males (objects) congregated in one place (condition) at JHHS (context), they became dangerous (status function) and were obligated to break up into smaller groups (deontic power). It wasn't until this logic was disrupted by protests and the Speak Out that school administrators began to see and be able to talk about the racial disparities and othering the Black community was experiencing.

2.3 Professional Organization: Defining Organizational Legitimacy

In our final illustration, we turn to Fernández and Scribner's (2015) study of a Latin@ parent organization at Martin Elementary, a Midwestern elementary school. This parent organization, named *Adelantando Familias en la Comunidad*/Advancing Families in the Community (AFC) was organized for the purpose of supporting immigrant parents with three specific aims: to learn about the educational system so that they could advocate and support their children, to access community resources to support families, and to network and access information and resources to address anti-immigrant policies. While the parents' presence signified parent involvement by virtue of their regular attendance to school activities and visibility within the school, the principal dismissed the parents' espoused aims (networking related to immigration advocacy, in particular) as a legitimate enactment of parent engagement with the school.

Organizational Legitimacy Fernández and Scribner's study allows us to more explicitly connect the linguistic foundations of social institutions to institutional theory. One of the central concepts of institutional theory is legitimacy. Organizations work toward legitimacy, toward winning legitimacy from the social environments in which they are embedded (Meyer and Rowan 1977). Winning legitimacy is key to organizational survival; thus survival is a driving force for decision- and policy-making (DiMaggio and Powell 1983; Scott 2008).

Martin Elementary School's legitimacy as an effective school was threatened. In 2010, it was deemed a "turnaround school" for failing to meet state accountability requirements. In 2014, the school received an "F" letter grade from the state, down from a "C" the previous year (Fernández and Scribner 2015). The turnaround status led to a great deal of turnover from year to year in the principalship and in teacher positions, another indicator that the school's legitimacy was threatened.

From school administrators' professional logic, the AFC had the status function of a social group of parents who volunteered in the school, and "viewing the AFC as 'just' a social group benefitted the school" (Fernández and Scribner 2015, p. 29). In fact, the AFC met regularly to organize mothers around serious issues that their families faced: anti-immigration policies and practices, their children's welfare in schools; domestic violence; healthcare; employment exploitation, etc. Because parental involvement is an accountability requirement, school officials used the existence of the AFC as evidence of parental involvement. This status function led to school officials assigning deontic powers to the AFC that limited the access these parents had to policy-making and removed the school officials' obligations to take the AFC seriously as an advocacy organization. Thus the school gained legitimacy from having the AFC members present and accounted for in the school building, but they decoupled their advocacy work from their symbolic use as evidence of a "welcoming" school.

However, the AFC benefited from not being legitimized as a formally recognized parent group (Fernández and Scribner 2015). "On the one hand, a lack of formal recognition from school administrators and staff means that there were fewer formal controls over the group's agenda" (Fernández and Scribner 2015, p. 22). Again, professional logics of school administration lead administrators toward attempts to control the school's internal activities for the sake of order and predictability (Larson and Ovando 2001). Had the AFC been formally recognized as a legitimate parent group, that status function would have then conferred the right (deontic power) to control the AFC's agenda, operations, and position within the school organization. Instead, the AFC enjoyed a great deal of autonomy and "had the freedom to discuss and organize around issues that extended far beyond schooling and academic issues" (Fernández and Scribner 2015, p. 22).

3 Synthesis and Implications

Viewed through a framework of institutional logics, we can see how historically marginalized communities assert themselves in spaces dominated by professional logics and language of school administration. Broadly speaking, actors in the three cases demonstrated attempts to negotiate policy. One way of doing this was to get at the linguistic foundations of administrators' logic. The Vietnamese community (Nguyễn and Maxcy 2010) contested the meaning of the meeting in order to resist decisions deemed settled by administrators; the Black community (Larson 1997) raised consciousness of their lack of access to schooling their White peers enjoyed; and the Latin@ community (Fernández and Scribner 2015) claimed legitimacy as a parent organization whose advocacy raised issues administrators interpreted beyond the scope of schooling. In each case, community members resisted marginalization and asserted their collective agency. Within these negotiations, school officials relied on their own professional logics, in which expertise and positional authority was a source of legitimacy in the policymaking arena (Thornton et al. 2012).

Institutional theories are often decried for a lack of attention to agency (Thornton et al. 2012). The framework we propose here does account for individual agency, though agency is clearly conditioned in particular ways by social institutions. Institutions therefore provide individuals both opportunities and constraints (Friedland and Alford 1991; Thornton et al. 2012). The framework helps to surface the manner in which opportunities and constraints are linguistically constituted and contingent upon a broadly shared network of status functions, deontic powers, constitutive rules, and institutional facts (Searle 2009). In the illustrations above, community members' attempts to claim agency were mediated through an administrative professional logic—one shaped in and shaping of a racialized bureaucracy (Larson and Ovando 2001). In each instance, members of historically marginalized groups seeking to advance their interests were positioned as aggressors (status function) who have no right to disrupt (deontic power) administrators' professional work. What these communities saw as legitimate and socially just actions in a democratic space were recast by school officials as intrusive attempts to undermine administrative authority (institutional fact).

Moreover, the institutional context in which these negotiations were operating afforded school officials certain opportunities to frame these situations in ways advantageous to them. When presented with a situation interpreted as instability, disruption, or chaos (institutional fact), school officials tended to fall back on a professional logic that authorized them to respond according to the bureaucratic rules of their organizations and field (Bacharach and Mundell 1993; Larson 1997). Thus, administrators at Jefferson Heights High School, Pecan Springs, and Martin Elementary objectified and assigned statuses with historically marginalized communities, and characterized the situations as warranting managerial rather than deliberative responses (Grint 2005). These school officials positioned these interactions as problems to solve, rather than opportunities to ask questions and meaningfully engage these communities. At the same time, these communities also strategically took insider and outsider positions relative to administrators' institutional logics to advance their interests.

3.1 *Implications for Educational Leadership*

It is important to remember that collective intentionality does not require agreement or consent; it simply requires enough recognition of status that others can understand the intended meaning. This mutually-understood intended meaning is based on a network of more or less backgrounded claims about the world that a speaker assumes others will consider valid (Habermas 1984, 1987).

The claims about the world an actor makes come from somewhere. For others to understand the speaker, those others must have a shared repertoire of meanings and understandings. Therefore, an actor's intentions cannot come solely from within the actor; the actor must draw from the shared institutional environment into which s/he is born (Carspecken 2003; Foster 1980; Habermas 1984, 1987). The institutional logics framework highlights the ways speakers draw from the interinstitutional system, which operates at the individual, organization, organizational field, and societal levels (Thornton et al. 2012). Each institutional order has its own "vocabulary of practice," which is a "common and distinct language" (Thornton et al. 2012, p. 94).

Applying institutional facts from logics institutionalized in the school administration profession would not necessarily sensitize administrators in these three studies—or in the profession more broadly—to the particular daily experiences and meanings of the range of students, parents, and teachers in their schools. As Larson (1997) and Larson and Ovando (2001) argued, the logics of action guiding school administrators are too often couched in a depoliticized language that masks the racial and cultural biases that inform and infect their logics. This may be exacerbated for those from dominant groups who may not have even realized that they, themselves, are racialized (Kendall 2006; Leonardo 2002). Even as our communities and schools become more diverse, school leaders are prepared under standards that do not even acknowledge that students of color exist (Davis et al. 2015) and shy away from explicit use of race vocabulary (Carpenter and Diem 2014).

Indeed, the legal system endorses this color-blind and homogenizing perspective (Parker and Villalpando 2007), with Chief Justice John Roberts claiming, "the way to stop discrimination on the basis of race is to stop discriminating on the basis of race" (*Parents Involved in Community Schools v. Seattle School District No. 1, et al.*, 2007, p. 40–41). Chief Justice Roberts's view seems to align well with the principals in Larson's study, one of whom said, "You have to treat all kids the same. White, Black, Red, Purple. You can't have different rules for different kids" (p. 324). Espoused neutrality had a homogenizing effect on the AFC in that they could only count as a legitimate parent organization if it operated in the same way all other parent organizations did (Fernández and Scribner 2015). A constitutive rule (Searle 2009) of that sort neglects the parents' interests and privileged the school's interests.

The proposed framework helps surface the subtle ways colorblindness and neutrality are laden with status functions linguistically assigned to different students based on race, ethnicity, linguistic status, and legal status. Declaring that policies apply to and serve all may be rhetorically appealing, but appears not to be enacted in practice. As a tool in "policy archeology" (Scheurich 1997), the framework helps to unearth aspects of an institutional order that actively ignore race and racism in schools by venerating colorblindness and neutrality. By surfacing the linguistic determinants of that order, the framework reveals the play and persistence of professional logics that continue the historic underserving of students of color— and suggest leverage points to reform these in leadership preparation and in practice.

3.2 Implications for Critical Policy Analysis

The framework suggested here aligns with the interpretivist, communicative turn in policy analysis suggested by Fischer and his colleagues (see Fischer 2003; Fischer and Forester 1993b; Fischer and Gottweis 2012b). Through the analysis of language that structures institutional orders and their logics (Bacharach and Mundell 1993; Searle 2009), we can see not only how power operates in and through institutional talk, but also ways in which agents attempt to resist being positioned by powerful institutional actors (Larson and Ovando 2001; Thornton et al. 2012). Furthermore, we can begin to reconstruct meanings and the taken-for-grantedness of language and claims to truth embedded in institutional talk. Thus our argument is methodological as well as epistemological.

We have also suggested an alternative to technical-rational, postpositivist analysis of policy formation, implementation, and outcomes (Diem et al. 2014; Fischer 2003). Given the ways institutions condition the political contestation of policy by differently positioned groups, outcomes are not wholly predictable and analysis must attend to the political dynamics of policy enactments in real settings. Because meanings always have the potential to be negotiated (Habermas 1984, 1987), we must avoid the presumption that institutions are static or that outcomes are determined.

When this framework is used to interpret the cases above, we see that marginalized groups retain agency in policy enactment, and that agency is conditioned in ways that may limit influence and create opportunities for political gains. In the case of the Pecan Springs, the Vietnamese community did force school officials to acknowledge the school's interpretation of law was incorrect (Nguyễn and Maxcy 2010), in the process realizing and revealing their collective ability to press community interests. In Jefferson Heights, school officials eventually listened to the Black community, heard some accusations and personal stories that were difficult to hear, and eventually "learned some things that we did not know. And we made some changes that needed to be made" (Larson 1997, p. 341). Contests over meaning, perhaps with continued pressure or more organized collective action, can create opportunities for the exercise of strategic agency and power (Thornton et al. 2012).

As a final observation, the transformative possibilities of critical policy analysis cannot be fully realized if these tools are used only to critique. The framework we described here does provide means of critique, but it also provides means of identifying and validating agency. Neither institutions nor organizations are static; they are dynamic, unpredictable, and full of contradictions. These contradictions create space for strategic agency and institutional and organizational change (Thornton et al. 2012). Those hoping to create change in schools can familiarize themselves with the professional logics and language of school administration. The administrators' own logics and language can then be leveraged for change as change agents seek and exploit contradictions inherent in these negotiated spaces. These change agents need not be outsiders; they could be equity-minded educators or faculty in equity-focused preparation programs. Additionally, negotiation and change need not be zero-sum, as schools and the communities they serve can both benefit from changes in the institutional logics structuring school organizations and schooling practices.

References

Abbott, A. D. (1988). *The system of professions: An essay on the division of expert labor.* Chicago: University of Chicago Press.

Bacharach, S. B., & Mundell, B. L. (1993). Organizational politics in schools: Micro, macro, and logics of action. *Educational Administration Quarterly, 29*(4), 423–452. http://doi.org/10.1177/0013161X93029004003.

Ball, S. J., Maguire, M., & Braun, A. (2012). *How schools do policy: Policy enactments in secondary schools.* Abingdon/New York: Routledge.

Bates, R. J. (1987). Corporate culture, schooling, and educational administration. *Educational Administration Quarterly, 23*(4), 79–115. http://doi.org/10.1177/0013161X87023004007.

Bidwell, C. E. (1965). The school as a formal organization. In J. G. March (Ed.), *Handbook of organizations* (pp. 972–1022). Chicago: Rand McNally & Company.

Carpenter, B. W., & Diem, S. (2014). Guidance matters: A critical discourse analysis of the race-related policy vocabularies shaping leadership preparation. *Urban Education.* http://doi.org/10.1177/0042085914528719

Carspecken, P. F. (2003). Ocularcentrism, phonocentrism and the counter Enlightenment problematic: Clarifying contested terrain in our schools of education. *Teachers College Record, 105*(6), 978–1047.

Czarniawska, B. (2008). *A theory of organizing*. Cheltenham: Edward Elgar.

Davis, B. W., Gooden, M. A., & Micheaux, D. J. (2015). Color-blind leadership: A critical race theory analysis of the ISLLC and ELCC standards. *Educational Administration Quarterly, 51*(3), 335–371. http://doi.org/10.1177/0013161X15587092.

Diem, S., Young, M. D., Welton, A. D., Mansfield, K. C., & Lee, P.-L. (2014). The intellectual landscape of critical policy analysis. *International Journal of Qualitative Studies in Education, 27*(9), 1068–1090. http://doi.org/10.1080/09518398.2014.916007.

DiMaggio, P. J., & Powell, W. W. (1983). The iron cage revisited: Institutional isomorphism and collective rationality in organizational fields. *American Sociological Review, 48*(2), 147–160. http://doi.org/10.2307/2095101.

Edelman, M. J. (1977). *Political language: Words that succeed and policies that fail*. New York: Academic.

Fernández, E., & Scribner, S. M. P. (2015). Micro-politics of parent engagement in an urban community school: Examining the intersection of school reform, anti-immigration policies, and Latin@ parent organizing. In *Annual meeting of the American Educational Research Association*, Chicago.

Fischer, F. (2003). *Reframing public policy: Discursive politics and deliberative practices*. Oxford: Oxford University Press.

Fischer, F., & Forester, J. (1993a). Editors' introduction. In F. Fischer & J. Forester (Eds.), *The Argumentative turn in policy analysis and planning* (pp. 1–17). Durham: Duke University Press.

Fischer, F., & Forester, J. (Eds.). (1993b). *The argumentative turn in policy analysis and planning*. Durham: Duke University Press.

Fischer, F., & Gottweis, H. (2012a). Introduction. In F. Fischer & H. Gottweis (Eds.), *The argumentative turn revisited: Public policy as communicative practice* (pp. 1–27). Durham: Duke University Press.

Fischer, F., & Gottweis, H. (Eds.). (2012b). *The argumentative turn revisited: Public policy as communicative practice*. Durham: Duke University Press.

Foster, W. P. (1980). Administration and the crisis in legitimacy: A review of Habermasian thought. *Harvard Educational Review, 50*(4), 496–505.

Friedland, R., & Alford, R. L. (1991). Bringing society back in: Symbols, practices, and institutional contradictions. In W. W. Powell & P. J. DiMaggio (Eds.), *The new institutionalism in organizational analysis* (pp. 232–263). Chicago: University of Chicago Press.

Grint, K. (2005). Problems, problems, problems: The social construction of "leadership". *Human Relations, 58*(11), 1467–1494. http://doi.org/10.1177/0018726705061314.

Habermas, J. (1984). *The theory of communicative action: Reason and the rationalization of society* (T. McCarthy, Trans.) (Vol. 1). Boston: Beacon Press.

Habermas, J. (1987). *The theory of communicative action: Lifeworld and system a critique of functionalist reason* (T. McCarthy, Trans.) (Vol. 2). Boston: Beacon Press.

Habermas, J. (1988). *On the logic of the social sciences* (S. W. Nicholson & J. A. Stark, Trans.). Cambridge, MA: The MIT Press.

Harré, R., & van Lagenhove, L. (Eds.). (1999). *Positioning theory: Moral contexts of intentional action*. Malden: Blackwell.

Kendall, F. E. (2006). *Understanding white privilege: Creating pathways to authentic relationships across race*. New York: Routledge.

Larson, C. L. (1997). Is the land of Oz an alien nation? A sociopolitical study of school community conflict. *Educational Administration Quarterly, 33*(3), 312–350. http://doi.org/10.1177/0013161X97033003004.

Larson, C. L., & Ovando, C. J. (2001). *The color of bureaucracy: The politics of equity in mulicultural school communities*. Belmont: Wadsworth.

Leonardo, Z. (2002). The souls of white folk: Critical pedagogy, whiteness studies, and globalization discourse. *Race Ethnicity and Education, 5*(1), 29–50. http://doi.org/10.1080/13613320120117180.

Levinson, B. A. U., & Sutton, M. (2001). Introduction: Policy as/in practice – A sociocultural approach to the study of educational policy. In M. Sutton & B. A. U. Levinson (Eds.), *Policy as practice: Toward a comparative sociocultural analysis of educational policy* (pp. 1–22). Westport: Alex.

Levinson, B. A. U., Sutton, M., & Winstead, T. (2009). Education policy as a practice of power: Theoretical tools, ethnographic methods, democratic options. *Educational Policy, 23*(6), 767–795. http://doi.org/10.1177/0895904808320676.

Meyer, J. W., & Rowan, B. (1977). Institutionalized organizations: Formal structure as myth and ceremony. *American Journal of Sociology, 83*(2), 340–363.

Nguyễn, T. S. T., & Maxcy, B. D. (2010). Revisiting distributed leadership: Examining the risks of leaderhip for and from a Vietnamese diasporic community. *International Journal of Urban Educational Leadership, 4*(1), 187–205.

Parker, L., & Villalpando, O. (2007). A race(cialized) perspective on education leadership: Critical race theory in educational administration. *Educational Administration Quarterly, 43*(5), 519–524. http://doi.org/10.1177/0013161X07307795.

Perrow, C. (1970). *Organizational analyses: A sociological view*. Belmont: Wadsworth.

Rury, J. L. (2013). *Education and social change: Contours in the history of american schooling* (4th ed.). New York: Routledge.

Scheurich, J. J. (1997). *Research method in the postmodern*. Washington, DC: Falmer Press.

Scott, W. R. (2008). *Institutions and organizations: Ideas and interests* (3rd ed.). Thousand Oaks: Sage.

Searle, J. R. (1995). *The construction of social reality*. New York: Free Press.

Searle, J. R. (2009). *Making the social world: The structure of human civilization*. Oxford: Oxford University Press.

Thorius, K. A. K., & Maxcy, B. D. (2014). Critical practice analysis of special education policy: An RTI example. *Remedial and Special Education*, 0741932514550812. http://doi.org/10.1177/0741932514550812

Thornton, P. H., Ocasio, W., & Lounsbury, M. (2012). *The institutional logics perspective: A new approach to culture, structure, and process*. Oxford: Oxford University Press.

Tyack, D. B. (1974). *The one best system: A history of American urban education*. Cambridge, MA: Harvard University Press.

Tyack, D. B., & Hansot, E. (1982). *Managers of virtue: Public school leadership in America, 1820–1980*. New York: Basic Books.

Ontario's Fourth 'R': A Critical Democratic Analysis of Ontario's Fund-'R'aising Policy

Michelle Milani and Sue Winton

Abstract School fundraising, for the purpose of supporting school programs and resources, has become widespread within Ontario, Canada's elementary and secondary schools; however, there exists a paucity of research exploring its implications on public education and democracy. In this study, we conduct a critical democratic analysis of Ontario's school fundraising policy by examining the context of influence, texts, and practices within the policy cycle to determine the ways in which Ontario's fundraising policy either supports or subverts critical democratic values including equity, inclusion, participatory decision-making, and critical mindedness. The findings indicate that school fundraising undermines public education and democratic values that aim to support social justice and the common good. Specifically, school fundraising is resulting in great inequities among students and schools and the increased reliance on fundraising is undermining commitments to publicly funded education as a whole as it shifts the responsibility of funding education from the government to private citizens and constructs education as a private rather than a public good. Our findings demonstrate that in order to achieve critical democracy, the practice of fundraising to subsidize and enrich Ontario's schools must be eradicated.

Keywords School fundraising • Fundraising policy • Critical democracy • Critical policy analysis • Ontario

"Publicly funded education is a cornerstone of our democratic society" (Ontario Ministry of Education 2009, p. 6). These words spoken by Ontario's Ministry of Education are currently challenged by elementary and secondary school fundraising practices in Ontario, Canada. School fundraising takes place in nearly all of the province's publicly funded elementary and secondary schools, and many allege it is resulting in great inequities between schools and boards (Alphonso and Hammer 2014; Froese-Germain et al. 2006; People for Education 2013b). Schools in affluent neighbourhoods raise about $900 per student within an academic year, while

---

M. Milani (✉) • S. Winton
Faculty of Education, York University, Toronto, ON, Canada
e-mail: michelle_milani@edu.yorku.ca

schools in modest neighbourhoods may raise as little as $3 (Alphonso and Hammer 2014). Ontario's Ministry of Education defines school fundraising as "any activity, permitted under a school board's policy, to raise money or other resources, that is approved by the school principal, in consultation with, and upon the advice of the school council, and/or a school fundraising organization operating in the name of the school, and for which the school provides the administrative processes for collection" (Ontario Ministry of Education 2012, p. 2).

In this chapter we present findings from our critical analysis of Ontario, Canada's fundraising policy and highlight how fundraising in Ontario's public schools is undermining critical democracy in education. An analysis of Ontario's fundraising policy is necessary because fundraising in public schools, although a prevalent practice, has not been widely explored or examined in Ontario or beyond. Ontario's school fundraising policy is explored from a critical lens because unlike traditional approaches to policy analysis, critical policy analysis (CPA) acknowledges that policy is inherently political and complex, and it provides the opportunity to interrogate the policy process, social structures, and power dynamics within the policy field (Diem et al. 2014). Further, Ontario's Ministry of Education has introduced two guidelines that challenge notions of public education within a democratic society: the *Fees for Learning Materials and Activities Guideline* (2011) and the *Fundraising Guideline* (2012) – and a third guideline, a *Corporate Partnership Guideline*, is under development. The guidelines outline the government's expectations for school boards' fees and fundraising policies and practices. The very presence of the guidelines affirms the Ontario Ministry of Education's support and endorsement of private funds in public education.

The chapter begins with an introduction to the context of education in Ontario, Canada, before turning to a brief review of the scholarly literature on school fundraising in Canada and the USA. We then discuss our conception of policy and the critical democratic lens we use in our critical policy analysis as well as explain why this lens is appropriate for examining Ontario's fundraising policy. Next, we describe our methodological approach and turn to a discussion of our findings. We describe Ontario's fundraising policy in detail and examine its consequences for critical democracy. We close with suggestions for ways parents, educators, and other citizens can engage in fundraising policy to enhance, rather than undermine, democracy.

1 Education in Ontario, Canada

All children in Canada are promised an education "free of charge" (Government of Canada 2012, para. 1), and each province and territory in the country is responsible for providing education to its citizens. Ontario is Canada's largest province; it is home to one-third of the nation's population with about 13.6 million residents. The province has four publicly funded school systems: English Public (i.e., non-denominational), English Catholic, French Public, and French Catholic; there are a total of 72 school districts. Ninety-five percent of all Ontario students attend public schools (People for Education 2013b). There are more than 2 million elementary and secondary students in the four systems, with the vast majority consisting of elementary school students (approximately 1.3 million children). Schools are funded through a combination of municipal property taxes and provincial grants based on a funding formula introduced by the Progressive Conservative government led by Mike Harris (Gidney 1999). Prior to 1997, school boards, rather than the provincial government, determined how much money would be raised through municipal property taxes (Gidney 1999). This meant that school boards with richer tax bases were able to collect more funds than those with lower tax bases and as such the Harris government implemented the new funding formula claiming that it would ensure equitable funding throughout the province (People for Education 2007). As we discuss below, this change in school funding played an important role in fundraising policy across the province. Indeed, schools have increasingly relied on school-generated funds since the new funding approach was introduced (Pistiolis 2012). Ontario is not unique in this regard, however. We turn now to a brief review of what is known about fundraising in Canada and the USA.

2 Literature Review

The need for schools across the USA and Canada to raise private funds has increased over the past few decades as governments have reduced overall funding to schools and, at the same time, increasingly regulated where government funds are to be spent (Brent and Lunden 2009; Froese-Germain et al. 2006; Zimmer et al. 2003). In Ontario, math, science, and literacy (reading and writing), receive the greatest concentration of government funds (Pistiolis 2012). In addition to meeting basic educational requirements, schools aim to provide enriched programs to attract and retain students in individual schools and in publicly funded schools in general (Sattem 2007). As government and citizen expectations for more and improved educational services have risen, so too have costs for goods and services (Brent and Lunden 2009; Froese-Germain et al. 2006). Large scale testing programs adopted in the name of greater accountability during this period, which are time consuming and costly to administer, have exacerbated this situation (Pistiolis 2012).

Limited research focused on school fundraising exists in general (Brent and Lunden 2009) and even less examines fundraising in Ontario or Canada specifically. However, a few US and Canadian studies identify sources of private funding, different kinds of private funding mechanisms, the extent of private funding, and the goods and services purchased with private funds in public schools. Raising private funds is commonplace in public schools (Brent and Lunden 2009; Froese-Germain et al. 2006), and in Ontario there is no cap on the amount that can be raised. Sources of private funding include parents, not-for-profit organizations, businesses, alumni, colleges and universities, and, in the USA, philanthropic organizations (Miller 2012; Pistiolis 2012; Scott 2009; Zimmer et al. 2003). Mechanisms used by schools to attract private funds include product sales, corporate-sponsored educational materials, sale of services, incentive programs, personal contacts and relationships, special events, exclusive marketing agreements with corporations, grant applications, mail solicitations, selling advertising space, and school-business partnerships (Brent and Lunden 2009; Froese-Germain et al. 2006; Zimmer et al. 2003).

Goods and services purchased with private funds in Canadian schools include athletic and academic programs, school supplies, transportation, field trips, clubs, books, technology, musical instruments, schoolyard revitalizations, sports equipment, guest speakers, professional performers, and extracurricular activities (Froese-Germain et al. 2006; Pistiolis 2012). In California, this list also includes non-teacher staff salaries, professional development, instructional materials, building enhancements, furniture, school beautification, and health services (Zimmer et al. 2003). Money raised may also be used to free up funds in school budgets that can be used to purchase items that cannot be obtained using private dollars, such as textbooks (Pistiolis 2012).

A few studies examine how fundraising specifically varies by the socioeconomic status of school neighbourhoods. For example, Zimmer et al.'s (2003) study of ten California schools found that parents provided monetary support in both affluent and poor neighbourhoods and that schools in poorer neighbourhoods had more options for private support than did schools in affluent areas (especially from corporations, community-based organizations, and philanthropic foundations). However, affluent schools had a greater level of monetary support from parents and could more readily depend on funds from this source whereas schools in poor neighbourhoods depended more heavily on dynamic principals to attract private support from sources other than parents (Zimmer et al. 2003). An investigation by journalists, Patty Winsa and Kristin Rushowy, at the *Toronto Star*, one of Canada's largest newspapers, reported that in the "Toronto public board alone, the top 20 money generating schools, primarily in wealthy neighbourhoods, collected a total of $4.4 million compared to just $103,000 for the bottom 20 schools, most in needy areas" (2011, para. 3). In another study, principals in eight Ontario schools report that the socioeconomic status of the school's neighbourhood affects its ability to raise funds (Pistiolis 2012). Other factors that influence how much money schools can raise through fundraising include school size, the social status of parents on school councils, the level of education of parents at the school, corporate partnerships, and fundraising strategies implemented by principals and teachers (Disparity in school fundraising 2012; People for Education 2012; Pistiolis 2012; Posey-Maddox 2013).

Fundraising is not only a financial challenge for low-income families, however; many middle-class families have a difficult time keeping up with the extra costs as well (Rushowy et al. 2011). Families within wealthier neighbourhoods are expected to contribute even more private dollars to support schools, perhaps because it is assumed that they can afford to do so (Alphonso and Hammer 2014). Indeed, the pressure to fundraise is widespread and experienced by families in all communities.

A number of concerns have been raised about school fundraising. One of the most frequent charges is that it produces inequities between schools because schools in different neighbourhoods are able to raise different amounts of money due to differences in families' socioeconomic status (Zimmer et al. 2003). In response to these concerns, some contend that these differences are addressed through federal and/or state/provincial grants designated for schools in low income neighbourhoods (Sattem 2007) or that the amounts raised are negligible. Data from Ontario's Toronto District School Board (TDSB) shows, however, that these grants do not make up for funds raised by schools in affluent communities; rather, their "equalizing effects ... are wiped out by private funding" (Inner City Advisory Committee [ICAC], 2012, slide 27). Further, only a small proportion of provincial funds designated to improve the academic achievement of low income students in the TDSB are spent as intended. In the USA, funds from federal grants can only be spent on academic programs in reading and math (Sattem 2007), whereas money raised through fundraising in affluent schools may be spent on a range of programs and individuals to enhance students' education and be used to improve school facilities (Disparity in school fundraising 2012; People for Education 2013b).

The practice of school fundraising has also been criticized for the way that it increases competition among students and between schools (Froese-Germain et al. 2006). Some schools use incentives to encourage greater fundraising participation among students and those who collect the highest sums are awarded prizes, such as bikes, helmets, movie tickets, and the likes (Disparity in school fundraising 2012; Pistiolis 2012). This practice encourages competition between students and increases the pressure to fundraise (Disparity in school fundraising 2012; Pistiolis 2012). In addition, when schools seek private funds to support education programs and resources, they may have to compete with one another as they pursue the same sources for monetary support (Froese-Germain et al. 2006). Competition between schools also arises from parents' desire to send their children to better resourced-schools. Competition between students and schools promotes the interests of individuals and "individual responsibility" rather than fostering concern for all citizens and a sense of collective responsibility for the well-being of all communities. Further, there are concerns about the amount of time and energy fundraising takes – time that might otherwise be spent on learning activities when fundraising is organized by school staff and by students (Pistiolis 2012).

Despite criticisms, many parents support fundraising since they "want their children to have the best educational experience possible" (CTV investigates 2013, part 3, para. 11). Some argue parents should be able to support their kids' schools if they wish (CTV investigates 2013). This idea, however, helps to recast education as a private rather than a public good. Annie Kidder, Executive Director of People for Education, explains that it is "hard to resist [fundraising] as a parent, but it really undermines the overall ideal of public education" (Winsa and Rushowy 2011, para. 7). Furthermore, while it has been suggested that parents pool together all or part of funds collected, parents have spoken against this suggestion either because it sends the message that school officials have accepted the need for private support or because they believe that they should not have to share hard-earned fundraised dollars (Alphonso and Hammer 2014; Disparity in school fundraising 2012).

3 Policy Analysis for Democracy

Policy is a complex and multifaceted concept that is understood and defined in various ways and therefore, offering one single, "fixed" definition of policy is an unfeasible endeavor (Ozga 2000, p. 2). Policy researchers have traditionally regarded policy as a rational, "linear process from formation through implementation" (Monkman and Hoffman 2013, p. 67); however, policy can also be viewed as a value-laden, "complex cyclical process, which is messier, contested, and nonlinear" involving negotiation and struggle between different individuals and groups who may lie within or outside of the formal arena of policy making (Monkman and Hoffman 2013, p. 67; Ozga 2000). Ozga (2000) argued that it is important to "remove 'policy' from its pedestal, and make it accessible to the wider community... because [doing so] contributes to a democratic project in education, which in turn contributes to democracy" (p. 2).

Policy scholars in the field of Critical Policy Analysis (CPA) share Ozga's interest in policy's relationship to democracy. Specifically, they are interested in the ways in which policy, as a practice of power, can work to benefit some while disadvantaging others by reproducing "existing structures of domination and inequality" (Levinson et al. 2009, p. 769; Tierney and Rhodes 1993). Like Chase et al. (2014) and many other critical policy researchers, we view the creation of knowledge as a subjective process and view truth as socially constructed, often in ways that supports certain class, racial, and gender groups. CPA understands that policy decisions are influenced by values, beliefs, resources, information, information processing capabilities, and the external environment and thus policy is not an objective process (Chase et al. 2014). It recognizes that individuals and groups have competing interests (Tierney and Rhodes 1993); so, critical policy researchers explore the power struggles in policy creation and enactment in order to understand the role policy plays in sustaining the status quo.

Our conception of policy reflects Bowe et al.'s (1992) continuous policy cycle, a cycle comprised of three contexts, and its effects (Ball 1994). The policy cycle's "first context, the *context of influence*, is where public policy is normally initiated. It is here that policy discourses are constructed... [and] that interested parties struggle to influence the definition and social purposes of education" (Bowe et al. 1992, p. 19, emphasis in original). The second context is the *context of policy text production.* Policy texts "*represent* policy" and "these representations can take various forms: most obviously 'official' legal texts and policy documents; also formally and informally produced commentaries... the media... [and] also speeches by and public performances of relevant politicians and officials... and videos are another recently popular medium of representation" (Bowe et al. 1992, p. 20–21, emphasis in original). Texts are "the outcome of struggle and compromise" and are used to "control the meaning of policy through its representation" (Bowe et al. 1992, p. 21). The consequences of these texts bring us to the third context, the *context of practice*, where policy is interpreted and "recreated" as opposed to simply being "received and implemented" since people do not "confront policy texts as naïve readers, they come with histories, with experience, with values and purposes of their own" (Bowe et al. 1992, p. 22). Thus "policy writers cannot control the meanings of their texts... [since] interpretation will be in contest, as they relate to different interests" further exemplifying the complexity involved with the policy process (Bowe et al. 1992, p. 22). In the current study we examined influences, texts, and practices in Ontario's fundraising policy cycle.

Effects of activities in the policy cycle are of two kinds (Ball 1994): "first-order effects are changes in practice or structure... and second order effects are the impact of these changes on patterns of social access, opportunity, and social justice" (pp. 25–26). It is the second-order effects that are of particular interest to us and other critical policy scholars as we share a commitment to understanding how policies challenge or perpetuate the status quo (Diem et al. 2014).

4 Democracy in Education

The Ontario government frequently acknowledges its commitment to democracy (Ontario Government 2003–2014). In order to achieve a democratic society, however, democracy and democratic practices must be reflected and entrenched within the education system as well (Sabia 2012). A primary purpose of *public* schooling is to prepare students to become informed and responsible democratic citizens (Knight and Pearl 2000; Osborne 2001). However, the meaning and purpose of democracy are contested (Apple 2011; Cook and Westheimer 2006; Garrison and Schneider 2008; Kurki 2010). Some researchers advocate liberal democratic models of democracy whereby individualism is valued as are the rights and freedoms of the individual (Kurki 2010). Others suggest a radical democratic approach whereby empowerment and equality for all are pivotal aims (Knight and Pearl 2000), and some have proposed an inclusive democratic approach, which requires that all be included in the distribution of power (Fotopoulos 2008).

In market democracies there is enthusiasm for free markets and increasing privatization (Pinto 2012a). Within this conception of democracy, "economic 'choice' and 'consumption' of public goods and services (including education) are taken to be components of 'citizenship'" (Pinto 2012a, p. 10). Education within this framework is viewed as a commodity that can be bought and sold. Unlike the aforementioned models of democracy, this model fails to address characteristics such as social justice or equity (Pinto 2012a).

Critical democracy stands in contrast to market models. Democracy within a critical democratic framework is not limited or bound by capitalism or the economy, but rather within this model of democracy, there is a "concern for the welfare of others and 'the common good'" (Beane and Apple 1995, p. 7). Thus, critical democracy transcends "minimalist, protectionist, and marginalist" notions of democracy that promote narrow ideas of individualism (Portelli and Solomon 2001, p. 17). Critical democracy is understood and recognized as a "personal experience [that] concerns itself with a set of values, dispositions, and behaviours that go far beyond citizen involvement in official, narrow, political functions" (Pinto 2012a, p. 7). Thus, "within the critical-democratic ideal, democracy is a personal, social, and political experience rather than a form of government" (Blaug 2002 as cited in Pinto 2012a, p. 6).

Portelli and Solomon (2001) express that although democracy is ever-changing and thus indefinite in how it is defined and contextualized, there are core qualities and values that are associated with democracy. These values include: social justice, equity, inclusion, diversity, participation and participatory decision-making processes, knowledge inquiry and critical mindedness, community, dialogue, creativity, free and reasoned choices, citizen engagement and involvement, empowerment, and the redistribution of power (Pinto 2012a; Portelli and Solomon 2001). While all of these values contribute to a democratic way of life, due to space limitations and CPA's interest in examining power relations we focus on equity, inclusion, participatory decision-making processes, knowledge inquiry, and critical mindedness in this chapter. We briefly describe the meanings of these values that we adopt and aspects of their relationship to critical democratic education.

Equity is related to both fairness and equality. Fairness is a requisite to achieving equity and justice (Nelson et al. 1993); thus, practices must be fair to all students and this involves more than equal treatment. Equality suggests that individuals have equal distribution of goods and equal opportunity whereas equity involves distributing goods in a fair way that may not be equal but instead compensate for differences that disadvantage an individual or group over another (Pinto 2012a). Therefore, while equality and equity are often viewed as similar, in fact, equity allows for inequality, when it is fair to do so (Nelson et al. 1993). Overall, within the critical democratic ideal, social justice aims to achieve equity over equality (Pinto 2012a). Although this may be difficult to achieve in practice since people may define and decipher what is fair differently, it is important to consider that equity involves more than a "one-size-fits-all" application.

Inclusion involves increasing the participation of all in education and in society as a whole by eliminating exclusionary and discriminatory practices (Polat 2011). Inclusion means including everyone despite any characteristic that is perceived as different – it involves including all people regardless of race, ethnicity, gender, sexual orientation, disability, language, socio-economic status, and all other characteristics (Polat 2011). To ensure that inclusion is achieved, education settings must be responsive to diversity in such a way that all individuals are valued equally and respectfully (Booth 2005). Diversity involves respecting, embracing and being open-minded to what is different and to those who may be perceived as different. While tolerance was commonly promoted as an important characteristic in supporting and cultivating diversity in education in the past, this concept has been furthered with the intention to go beyond tolerance and toward acceptance which is an important push forward in the concept of diversity. Accepting and embracing diversity involves an understanding and respect for difference as opposed to simply being tolerant of difference. Thus, inclusion and diversity are inherently linked since without a sincere respect and understanding of difference, inclusion cannot be fully achieved.

Central to a critical democratic process in education is the participation of citizens in public decision-making (Pinto 2012a). Including students within this process is vital especially when these decisions concern the students themselves (Raby 2012). In a "democracy everybody should be given the tools to participate in society and encouraged to have a voice, especially young people" (Edmonds 2012, p. 42). Participation involves collaborating with others and being actively engaged and involved in the decision-making process (Booth 2005). Participation also involves understanding and valuing various types of identities so that people are accepted for who they are, and as a result, difference is embraced (Booth 2005).

Knowledge inquiry and critical mindedness are necessary for achieving critical democracy. The education setting should involve critically inquiring about social structures and social phenomena – questions inevitably lead to more questions and this is an important part of the active learning process necessary for social change. Thus, developing the classroom into a community of inquiry is essential for critical thinking to transpire (Portelli 1994). It is vital that students as citizens of a democratic society become active participants who question their own ideas, those of their peers, and those of their surroundings as opposed to passive participants who accept what they are told to believe (Portelli 1994). Since a "spectator citizenry is inconsistent with critical democracy," it is important that students become involved and engaged in critically inquiring so as to challenge the status quo (Martin 1992 as cited in Portelli and McMahon 2004, p. 40). Furthermore, "thought and action should not be separated" and therefore it is important that the dispositions and values held become a way of life and are put into action (Portelli and McMahon 2004, p. 40). Within this process, it is essential that schools are liberating places where silence is broken and voices are used to question and challenge dominant discourses so as to bring about positive social change (Portelli and McMahon 2004).

Taken together, the above values help us understand the ideals of schooling, decision-making, civic engagement, and living together in a critical democracy. To determine how Ontario's fundraising policy supports and/or hinders the achievement of these ideals, we adopt a critical democratic lens. This perspective directs us to examine the policy in relation to each democratic value. It is an appropriate lens for our analysis of Ontario's fundraising policy for a number of reasons. First, the critical democratic perspective shares our view of the social world as socially constructed and dynamic. Neither our view of policy nor of critical democracy deem that there is a single "best" reality. In fact, we view critical democracy, like policy, as always "becoming" and never fully "realized" since the world is always changing. Second, this lens enables us to identify which conception of democracy is supported through actors' practices and anticipate effects of these practices. Governments in particular often claim to make policy decisions in the name of enhancing democracy, yet, as discussed above, there are many conceptions of democracy with diverse and sometimes conflicting emphases. Using a critical democratic lens enables us to identify which conception of democracy is advocated by the Ontario Ministry of Education's fundraising policy as well as the conception supported and enacted by other policy actors in the province. Thus, the critical democratic lens aligns with the aims of CPA: to "offer a critique of the assumptions built, either explicitly or implicitly, into any given policy with a view to showing how they might either support or undermine the values of democracy and social justice" (Rizvi and Lingard 2010, p. 70). Ultimately, analyzing Ontario's school fundraising policy from a critical democratic perspective enables us to ascertain the ways Ontario's school fundraising policy supports and/or challenges the ideals of critical democracy in education and society more broadly.

5 Methodology

This chapter presents findings from our critical analysis of Ontario's fundraising policy. We were drawn to the analysis initially by media reports of the vast differences in amounts of money raised in schools across the province, our personal experiences with fundraising in Ontario schools, and our commitments to equity and social justice. Data collection was guided by our conception of policy as a cycle and its effects (Ball 1994; Bowe et al. 1992). Thus, we aimed to understand what was occurring in the policy's contexts of influence, text production, and practice as well as the effects and outcomes of these practices. Since it is normally impossible to identify when a policy was initiated, we focused on Ontario's fundraising policy cycle since changes were introduced to the funding of Ontario schools in 1997.

Data collection involved several phases. To understand what was occurring in the context of influence we conducted a broad review of the scholarly literature to identify studies of school fundraising in particular as well as research that examined Ontario and Canada's social, economic, political, cultural, and historical contexts. We also collected related government documents and news articles that addressed school fundraising in Ontario. We identified policy actors engaged in fundraising by conducting online searches, reading through news articles, and drawing on our knowledge of education in Ontario. We then collected relevant texts produced by these actors. These texts provided information about activities taking place in the context of practice as well as served as data in the policy cycle's context of text production. The texts include: the Ontario Ministry of Education's (2012) *Fundraising Guideline*; reports and other texts produced by non-governmental organizations including People for Education and the Canadian Centre for Policy Alternatives; a television news program; news articles published in local and national newspapers; transcripts of parliamentary debates; and numerous articles, books, and book chapters published by academic researchers.

Next, we asked *how does Ontario's school fundraising policy support equity, inclusion, participatory decision-making processes, and knowledge inquiry and critical mindedness?* We examined the texts listed above to help answer this question. We considered all three contexts of the policy cycle to understand the various ways the policy supports and undermines these values. Below we present the findings of our analysis.

6 School Fundraising Policy in Ontario and Critical Democracy

The past few decades witnessed intensified activity in Ontario's fundraising policy. While not a new policy, school fundraising became more prevalent, prominent, and important for schools. The ways fundraising undermined the ideals of critical democracy also became more apparent. Important influences in the policy's context of influence include the rising dominance of neoliberalism and neoconservatism globally and in Ontario, the election of Ontario's Progressive Conservative party in 1995, the introduction of a new approach to funding the province's public schools, and the emergence of People for Education (P4E), a parent advocacy group in Toronto, Ontario. Key texts in the context of text production include: reports on the prevalence, variation and diverse outcomes of school fundraising published annually by P4E; media reports; and fundraising guidelines introduced in 2012 by Ontario's Ministry of Education. The challenge of fundraising to the ideals of equity, inclusion, participatory decision-making, and critical mindedness are most clearly evident in the context of practice since while the pressure, reliance, and the overall amount of money raised by schools has risen, the astonishing disparities raised by different schools has not diminished.

6.1 Context of Influence

Fundraising policy in Ontario is situated within hegemonic political rationalities of neoliberalism and neoconservatism (Brown 2006). A political rationality is "a specific form of normative political reason organizing the political sphere, governance practices, and citizenship....[It] governs the sayable, the intelligible, and the truth criteria of these domains" (Brown 2006, p. 693). Neoliberalism celebrates the principles of the free market and aims to reorganize and transform economies, societies, and individuals by creating new markets and expanding existing ones, liberalizing trade, reducing government regulations over market activity, and privatizing public services (Connell 2013; Hursh 2007). Neoliberalism advocates and celebrates competition, efficiency, standardization, privatization, and individualism and is a key influence on contemporary education policy in Ontario and around the world (Carpenter et al. 2012; Connell 2013). Operating concurrently with neoliberalism is neoconservatism (Apple 2006; Benze and Carter 2011; Pinto 2012a; Winton 2008). Among other social and political concerns, neoconservatism includes an interest in reducing the size, influence and spending of government while better supporting the private sector (Brown 2006; Nevitte and Gibbins 1984). Neoliberal and neoconservative values and goals conflict with critical democratic commitments to equity, inclusion, diversity, participatory decision-making and social justice (Pinto 2012b; Winton and Tuters 2015).

It was within this larger ideological context that a new approach to funding Ontario's public schools was introduced by the Progressive Conservative government led by Mike Harris (Gidney 1999). The new approach was introduced in 1997 ostensibly as a way to equalize funding across the province so that all students would receive the same resources (Baillie 2002; Mackenzie 2009). This was to be achieved by funding schools based on student enrollment rather than on how much could be raised by municipalities through taxes as had been the previous practice (Baillie 2002; Ontario Ministry of Education 2008). Instead, the Ontario government, rather than school boards, would determine the amount to be collected from local property tax to support local schools (Gidney 1999).

The changes to the funding model and to provincial education grants resulted in overall reductions in government spending on education, and this impacted school boards differently throughout the province (Gidney 1999; Mackenzie 2009). For example, some schools became overcrowded while others were forced to close due to low enrollment; older schools lacked the necessary funds to upgrade; school boards in areas facing socioeconomic challenges were further disadvantaged; rural schools and schools in the north went without specialist teachers and Special Education supports; many small schools did not have full-time principals and librarians; and students with unique and diverse needs were not adequately supported (Campbell 2002; Charette 1998; People for Education 2001; School funding formula challenged 2002). Public funding shortfalls pressured school boards to become more financially self-reliant and as such schools and boards turned to private sources to supplement expenses through school-generated funds (Mackenzie 2009; People for Education 2001).

Indeed, a principal at an elementary school in Toronto approached parents and asked them to raise funds for books, maps, and microscopes (People for Education 1996). The parents agreed to do so but were determined to make their concerns about fundraising and the impact of the changes to school funding widely known (Evans et al. 2015; Winton and Brewer 2014). The group set out to learn how to have their voices heard, and they did so in part through staging dramatic protests at the Ontario legislature, engaging with the media, speaking to elected officials, and collecting and disseminating data on the effects of funding on schools throughout the province (Winton and Brewer 2014). The group, People for Education, has since become a key actor in Ontario's education policy landscape (Evans et al. 2015).

While funding in education increased during the Liberal period led by Dalton McGuinty in the mid-millennium, funding efforts were focused on new priorities such as reducing class sizes, increasing elementary and secondary teacher preparation time, and hiring support teachers in secondary schools (Mackenzie 2009). Although the Liberal government acknowledged various problems within education and successfully increased the overall average per-student funding, they neglected to re-evaluate the funding formula thus "leaving basic funding problems unaddressed" (Mackenzie 2009, p. 11). A media release published by People for Education in 2006 reported that Ontario's schools were increasingly relying on fundraising and that school fundraising amounts had increased each year since 1999. Pinto (2015) explains: "Since the election of a Liberal party government in 2003, Ontario's core education policy has remained largely unchanged while the neoliberal rhetoric has persisted" (p. 4).

6.2 Context of Text Production

A number of key texts exist in the Ontario fundraising context of text production. People for Education's Annual Reports and related reports on school fundraising especially stand out. From 1998–2013, P4E has published reports of Ontario schools' fundraising practices. The group collected this data annually through surveys of elementary and secondary schools and school councils across the province. Their findings are disseminated widely through news articles in major Canadian newspapers and by other non-governmental organizations and members of provincial parliament (Winton 2015). P4E's annual reports have highlighted how much money schools raise, how they raise it, and what the school-generated funds purchase. The group has argued that inadequate government funding has given rise to inequities in the school system. In 2010, for example, P4E reported that "[f]or some parents, the combination of [student] fees and the pressure to participate in fundraising can be experienced as a form of exclusion or built-in inequity" (People for Education 2010, p. 2). The group's 2012 Annual Report explains that "A reliance on fees and fundraising in Ontario schools increases the gap between 'have' and 'have-not' schools" (People for Education 2012, p. 31).

Other important texts include the *Fundraising Guideline* (Ontario Ministry of Education 2012) and the *Guideline for Fees for Learning Materials and Activities* (Ontario Ministry of Education 2011). The Ontario Ministry of Education released the *Fundraising Guideline* in May 2012 in a supposed effort to create a province-wide standard for fundraising at schools. Funds that are raised by individual boards and schools must adhere to the guidelines set out by the Ontario Ministry of Education's *Fundraising Guideline.* The *Fundraising Guideline* provides 'guiding principles' concerning fundraising within Ontario schools which elucidate that funds raised should only be used to complement education funding, not replace it. It also asserts that fundraising should be voluntary, safe, and transparent (Ontario Ministry of Education 2012). Furthermore, the *Guideline* explicitly states that fundraising activities must comply with the government's Equity and Inclusive Education Strategy and that when engaging in fundraising activities schools should "consider the purposes and principles of public education, including diversity, accessibility, and inclusivity" (Ontario Ministry of Education 2012, p. 1). Thus, the *Guideline* appears to support critical democratic values of equity and inclusion, although, the absence of consequences of failing to comply with the *Guideline's* principles suggests it is a symbolic policy (Rizvi and Lingard 2010). Indeed, this is what was alleged in an Editorial in the *Toronto Star* shortly after the *Guideline* was released: "it appears the government wants to look as though it's cracking down on excessive school fundraising, without actually doing it" (Toronto Star Editorial 2012).

6.3 Context of Practice

There is no doubt that fundraising is now commonplace in Ontario schools. People for Education's 2013 Annual Report states that 83 % of secondary schools and nearly all elementary schools fundraise. Although Ontario's *Fundraising Guideline* (2012) asserts that schools must not use collected funds to "replace public funding for education" (Ontario Ministry of Education 2012, p. 1), "Ontario schools continue to rely on... fundraising to augment school budgets and cover the cost of enrichment" (People for Education 2013b, p. 8). Fundraising mechanisms include pizza lunches, bake sales, chocolate sales, school performances, fun fairs, book sales, magazine subscriptions, and direct requests for donations from parents (Alphonso and Hammer 2014; Disparity in school fundraising 2012; Winsa and Rushowy 2011). Money is used to purchase library materials, sports equipment, team uniforms, musical instruments, gym facilities, school excursions, playground equipment, gardens, scoreboards, and more (Froese-Germain et al. 2006; Fundraising creating 2012; Fundraising fever 2012). Furthermore, school fundraising is a top priority for school councils and the activity they spend the most of their time on (People for Education 2010).

Ontario's fundraising practices produce a range of effects for students, schools, and democratic society. Of particular concern to us are the inequities that are created and perpetuated by school fundraising. Schools in the province raised vastly different amounts of funds. P4E (2013b) reports that the "top 10 % of fundraising schools raise as much as the bottom 81 %" (p. 8). This finding is virtually unchanged from 2007 (People for Education 2007). However, the difference in amounts raised has changed; in 2007, the highest fundraised amount reported was $400 000 and by 2013 this figure was $500 000. The lowest amount raised remained the same, however: $0 (People for Education 2007, 2013b). While the *Fundraising Guideline* prohibits schools from spending fundraised dollars on items such as classroom learning materials and textbooks, principals report using fundraised dollars to purchase necessities allowed by the *Guideline* and using government dollars to purchase the extras not allowed by the *Guideline* (Pistiolis 2012). This appropriation of the *Guideline* contributes to inequities in education since not all schools have these extra funds to spend.

Students who attend schools that collect money through fundraising have access to resources and opportunities not available to students whose schools do not or cannot collect additional funds. These additional resources provide students with more rewarding school experiences, activities known to engage students in schooling, and an overall higher quality education (Disparity in school fundraising 2012; Froese-Germain et al. 2006; Fundraising fever 2012). Benefits and additional resources are enjoyed by a relatively small number of students, however (Pistiolis 2012). The schools raising the largest amounts of money are ones with the highest family incomes (People for Education 2013b); in fact, schools with families with high incomes raise five times as much as those in schools with low income families (People for Education 2013a). Students at these high income schools are also more likely to participate in band or in choir (People for Education 2013a). Fundraising, then, creates a "double disadvantage" for low-income families since these families cannot afford to "provide the funds to help buy the extras that schools in wealthy neighbourhoods can buy" (Fundraising fever 2012, para. 6). Thus, the irony of school fundraising is that the schools in greatest need for additional funds are the ones that do not have the capacity to raise them (Fundraising creating 2012). Fundraising creates "have" and "have not" schools that reflect the growing disparity between the wealthy and poor in Ontario (Mackenzie 2011) and globally (Fotopoulos 2008).

In addition to equity, fundraising practices and Ontario's *Fundraising Guideline* undermine the critical democratic principle of inclusion. First, although the *Guideline* states that fundraising must be voluntary, many students and schools are faced with the reality that there are no funds to collect; thus, there really is no choice to be made. Further, as discussed above, since schools raise vastly different amounts of money and because schools keep what they raise, some students are included in the advantages that fundraising can buy while others are excluded. Excluding some students from the benefits of public education (now augmented by private funding) undermines critical democracy. As explained by Osborne (2001): "No society can properly be called democratic if it denies its citizens, whether deliberately or otherwise, equal access to the highest possible quality of education" (p. 49).

In addition to equity and inclusion, critical democracy requires citizen participation in decision-making. Aspects of school fundraising may be undermining this process. First, there is the question of whether a school should fundraise or not. As discussed above, for some schools the decision is determined by their communities' inability to afford to fundraise. There is also the question of which fundraising activities schools will pursue. The *Guideline's* principle that fundraising should be accountable and transparent includes the following element: "Fundraising activities are developed and organized with advice and assistance from the school community, including students, staff, parents, and community organizations" (Ontario Ministry of Education 2012, p. 3). Froese-Germain et al.'s (2006) study of fundraising across Canada found, however, that fundraising decisions are mainly made by parent groups and school councils. Students were involved to a "lesser extent" (p. 12); more precisely, only 23 % of schools reported that students were also involved with school fundraising decisions. Participatory decision-making by everyone, including students, is necessary as it supports democratic values of inclusion, participation, and dialogue.

If a school does fundraise the option not to participate may exist, but in reality students and parents are expected to fundraise (TVO Parents 2012). Pressure to participate is achieved by various tactics practiced in schools (Pistiolis 2012). For example, top student-fundraisers are recognized and commended by having their names published in school newsletters or are presented with a prize in front of their peers. Highest-earning classes may be rewarded with pizza parties. These practices identify those who have fundraised large sums as well as those who have not (Pistiolis 2012) and pressure students to fundraise. They also promote competition between students and classrooms within the same schools while also fostering competition between schools (Canadian Centre for Policy Alternatives 2006; Ricci 2009). Students, as well as parents and schools, who are unable to raise funds may experience a loss of dignity (Pistiolis 2012).

Promoting competition, rewarding individuals who raise large sums, and institutionalizing private money in public schools reflect and support neoliberal and neoconservative values of competition, individualism, productivity, and reduced spending on public services. The reliance of schools on fundraising undermines commitments to publicly funded education as a whole as it shifts the responsibility of funding education from the government to private citizens and constructs education as a private rather than a public good. These values contradict critical democratic commitments to equality, equity, social justice, and community. Critical democratic education should involve students in critical analysis of existing social systems rather than prepare students to fit into them. Given the reliance of schools on fundraising, its widespread practice, and the pressure to participate, it is difficult to imagine critical analysis of fundraising and its effects taking place in schools. Even if such dialogues are occurring they are undermined by the normalization of fundraising in Ontario schools. The importance of raising money to benefit one's self and one's local community is emphasized through the time devoted to fundraising in and out of schools – time that could otherwise have been spent engaged in extracurricular activities or school work.

7 Toward Critical Democratic Education Through Fundraising Policy Change

We are not the first to raise concerns about fundraising. Various options have been proposed to address our and others' concerns. One suggestion is to pool funds raised and distribute them equally between schools within each school board across the province. This idea was proposed in the Toronto District School Board, however, the idea was a "hot potato" and was dropped (Winsa and Rushowy 2012, para. 16). Some school councils suggest that pooling funds be voluntary and based on the discretion of the school (Winsa and Rushowy 2011), but other school councils oppose a shared model arguing they "worked hard for that money" (Fundraising fever 2012, para. 38). Others have proposed pooling a percentage of funds raised by schools and redistributing those funds based on the individual needs of schools (Rushowy and Winsa 2011). However, all of these options institutionalize private money in public schools and reduce the responsibility of the government to adequately fund public education.

The findings of our CPA demonstrate that in order to achieve critical democracy, the practice of fundraising to subsidize and enrich Ontario's public schools must be abolished. A central concern of CPA is to understand how policies challenge or reproduce power relations and inequities. Adopting a critical democratic perspective is a useful means of achieving this understanding. Our analysis of Ontario's fundraising policy through a critical democratic lens finds that the policy undermines commitments to equity, inclusion, participatory decision-making, and critical mindedness and instead promotes competition, individualism, and inequality. Schools across the province, like those in other Canadian provinces, raise private funds for athletic and academic programs, school supplies, transportation, field trips, clubs, books, technology, musical instruments, schoolyard revitalizations, sports equipment, guest speakers, professional performers, and extracurricular activities (Froese-Germain et al. 2006; Pistiolis 2012). Schools located in high socioeconomic neighbourhoods or whose students come from affluent families are able to raise substantially more money than less affluent schools or students (People for Education 2007, 2013b; Pistiolis 2012; Winsa and Rushowy 2011). This money is in turn used by affluent schools to provide enhanced experiences for their students, ultimately leading to enhanced educational experiences and outcomes for already advantaged social groups. Therefore, fundraising must be eliminated from Ontario's public school system and schools need to be adequately funded by the Ontario government. Advocacy and changes in practice by parents, students, educators, administrators, and citizens alike are necessary for fundraising policy change to transpire.

References

Alphonso, C., & Hammer, K. (2014, November 03). Toronto school fundraising raises questions about equity in public-education system. *The Globe and Mail*. Retrieved from http://www.theglobeandmail.com/news/national/education/fundraising-clout-gives-torontos-affluent-schools-a-wider-edge/article21421933/

Apple, M. W. (2006). Understanding and interrupting neoliberalism and neoconservatism in education. *Pedagogies: An International Journal, 1*(1), 21–26.

Apple, M. W. (2011). Democratic education in neoliberal and neoconservative times. *International Studies in Sociology of Education, 21*(1), 21–31.

Baillie, A. (2002, November 30). School funding formula. *Pembroke Observer*. Retrieved from Canadian Newsstand.

Ball, S. J. (1994). *Education reform: A critical and post-structural approach*. Buckingham: Open University Press.

Beane, J. A., & Apple, M. W. (1995). The case for democratic schools. In M. W. Apple & J. A. Beane (Eds.), *Democratic schools* (pp. 1–25). Alexandria: Association for Supervision and Curriculum Development.

Benze, L., & Carter, L. (2011). Globalizing students acting for the common good. *Journal of Research in Science Teaching, 48*(6), 648–669.

Booth, T. (2005). Keeping the future alive: Putting inclusive values into action. *FORUM, 47*(2&3), 151–158.

Bowe, R., Ball, S. J., & Gold, A. (1992). *Reforming education and changing schools: Case studies in policy sociology*. London: Routledge.

Brent, B. O., & Lunden, S. (2009). Much ado about very little: The benefits and costs of school-based commercial activities. *Leadership and Policy in Schools, 8*(3), 307–336.

Brown, W. (2006). American nightmare: Neoliberalism, neoconservatism, and de-democratization. *Political Theory, 34*(6), 690–714.

Campbell, M. (2002, May 06). Tories' funding formula hits hard at older schools. *The Globe and Mail*. Retrieved from http://www.theglobeandmail.com/news/national/tories-funding-formula-hits-hard-at-older-schools/article754457/

Canadian Centre for Policy Alternatives. (2006). *Commercialism in Canadian schools: Who's calling the shots?* (Summary). Retrieved from https://www.policyalternatives.ca/sites/default/files/uploads/publications/National_Office_Pubs/2006/Commercialism_in_Canadian_Schools_summary.pdf

Carpenter, S., Weber, N., & Schugurensky, D. (2012). Views from the blackboard: Neoliberal education reforms and the practice of teaching in Ontario, Canada. *Globalisation, Societies and Education, 10*(2), 145–161.

Charette, R. (1998, December 11). Funding formula is flawed. *The Ottawa Citizen*. Retrieved from Canadian Newsstand.

Chase, M. M., Dowd, A. C., Pazich, L. B., & Bensimon, E. M. (2014). Transfer equity for "minoritized" students: A critical policy analysis of seven states. *Educational Policy, 28*(5), 669–717. doi:10.1177/0895904812468227.

Connell, R. (2013). The neoliberal cascade and education: An essay on the market agenda and its consequences. *Critical Studies in Education, 54*(2), 99–112.

Cook, S., & Westheimer, J. (2006). Democracy and Education. *Canadian Journal of Education, 29*(2), 347–358.

CTV investigates school support. (2013, March 25). *CTV News*. Retrieved from http://kitchener.ctvnews.ca/ctv-investigates-school-support-1.1210738

Diem, S., Young, M. D., Welton, A. D., Mansfield, K. C., & Lee, P. (2014). The intellectual landscape of critical policy analysis. *International Journal of Qualitative Studies in Education, 27*(9), 1068–1090.

Disparity in school fundraising is more than just an academic concern. (2012, June 06). *The Record*. Retrieved from http://www.therecord.com/news-story/2605207-disparity-in-school-fundraising-is-more-than-just-an-academic-concern/

Edmonds, K. (2012). Young people's engagement in society, how government policy has ignored the role of youth work in citizenship education: A critical analysis of Britain's future, the citizenship and the state, in the Governance of Britain Green paper. In M. Lall (Ed.), *Policy, discourse and rhetoric: How new labour challenged social justice and democracy* (pp. 41–58). Rotterdam: Sense Publishers.

Evans, M. P., Newman, A., & Winton, S. (2015). Not your mother's PTA: Hybridity in community-based organizations working for educational reform. *The Educational Forum, 79*(3), 263–279. doi:10.1080/00131725.2015.1037510.

Fotopoulos, T. (2008). Inclusive democracy. In D. Gabbard (Ed.), *Knowledge & power in the global economy* (pp. 435–448). New York: Taylor and Francis Group, LLC.

Froese-Germain, B., Hawkey, C., Larose, A., McAdie, P., & Shaker, E. (2006). *Commercialism in Canadian schools: Who's calling the shots?* Retrieved from https://www.policyalternatives.ca/sites/default/files/uploads/publications/National_Office_Pubs/2006/Commercialism_in_Canadian_Schools.pdf

Fundraising creating an uneven playing field in Ontario schools. (2012, June 6). *York Region News*. Retrieved from http://www.yorkregion.com/community-story/1463210-fundraising-creating-an-uneven-playing-field-in-ontario-schools/

Fundraising fever: The have-not schools in Durham and Ontario. (2012, June 6). *Durham Region: Metroland Media Report*. Retrieved from http://www.durhamregion.com/community-story/3505339-fundraising-fever-the-have-not-schools-in-durham-and-ontario/

Garrison, J. W., & Schneider, S. (2008). Democracy. In D. Gabbard (Ed.), *Knowledge & power in the global economy* (pp. 5–12). New York: Taylor and Francis Group, LLC.

Gidney, R. D. (1999). *From hope to Harris: The reshaping of Ontario's schools*. Toronto: University of Toronto Press.

Government of Canada. (2012). *Education*. Retrieved from http://www.cic.gc.ca/english/newcomers/after-education.asp

Hursh, D. (2007). Assessing no child left behind and the rise of neoliberal education policies. *American Educational Research Journal, 44*(3), 493–518.
Inner City Advisory Committee. (2012, September 12). *Funding model schools and inner-city programs*. Retrieved from http://webcache.googleusercontent.com/search?q=cache:FuAPsGxmEfQJ:www.tdsb.on.ca/Portals/0/Community/Community%2520Advisory%2520committees/ICAC/Subcommittees/ICAC%2520on%2520LOS%2520and%2520SBFR.ppt+&cd=1&hl=en&ct=clnk&gl=ca
Knight, T., & Pearl, A. (2000). Democratic education and critical pedagogy. *The Urban Review, 32*(3), 197–226.
Kurki, M. (2010). Democracy and conceptual contestability: Reconsidering conceptions of democracy in democracy promotion. *International Studies Review, 12*, 362–386.
Levinson, B. A. U., Sutton, M., & Winstead, T. (2009). Education policy as a practice of power: Theoretical tools, ethnographic methods, democratic options. *Educational Policy, 23*(6), 767–795. doi:10.1177/0895904808320676.
Mackenzie, H. (2009). No time for complacency: Education funding reality check. *Canadian Centre for Policy Alternatives*. Retrieved from https://www.policyalternatives.ca/sites/default/files/uploads/publications/reports/docs/Education%20Funding%20Formula%20Review_0.pdf
Mackenzie, H. (2011). *Rich getting richer: Gap in Ontario, Canada*. Retrieved from http://mydailyconcerns.com/hugh-mackenzie-rich-getting-richer-gap-in-ontario-canada/
Miller, V. W. (2012). The broad challenge to democratic leadership: The other crisis in education. *Democracy and Education, 20*(2), 1–11.
Monkman, K., & Hoffman, L. (2013). Girls' education: The power of policy discourse. *Theory and Research in Education, 11*(1), 63–84. doi:10.1177/1477878512468384.
Nelson, J. L., Carlson, K., & Palonsky, S. B. (1993). *Critical issues in education: A dialectic approach* (2nd ed.). New York: McGraw-Hill, Inc.
Nevitte, N., & Gibbins, R. (1984). Neoconservatism: Canadian variations on an ideological theme? *Canadian Public Policy, 10*(4), 384–394.
Ontario Government. (2003–2014). (Various texts). Retrieved from http://news.ontario.ca/mag/en/2003/12/mcguinty-government-to-strengthen-our-democracy-and-improve-the-way-government-serves-people.html; http://news.ontario.ca/opo/en/2004/06/mcguinty-government-takes-bold-action-to-strengthen-our-democracy.html; http://news.ontario.ca/archive/en/2004/06/01/McGuinty-government-takes-bold-action-to-strengthen-our-democracy.html; http://www.ontario.ca/government/progress-report-2014-education
Ontario Ministry of Education. (2008). *A guide for parents: How does school funding support my child's education?* Retrieved from http://www.edu.gov.on.ca/eng/parents/funding/How_Education_WebE2008.pdf
Ontario Ministry of Education. (2009). *Ontario's equity and inclusive education strategy*. Retrieved from http://www.edu.gov.on.ca/eng/policyfunding/equity.pdf
Ontario Ministry of Education. (2011). *Fees for learning materials and activities guideline*. Retrieved from http://www.edu.gov.on.ca/eng/parents/feesguideline.pdf
Ontario Ministry of Education. (2012). *Fundraising guideline*. Retrieved from http://www.edu.gov.on.ca/eng/parents/Fund2012Guideline.pdf
Osborne, K. (2001). Democracy, democratic citizenship, and education. In J. P. Portelli & R. P. Solomon (Eds.), *The erosion of democracy in education: From critique to possibilities* (pp. 29–62). Calgary: Detselig Enterprises Ltd.
Ozga, J. (2000). *Policy research in educational settings: Contested terrain*. Philadelphia: Open University Press.
People for Education. (1996, May 14). *Submission to Ontario's standing committee on social development*. Retrieved from http://www.ontla.on.ca
People for Education. (2001). *The 2001 tracking report: The effects of funding and policy changes in Ontario's elementary schools*.
People for Education. (2006). *Ontario schools increasingly relying on fundraising*. Retrieved from http://www.peopleforeducation.ca/wp-content/uploads/2011/08/Ontario-Schools-Increasingly-Relying-on-Fundraising.pdf

People for Education. (2007). *The annual report on Ontario's public schools*. Retrieved from http://www.peopleforeducation.ca/wp-content/uploads/2011/07/Annual-Report-on-Ontario-Schools-2007.pdf

People for Education. (2010). *Private money in public schools*. Retrieved from http://www.peopleforeducation.ca/wp-content/uploads/2011/07/Fees-and-Fundraising-in-Schools-2010.pdf

People for Education. (2012). *Making connections beyond school wall. People for Education annual report on Ontario's publicly funded schools 2012*. Retrieved from http://www.peopleforeducation.ca/wp-content/uploads/2012/05/Annual-Report-2012-web.pdf

People for Education. (2013a, May 26). *In Ontario schools, higher income = higher opportunity*. Retrieved from http://www.peopleforeducation.ca/pfe-news/annual-report-shows-in-ontario-schools-high-income-high-opportunity/

People for Education. (2013b). *Mind the gap: Inequality in Ontario's schools. People for Education annual report on Ontario's publicly funded schools 2013*. Retrieved from http://www.peopleforeducation.ca/wp-content/uploads/2013/05/annual-report-2013-WEB.pdf

Pinto, L. E. (2012a). *Curriculum reform in Ontario: 'Common sense' policy processes and democratic possibilities*. Toronto: University of Toronto.

Pinto, L. E. (2012b). Hidden privatization in education policy as 'quick fixes' by 'hired guns': Contracting curriculum policy in Ontario. *Critical Policy Studies, 6*(3), 261–281.

Pinto, L. E. (2015). Fear and loathing in neoliberalism: School leader responses to policy layers. *Journal of Educational Administration and History*. doi:10.1080/00220620.2015.996869.

Pistiolis, V. (2012). *The results and implications of fundraising in elementary public schools: Interviews with Ontario Principals*. (Master's thesis). Retrieved from https://tspace.library.utoronto.ca/bitstream/1807/32507/1/Pistiolis_Ioanna_V_201206_MA_thesis.pdf

Polat, F. (2011). Inclusion in education: A step towards social justice. *International Journal of Educational Development, 31*, 50–58.

Portelli, J. P. (1994). The challenge of teaching for critical thinking. *McGill Journal of Education, 29*(2), 137–152.

Portelli, J. P., & McMahon, B. J. (2004). Why critical-democratic engagement? *Journal of Maltese Education Research, 2*(2), 39–45.

Portelli, J. P., & Solomon, R. P. (2001). Introduction. In J. P. Portelli & R. P. Solomon (Eds.), *The erosion of democracy in education: From critique to possibilities* (pp. 15–27). Calgary: Detselig Enterprises Ltd.

Posey-Maddox, L. (2013). Professionalizing the PTO: Race, class, and shifting norms of parental engagement in a city public school. *American Journal of Education, 119*(2), 235–260.

Raby, R. (2012). *School rules: Obedience, discipline, and elusive democracy*. Toronto: University of Toronto Press.

Ricci, C. (2009). "Partners" in education? Why school parent councils should not be fundraising and what they should be doing instead. *Our Schools, Our Selves, 18*(4), 75–81.

Rizvi, F., & Lingard, B. (2010). *Globalizing education policy*. New York: Routledge.

Rushowy, K., & Winsa, P. (2011, September 12). Ban school fundraising, province urged. *The Toronto Star*. Retrieved from http://www.thestar.com/life/parent/2011/09/12/ban_school_fundraising_province_urged.html

Rushowy, K., Winsa, P., & Ferguson, R. (2011, March 01). Province needs to set school fundraising limits, groups say. *The Toronto Star*. Retrieved from http://www.thestar.com/life/parent/2011/03/01/province_needs_to_set_school_fundraising_limits_groups_say.html

Sabia, D. (2012). Democratic/utopian education. *Utopian Studies, 23*, 374–405.

Sattem, J. L. (2007). *Publicly funded, privately assisted: The role of giving in Oregon K-12 education*. (Master's thesis). Retrieved from https://ir.library.oregonstate.edu/xmlui/bitstream/handle/1957/6193/Sattem%20MPP%20Essay.pdf?sequence=1

School funding formula challenged. (2002, September 20). *The Record*. Retrieved from Canadian Newsstand.

Scott, J. (2009). The politics of venture philanthropy in charter school policy and advocacy. *Educational Policy, 23*(1), 106–136.

Tierney, W., & Rhodes, W. (1993). Postmodernism and critical theory in higher education: Implications for research and practice. In S. John (Ed.), *Higher education handbook of theory and research* (Vol. IX, pp. 308–343).

Toronto Star Editorial. (2012, May 7). Excessive school fundraising is creating two-tiered public education in Ontario. *Toronto Star*. Retrieved March 10, 2015, from http://www.thestar.com/opinion/editorials/2012/05/07/excessive_school_fundraising_is_creating_twotiered_public_education_in_ontario.html

TVO Parents (Producer). (2012). *Private money in public schools?* [online video]. Available from http://tvoparents.tvo.org/blog/tvoparents-blog/new-fundraising-guidelines-ontario-schools

Winsa, P., & Rushowy, K. (2011, February 28). Rich schools get richer thanks to private cash. *The Toronto Star*. Retrieved from http://www.thestar.com/life/parent/2011/02/28/rich_schools_get_richer_thanks_to_private_cash.html

Winsa, P., & Rushowy, K. (2012, May 4). Province's new school fundraising rules don't address rich/poor gap, say critics. *The Toronto Star*. Retrieved from http://www.thestar.com/news/ontario/2012/05/04/provinces_new_school_fundraising_rules_dont_address_richpoor_gap_say_critics.html

Winton, S. (2008). The appeal(s) of character education in threatening times: Caring and critical democratic responses. *Comparative Education, 44*(3), 305–316.

Winton, S. (2015). *Resisting "a system of 'have' and 'have not' schools": Engaging in the struggle over the meaning of fundraising for policy change.* 1–23. [unpublished manuscript] York University.

Winton, S., & Brewer, C. (2014). People for Education: A critical policy history. *Qualitative Studies in Education, 27*(9), 1091–1109.

Winton, S., & Tuters, S. (2015). Constructing bullying in Ontario, Canada: A critical policy analysis. *Educational Studies, 41*(1 & 2), 122–142.

Zimmer, R. W., Krop, C., & Brewer, D. J. (2003). Private resources in public schools: Evidence from a pilot study. *Journal of Education Finance, 28*(4), 485–521.

Examining the Theater of "Listening" & "Learning"

Bradley W. Carpenter

Abstract The purpose of this chapter is to provide an example of how critical policy analysis, specifically the dramaturgical analysis of policymaking, is able to broaden the examination of discourses in isolation. This chapter expands the field of the discourse analyses often found within critical policy work by examining how dominant discourses (privileged and inscribed language) are constructed through the deliberative performance of politics (performative act of policymaking). The focus for analysis in this chapter is the Obama/Duncan Administration's Listening & Learning Tour (L&L Tour). By examining the orchestrated interaction between discourses and performative politics during the L&L tour this chapter provides readers with a critical policy analysis of how dominant discourses and deliberative politics codetermined which definition of school improvement would shape the Obama/Duncan revision of the Title I School Improvement Grant (SIG).

Keywords Critical policy analysis • Discourse analysis • School turnaround • School reform • Title I School Improvement Grant • Educational leadership

The interconnectedness of global economies and the perpetual threat of economic instability have shaped public policy debates in the United States since the economic crises experienced in the late 1970s. International events such as OPEC's dramatic increase in the price of crude oil during the presidency of Jimmy Carter undermined the authority of once sovereign polities by destabilizing domestic economies and facilitating the rearrangement of institutional politics. Hajer (2006b) described this political reorganization as "institutional ambiguity" (p. 43). Hajer (2006b) claims, institutional ambiguity takes place when governing institutions no longer have the centralized power to deliver policy results on their own. Subsequently, as this power subsides governance evolves from a traditional party system focused

---

B.W. Carpenter (✉)
Department of Educational Leadership & Policy Studies, University of Houston, Houston, TX, USA
e-mail: bcarpen2@Central.UH.EDU

on a priori knowledge of easily identifiable issues into a system defined by multi-party convergences, rapidly shifting issue landscapes, and polycentric networks (Hajer 2006b).

Although Hajer's insights speak to the rearrangement of Western politics, the concept of institutional ambiguity captures the way in which the continual threat of economic crisis and a globally connected marketplace dislocated the traditional rules guiding domestic and international policymaking in the United States. Particularly, within periods of institutional ambiguity, solutions for the pressing problems of education cannot be found exclusively within the traditional constitutional authority of the federal government. Rather, a new politics of education emerges, one that is characterized by the phenomenon of multisignification (Hajer 2006b), wherein a multitude of varied interests battle and collaborate to define the significance of what is necessary to solve public policy issues; each interest operating from a biased system of signification (i.e. ideological reading of issues). Consequently, during an era where the regulatory boundaries for a global marketplace are still being developed, rules for federal decision-making are not made in advance (a priori), and thus are continually subjected to reinterpretation and renegotiation in the deliberative enactment of policymaking.

Furthermore, in an environment of an enhanced globally interdependent economy, issues such as trade, energy, environment, labor, health care, welfare, taxation, and education must appear as credible responses to the pursuit of economic growth and stability in order to secure top billing on the political agendas of federal policy makers. Although each of these issues received recognition at different points in U.S. history, education, specifically the "chronic failure" of public schools, emerged as an emblematic issue, one that serves as an effective metaphor for the nation's economic crisis. Within this context, a discursive chain of reasoning has prevailed suggesting the following: If educators simply had the courage to make difficult decisions and do what is morally necessary to turn around the lowest performing schools, then the United States could provide the educational opportunities necessary to secure its dominant position in the global economy.

Former Secretary of Education Arne Duncan offered a preview of this reasoning during his Senate confirmation hearing: "The President-elect views education as both a *moral obligation and an economic imperative*. In the face of rising *global competition*, we know that education is the *critical*, some would say the only, road to *economic security*" (*Confirmation of Arne Duncan* 2009a, para. 9), (emphasis added). Though Duncan's testimony also cited issues of social justice as the moral justification for education reform, the global reconfiguration of educational purposes emerged as a dominant storyline through Duncan's rhetorical linking of urgency ("imperative," "critical"), global competition and economic security with educational reform priorities. Thus, Secretary Duncan's Senate confirmation testimony served as an effective introduction for the discourse of educational globalization, which functioned as the dominant discourse during the Obama/Duncan school reform agenda.

The purpose of this chapter is to provide an example of how critical policy analysis, specifically the dramaturgical analysis of policymaking, is able to broaden the examination of discourses in isolation. This chapter expands the field of the discourse analyses often found within critical policy work by examining how dominant discourses (privileged and inscribed language) are constructed through the deliberative performance of politics (performative act of policymaking). In speaking to the importance of looking beyond the isolated analysis of language, Hajer (2006a) cites the Wittgensteinian idea that language does not simply "float" but is related to the practices of policymaking as well as the operational routines endorsed through governance. Therefore, Hajer (2006a) explained that whereas language (e.g., discourses, story lines, policy vocabularies) is certainly a powerful element in the politics of deliberative policy making, it is the performing of politics that convey particular meanings. Also of importance, these performance-specific meanings are constantly re-produced and re-enacted in particular settings (Hajer 2005a). The focus for analysis in this chapter is the Obama/Duncan Administration's Listening & Learning Tour (L&L Tour). By examining the orchestrated interaction between discourses and performative politics during the L&L tour this chapter provides readers with a critical policy analysis of how dominant discourses and deliberative politics codetermined which definition of school improvement would shape the Obama/Duncan revision of the Title I School Improvement Grant (SIG).

Although one could argue that each time national leaders speak publicly about education their actions would count as a performance, some performances are afforded more significance than others. In the case of the Listening & Learning Tour, Secretary of Education Arne Duncan's series of performances in his travels across the United States provided the performative and symbolic politics necessary to help build consensus amongst the multitude of differences seeking to define how exactly education policy should be crafted to better address the persistent issue of failing schools. The deliberative performances of the Obama/Duncan Administration were purposefully constructed to bring stability to a political environment characterized by Hajer's (2006a) concept of multisignification. As a result, Secretary Arne Duncan's L&L Tour helped build the initial support necessary for the launching of a bold reform agenda intended to "turnaround" the nation's chronically low-performing schools.

In the remaining sections of this chapter, I provide an overview of the theoretical framework used in my analysis of the Listening & Learning Tour, giving particular attention to the dramaturgical functions of scripting, staging, setting and performance. I then describe the players associated (both government and nongovernment) with the Listening & Learning tour, details about the settings, and specific texts pertaining to the coverage of each event. In order to illustrate how storylines used to support the Obama/Duncan educational reform agenda were reinforced throughout the performances of the Obama/Duncan Administration, I coded for words/phrases drawn from each of the three dominant story lines that surfaced during President Obama's run for presidency and during Secretary

Arne Duncan's confirmation process: *Global Competitiveness, Unprecedented Opportunity*, and *Disrupt Complacency*.[1] After examining each of the performances, I highlight the unveiling of the Obama/Duncan turnaround reform agenda and then conclude with a discussion of how the scripts, staging, setting, and performative aspects of the events analyzed further solidified the Title I SIG of 2009 as a credible policy solution for the nation's chronically low performing schools.

1 Theoretical Background

Hajer (2006b) argued that discourse analysis alone is insufficient for policy studies:

> A problem with much work on discourse is, however, that it is too much focused on language, whereas linguistic analysis should ideally be related to the analysis of the practices in which a particular language or languages is/are employed. (p. 46)

The beliefs put forth in this statement provide the impetus for the dramaturgical dimension of Hajer's policy framework and confirm the critical interpretive belief in how the socially constructed act of sense making are influenced throughout deliberative politics. This framework both supports and extends the focus of critical policy analysis examining the act of policymaking as a struggle over discursive meaning. The critically interpretive examination of policy making provides insights into particular policy environments by interpreting the connections between policy making and the purposeful construction of political narratives (Hajer and Wagenaar 2003). The next section outlines the dimensions of performance in Hajer's analytical framework.

1.1 *The Role of Performance in Hajer's Analytical Framework*

The centrality of performance to Hajer's analytical framework is founded upon the critical interpretive belief that contemporary policy studies attempting to examine the "nature of modern democracy" should be founded upon the three pillars of interpretation, practice, and deliberation (Hajer and Wagenaar 2003, p. 16). This focus on performance is founded upon the second dimension of contemporary policy sciences, which calls into question the positivistic notion that the actions of political actors are a natural byproduct of a certain understandable (a priori) knowledge. Specifically, positivistic analyses of policy assume the performance of policy making can be analyzed without considering the socially constructed and contested views of irrational actors. Instead, actors from Hajer's viewpoint "learn about the world in public, shared processes in which they test what they

---

[1]The discourse analysis that surfaced these storylines is embedded in a separate study article submitted for publication.

have learned" (Hajer and Wagenaar 2003, p. 20). Indeed, this suggests that actors learn in real-time through the performative interactions involved in deliberative policymaking.

1.2 Hajer's Terms of Policy Performance

Hajer (2005a) coined the performance dimension of his analytical framework as "dramaturgy" (p. 449). Deliberative politics from this perspective consists of a sequence of "staged" performances in which deliberative actors collaboratively determine the rules of policy making. In an attempt to examine the artful practice of deliberative politics, Hajer's (2005a, 2006b) framework focuses on four aspects of political performance: *scripting*, *staging*, *setting*, and *performance*. Together, the explorations of these political performances enrich policy studies depending solely on the methodologies available in discourse analysis.

1.2.1 Scripting

Hajer (2005a) described scripting as the deliberative actions of actors who, by determining the "settings" of a political performance, define the play's characters and therefore provide "cues for appropriate behavior" (p. 449). This conceptualization of scripting captures the ways in which the rules of deliberative policy making are constantly being defined and redefined by the actions of political actors. In this sense, depending upon the policy director and the script being presented, actors assume a role as active or passive, collaborator or protestor, or competent or incompetent (Freeman and Peck 2007).

1.2.2 Staging

Hajer (2005a) described staging as the purposeful management of political interactions; thus actors in this sense draw from "existing symbols and the intervention of new ones, as well as to the distinction between active players and (presumably passive) audiences ('mis en scene')" (p. 449). This understanding of staging was adapted from the work of Murray Edelman (as cited in Hajer 2005a), who considered politics as a drama where the setting and staging of political events were key elements in the performance of governmental interactions. Specific to Hajer's analytical framework, staging can be interpreted as the active manipulation of policy settings such as presentations, town hall forums, conferences, and colloquiums.

1.2.3 Setting

Hajer (2005a) described setting as the physical structuring of political interactions through the use of specific "artifacts" used during the enactment of deliberative policy making (p. 449). The political setting from this perspective is considered to be influential in the shaping of deliberative interactions through the reproduction of political meanings, the enactment of political significations, and the overall performativity of deliberative policy making (Hajer 2006a). For Hajer (2005b), the idea of setting cannot be limited to the recognizable norms enacted in deliberative forums; instead, setting should be understood as the "actual things" (stage set, artificial devices) that provide structure to such forums (p. 629).

1.2.4 Performance

Hajer (2005a) described performance as the "contextualized" interactions that shape social realities such as the "understandings" of social issues (p. 449). This understanding of performance was adapted from Kenneth Burke's 1969 analysis (as cited in Hajer 2005b) of how the "grammar of dramatism" could be used to explain the actions and motives of actors. Hajer's analytical framework considers performances as purposefully sequential and collaboratively shaped by both the actors and those invited to participate in the play that is deliberative politics. This particular focus on performances allows policy studies to untangle the conditions that must be present in order for actors to be recognized in the act of deliberation. Additionally, it provides policy studies insight as to how the actions of political actors relate to each other in the performance of deliberative policy making, thus helping to provide clarity as to which actions actually influence the final composition of policy solutions (Hajer 2005b).

Hajer (2003) suggests policy analysts should elucidate how the examination of the performative aspects of deliberative politics might fulfill a role in renewing democratic governance in a new modernity. As such, for the purposes of this chapter, the examination of deliberative politics provides value to the field of critical policy analysis by offering a purposeful exploration of discourses and participatory processes in policy studies, such as those that have shaped the Title I SIG of 2009.

2 Methodology

The performance, or dramaturgical, dimension of Hajer's analytical framework focuses on a sequence of "staged" performances through which policymakers co-construct the rules of policy making. This framework investigates the four specific aspects of political performance introduced in the previous section: *scripting*, *staging*, *setting*, and *performance*. Together, the exploration of these performances provides an extension to policy studies relying solely upon discourse analysis. In particular, Hajer's concept of *scripting* is used to examine how the rules of deliberative politics are continuously being redefined by the actions of political actors.

2.1 Data Collection

This project was guided by Hajer's (2006a) 10-step prescription for data collection. This particular approach was designed to provide policy analysts with an iterative inquiry model able to examine the social and discursive formation of policy solutions. This iterative approach is based upon the belief that a discourse analysis is an investigation of "what is being said to whom, and in what context" (Hajer 2006a, p. 72). Specifically, this approach examines the socially constructed learning taking place as people react to one another in deliberative settings. Hajer's (2006a) 10 steps of data collection are the following:

1. *Desk research* involves an initial survey of the documents and positions in a given field. This step is meant to provide the researcher with a first chronology and first reading of events.
2. *Helicopter interviews* involve targeting a select group (three or four) of initial actors who can provide an overview of the field from different viewpoints.
3. *Document analysis* involves the analysis of documents in an attempt to understand the story lines, metaphors, and sites of discursive struggle.
4. *Interviews with key players* involve interviewing a broader group of key players and using the questions and interviewer–interviewee interactions as a way to develop generative learning that will serve to uncover shifts in recognition, moments of learning, and reversals of opinion.
5. *Sites of argumentation* involve the search of data that can be used to account for the argumentative exchanges.
6. *Analyze for position effects* means sifting through the collected data to find instances when the involved actors get caught up in interplay or positioning.
7. *Identification of key incidents* involves the identification of incidents that help the researcher to understand the discourse-related dynamics in a chosen case.
8. *Analysis of practices in particular cases of argumentation* involves going back to the data to see if the meaning of what is being said can be related to the practices in which it was said.
9. *Interpretation* involves creating an account of the discourse-related structures of a particular discussion, of practices, and of the sites of production.
10. *Second visit to key actors* involves revisiting a select group of key actors and presenting them with the initial findings to see if they might recognize some of the hidden structures of language.

By working through each of these 10 steps, a qualitative researcher is able to iteratively identify and highlight a narrative of the discursive formations and deliberative actions that give rise to particular policy solutions.

2.1.1 Documentary Review

Review of primary and secondary resources, which is part of stages one and three, allowed me to develop an overview of the positions in the debate on the Title I SIG and helped to cultivate an initial chronology of important events contributing to the final revision of the Title I SIG program of 2009. The review of resources included past Title I SIG policy documents, the current Title I SIG program, the scholarly and technical reports cited by the U.S. Department of Education as the foundation of the current Title I SIG program, technical and research reports distributed by special interests and advocacy organizations targeting both the past and current versions of the Title I SIG program, and media accountings of the debate surrounding the final iteration of the Title I SIG program. This documentary review provided a detailed overview of the numerous viewpoints that shaped the debate surrounding the Title I SIG program. As the analysis progressed, the continued review of documents formed my initial conceptualizations of the story lines and policy vocabularies used to support the Title I SIG program. In the final stages of analysis I was able to develop an interpretive understanding of the ways in which discourses and deliberative performances structured the discussion, practices, and final production of the Title I SIG of 2009.

2.1.2 Interviews

All interviews, including those conducted during stages two and four, were conversational and thus semistructured. A total of 26 interviews were conducted with three categories of actors: (1) government actors, (2) special-interest or advocacy actors and (3) university actors. Data collected from initial helicopter interviews[2] provided a broad overview of the education reform environment in which the Title I SIG program was developed and assisted in the identification of key informants and key documents for analysis. Each of the interviews was conducted over a 6-month period, between September 2010 and February 2011. Due to requests for anonymity, a comprehensive listing of interview participants is not provided; however, each source is cited appropriately throughout the analysis. Additionally, because several interview participants fit within multiple categories, the total number of actors from each of the three target populations appears larger than the total number of actors interviewed. Table 1 provides a listing of the number of interviews that can be attributed to each category.

---

[2] See the Appendix for a detailed listing of all interviewees and their roles.

Table 1 Number of interviews in each category

Role	Number
Government actors (Carter, G.W. Bush, Clinton, & Obama Administrations)	12
Special-interest & advocacy actors	13
University actors	6

2.1.3 Helicopter Interviews and Sampling Techniques

Participants involved in the first round of informal helicopter interviews were chosen after the extensive survey of the documents and were selected through confirming/disconfirming case sampling. Patton (1990) described this style of sampling as important during the early stages of fieldwork, as the researcher is attempting to gather data and confirm the importance of emergent patterns. Specifically, the three categories of actors under examination were developed through the textual analysis of the Title I SIG of 2009. Initial analyses revealed that actors from the three categories mentioned were often provided with the greatest access to the deliberative spaces in which this policy was crafted.

2.1.4 Key Informant Interviews and Sampling Techniques

The second round of interviews, with key informants, took place after I had completed additional textual analyses, allowing me to develop an initial understanding of the discourses structuring the Title I SIG debate. Key informants were selected primarily through the snowball technique, as a convergence of specific policy actors appeared during the conversations in the initial helicopter interviews. Snowball sampling allows a qualitative researcher to pinpoint information-rich informants by asking initial contacts to locate key actors or incidents that play an important role in the issues under investigation (Patton 1990). Key informants were also chosen through the use of the opportunistic sampling method. This method for sampling allows qualitative researchers to make "on-the-spot" decisions and emphasizes the "primary strength" of qualitative inquiry, which is to remain open to new investigatory opportunities as they emerge (Patton 1990, p. 179). This method of sampling worked particularly well within the iterative framework guiding this study, as the back-and-forth analysis of primary and secondary data brought forward new sets of actors as my understandings of the story lines and policy vocabularies structuring the Title I SIG program continued to evolve.

The final round of interviews, the second visit with key informants, was conducted after I had moved through several iterative stages of coding, which involved searching the performative aspects of argumentation, analyzing the collected data for positioning effects, identifying key incidents, and examining the practices in particular cases of argumentation. These interviews allowed me to present key actors with my initial findings and check their understandings of the story lines and policy vocabularies I had identified as structuring the deliberative creation of the Title I SIG program.

2.2 Critical Interpretation of Data

Data analysis focused on the performance dimension of deliberative politics. During this phase, I recoded data (both interview transcripts and documents) in an attempt to uncover the ways in which performative practices—scripting, staging, setting, and performance— were used to promote the Title I SIG revision. This process allowed me to develop a historical understanding of the performative collaborations that structured the deliberative politics of the Title I SIG program. Additionally, I was able to highlight emergent trends as to which actions seemed to have directly and indirectly influenced the final composition of the Title I SIG program.

The second phase of data analysis brought together the critical interpretive linkages between the discourse and performance dimensions of policy making (i.e., this phase of analysis focused on what was communicated verbally and/or in text versus what was enacted). This phase was characterized by the triangulation of large quantities of data as I revisited multiple sources – interview data and archival data. Wodak (2008) suggested that biases in discourse analysis, although always present, could be minimized by the examination of a wide range of historical, organizational, and political sources, providing the researcher with insight as to the social and political discursive fields in which events are embedded. Thus, my revisiting of the diverse range of primary and secondary sources used to interpret the story lines, policy vocabularies, and performative dimensions of this study helped reduce potential limitations of validity caused by an overreliance on limited data sets.

3 Findings

3.1 The L&L Tour: Setting 1

The Listening & Learning Tour (L&L Tour) was the most publicized and time-consuming political performance authorized by the Obama/Duncan Administration prior to the unveiling of their educational policy agenda, as the tour visited a dozen different states and lasted 8 months. The intent of the tour was embedded within the title as presented in the U.S. Department of Education (2009a) press release: "Education Secretary Launches National Discussion on School Reform: 'Listening and Learning Tour' Seeks Grassroots Input on Improving America's

Schools." The L&L Tour was promoted as a deliberative vehicle that would allow the Obama/Duncan Administration to meaningfully engage with "parents, teachers, and administrators," from both "rural" and "urban" communities. Offering insight as to the primary purposes of the L&L Tour, the U.S. Department of Education (2009a) released the following statement, quoting Duncan:

> The primary purpose of the Listening and Learning tour is to, "Have a national dialogue about how to best deliver a *complete and competitive education to all children* [Global Competitiveness][3]—from cradle through career. We want to hear directly from people in the classroom about how the federal government can support educators, school districts and states to drive education reform. Before crafting education law in Washington, we want to hear from people across America—parents, teachers and administrators— about the everyday issues and challenges in our schools that need our national attention and support." (para. 4)

Suggesting the tour's purpose had been realized, a former U.S. Department of Education employee offered the following:

> I think that is what really shaped a lot of his ideas on reform and really what things need to happen across the country. And he went to most of the 50 states. Someone from the senior staff or the Secretary went to all 50 states and talked to education stakeholders, state leaders, teachers, families. All sorts of folks everywhere and really got a sense of what's happening on the ground in lots of different areas and how federal policy can impact different areas in different ways. (Personal communication, January 31, 2011)

Yet, it is important to note that the L&L Tour was launched just a month prior to Secretary Duncan's unveiling of the Title I SIG program at the National Alliance for Public Charter Schools Conference. Of the 13 scheduled L&L Tour stops, only five had taken place (West Virginia, rural; Detroit, urban; Vermont, rural; Montana, rural; and New Jersey, urban) before Secretary Duncan officially revealed the Department of Education's revision of the Title I SIG program of 2009. Thus, Duncan's claim that "before crafting education law in Washington" the L&L Tour would provide "parents, teachers, and administrators" of the nation's schools with a deliberative role in policy formation appears problematic.

In the following subsections, I provide the performative details of the first five stops. The events are shared in the order in which they occurred and they are convey either through the words of the persons in the department, key informants, media coverage, and/or documents produced by the U.S. Department of Education. Within each section, I offer a brief description of the settings and participants involved at each L&L Tour event. When available, I also provide the reasons shared for choosing particular tour events and the Department of Education's synopses of what participants shared at specific sites.

---

[3] The dominant storyline will be placed in brackets to highlight the ways in which this language was during the crafting of a narrative supporting the Obama/Duncan revision of the Title I School Improvement Grant.

3.1.1 Tour Stop 1: West Virginia, Rural, May 5, 2009

The Duncan team launched the L&L Tour in West Virginia as the first of several visits targeting rural constituencies. The West Virginia stop included visits to three schools chosen by Duncan's team after receiving recommendations from West Virginia Governor Joe Manchin (McVey 2009) and State Superintendent of Schools Steven Paine (Kesner 2009). West Virginia's first lady Gayle Manchin, State Superintendent of Schools Steven Paine, and Berkeley County Schools Superintendent Manny Arvon accompanied Secretary Duncan during each of the three tour stops. The first two events were held at Berkeley County schools, Bunker Hill Elementary and Eagle School Intermediate. Avron, speaking to the quality of schools selected by Duncan's team, claimed the administration chose "two outstanding schools, one of which [Eagle School] has received national recognition because they have been able to overcome challenges that face schools across the country with excellent results" (Kesner 2009, para. 13).

The Bunker Hill tour event was labeled as a "private discussion with teachers, administrative personnel and parents" (McVey 2009, para. 8). The 2008–2009 NCLB Report Card classified Bunker Hill as successful on AYP measures, scoring above the district and state average in both reading and math assessments, and identified the school's student population as 43.5 % meeting the qualifications for free and reduced-price lunch, 93.9 % White (*2008–2009 NCLB Report Card: Bunker Hill Elementary School* 2009).

The second stop in West Virginia, labeled as a "roundtable discussion" (Winters 2009), took place at Eagle Intermediate School. At Eagle Intermediate, Duncan conversed with staff members about "what works and what doesn't work in the school system" (Kesner 2009, para. 5). The 2008–2009 NCLB Report Card classified Eagle Intermediate as successful on AYP measures, scoring above the district and state average in both reading and math assessments, and identified the school's student population as 57.3 % meeting the qualifications for free and reduced-price lunch, 66.8 % White (*2008–2009 NCLB Report Card: Eagle Intermediate School* 2009).

The highlight of the final L&L Tour event in West Virginia was a panel discussion located at Blue Ridge Community and Technical College located in Martinsburg. Conducted by Secretary Duncan and moderated by Peter Checkovich (President of Blue Ridge Community and Technical College), the town-hall style meeting allowed Duncan and fellow dignitaries to interact with students, instructors, administrators, and local employers. Blue Ridge Community and Technical College (2011) is a state-supported institution within the West Virginia Community and Technical College System and offers education in the areas of liberal arts, business administration, and a variety of health fields.

"Heard on the Tour": U.S. Department of Education Synopsis of Participant Input

Secretary Duncan's chief of staff, Margot Rogers, summarized the West Virginia L&L Tour participants' contributions:

One of the most important things we can do as policymakers is stay connected with the people who will be affected by the decisions we make. Our first listening tour stop was a powerful reminder of the value of listening to teachers, parents, and students. The elementary school teachers and parents reminded us of three things:

- Leadership matters. In both schools, teachers told us that they stayed because their principals allowed them to perfect their craft, *removed barriers*[4] [Disrupt Complacency], effectively brokered resources, and supported them. Parents felt welcomed by the principals and recognized that great principals attract and retain great teachers.
- The use of formative assessments – and the resulting data – can be transformative. In both schools, teachers used formative assessments frequently to gauge student progress, shuffle student groupings, determine who needed extra support (including Response to Intervention) and extra challenge, and to otherwise drive their instruction. They painted an incredibly clear before picture ("we told parents that their children couldn't read, but that was all") and after picture ("we can tell parents that their child can't read because he has a specific challenge decoding a short 'a' sound") and spoke passionately about how their use of data made them better at their jobs. Parents commented on how this specific information was much more helpful to them.
- *Preparation matters. Teachers generally agreed that their education had not prepared them to be highly effective in the classroom* [Disrupt Complacency]. Many teachers commented that they felt like they got an education that taught them how to teach 25 years ago, and not one that prepared them for teaching in the 21st century. (Rogers 2009, emphasis added)

Taking the Tour Online, May 11, 2009

A week after the L&L Tour event began in West Virginia, the Obama/Duncan Administration introduced a new website meant to offer all school communities with an opportunity to provide input on a specific range of questions about "what's working, and what's not" in public schools. Secretary Duncan introduced the website through the release of the following statement:

> Last week I went to Berkeley County, West Virginia, to begin an open, honest conversation about education reform. I wanted to hear ideas about how we can accomplish President Obama's goal of providing every child in America a complete and *competitive education* [Global Competitiveness], from cradle through career. As we prepare for the reauthorization of No Child Left Behind, I want to hear from classroom teachers and other educators, parents and students, business people and citizens. What's working, and what's not? What do we need to do that we're not doing, and what do we need to stop doing— or do differently? I will be going to 15 other places across the country to continue this conversation. There is one more place I will be going to listen and learn. Here. In the coming weeks, I will ask questions here. *Topics will include raising standards, strengthening teacher quality, using data to improve learning, and turning around low-performing schools.* I will be reading what you say. So will others here at the U.S. Department of Education. Today, I want to start with a simple set of questions: Many states in America are independently considering adopting internationally benchmarked, college and career-ready standards. Is raising standards a good idea? How should we go about it? Let the conversation begin! (Winters 2009, para. 1–9, emphasis added)

---

[4]To highlight some of the words used to inscribe dominant storylines the author uses italicized wording.

This introductory passage highlights how Duncan framed the Listening & Learning Tour as the deliberative vehicle necessary to garner input from the common populous - classroom teachers and other educators, parents and students, business people and citizens. Additionally, the text in this passage outlines the Obama/Duncan educational reform agenda, while effectively linking global competition and economic security with the impetus to reauthorize No Child Left Behind.

3.1.2 Tour Stop 2: Detroit, Urban, May 13, 2009

The second leg of Secretary Duncan's L&L Tour was in Detroit, Michigan, and was the first of tour stops to target urban school communities. The choice to hold an event in Detroit was strategic in nature, as the "poor quality of education" offered by Detroit's public schools had become a "huge focus" (Mrozowski and Wilkinson 2009) during Duncan's promotion of mayoral takeovers in low-performing districts and the broader turnaround reform agenda. This support was voiced a month prior to the L&L Tour events in Detroit when Duncan addressed the nation's mayors at the Mayors' National Forum on Education: "At the end of my tenure, if only seven mayors are in control [of big-city school districts] I think I will have failed" (as cited in Quaid, 2009, para. 5).

The Detroit L&L Tour began with a series of meetings during which Secretary Duncan visited with Michigan Governor Jennifer Granholm, Detroit Federation of Teachers President Keith Johnson, community leaders, and Detroit officials to "discuss challenges facing Detroit public schools and possible solutions to the problems, including mayoral control and strategies for turning around underperforming schools" (Duncan 2009b, para. 2).

The second event was a student forum held at Cody High School, where the Duncan team and dignitaries such as Mayor Dave Bing and State Superintendent Mike Flanagan allowed high school seniors to voice their concerns about education. Though the "Heard on the Tour" blog claimed that Duncan and his team listened to the "heart wrenching stories" (Ali 2009, para. 2) of policy makers, community leaders, educators, parents and students, the official press release (U.S. Department of Education 2009d) did not explicitly mention any such interactions with educators or parents and only detail communications with policy makers, community leaders, and students. At the time of Duncan's visit, Cody High School had been under intense scrutiny by district and city officials due to its consistent failure to meet federal AYP standards. As of the 2007–2008 school year, approximately 97 % of Cody High School's juniors were below proficiency on state math tests and 80 % on the English assessment (Glod 2009). Although the student demographics for Cody High School during Duncan's visit are unclear, the school has since been reconstituted as five separate school academies where, on average, 98.4 % of the student population were labeled as Black or African American (Detroit Public Schools 2009).

Duncan concluded the L&L Tour in Detroit with a keynote speech at the United Way Leaders Conference, addressing over 1500 chief executive officers of United

Way organizations from across the United States. Reinforcing the need for dramatic school reforms targeting the nation's lowest performing schools, Duncan told leaders to "ensure that all children get the education they need and deserve, we must demand fundamental change across the education system and push a strong reform agenda" (Duncan 2009a).

"Heard on the Tour": U.S. Department of Education Synopsis of Participant Input

Russlynn Ali, Assistant Secretary of Education in the Office for Civil Rights summarized the contributions of Detroit L&L tour participants:

> This week we went to "ground zero" for our second stop on the listening and learning tour. We listened to a community hobbled by the decline of an industry that was once the engine of the city's economy, a housing market bust as bad as it gets, recent political strife the likes of which one couldn't make up in a Hollywood screenplay, and a school system suffering beyond compare. Today we listened to Detroit.
>
> We heard heart wrenching stories about unfulfilled dreams from policy-makers, community leaders, educators, parents, and student themselves. We heard from teachers struggling to teach with few needed supports. Teaching, for example, rigorous high school science using a laboratory that is devoid of even the basics, like running water. We listened as high schools seniors told us that more than half of their peers starting with them in the 9th grade were either dead or in jail by the 12th grade. *We heard from community activists and elected officials begging for national attention and support in their moment of urgent crisis* [Unprecedented Opportunity].
>
> But today, we also witnessed hope, responsibility and courage. Hope that finally the forces were aligning for positive change and sustainable reform. *Hope in a new Mayor with the will to do whatever it takes to fix an utterly broken school system* [Disrupt Complacency]. Hope in a Governor with the passion and commitment to help an ailing people. We witnessed courage by everyone to confront the challenges head on; steely determination by students to thrive, no matter what; parents taking ultimate responsibility for their children's future; and teachers finding creative ways to restructure their schools to meet their students' needs. More than anything, we saw an entire community united with the spirit of survival.
>
> *Today we listened to a city ready to transform its schools from a national disgrace to a national model* [Disrupt Complacency]. And, albeit with a heavy heart, we were inspired. (Ali 2009, emphasis added)

The text from the *"Heard on the Tour"* synopses passages pinpoint Duncan's attempt to build a sympathetic constituency for the Obama/Duncan Title I SIG revisions. Specifically, the use of language such as "ground zero," "heart wrenching," and "unfulfilled dreams" highlights Duncan's efforts to position the soon to be released turnaround reform policies as an act of compassion that would counter previous federal efforts to improve public schools.

3.1.3 Tour Stop 3: Vermont, Rural, May 14, 2009

The Duncan team once again sought to involve rural communities, selecting Vermont as the third stop on the L&L Tour. The first event in Vermont took place at St. Michael's College in Colchester, where Secretary Duncan delivered the commencement speech to members of the graduating class, Governor of Vermont Jim Douglas, St. Michael's President John Neuhauser, the St. Michaels Board of Trustees, and members of the faculty (U.S. Department of Education 2009b). St. Michaels College is a small liberal arts college offering 29 majors and serving 2000 undergraduate and 500 graduate students (St. Michaels College 2011). The U.S. Department of Education (2009b) released the following statement regarding Duncan's address at St. Michaels:

> Duncan called education the civil rights issue of our time and said, "All of the anti-poverty programs in the world will never do as much as an education to make people successful." He commended St Michael's graduating class for its commitment to service and challenged them to choose the classroom to continue their service, noting that more than a million teachers from the baby- boom generation are expected to retire in the next five years. "I believe that access to a high-quality education is the difference between a life lived on the margins and a life lived in fulfillment of the American dream," Duncan said. (para. 3–4)

After the commencement ceremonies, the Duncan team visited Lawrence Barnes Elementary School in Burlington. Secretary Duncan first ate lunch with Senator Patrick Leahy, Burlington Mayor Bob Kiss, and Vermont's Education Commissioner Armando Vilaseca ("Secretary Arne Duncan Takes Listening Tour," 2009) and then visited with teachers, parents, and students about the particular educational challenges facing rural communities. In 2008 the Burlington School Board designated Barnes Elementary as one of the nation's first K-5 magnet schools to endorse a sustainability theme (Cirillo 2010). Before its conversion to a magnet school, Barnes Elementary did not have enough Asian, Hispanic, or Black students to register on the state assessment report; however, after its conversion to a magnet school, 25 % of students were categorized as Black (Burlington School District 2011).

The third stop of the Vermont tour took place at the Muddy Waters Café in Burlington, where Secretary Duncan participated in an open-ended conversation with 10 elementary and high school teachers. Tim Tuten (2009), Duncan's director of events, summarized the content of the "teachers coffee":

> Teachers talked about everything from their personal reasons for becoming teachers, to experiences with their students, dealing with discipline, pressure to "teach to the test," national standards, media perceptions of teachers, parents who are intimidated by teachers and schools, cooking for their families after working all day, class sizes, what to wear to school, music, support for teachers who want to be principals, "loan forgiveness" and more. The conversation kept running for a couple hours, even after the Secretary had to leave for his next appointment. (para. 3)

The Duncan team's final stop in Vermont was at Westford Elementary School in Westford. David Wells, principal of Westford Elementary, blogged about the federal government's staging of the "big day":

> I got a call the next day that it was definite, Arne Duncan would be visiting my school. Tim [Duncan's advance man] came out again that Thursday morning to go over how he would enter the building, who he would meet with, which rooms he would use and how they would be set up. I assured Tim that everything would be fine and we were all ready for the visit. As the time drew near, we had more visitors—a security detail, a photographer, and

a videographer. Tim came back to double check our room arrangements and put up banners from the Department of Education. Finally, Arne Duncan came, my students greeted him at the door and escorted him to his meetings. (Wells 2009a, para. 3)

Duncan's time at Westford would be split into two 30-min meetings, one with a group of school stakeholders (school board, district administrators, and parents), the other with Principal Wells and his immediate staff. Wells (2009b) offered commentary on the content of his staff's conversation with Duncan:

> I found that Arne Duncan is interested in keeping the best and brightest in the teaching field and told my young music teacher with many school loans to pay back that his administration was looking into loan forgiveness for educators. When the topic of NCLB came up, *Arne Duncan said that he favored the idea of a global achievement measures over the patchwork of standards and assessments that schools wrestle with today* [Global Competitiveness, Disrupt Complacency]. I was also glad to hear that Arne Duncan spoke about the importance of measuring academic growth rather than penalizing students who have seen real gains but haven't yet met the high bar of state standards. I had heard in the news that President Obama and Secretary Duncan favor the idea of incentive pay for teachers. One of my teachers who had lived with such a system spoke of her concern that teacher by teacher incentive pay had resulted in divisions among educators. Arne Duncan acknowledged that and spoke about his desire to provide incentives to schools where teachers have worked as a team to raise student achievement. (para. 2)

"Heard on the Tour": U.S. Department of Education Synopsis of Participant Input

The only "Heard on the Tour" synopsis of Vermont participant input was that of the conversations taking place at the Muddy Waters Café. Tuten (2009, para. x) summarized the contributions of participants:

> Two weeks ago In West Virginia, our first listening tour stop, teachers told me they would have liked to have met Secretary Duncan after school for coffee. They said the conversation he'd started at their school could have gone on for hours. They'd have time for that after school, when they could relax and just let the conversation roll.
>
> We took that advice to heart. Before arriving in Vermont last week, we contacted a teacher at Colchester High School and asked where her teacher friends hang out. She mentioned a café in nearby Burlington, a few blocks from the university.
>
> That's where 10 elementary and high school teachers stopped in right after school got out, grabbed a coffee, and sat down for an hour with Secretary Duncan for an open-ended conversation. Support for teachers who want to be principals, "loan forgiveness" and more. The conversation kept running for a couple hours, even after the Secretary had to leave for his next appointment.
>
> Something that kept coming up again and again throughout the conversation was the realization that teachers laugh and cry a lot. We cry mostly in the first few years, then we learn to laugh more, and as we get older we cry with joy when our students succeed and graduate. Maybe the teachers in Vermont are just highly emotional, but I don't think so. The teachers in West Virginia told us similar stories, with similar emotional reactions. It seems that if you're going to have a free-wheeling conversation with teachers, you better bring some Kleenex, or if you're in a café, stock up on the napkins. You're going to laugh until you cry, and you're not leaving until everybody hugs each other. This "meeting" really set the tone for the next day's school visits.

The *"Heard on the Tour"* synopsis from the Vermont portion of the Listening and Learning Tour were limited to the seemingly informal "coffee shop" conversation set up by one of Duncan's assistants. Without mentioning the commencement speech or the visit to the local elementary school, the summary of the Vermont stop focused on the emotional state of teachers without providing any details as to the context of the conversation.

3.1.4 Tour Stop 4: Montana, Rural, May 27, 2009

Montana was chosen by the Duncan team as the fourth stop of the L&L Tour, providing Secretary Duncan with a third opportunity to interact with constituents about the issues confronting rural education. The first event was held at Lame Deer High School in Billings, where Duncan, U.S. Housing and Urban Development (HUD) Secretary Shaun Donovan, Senator Jon Tester, and Montana Governor Brian Schweitzer visited with 20 education and school officials, students, parents, and Larry Medicine Bull (Lame Deer's American Indian Culture and Government teacher). In a profile written about Secretary Duncan, the *Christian Science Monitor* described his interactions with the Lame Deer community:

> Sitting in a circle with students and teachers and, in the Native American tradition, passing a feather to the person who had the floor, Duncan listened to the usual litany of requests for computers and fancy equipment. But an air of defeatism pervaded the place: In the past six years, only eight students have gone on to four-year colleges. Duncan was incredulous. (Paulson and Teicher Khadaroo 2010, para. 3)

The article then described Duncan's reaction to the state of poverty witnessed during his visit:

> Duncan says he was hit by how mentally crushing it is to grow up surrounded by poverty—70 percent of the reservation's adults are unemployed—and a sense that even school, the one place that might afford the opportunity to climb out of it, was letting kids down. (Paulson and Teicher Khadaroo 2010, para. 5)

The 2008–2009 NCLB Report Card classified Lame Deer High School as failing to meet both reading (81 % of students failing to meet proficiency) and math standards (95 % of students failing to meet proficiency) on federal AYP measures, and 100 % of the school's students were labeled as American Indian or Native American (Web Report Card: Lame Deer High School 2009).

The second event in Montana took place at the Northern Cheyenne Tribal Council, where Duncan, Donovan, and Schweitzer participated in a "Friendship Ceremony" (U.S. Department of Education 2009c). It appears the primary purpose of this visit was for U.S. HUD Secretary Shaun Donovan to speak with tribal leaders about governmental aide and the persistence of poverty under HUD policies. The Northern Cheyenne Tribal Housing Authority (2010) released the following statement in regards to the visit:

In May, the new U.S Department of Housing and Urban Development Secretary, Shaun Donovan, made a "first-ever" visit to the Northern Cheyenne Reservation along with the Education Secretary, Arne Duncan. This visit was historic as Secretary Donovan was able to see first-hand the issues that have plagued reservations since the inception of HUD funding. Secretary Donovan vowed that he would do all he could to help Native Americans address issues related to Housing. The Tribe had a very nice welcoming for these dignitaries and a Friendship Ceremony was performed by one of our very own Societies. (para. 4)

The final two events on the L&L Tour in Montana included a visit to Broadwater Elementary School and a joint press conference for Secretary Duncan, HUD Secretary Donovan, Senator Jon Tester, and Governor Brian Schweitzer. The Broadwater visit was primarily ceremonial, as Montana Senator Jon Tester's press release and local media coverage suggested the primary purposes of Duncan's visit were to honor Broadwater's 100th birthday celebration (*Tester Hosts Housing, Education Secretaries in Montana* 2009) and to take photos with students (Shay 2009). Although a short promotional video was provided, there was no "Heard on the Tour" synopsis provided for the L&L Tour events in Montana.

3.1.5 Tour Stop 5: New Jersey, Urban, June 5, 2009

The fifth overall L&L Tour stop took place in New Jersey. As the second visit targeting urban school communities, Senator Frank Lautenberg, Senator Robert Menendez, Representative Rush Holt, Representative Donald Payne, and New Jersey Governor Jon Corzine joined Duncan during his visit to North Star Academy-Clinton Hill charter school. North Star Academy was chosen because of its success with students in Newark (U.S. Department of Education 2009d), thus supporting an Obama/Duncan reform agenda that promotes the expansion of charter schools as an integral solution for the nation's consistently low-performing urban school districts. Duncan offered the following response when asked during his visit to New Jersey about those opposed to the expansion of the charter school network as a solution to low-achievement in urban school districts:

> The data on charters is very clear. The highest-performing charters are a huge part of the solution. There are some in the middle, and there are some that are part of the problem. The key for Newark is to bring in more of the high-performing charters [Disrupt Complacency]. There are some amazing players out there who can help. And at the end of the day, it's a false argument against charters. These are public schools, public dollars, public school children and should be part of any reform. (*A Q&A With ... Arne Duncan* 2011)

In anticipation of Duncan's visit, Paul Bambrick-Santoya, managing director of North Star Academy, said he hoped to "share with Duncan their methodology" as a way to contribute to the "massive movement to force change in urban education" (Nutt 2009, para. 5).

During Duncan's stay at North Star, he and fellow dignitaries visited English and math classes, attended a school-wide celebration of academic achievement, and participated in a forum with students and parents (U.S. Department of Education

2009c). At the time of the Duncan team's visit, North Star Academy met the administration's criterion as a high-performance charter school, as it continuously posted achievement scores higher than schools in the same community and based upon the 2008 NCLB data was considered to be the second highest performing urban school in New Jersey (Epstein 2009).

"Heard on the Tour": U.S. Department of Education Synopsis of Participant Input

Todd May, senior director in the U.S. Department of Education Office of Communications and Outreach, provided a brief reflection of the previous L&L Tour stops and summarized the contributions of New Jersey participants:

> Everywhere Secretary Duncan has visited on his listening tour—a Montana Indian reservation, a high school in Detroit, a middle school in West Virginia—students are saying, *"Challenge me, push me, make me work, and I will do it"* [Disrupt Complacency].
>
> He heard the same message in Newark, N.J., one of America's poorest cities. Many families there face so many challenges: rising unemployment, foreclosures, an overburdened social services system. One in three children lives in poverty. No more than half of the 8th grade students pass state tests. A quarter of high school seniors do not graduate.
>
> Yet parents and students find hope in the form of a promise of a better life through education. In Newark, nowhere does that hope shine brighter than at North Star Academy. Children enter this public charter school at the 5th grade often significantly behind their state peers. Less than 35 percent of entering students are proficient in literacy and 15 percent are proficient in math. Yet over 95 percent of 7th graders—who have been in the school less than 2 full years—scored proficient or advanced in language arts literacy and math. Based on these results, North Star is the highest performing school in Newark and 2nd highest among all urban schools in New Jersey.
>
> The secretary and those of us traveling with him observed classes, participated in the all-school "community circle," and heard students and parents testify to the passion and commitment of the teachers and administrators at North Star. We heard how educators take the time to really know their students, and students and parents really know teachers and staff. We saw how teachers challenge students not to just learn but to make good choices— the right choices—and thereby develop their character and an ethos of service. Students talked about their teachers as their second parents— available to them at all hours, on weekends, and whenever they really need them. The passion and commitment of the North Star community has students believing that failure is not an option.
>
> The youth of North Star understand that despite the unwavering efforts of dedicated teachers and supportive staff, the responsibility for learning, achieving and growing ultimately depends on them. These young scholars commit to a schedule that has them attending class or involved in enrichment and remediation activities far after the regular school day ends for other students in the city. And, to avoid the summer slide in academic skills, North Star students have a longer school year and a shorter summer break, with students in class for 200 days a year. Students said this helps build confidence and character and an understanding of the expectations that lie ahead: college. For the North Star student, college is not a "dream, an aspiration or a goal; it is their destiny."
>
> Parents in the North Star community believe fervently in their role as advocates for their children and the children of Newark. *They believe in being more accountable and responsible for their children's academic success* [Disrupt Complacency]. They embrace it

and feel passionately about it. As one parent said, "the happiest day of my life was when I knew my son would be enrolled in North Star and he would have an opportunity to receive a great education." They believe that charter schools like North Star are beacons of hope for parents and students. As one parent said "build on what works, expand it to benefit the entire public education system, and, in turn, renew and revitalize Newark." (May 2009)

These remarks conclude Secretary of Education Arne Duncan's preliminary series of scripted and staged performances of his initial Listening & Learning Tour. The central theme of this concluding synopsis focused on the Disrupt Complacency storyline, as Duncan and his staff framed the success of the Newark North Star Charter as the preferred alternative to public schools that were less "accountable and responsible" for the overall success of children. In the following sections I work through the intimate connection between dominant and privileged storylines and the performative construction of deliberative politics.

4 Intent vs. Reality

According to government officials, the "primary purpose" (intent) of Secretary Duncan's L&L tour was to engage the nation's "parents, teachers and administrators" in a discussion about the ways in which the federal government should support educators in their efforts to "deliver a *complete and competitive education to all children* [Global Competitiveness]—from cradle through career" (U.S. Department of Education 2009a, para. 4, emphasis added). Officials claimed the L&L Tour was intended to engage constituents in a direct manner "before crafting education law in Washington" (U.S. Department of Education 2009a, para. 4). Given the widely publicized intentions of the L&L Tour, I carefully examine this claim in light of the USDOE's political performances. Specifically, I sought to understand how the L&L Tour was enacted vis-a-vis the written and spoken purposes of the tour.

Of the five L&L Tour events staged before the Obama/Duncan Administration introduced the Title I SIG program of 2009, only eight public school communities were visited. Of these eight schools, four were classified as elementary schools, two as intermediate or middle schools, and two as high schools. Additionally, of the campuses selected, only two schools were considered to be low performing (Cody High School and Lame Deer High School) at the time of Duncan's visit.

Consequently, Sargrad's earlier claim that the L&L Tour "shaped a lot of his [Duncan's] ideas on reform" appears problematic (reality). Certainly, even without considering the qualitative depth of conversational dialogue during the first five tour stops, the simple quantity of "deliberative" interactions Duncan and his team shared with dignitaries and school stakeholders fail to serve as an adequate representation of the nation's parents, teachers and administrators that would soon be directly affected by the Title I SIG program.

5 Conclusion

Again, the purpose of this chapter is to provide the field of critical policy analysis with an example of how the dramaturgical analysis of policymaking can add value to our understanding of how discourses and performative politics can be strategically joined to shape educational policy. Traditional interest analysis frameworks are often criticized for their reliance on rationalist assumptions. Critical scholars have argued that rationalistic frameworks rely upon the observance of natural occurrences (Scheurich 1994; Young 1999), overlook the social construction of political questions in the search for a scientifically based solution (Fischer 2003b), and fail to consider the value orientation inherent within research (Hajer 2003; Marshall 1997). Given the increased politicization of the federal government's role in education and the growing number of interests attempting to influence the debates concerning school reform, education policy scholars have recognized the need to extend the field of policy studies by using analytical frameworks that consider both the discourse and performative dimensions of deliberative policy making. This chapter addresses this particular need by employing a critical interpretive policy analysis that illustrates how both dominant discourses and the deliberative performances of the federal government framed the Title I School Improvement Grant program of 2009 as the commonsense solution for the nation's chronically low-performing schools.

Expanding on the field of the rich history of discourse analyses in critical policy analysis, this chapter examines how the Obama/Duncan administration used dominant discourses (privileged and inscribed language) and the deliberative performance of politics (performative act of policymaking) to construct how low performing schools should be addressed in the revision of the Title I School Improvement Grant.

Two primary issues arose during the examination of political performances that helped structure the final revision of the Title I SIG program. First, and most glaring, is the obvious disconnect between the government's stated desire to seek deliberative input on the shaping of education reform and the abbreviated timeline upon which deliberative performances were scheduled. Secretary Duncan promoted the L&L Tour and the Educational Stakeholders Forums as two of the deliberative vehicles that would allow the Obama/Duncan Administration to meaningfully engage with parents, teachers, and administrators when gathering valuable input on the policies targeting the improvement of America's lowest performing public schools. Explicitly outlining the purposes of the tour, Duncan offered that the purpose was to:

> have a national dialogue about how to best deliver a complete and competitive education to all children from cradle through career. We want to hear directly from people in the classroom about how the federal government can support educators, school districts and states to drive education reform. *Before crafting education law in Washington, we want to hear from people across America parents, teachers and administrators about the everyday issues and challenges in our schools that need our national attention and support.* (as cited in U.S. Department of Education 2009a, para. 4, emphasis added)

Certainly, if Secretary Duncan were referring only to the future reauthorization of ESEA, this timeline might have been conducive for gathering such input. However, Duncan joined the deliberative activities of the tour and forum with the shaping of the Title I SIG program, even though only 5 of the 13 tour stops had been conducted and only 1 of the 9 forums had taken place. This abbreviated timeline sheds light on why persons from both parties expressed concerns about the precipitous authoring of the Title I SIG. Specifically, the Obama/Duncan Administration failed to sufficiently vet the revision of the Title I SIG program with persons in the education reform community, members and staffers of Congress, those participating in the L&L Tour, or those invited to participate in the series of Education Stakeholders Forums.

Second, consideration of the L&L Tour and Education Stakeholders Forum performances must be viewed within the context of an administration that considers the nation as mired in an economic and education crisis. This was an important point for Hajer and Uitermark (2007), who maintained that, during crises, standard classifications are inadequate, as authoritative systems are ill equipped to differentiate among competing claims. In this view, the performative acts of education policy makers reflect that they must recognize and maneuver between the multitudes of interests seeking to impose a specific view as to what works in low-performing public schools. The examination of data in this chapter suggests the Obama/Duncan Administration defined the performance specific rules of deliberation and were thus able to determine which turnaround meanings gained credibility during the performative enactment of politics. Therefore, turnaround meanings were directly shaped by the Obama/Duncan Administration's ability to develop the support of discourse coalitions that endorsed a specific way of considering the crisis of low-performing schools, thus neutralizing critics who might question the intricacies of implementing the policies embedded within the turnaround reform agenda.

Roger Ebert (1998) described Barry Levinson's political satire "Wag the Dog" as a cinematic portrayal of how easy it is for the federal government to "whip up a patriotic frenzy," thus warning viewers of the sometimes "dubious" intentions of authority. Note that *dubious* means questionable or suspect as to the true nature or quality. Addressing the "absurd" yet "convincing" themes broached in the script adapted from the Larry Beinhart book, *American Hero*, Ebert offered the following:

> Levinson, working from a smart, talky script by David Mamet and Hilary Henkin, based on the book "American Hero'" by Larry Beinhart, deconstructs the media blitz that accompanies any modern international crisis. Even when a conflict is real and necessary (the Gulf War, for example), the packaging of them is invariably shallow and unquestioning; like sportswriters, war correspondents abandon any pretense of objectivity and detachment, and cheerfully root for our side.

The purpose of this study was not to question the personal motives of President Barack Obama or Secretary of Education Arne Duncan, yet the findings in this chapter seem to resemble the themes brought forward in Ebert's commentary on the issues addressed in "Wag the Dog." Ebert framed "Wag the Dog" as a theatrical illustration of the effectiveness of a government manufactured media blitz when attempting to package crises or conflicts. Ebert's comments seem to suggest that, while shallow, the effectiveness of such "packaging" is that it creates a seductive layer of spin, detaching individuals tasked with covering such crises or conflicts from the deep scrutiny deserved by the general public. The examination of political performances in this chapter illustrates the effectiveness of the federal government's manufactured "deliberative" blitz and the ways in which scripted and staged performances packaged what could be "heard" from parents, teachers, administrators and educational stakeholders. The seductive premise that the government would "listen and learn" to those closest to the issue of low-performing public schools before crafting federal policy provides the pretense that the Title I SIG program and other policies are founded directly upon the ideals that were revealed through deliberative and democratic engagement.

Yet, the findings in this chapter suggests that the federal government's shallow enactment of deliberative politics and constant reiteration of strategic story lines determined the discursive meanings of the issues and challenges used to justify the policy vocabularies and policy solutions embedded within the Title I SIG program. Consequently, such performative politics shaped the meanings of the issues that informed the frenzy surrounding the perceived crisis of persistently low-performing public schools, allowing the Obama/Duncan turnaround reform agenda to initially evade deeper scrutiny as to the potential impact of policy solutions on local communities and the lack of empirical research supporting the turnaround strategies being promoted.

Appendix: Participants & Roles[5]

Participant	Description
Advocacy/interest actors	
Beth Antunez	Beth Antunez was the assistant director in educational issues at the American Federation of Teachers, an affiliate of the AFL-CIO that represents preK-12 teachers; paraprofessionals and other school- related personnel; higher education faculty and professional staff; federal, state, and local government employees; and nurses and other healthcare professionals.
Justin Cohen	Justin Cohen was the President of the School Turnaround Group at Mass Insight Education and the former director of the Office of Portfolio Management and senior advisor to Chancellor Michelle Rhee at the District of Columbia Public Schools. The Mass Insight Turnaround Group is a nonprofit organization that partners with school districts and state education agencies to redesign the ways they support low- performing schools.

(continued)

---

[5] Actors (both helicopter interviews and key informants) whose ideas shaped both the formative and summative stages of sense making, but whose direct comments did not appear in this portion of a larger study.

Participant	Description
Daria Hall	Daria Hall was the director of K-12 policy development at the Education Trust, where she focuses on issues pertaining to accountability; high school graduation; standards; and the identification of high-poverty, high-minority, high-performing schools. The Education Trust is a policy organization that focuses on issues pertaining to academic achievement for all students.
William Mathis	William Mathis was the managing director of the National Education Policy Center at the University of Colorado at Boulder and the former superintendent of schools for the Rutland Northeast Supervisory Union in Brandon, Vermont. The National Education Policy Center employs scholars and policy analysts who produce and disseminate peer-reviewed research on a variety of educational issues.
Vicki Phillips	Vicki Phillips was the director of the Education, College Ready in the United States Program at the Gates Foundation and a former education specialist at the U.S. Office of Education in Washington, DC. The Gates Foundation funds a variety of initiatives that focus on the preparation of college- and career-ready students and the attainment of postsecondary education.
Cynthia Brown	Cynthia G. Brown was the vice-president for education policy at the Center for American Progress, a former director of the Resource Center on Educational Equity of the Council of Chief State School Officers, and the former assistant secretary for civil rights in the U.S. Department of Education (appointed by President Carter). The Center for American Progress is a policy advocacy organization supportive of the "progressive movement." Brown's work focuses on issues pertaining to the education of low-income and minority students, standards-based education, federal education programs, state education agency operations, state education policy, federal civil rights enforcement in education, and preschool education.
Diane Stark Rentner	Diane Stark Rentner was the director of national programs for the Center on Education Policy and a former legislative associate for the U.S. House of Representatives' Committee on Education and Labor. The Center on Education Policy is an independent advocacy organization that focuses on issues pertaining to the role of public education in a democracy and the need to improve the academic quality of public schools.
Advocacy/interest & federal actors	
Andy Rotherham	Andy Rotherham is a cofounder and partner at Bellwether Education and a former White House Special Assistant to President Clinton for Domestic Policy. Bellwether Education Partners is a national nonprofit organization that focuses on issues pertaining to the achievement of low-income students.
University Actors	
Daniel Duke	Daniel Duke is a professor at the University of Virginia, where he is recognized as a nationally recognized expert on educational change and reform, school leadership and accountability policy, and issues pertaining to the turnaround of low-performing schools.

(continued)

Participant	Description
Betty Malen	Betty Malen is a professor at the University of Maryland, where she is recognized for her work in education politics, policy, and leadership and issues pertaining to reconstitution reform efforts targeting low- performing schools.
Joseph Murphy	Joseph Murphy is the chair of education and associate dean at Peabody College, Vanderbilt University, where he focuses on issues pertaining to school improvement, turnaround reform, leadership, and policy.
Joe Johnson	Dr. Joseph Johnson is the executive director of the National Center for Urban School Transformation and the former director of student achievement and school accountability at the U.S. Department of Education, where he was responsible for directing the federal Title I program and several related programs.
Diane Ravitch	Diane Ravitch was a professor at New York University, where she focuses on the history of education and education reform. She was Assistant Secretary of Education during the presidency of George H. W. Bush.

References

A Q&A with… Arne Duncan: The eyes of America are on Newark's school reform. (2011, April 3). Retrieved from http://blog.nj.com/perspective/2011/04/a_qa_with_arne_duncan_the_eyes.html

Ali, R. (2009, May 15). *Heard on the tour: Detroit.* Retrieved from the U.S. Department of Education Learning & Listening Tour website: http://www.ed.gov/blog/topic/listening-tour/page/3/

Burlington School District. (2011). *About us.* Retrieved February 20, 2011, from http://bsdweb.bsdvt.org/aboutus.php

Cirillo, J. (2010). *Vermont boasts first sustainability-themed elementary magnet school.* Retrieved from http://www.sustainableschoolsproject.org/news/vermont-boasts-first-sustainability-themed-elementary-magnet-school

Confirmation of Arne Duncan: Hearing of the Committee on Health, Education, Labor, and Pensions, 111th Congress, 1st session (2009a, January 13) (statement of Arne Duncan).

Detroit Public Schools. (2009). *Welcome to DPS.* Retrieved February 20, 2011, from http://detroitk12.org/schools

Duncan, A. (2009a, June 8). *Robust data gives us the roadmap to reform* [Speech]. Retrieved from the U.S. Department of Education website: http://www2.ed.gov/news/speeches/2009/06/06082009.html

Duncan, A. (2009b, September 8). *Secretary Duncan joins AFT president for kick-off of AFT Back-to-School'09* [Transcript]. Retrieved from the U.S. Department of Education website: http://www2.ed.gov/news/av/video/youtube/index.html

Ebert, R. (1998, January 2). Wag the Dog [Film review]. *Chicago Sun Times.* Retrieved from http://rogerebert.suntimes.com/apps/pbcs.dll/article?AID=/19980102/REVIEWS/801020302/1023

Epstein, V. (2009). *NJ to get $891 M in education stimulus funding.* Retrieved from http://www.mycentraljersey.com/article/20090606/STATE/90606003/NJ+to+get++891M+in+education+stimulus+funding

Fischer, F. (2003b). *Reframing public policy.* New York: Oxford University Press.

Freeman, T., & Peck, E. (2007). Performing governance: A partnership board dramaturgy. *Public Administration, 85*(4), 907–929.

Glod, M. (2009, May 16). Duncan delves behind grim statistics: Detroit students go face to face with education chief on what they need to succeed. *The Washington *Post*, Retrieved from http://www.washingtonpost.com/wp-dyn/content/article/2009/05/15/AR2009051503152.html?wpisrc=newsletter&sid=ST2009051301564

Hajer, M. A. (2003). A frame in the fields: Policymaking and the reinvention of politics. In M. A. Hajer & H. Wagenaar (Eds.), *Deliberative policy analysis: Understanding governance in the network society* (pp. 88–112). Cambridge: Cambridge University Press.

Hajer, M. A. (2005a). Rebuilding ground zero: The politics of performance. *Planning Theory and Practice, 6*(4), 445–464.

Hajer, M. A. (2005b). Setting the stage: A dramaturgy of policy deliberation. *Administration and Society, 36*(6), 624–647.

Hajer, M. A. (2006a). Doing discourse analysis: Coalitions, practices, meaning. In M. van den Brink & T. Metze (Eds.), *Words matter in policy and planning: Discourse theory and method in the social science* (pp. 65–74). Utrecht: Koninklijk Nederlands Aardrijkskundig Genootschap.

Hajer, M. A. (2006b). The living institutions of the EU: Analysing governance as performance. *Perspectives on European Politics and Society, 7*(1), 41–55.

Hajer, M. A., & Uitermark, J. (2007). Performing authority: Discursive politics after the assassination of Theo Van Gogh. *Public Administration, 86*(1), 1–15.

Hajer, M. A., & Wagenaar, H. (Eds.). (2003). *Deliberative policy analysis: Understanding governance in the network society*. Cambridge: Cambridge University Press.

Tester hosts Housing, Education Secretaries in Montana. (2009, May 27). Retrieved from http://tester.senate.gov/Newsroom/pr_052709_secretaries.cfm

Kesner, J. E. (2009, May 5). U.S. Secretary of Education to visit area today. *The Journal*. Retrieved from http://www.journal-news.net/page/content.detail/id/519203.html

Marshall, C. (Ed.). (1997). *A perspective from primary and secondary schooling*. London: Falmer Press.

May, T. (2009, June 17). *Heard on the tour: North Star Academy, Newark*. Retrieved from the U.S. Department of Education Learning & Listening Tour website: http://www.ed.gov/blog/topic/listening-tour/page/3/

McVey, J. (2009). Stopping to listen, learn: Education secretary pays visit to Berkeley County on his tour. *The Journal*. Retrieved from http://www.journal-news.net/page/content.detail/id/519245.html?nav=5006

Mrozowski, J., & Wilkinson, M. (2009, February 14). DPS fails kids, fed school chief says: Education secretary says district must be improved. *The Detroit News*. Retrieved from http://detnews.com/article/20090214/POLITICS/902140377/DPS-fails-kids--fed-school-chief-says

2008–2009 NCLB Report Card: Bunker Hill Elementary School. (2009). Retrieved from http://wveis.k12.wv.us/nclb/pub/rpt0809/printrp/test.cfm?cn=004&school=204&sn=204&coname=BERKELEY&rpage=index.cfm&rptnum=rpt09

2008–2009 NCLB Report Card: Eagle Intermediate School. (2009). Retrieved from http://wveis.k12.wv.us/nclb/pub/rpt0809/printrp/test.cfm?cn=004&school=218&sn=218&coname=BERKELEY&rpage=index.cfm&rptnum=rpt09

Northern Cheyenne Tribal Housing Authority. (2010). *2009 in a nutshell*. Retrieved from http://nctribalhousing.org/?p=486

Nutt, C. (2009, June 5). *U.S. education secretary to visit Newark charter school North Star Academy*. Retrieved from http://www.nj.com/news/index.ssf/2009/06/us_education_secretary_to_visi.html

Patton, M. (1990). *Qualitative evaluation and research methods* (2nd ed.). Newbury Park: Sage.

Paulson, A., & Teicher Khadaroo, S. (2010, August 30). Education secretary Arne Duncan: Headmaster of US school reform. *The Christian Science Monitor, 7*.

Quaid, L. (2009, March 31). School chief: Mayors need control of urban schools. Associated Press.

Rogers, M. (2009, May 11). *Heard on the tour*. Retrieved from the U.S. Department of Education Learning & Listening Tour website: http://www.ed.gov/blog/topic/listening-tour/page/3/

Scheurich, J. J. (1994). Policy archeology: A new policy studies methodology. *Journal of Education Policy, 9*(4), 297–316.

Secretary Arne Duncan takes Listening Tour to Vermont, invites comments. (2009, May 18). Retrieved from the U.S. Department of Education Learning & Listening Tour website: http://www.ed.gov/blog/topic/listening-tour/page/3/

Shay, B. (2009). Broadwater visit may be on tap. *Billings Gazette.* Retrieved from http://billingsgazette.com/news/local/article_078f16b5-5ec6-5d19-9afe-a262ce0127c1.html

St. Michaels College. (2011). *At a glance.* Retrieved February 20, 2011, from http://www.smcvt.edu/about/

Tuten, T. (2009, May 21). *Heard on the tour: Vermont coffee house.* Retrieved from the U.S. Department of Education Learning & Listening Tour website: http://www.ed.gov/blog/topic/listening-tour/page/3/

U.S. Department of Education (2009a, May 28). Montana students call for higher standards on Listening Tour. Retrieved from http://www2.ed.gov/news/ pressreleases/2009/05/05282009.html

U.S. Department of Education. (2009b, May 5). U.S. Education Secretary launches national discussion on school reform: "Listening and Learning Tour" seeks grassroots input on improving America's schools [Press release]. Retrieved from http://www.ed.gov/news/press-releases/education-secretary-launches-national-discussioneducation-reform

U.S. Department of Education. (2009c, May 14). U.S. Education Secretary delivers commencement address at St. Michael's College and continues "Listening and Learning" Tour in Vermont [Press release]. Retrieved from http://www2.ed.gov/news/pressreleases/2009/05/05142009.html

U.S. Department of Education. (2009d). U.S. Education Secretary takes his "Listening and learning" Tour to New Jersey: Announces that state now has more than $891 million available for reform and to help save jobs. Retrieved from http://www2.ed.gov/news/pressreleases/2009/06/06052009.html

U.S. Department of Education. (2009e). U.S. Education Secretary takes Listening and Learning Tour to Detroit: Fundamental change in education and strong reform agenda needed. Retrieved from http://www.ed.gov/news/press-releases/us-education-secretary-takes-listening-and-learning-tour-detroit

Web Report Card: Lame Deer High School. (2009). Retrieved from the Montana Office of Public Instruction website: http://data.opi.mt.gov/WebReportcard/disagg.svg

Wells, D. (2009a, May 25). *When the U.S. Secretary of Education visits your school.* Retrieved February 20, 2011, from http://principalofchange.wordpress.com/page/2

Wells, D. (2009b, May 17). *Who is this Arne Duncan?* Retrieved from http://principalofchange.wordpress.com/tag/school/

Winters, K. (2009, May 11). *Secretary Arne Duncan takes listening tour online, invites comments on raising standards.* Retrieved from the U.S. Department of Education Learning & Listening Tour website: http://www.ed.gov/blog/topic/listening-tour/page/3

Wodak, R. (2008). Introduction: Discourse studies—Important concepts and terms. In R. Wodak & M. Krzyzanowski (Eds.), *Qualitative discourse analysis in the social sciences* (pp. 1–29). New York: Palgrave Macmillan.

Young, M. D. (1999). Multifocal educational policy research: Toward a method for enhancing traditional educational policy studies. *American Educational Research Journal, 36*(4), 677–714.

Utilizing Michel De Certeau in Critical Policy Analysis

Curtis A. Brewer and Amanda Bell Werts

Abstract In this chapter we argue that the use of Michel de Certeau's concept of *consumption* offers a complementary analytical tool for the critical study of policy in education. We assert that there is a gap in critical policy analysis regarding the need to understand educators as simultaneously active democratic subjects and governed subjects. Therefore we contextualize Certeau's theory by explaining the theoretical, historical, and experiential forces that engendered his desire to theorize the power of the passive. Then we delineate the broad initial framework explained by Certeau for the study of the practice of everyday life. We conclude with a hypothetical example of the possibilities of application of Certeau's concepts of *consumption* in *everyday* life in critical policy analysis in education.

Keywords Critical policy analysis • Democratic subjects • Governed subject • Certeau • Consumption • Everyday

In this chapter, we explore Certeau's (1984) theory of *consumption* in the *everyday* and the subsequent narrators of the theory (see Ahearne 1995; Buchanan 2000; Giard 2000; Roberts 2006; Ward 2000). Specifically, we argue that using the concept of *consumption* offers a complementary analytical tool for the critical study of policy in education. The foregrounding of this concept helps elucidate the active democratic subject working through schools (Rancière 1991). Such an approach might help educators find possibilities for radical forms of democracy through the appropriation or use of policy in ways that are not completely prescribed, locked down, normative, or separated from their practice.

Certeau (1984) dedicated his book, *The Practice of Everyday Life*, to the recurring subjectivities of "an anonymous hero" and the "murmuring voice of societies"

C.A. Brewer (✉)
Department of Educational Leadership and Policy Studies, The University of Texas at San Antonio, San Antonio, TX, USA
e-mail: curtis.brewer@utsa.edu

A.B. Werts
Reich College of Education, Appalachian State University, Boone, NC, USA

who do "not expect representations" (p. v): anonymous because they work from within, murmurs because they share quietly in a fog of domination and they do not seek representation because they know the power of surveillance. In the same vein, key to our exploration of Certeau's theoretical framework is an assumption that the subjectivities of educators vary across social and temporal contexts and the enactment of these subjectivities are enacted through various forms of governance (Stoker 2003). Such a starting point allows us to critically study how people, at the turn of the twenty-first century, continue to practice education amidst a policy hyperactivity that works to crudely quantify the outcomes of education (Ball et al. 2011a). Our concerns echo the tradition of critique that illuminated the dilemma of the practice everyday life after the quantification and commodification of culture unleashed by the growth of capitalist mass production during the nineteenth and twentieth centuries (Benjamin 1999; Foucault 1977; Lefebvre 1947).

Our work coincides with critical policy analysts who deployed the concept of *policy enactment* (Ball et al. 2012; Singh et al. 2014). The concept proved fruitful in helping explore how "putting policies into practice is a creative, sophisticated and complex but also constrained process" (Braun et al. 2011a, b, p. 568). Differing from past implementation studies, *policy enactment* research hopes to illuminate how policy is not simply adopted but instead enacted through productive processes of translation, elaboration and embedding in the local cultures and situated necessities (Maguire et al. 2011). In order to "generate some theoretical leverage for making sense of education policies in process in schools" (Braun et al. 2011a, b, p. 581), we build on the idea of policy enactment and offer a reading of Certeau's (1984) theoretical concept of *consumption* through the *everyday*.

Consumption through the *everyday* refers to a social process of usage of the context by groups of social subjects that may be divergent from the dominant forms of representation and organization in a historical moment. These divergences of use are attempts by social groups to satisfy a desire to practice everyday life that escapes forms of alienation resulting from dominant institutional practices. Attention to usage allows us to ask, as Certeau (1984) asked, "what popular procedures (also miniscule and quotidian) manipulate the mechanisms of discipline and conform to them only in order to evade them" (p. xiv)?

In order to evaluate the possible utility of Certeau's approach we structured the paper as follows. First, we will point to a gap in the theorizing of critical policy analysis regarding the need to understand educators as simultaneously active democratic subjects and governed subjects. Next, we contextualize Certeau's theory by explaining the theoretical, historical, and experiential forces that engendered his desire to theorize the power of the passive. Third, we delineate the broad initial framework explained by Certeau for the study of the practice of everyday life. Finally, we offer a hypothetical example of the possibilities of application of Certeau's concepts of *consumption* in *everyday* life in critical policy analysis in education.

1 Policy Enactment and Active Subjects

Critical policy analysis (CPA) scholars offer their readers glimpses of moments of opportunities for resistance within the dominant educational accountability policy regime. They do so in part by reframing our understanding of the educator or student as a governed subject (Ball 2005; Ball et al. 2011a, b; Carpenter et al. 2014; Thompson 2008; Welton 2011). As part of this reframing, authors record the affective results of accountability in specific schooling environments (Maguire et al. 2011), and how the accountability policies themselves are actually enacted in schools (Maguire et al. 2012; Werts et al. 2012). Key to this reframing is a recognition that we need to treat the policy process as complex and incoherent and that we should attend to the discourses and policy technologies "producing (teacher and student) subjects as their effects" (Braun et al. 2011a, b p. 581).

Stephen Ball and his research team have consciously attended to the educators as policy subjects. They propose three theoretical statements regarding how current education policy in the UK works to discursively and materially construct the educator subject through "a network of social practices which are infused with power relations" (Ball et al. 2011a, p. 611). First, they propose that different kinds of policy, such as imperative policies compared to exhortative policies, produce different kinds of policy subjects; the former producing primarily passive subjects, the latter producing more reflexive subjects. Second, building on the first, they argue that teachers move through these contrasting subject positions through coping strategies where they are always "keeping up" as the definition of their professionalism is simultaneously constrained and extended (p. 616).

Finally, and maybe most importantly, they propose that in the current policy framework most critique by educators is reduced to "discomfort" and "murmurings" (Ball et al. 2011a, p. 617). The authors use the theoretical work of Foucault (1972) and explain "policies work to exclude statements which they characterise as false and they keep in circulation those statements which they characterise as true" (p. 618). If critiques cannot circulate, then what is in circulation is discomforting experiences and murmurs of discontent.

The authors go on to articulate: "Policy enactment involves different sorts of policy actors in the work of interpretation (decoding) and translation (recoding) of policy" (Ball et al. 2011a, p. 619). Supporting this proposition is a typology of *policy actors* with distinct forms of policy work (Ball et al. 2011b, p. 626). They explain that the *policy actors* or the positions "are not necessarily specific individuals"; people may be narrators who interpret the policies for the local school, and/or they may be entrepreneurs who work to integrate the policy to the local school (p. 626).

We applaud this work as it begins to outline a provocative theoretical approach to policy enactment; an approach that recognizes the past over-emphasis on egocentric cognitive reframing in policy implementation studies (see Werts and Brewer 2015). In addition, the authors take seriously the dialectical tension between the educators as governed subjects and educators as democratic subjects. While this work recognizes the importance of understanding how educators navigate the role of the governed subject, the analytical approach that Ball et al. (2011b) deploy (based on Foucault's (1972) archeology) does not take into account "the elaborations, connections, deductive series or style of texts" *produced* by the subject (p. 612). That is, the framework does not theorize how the governed subject used the forms of domination to evade governance.

To this end, we offer an analytical tool that was conceptualized in light of Foucault's critique of his own method (Ward 2000). Certeau's (1984) theorization of *consumption* offers a framework for thinking about "the models of action characteristic of the users" often under theorized as passive following Foucault's (1977) analysis of the exercise of power through disciplinary technologies. The goal of Certeau's (1984) work was precisely to "bring to light the clandestine forms taken by the dispersed, tactical, and make-shift creativity of groups or individuals already caught in the nets of 'discipline'" (p. xv).

Thus, we argue that such a theoretical augmentation offers methodological possibilities for understanding how teachers *keep up* with their institutional subjectivities in order to find, evade, or utilize them according to the exigencies of their everyday. We advocate for an approach that takes into account the practices that occur amongst the discomfort and murmuring. Our assertion is that the work of Certeau offers a approach to the study of educators that are caught in the nets of policy. Below, we first describe our general resonance with Certeau's work through a description of the context in which he was writing. Then, we look more specifically at the theoretical concepts he articulated to answer his questions.

2 The Everyday, Loss of Authority and the Pseudo-Believer

Certeau's work in the *Practice of Everyday Life* represents a conjunction of the Marxist philosophical respect[1] for the *everyday* in post-war twentieth century France and Certeau's own experiences with resistance in the late 1960s. Below, we will explain the philosophical roots of the concept of the *everyday* and historical contexts that shaped Certeau's perspective on the governed subject. Through this contextualization of the concept of the consumption of the everyday we hope to draw the reader's attention to the parallel between the historical moment in which Certeau was writing and our current one (or possibly ours is an extension of his), where society is governed less by modern forms of authority (bureaucracy, patriarchy, etc.) and more by constrained discretion facilitated through panoptic technologies (Foucault 1977; Stoker 2003).

---

[1] Although Roberts (2006) claims that the utilization of Certeau has diminished a full understanding of the philosophical concept of the everyday, we believe that Certeau's purposive use of it in his title shows his recognition of the centrality of the concept.

2.1 The Everyday as Revolution

In the first half of the twentieth century, Lenin, Trotsky, Lukács and others theorized the concept of the *everyday* as a site of social change (Roberts 2006). Building off the Marxist argument that the critique and eventual demise of capitalist forms of life were dependent on the "collective aesthetic and sensuous reappropriation of everyday experience," these authors attempted to theorize the conditions for the practice of everyday life in terms of re-appropriation (Roberts 2006, p. 13). However, blinded by the needs of a growing population, Lenin and other Soviet leaders felt that the everyday culture of the proletariat needed to be based in a narrow, self-conscious discipline of industrial labor modeled on Tayloristic approaches. Trotsky supported this assessment by pointing out that the aim of the revolution was not to "smash Fordism, but to socialize and purge it" (as cited in Roberts 2006, p. 23). Trotsky (1973) however, sensing the dilemmas raised by such a narrow definition of the everyday, attempted to mitigate the approach by theorizing the possibilities of the worker-correspondent. A worker-correspondent collected materials on problems occurring in the local workers lives and through acts of self-representation tied them to the wider issues of the revolution (Trotsky 1973). The self-representations of the workers (mostly understood as newspaper articles) served a dual purpose of connecting intellectual labor to manual labor in order to facilitate the historical consciousness of the proletariat as well as act as petitions for organizational change (Roberts 2006). The worker-correspondent movement as a strategy for collective aesthetic appropriation of everyday life was carried out for only a few years. In 1924, Stalin chose to regulate the worker's perspective and the party worked to sift out writers who could hurt the party's authority (Hicks 2007).

In Western Europe, in the middle of the twentieth century, the rise of fascism tempered the left's enchantment with the revolutionary possibilities of the everyday. As Roberts (2006) pointed out, only Benjamin (1999) offers a theorization of the everyday which contains two distinct parts. He theorizes that in everyday life there is a part, made up of moments, that are unregulated or prescribed by the authoritative order. However, these moments represent a remainder to the second part that is constituted by the "structured activities of science, technology and social administration which define and regulate daily experience" (Roberts 2006 p. 6). Following the Second World War, Lefebvre (1947) picks up this distinction and titles it *everydayness* as the mode of authoritative administration of productive forces and the *everyday* as that which is outside that administration. He describes this in his work *The Critique of Everyday Life*. Lefebvre saw the everyday as a place where "mass-mediated and industrialized everydayness is unable to completely regulate and reify the shared practices, customs, forms of resistance, self-identify and moments of subversion of a 'common culture'" (Roberts 2006 p. 67). Roberts (2006) contended Certeau engages this distinction in his own work and thus conceptualizes the *everyday* as "the irreducible remainder" pregnant with possibilities of resistance.

In other words, Certeau, like many of his contemporaries, treated the *everyday* as the site of resistance but were wary of both the Soviet and capitalist systems. As the twentieth century wore on it was clear that in both systems, the normal lives of people were run through with forms of domination (everydayness) that work to commodify and systematize all forms of cultural life in order to increase production and legitimate various hierarchies. As Certeau theorized the power of the governed, he located their non-regulated practices in the *everyday* alongside and underneath *everydayness*. Importantly, from his perspective these practices of resistance do not necessarily exist outside of dominant institutional frameworks and are possibly most exposed in times of institutional transition.

2.2 Studies of Shifting Authorities

Along with the theoretical arguments in his readings on the everyday as a site of resistance, Certeau's concerns with the complexity of the power of the governed were also visible in his first projects as a historian for the Roman Catholic Church. In one of his first studies, he looked at seventeenth century European history when ecclesial power broke down; the moment where "Christianity became privatized [...] leaving a vacuum that the political as such filled" (Ward 2000, p. 6). People of this time were faced with a question of who to follow, what to believe or how to continue. Ways of making meaning of the world needed reorganization as the new authoritative orders developed and the new authorities wanted ways of meaning making that were less spiritual. Certeau's specific subject of study was important: the new ecclesiastical order the Jesuits (of which he was a twentieth century member) and particularly a spiritual, mystical branch and their coincidence with the birth of modernity. These subjects were governed by an older authoritative order of the catholic church *and* the growing power of science, commerce, and information; and, yet at the same time, embraced a spiritual mysticism. Certeau studied how a modern collective developed a mystical sensibility at the exact moment when authority was being grounded in worldly epistemologies (Giard 2000).

The mystics wrote at the same moment as emergence of new sciences that claimed rational authority such as anthropology, ethnography, and engineering. His investigation of this era of social, cultural, and political change centered on questions concerning "the power of institutions to produce new knowledges and discipline its subjects" (Ward 2000 p. 4) and importantly, the power of the subjects to consume the disciplining practices. As his long time coauthor, Luce Giard, pointed out, Certeau's historical investigations into the "disenchanted world" of early modern Europe led him to investigate how a few social circles "tried to restore a communication with God" (Giard 2000 p. 21). That is, in a setting where the medieval spiritual culture gave way to the culture of the moderns and the church and her order lost authority, he wanted to investigate how modern people (Jesuits were a thoroughly modern sect) within the church practiced their everyday life and how they chose to narrate those practices.

We feel this early work is important because he draws our attention to the ways in which older forms of authority (the Catholic church) are present as newer forms of authority (sciences and risk-based economies of modernity) develop and how subjects (mystic Jesuits) who occupy institutional positions must practice everyday life (resistance) through them. Certeau's attention to this moment of transition in authority in Europe reveals the complexity of how governed subjects navigate networks of sanctioned practices.

Importantly, Certeau's investigations of the dawn of modernity made him particularly attuned to the demise of modern sources of authority in France in the late 1960s. Reflecting on this change, he wrote: "Believing is being exhausted. Or at least it takes refuge in the areas of the media and leisure activities. It goes on vacation" (de Certeau 1984, p. 180). He was concerned with how people continue to operate as a society calls into "question [its] entire system of representation" (Ward 2000 p. 5). Thus, he was interested in how people practice their everyday life while the power and disciplines that shaped much of their *everydayness* were being discredited.

As Certeau experienced the beginning of the death of the modern era in May of 1968 he realized the gravity of the change and his narration of the event was important to the movement (Buchanan 2000). Certeau wrote:

> Something happened to us. Something began to stir us. Emerging from who knows where, suddenly filling the streets and the factories, circulating among us, becoming ours but no longer being the muffled noise of our solicitude voices that had never been heard began to change us. At least that was what we felt. From this something unheard of was produced: we began to speak (as cited in Ward 2000 p. 4)

The "something" that Certeau begins this quote with had a subtle quality. In this historical moment people began to see through the *everydayness* mantle of authority that previous generations had worn. This meant that they began to narrate their *everyday* feelings. Certeau and others at the time felt a different culture struggling to be heard just beneath the "remnants of modernity's unquestioned powers and disciplines" (Ward 2000, p. 5). However it would become clear that they were not engaged in a full revolution as the systems of authority of modern France were not really changed or disregarded. In fact, by the end of the summer business as usual continued.

Certeau's engagement with this moment, his historical research, and the theoretical context in which he was educated resulted in his desire to theorize how people practice their everyday life as the cultural cohesion dissipates. He wanted to try to understand how people live out their lives still engaged with systems of knowledge and organization that they no longer trust or to which they do not completely adhere or endorse. What does a culture look like when it is practiced not by adherents but by "pseudo-believers" (Ward 2000, p. 7)?

2.3 Resonances

Certeau wrote the book *The Practice of Everyday Life* out of his theoretical concern for *everyday* as a site of resistance, his historical recognition of the complexity of the governed subject trajectory, and his own experience with social resistance. In fact, the book was the outcome of a large research grant funded by the French government through the Délégation Générale à la Recherche Scientifique et Technique (DGRST). The governing body wanted a broad study of culture that would allow a development of a futurology; one that would allow them to predict social upheaval. As a pseudo-believer himself, Certeau "had little taste" for the futurist goal and downplayed it (Buchanan 2000, p. 2). Instead, Certeau and his coauthors attempted to suggest an approach to the study of culture that allowed us to understand how the "everyday evidences a discernible form and conceals a knowable logic" (Buchanan 2000, p. 90). Rather than focusing on the power of institutions to constitute the subjects (as Foucault's approach offered) they chose to look to how people practice everyday life within the institutions or rather how people consume the institutions.

The acknowledgement of a knowable logic of resistance hidden amongst the dominant culture and its alienated pseudo-believers parallels our much more specialized recognition that just beneath the accountability culture that was born in the last gasp of the modern era, is a muffled noise. Accountability culture in education is rooted in modernist assumptions about the value of objective measures, Tayloristic efficiency, standardization, individualism, and meritocracy. The various educational accountability systems implemented through the U.S.A. and U.K. operate through and reinforce this network of beliefs. In doing so they tend to circumscribe educator work within these systems. Yet, just as this system begins to completely infiltrate and dominate educational institutions the underlying assumptions are being questioned. Educators, parents, and students, through their experience of both everydayness and the everyday, question the fantasy of objective measures and the over reliance on individualistic approaches to work (Porter 2015). Despite this questioning and dissonance, the systems continue to operate and are implemented by the very people who question their legitimacy (Carpenter and Brewer 2014).

We propose that educators are practicing the *everydayness* of accountability culture as pseudo-believers or alienated subjects. Our questions are similar to Certeau's in that we want to know if the everyday practices of the people living out "accountability" evidence a hidden cultural logic of resistance. We are interested in the combination of operations of those who consume the system or to state it differently, the power of the dominated. In order to begin the development of a project that understands the enactment of policy as a practice of consumption by the alienated or the pseudo-believers, we will first explore the concepts Certeau pointed to as important to the study of consumption.

3 Consumption: Ways of Operating

In his investigations of everyday life, Certeau was not concerned so much with the makeup of everyday life (e.g. that certain activities took place), but rather how it was that these everyday practices occurred—the usage rather than the use, function, or purpose. With the loss of modern modes of authority, Certeau pointed to a reawakening on the part of the alienated or the pseudo-believer in that a person was not rotely following a particular set of beliefs and consequently, a prescribed set of actions. In this section, we describe the particular qualities of this focus: the difference between use and usage and the hidden and particular nature of usage. We do so in order to illuminate what we see to be Certeau's unit of analysis in his investigation of everyday life.

3.1 Use v. Usage

Buchanan (2000) explained that "the measure of success of [Certeau's] project will be whether or not the practices of everyday life remain in the background or not, whether their specificity of operation is delineated and articulated" (p. 91). The distinction between use and usage is that of comparing a static picture to a dynamic one, where use or simply the practices of everydayness could be seen as a static, unmoving representation. Usage, on the other hand, points beyond that static representation to the operation, or the temporality of situated everyday practice.

The "specificity of operation" or *ways of use* suggests meaning or signification beyond the *use* or representation of the object; instead, one must pay attention to the ways that the object is used across time. This would be the difference between the intended function of a rocking chair (a particular artifact) and the act of rocking (a particular action) in a rocking chair. For example, the pace of rocking an infant could be a key *way of using* the rocking chair when trying to feed or calm them. For that matter, a rapid rocking pace may also indicate anger on a particular afternoon in a particular culture, intended or not. Certeau (1984) explained "these 'ways of operating' are similar to 'instructions for use'" (p. 30). The difference between use and usage can be seen in the idea of instructions for use that delineate steps taken that can also be modified, and are lived out, rather than an intended function or use. This focus on the living out of practices also opens the door to what Certeau refers to as "styles of action" (p. 30). He compares them to styles of literature: "just as in literature one differentiates 'styles' or ways of writing, one can distinguish 'ways of operating' ways of walking, reading ..." (p. 30); therefore, use as it is lived out (e.g. the pace of the rocking chair) can have a particular character that "create[s] a certain play ... through stratification of different and interfering kinds of functioning" (p. 30). In other words, focusing on ways of use allows a researcher to think about how the use of a particular object can be divided into different kinds of usage that are unique or at odds with the intentions of the dominant forms of organization.

For our purposes, the focus on everyday life helps us study the nuances of living through policy enactment, where educators continually live out "styles of action" or particular combinations of policy enactment and instructional expertise. Certeau's approach pushes us beyond investigating the abstraction of policy implementation, and instead insists that the usage or ways of use are understood as inhabited through a particular space and time as well as composed a of particular sequences.

3.2 Hidden Practices

The world of representation serves the dominant order by classifying and categorizing objects and actions and allowing those representations to stand in for their lived out expression. Signifying practices (e.g., the ways in which practices gain their significance or meaning) highlight the purpose or "material of these practices" (p. xviii). However, the dominant order's crystallization and codification of the functional meaning hide or steal many creative and interesting usages of available objects. For example, the dominant order might assume that content standards in education offer a guide for a successful scaling up of the production of an educated work force. However, the everyday use of those standards by a critical educator might engage a construction of the logic of justice for the subaltern (Gillen 2009). As we pointed out above, the everydayness "evidences a discernible form and [simultaneously] conceals a knowable logic" of the practice of the everyday (Buchanan 2000, p. 90).

Certeau also helped us see that the way that we not only make sense of (e.g. give meaning to) objects and actions, but also study them, conceals their ways of use. Statistical investigation, an example he used throughout his investigations of the practices of everyday life, "is satisfied with classifying, calculating, and putting into table the 'lexical' units ... in reference to its own categories and taxonomies" (p. xviii). The process of categorization references the materials that make up the object being studied (e.g., the units that make up the object being studied), but not particular formulation of the object. He explained "[statistical investigation] determines the elements used, but not the 'phrasing' produced by the *bricolage* (the artisan-like inventiveness) and the discursiveness that combine these elements" and in doing so "finds' only the homogenous" (p. xviii). Thus, the breaking down or classifying the material studied does not explain the ways in which they are used, acted out, and lived (e.g. the knowable logic); therefore, a fundamental quality of ways of use is that they are hidden or rather overlooked by our representational system and predominant modes of inquiry.

De Certeau (1984) explained, consumption is

> characterized by its ruses, its fragmentation (the result of circumstances), its poaching, its clandestine nature, its tireless but quiet activity, in short by its quasi-invisibility, since it shows itself not in its own products ... but in an art of using those imposed on it (p. 31).

Thus, if we momentarily separate the practice of everyday life from the signifying practices that constitute the everydayness of life, we can see that the former has a seemingly irregular logic that is not immediately knowable. Certeau (1984) describes this logic as following a trajectory similar to "Brownian movement" (p. xx). If we think for a moment about the epistemology of this perspective, it requires not allowing the logic of conventional signifying practices to stand in as explanation for how we live out our lives. At the same time, we cannot leave behind conventional signifying products and therefore must work within them (e.g. use the products "imposed on it"). In other words, our glimpses of consumption cannot be whole or complete as they are compromised by the system in which they exist and trace irregular trajectories through time. Importantly this does not suggest a systemic revolution because these logics would not exist outside of their "clandestine nature." Instead, the possibility of a separate, hidden logic must be investigated. For example, a creative dean of students practices student discipline through the application of school safety policies in ways that mollify the moral panic following school shootings. However the dean's practices might contain a logic that validates a student's struggle but also minimizes the destructive elements of the panic. This logic may be hidden to everyone except the offending student and the dean in that its exposition might only occur in a specific place and time such as behind the closed door of an office following the offense (Brewer and Lindle 2013).

The hidden nature of consumption should draw one's attention beyond the purpose of a given practice to consider the hidden logic behind various opportunities of that practice. Scholars of CPA such as Braun et al. (2010) have pointed out that focusing on the typologies of response to educational policy erases the inherent complexity, the "connected and dependent" (p. 558) quality of policy enactments in context. We wish to point out that we cannot completely turn the system on its head and ignore that which often silences educators, but rather acknowledge the silencing and attribute a particular hidden logic to educators working through silence within these policy systems.

3.3 *Strategies and Tactics*

Strategies and *tactics* are the terms Certeau uses to describe two types of ways of operating. They are possible modes of usage or making do that are deployed in multiple societies. These two concepts represent knowable logics of practice or, ways of using the world. For us, they are starting points for understanding the ways in which educators use the world (policies included) to practice education.

Specifically, we are interested in these ways of use within the context of the pseudo-believers. As Buchanan (2000) argues "strategy and tactics [in Certeau's work] are not so much modalities of power as indexes of belief" (p. 87). Certeau wanted to make possible a discussion of the practice of everyday life in the space between absolute belief in the disciplining practices of authority and the "despiritualized anarchy in which cynicism reigned supreme" (Buchanan 2000, p. 104). As such, one must understand strategies and tactics as forms of practice of everyday life that are dialectical. In the study of these practices, we may begin to understand the evidence of "a discernable form" and begin to see the "knowable logic" that the practice of everyday life conceals. (Buchanan 2000, p. 104). Certeau (1984) hoped to begin a discussion on the "continuing investigation of the ways in which users—commonly assumed to be passive and guided by established rules–operate" (p. xi). In doing so, he hoped to illuminate how people live (cook, create neighborhoods, walk the city) through the space between authority and absolute freedom. Certeau's discussion of strategies and tactics should not be understood as an exhaustive list of the forms of practice of everyday life, but rather reference points within a "schemata of action" (de Certeau 1984, p. xi). Below, we describe Certeau's conceptualizations of strategies and tactics and their place within the schemata of action he broadly described.

3.3.1 Strategies

As noted above, volume one of *The Practice of Everyday Life* was an attempt to make possible a conversation about "the ways in which users–commonly assumed to be passive and guided by established rules–operate." (p. xi). The goal was to provide a broad outline for the study of the "operational combination" that is often hidden; the "modes of action" characteristic of the users from all levels within society (p. xi). Inclusively, he wanted to bring into conversation the practices of the "dominated" who he felt past theorists ignored due to assumptions of docility or passivity. The seemingly passive engage in strategic and tactical everyday practices through the everydayness of the dominant order.

Strategies are practices of life that are engaged when a "subject of will and power (a proprietor, an enterprise, a city, a scientific institution) can be isolated from an 'environment'" (de Certeau 1984, p. xix). To put it another way, a strategy is a practice of everyday life that is enacted through an institution of authority. The institution of authority (i.e., school, plantation, city government) creates a place through strategic calculations that make one's fortune in life less random. Certeau (1984) writes that it is "a Cartesian attitude, if you wish: it is an effort to delimit one's own place in a world bewitched by the invisible powers of the Other" (p. 36). Users of the world who practice strategies engage in actions that allow them to "capitalize acquired advantages" and thus prepare for the future (p. 36). The strategic practice of everyday life then involves acting in ways that master time and space to create a place. For example, the rise of nation states in the modern era involved securing borders through military practices then using the future production of that land as collateral for diplomatic and fiscal recognition.

Certeau (1984) also highlighted that strategies are a form of practice that involves mastery through "sight" (p. 36). Specifically, he is referencing Foucault's work that explicated "panoptic practice." He writes that the division of space into places allows one to "transform foreign forces into objects that can be observed and measured, and thus control and 'include' them within its scope of vision" (p. 36). In the early twenty-first century, this dimension of strategies can be observed in examples ranging from the study of the vectors of infectious disease, to the development of test-based accountability movements in education, to the growth of cyber counter-intelligence. Each example involves practices of everyday life that measure threats to the established place (communities, taxpayers, corporations) and work towards eliminating the potential damage. Importantly, Certeau points out the users of this practice "run ahead of time by reading a space" (p. 36).

The establishment of place through panoptic practices elevates the production of a certain kind of knowledge. Strategic practices create a place for knowledge that claims to be neutral or disinterested. For example, in the west the state may fund private professional armies or scientific endeavors, but the actors enjoy certain autonomy from the state. However, their practices and the knowledge they produce are constituted by and support the state's strategic practices. Thus, a place (a city, a nation, a school) produces itself in and through the power of the knowledge (often scientific and military knowledge) that it supports.

Significantly, strategies are forms of consumption, or practices of everyday life that are characterized by a use of the world to create autonomous places that are not subject to the dangers of the surrounding environment or the passage of time. Certeau (1984) sums it up as follows:

> strategies are actions which thanks to the establishment of a place of power (the property of a proper), elaborate theoretical places (systems and totalizing discourses) capable of articulating an ensemble of physical places in which forces are distributed (p. 38).

Strategies are practices of everyday life, consumption of the world, that are essentially defensive. As Buchanan (2000) pointed out they are connected to a paranoia; paranoia that gets worked out through "building of castles" or institutions that can "domesticate the body" (p. 89).

It is important here to remind ourselves that our goal is not the analysis of "individuality" (p. xi). Rather, we are concerned with a broad culture that is constituted through the act of consumption across groups. Strategic consumption is a calculation of defense not made by one official, general or teacher but a practice enacted across culture. Different groups engage in different dimensions of this practice through enacting the practices common to students, teachers, scientists, bureaucrats, policy makers, overseers, nurses, doctors, counselors, financial planners, entrepreneurs, infantry, police, or generals.

Thus, we should understand that any group of actors in society can engage in practices beyond their regulated subjecthood and that at times these practices are strategic. However, it is important to remember the engagement of strategic practice bolsters its power through legitimation of other strategic actions deployed by the dominant: to create an alternative progressive school one must legitimate the organizing notion of schooling. If we are going to utilize this concept in critical policy analysis we should attempt to identify how educators engage in practices that may establish a place for student development yet be aware that this place's survival, in part, depends on the legitimation of larger strategic operations such as standardization and testing.

3.3.2 Tactics

Certeau (1984) names a practice a tactic if it is a "calculus which cannot count on a 'proper' (a spatial or institutional localization) nor thus on a borderline distinguishing the other as a visible totality." He continues, "A tactic insinuates itself into the other's place, fragmentarily, without taking it over in its entirety, without being able to keep it at a distance" (p. xix). Thus a tactic is a practice of "seizing opportunity," of "poaching," of "knowing how to get away with things" and of "appropriation" (p. xix). He identified tactics as the "ingenious ways in which the weak make use of the strong" (p. xvii).

So while strategic practices involve the creation of place out of space, tactical practices transform someone else's place into a "space borrowed for a moment" (xxi). Tactics "must play on and with a terrain imposed on it and organized by the law of a foreign power" (p. 37). For example, a student may use the time allotted for working on an assignment to write notes to a love interest or a graffiti artist may use advertisements at a bus stop to make social commentary on inequality in the city. The student and the artist consume the allotment (of space or time) but never own it.

Due to being within the place of the foreign power and not privy to (or disregarding the legitimacy of) the big picture, tactics are characterized by isolated actions; "blow by blow" (p. 37). A response to panoptic practices, tactical practices "vigilantly make use of the cracks that particular conjunctions open in the surveillance of the proprietary powers" (p. 38) That is, "strategies pin their hopes on the resistance that the establishment of a place offers to the erosion of time; tactics [pin their hopes on] a clever utilization of time" (p. 39). The student is clever in how she pursues her desires; the artist is clever in how she cries foul.

Therefore, the study of the practice of everyday life or the study of how governed subjects live out their lives as pseudo-believers must also include a recognition of tactical moments. Moments when the weak disrupt, contradict, and stall the will of the strong.

In CPA for education we must look for moments when groups of people such as teachers, students, and parents engage in practices that momentarily use dominant schooling spaces to critique, denaturalize, or debase dominant forms of governance. Given the theoretical description above, a critical policy analyst can assume that in any system of governance groups of people are engaged in patterns of practice that are at times strategic and at other times more tactical. The critical study of policy enactment therefore should focus on the styles of action or *usage* of dominant policies. It is in these dispersed and hidden actions that we see how the policies are evaded. Below we will offer a hypothetical application and show how the critical study of the *usage* of policies that work to standardize writing might help illuminate the styles of action that evade the limits of the writing policies.

4 A Hypothetical Application

As we described above, Ball and his colleagues offered very useful tools for the critical study of policy enactment. They have also theorized how educators must enact the various "contrasting subject positions" and how they are always "keeping up" as their role is redefined through legislation (Ball et al. 2011a, p. 616). We assert that the utilization of Certeau's work will offer a theoretical guide to this study of "keeping up." Below we will explicitly describe our vision of the application of the theory in order to extend the critical study of policy enactment.

As a starting point, a critical policy study that utilizes Certeau's theory of consumption through the everyday requires an assumption that those who enact policy at the local level are not only governed subjects. In addition, the analyst should build off of previous critical studies on the site at hand that have identified the mode of domination that is common within education in a given historical time and place. Finally, it would require the desire to understand a group's operational logics of resistance that developed over time out of the usage of the context rather than the establishment of a typology of abstract revolutionary practices.

Once a group of actors are identified the researcher would need to embed herself within the context in order to begin to record the erratic trajectories of their operational logics of resistance. That is, one would need to look for the practices, actions, or discursive performances that are distinct from the *everydayness*: to look for strategic or tactical practices that are normally hidden among regulated practices. In order to do so, one would need to observe members of this group across multiple physical and temporal settings. Given Certeau's emphasis on the importance of unique usage of each setting, a thick description would be required.

The analysis would require an explanation of the logic of these dispersed, varied usages of the context in relationship to strategic and/or tactical practices. The analyst would need to judge if the practices are strategically or tactically flavored. The following questions would guide the analysis: "Do the practices represent an attempt to establish time or place for alternative forms of education through the dominant forms of schooling?" and/or "Do the practices represent moments of tactical practices, radical ruptures that denaturalize dominant forms of schooling?" If it is the former, then one must ask "what ways do the practices support larger strategic practices?" and if the latter then one must ask "what conjunction of contextual elements provided the opportunity for such a disruption?" From these starting points one could begin to study the power of the pseudo-believer; the power of the governed.

As an example, we propose a critical analysis of a common education policy concerning student writing. At the turn of the twenty-first century, there was a proliferation of policies that attempted to standardize the definition of quality writing for secondary students and establish exams designed to certify that the secondary students could produce a quality product. By 2002, in the U.S.A., 15 states required students to pass such an exam in order to graduate from high school (Chudowsky et al. 2002). Much of this political focus on writing was couched in economic terms. It was assumed that the economic health of a society was dependent on the creation of information that could be leveraged for profit. As Brandt (2005) states, writers "put knowledge in tangible, and thereby transactional, form...Writing, we might say, is hot property" (p. 167). The commodification of writing through education policy fits with historical political positioning of public education in the U.S. as the state supported producer of human capital for private markets (Spring 2008).

The standardization of writing as a practice of creating transactional products introduces students to self-expression as an alienating process rather than one of intersubjective democratic identity creation. In addition, the testing format often results in students responding to a prompt and writing without presence of other texts. The assessment of the writing exam is conducted along standardized criteria, a phenomena which renders the content of the writing, the student's ideas, empty for all practical purposes.

Most of the teachers and students in the schools understand these issues and yet it is their enactment of the policy that brings it into the real. They are practicing pseudo-believers. A study of their resistance along the lines described above would require an ethnographic eye that is open to the cognitive, physical, and affective dimensions of the practice of schooling and the ways in which the policy enactment is woven into the lives of the students and the teachers.

In such a study, it would be imperative to pay attention to multiple locations and social interactions in order to understand how the policy is being simultaneously enacted and disturbed: the usage of the policy over and above the use of the policy. For example, an ethnographic treatment of the teacher's role might include attention to how they describe the test to students, the ways the stress engendered by the test is used to teach students about the role of evaluation in the creation of self, and the ways in which teachers use the pretext of the test to help students to experience writing for other purposes. Alongside the classroom, it would be important to watch how teachers proceed during peer-level meetings and meetings with administrators; for instance, the location of the assessment on the meeting agenda compared to the attention the test scores get in the meetings. Finally, one would need to pay attention to how teachers narrate their jobs to their families and friends and the degree to which their position on the policy changes once they are outside of the institution. Across all of these settings one would be looking for moments of strategic or tactical practice that attempts to impose a will that is contradictory to the policy intent through the enactment of the policy. However, most importantly an analysis of these moments would entail a sequencing of itinerant and stunted practices and the possible alternative logics that they indicate.

We must emphasize that one must look for more than a cognitive reframing of the policy (Werts et al. 2012). Instead one must also look at the range and trajectory of the emotional responses to the enactment of the policy. The physical experiences of stress, elation, fatigue, escape and other physical manifestations would need to be taken into account as these logics are constructed across time. To state it succinctly, the analyst would be looking for the embodied appropriation of the *everyday* as educators and students impress their democratic subjecthood amongst the noise of the *everydayness*.

5 Conclusion

In this chapter, we argue for the utility of Certeau's conceptualization of the *consumption* of the *everyday* as a theoretical guide in the practice of critical policy analysis. We assert that this approach helps augment the concept of *policy enactment* (Ball et al. 2011a). Importantly, the critical study of policy enactment utilizing the concept of *consumption* through the *everyday* should be understood, not as an approach to technocratic study of policy implementation with a desire towards fidelity, rather as part of the larger critique of the contradictions that arise in the practice of everyday life after the quantification and commodification of culture in the last moments of the modern era.

References

Ahearne, J. (1995). *Michel de Certeau: Interpretation and its other*. Stanford: Stanford University Press.
Ball, S. (2005). *Education policy and social class: The selected works of Stephen Ball*. London: Routledge.
Ball, S. J., Maguire, M., Braun, A., & Hoskins, K. (2011a). Policy actors: Doing policy work in schools. *Discourse: Studies in the Cultural Politics of Education, 32*(4), 625–639.
Ball, S. J., Maguire, M., Braun, A., & Hoskins, K. (2011b). Policy subjects and policy actors in schools: Some necessary but insufficient analyses. *Discourse: Studies in the Cultural Politics of Education, 32*(4), 611–624.
Ball, S. J., Maguire, M., & Braun, A. (2012). *How schools do policy: Policy enactments in secondary schools*. London: Routledge.
Benjamin, W. (1999). *The arcades project*. Cambridge: Harvard University Press.
Brandt, D. (2005). Writing for a living literacy and the knowledge economy. *Written Communication, 22*(2), 166–197.
Braun, A., Maguire, M., & Ball, S. J. (2010). Policy enactments in the UK secondary school: Examining policy, practice and school positioning. *Journal of Education Policy, 25*(4), 547–560.
Braun, A., Ball, S. J., & Maguire, M. (2011a). Policy enactments in schools introduction: Towards a toolbox for theory and research. *Discourse: Studies in the Cultural Politics of Education, 32*(4), 581–583.

Braun, A., Ball, S. J., Maguire, M., & Hoskins, K. (2011b). Taking context seriously: Towards explaining policy enactments in the secondary school. *Discourse: Studies in the Cultural Politics of Education, 32*(4), 585–596.

Buchanan, I. (2000). *Michel de Certeau: Cultural theorist*. London: Sage.

Brewer, C. A., & Lindle, J. C. (2013). Negotiation of care and control in school safety. In G. Muschert, S. Henry, A. Peguero, & N. Bracy (Eds.), *Responding to school violence: Confronting the Columbine effect*. Boulder: Lynne Reinner.

Carpenter, B. W., & Brewer, C. (2014). The implicated advocate: The discursive construction of the democratic practices of school principals in the USA. *Discourse: Studies in the Cultural Politics of Education, 35*(2), 294–306.

Carpenter, B. W., Diem, S., & Young, M. D. (2014). The influence of values and policy vocabularies on understandings of leadership effectiveness. *International Journal of Qualitative Studies in Education, 27*(9), 1110–1133.

Certeau, M. (1984). *The practice of everyday life* [Arts de faire.]. Berkeley: University of California Press.

Chudowsky, N., Kober, N., Gayler, K. S., & Hamilton, M. (2002). *State high school exit exams: A baseline report*. Washington, DC: Center for Education Policy.

Foucault, M. (1972). *The archaeology of knowledge*. London: Tavistock.

Foucault, M. (1977). *Discipline and punish: The birth of the prison* (A. Sheridan, Trans.). New York: Vintage Books.

Giard, L. (2000). Introduction: Michel de Certeau on historiography. In G. Ward (Ed.), *The Certeau reader* (pp. 15-15-23). Oxford: Blackwell Publishers.

Gillen, J. (2009). An insurrectionary generation: Young people, poverty, education, and Obama. *Harvard Educational Review, 79*(2), 363–369.

Hicks, J. (2007). Worker correspondents: Between journalism and literature. *The Russian Review, 66*(4), 568–585.

Lefebvre, H. (1947/2002). *Critique of everyday life*. London: Verso.

Maguire, M., Hoskins, K., Ball, S., & Braun, A. (2011). Policy discourses in school texts. *Discourse: Studies in the Cultural Politics of Education, 32*(4), 597–609.

Porter, E. (2015, March 25). Grading teachers by the test. *New York Times*, pp. B1.

Rancière, J. (1991). *The ignorant schoolmaster: Five lessons in intellectual emancipation*. Stanford: Stanford University Press.

Roberts, J. (2006). *Philosophizing the everyday: Revolutionary praxis and the fate of cultural theory*. London: Pluto Press.

Singh, P., Heimans, S., & Glasswell, K. (2014). Policy enactment, context and performativity: Ontological politics and researching Australian national partnership policies. *Journal of Education Policy, 29*(6), 826–844.

Spring, J. H. (2008). *The American school: From the puritans to no child left behind*. London: McGraw-Hill Humanities/Social Sciences/Languages.

Stoker, G. (2003). *Transforming local governance: From thatcherism to new labour*. London: Palgrave Macmillan.

Thompson, D. F. (2008). Deliberative democratic theory and empirical political science. *Annual Review of Political Science, 11*, 497–520.

Trotsky, L. (1973). *Problems of everyday life and other writings on culture and science*. New York: Pathfinder Press.

Ward, G. (Ed.). (2000). *The certeau reader*. Oxford: Blackwell Publishers.

Welton, A. (2011). The courage to critique policies and practices from within: Youth participatory action research as critical policy analysis. A response to "Buscando la Libertad: Latino Youths in Search of Freedom in School". *Democracy and Education, 19*(1), 1–5.

Werts, A. B., & Brewer, C. A. (2015). Reframing the study of policy implementation lived experience as politics. *Educational Policy, 9*(1), 206–229.

Werts, A. B., Brewer, C. A., & Mathews, S. A. (2012). Representing embodiment and the policy implementing principal using photovoice. *Journal of Educational Administration, 50*(6), 817–844.

Policy Studies Debt: A Feminist Call to Expand Policy Studies Theory

Wanda S. Pillow

Abstract This chapter argues that the field of policy studies faces a policy debt, a debt created by theoretical absences and blind spots, a debt unaccounted for. Citing an expanse of data that details a debt of school inequity, Pillow argues this is data that requires an obligation of policy scholars to engage in theory and praxis differently. Women of Color theorizing is introduced as one analytic, which when centered theoretically, challenges ontological and epistemological foundations of Critical Policy Analysis and creates obligations of praxis. Demonstrating what this looks like in a policy studies project, Pillow argues for the necessity of analytics such as Women of Color theories to be seen as more than identity additive models if policy studies is going to face and begin to take responsibility for its education debts.

Keywords Policy studies • Women of color feminisms • Education disparity

> I don't understand how they do that...How can they just ignore history?...It's like we don't exist...This makes me angry, but I also feel sad.
>
> When I was wait'n for the bus and there's like these signs, posters showing a screaming baby and saying "mom, you won't graduate from high school now," and I just felt like everyone was look'n at me and thinking I'm stupid...I wish I could've just become invisible or be like y'know in a different body.

The above quotes—one from my then 10 year old son reacting to the lack of mention of slavery in a Lewis & Clark Interpretive Center[1] and the other from a pregnant high school student—speak to the embodied violences, the "racial-micro-aggressions" (Smith et al. 2011) youth of color experience on a daily basis

---

[1]Clark brought his slave, York, on the 1804–1806 Corps of Discovery expedition. For discussion of lack of attention to York see: Betts 1985; Pillow 2016.

W.S. Pillow (✉)
Department of Education, Gender Studies/Education Culture and Society, University of Utah, Salt Lake City, UT, 84112-0442 USA
e-mail: wanda.pillow@utah.edu

as they navigate organizations, institutions, and communities that let them know their histories and lives do not matter, that they do not belong.

Experiences of micro-aggressions are well documented in school ethnographies and can be seen in local, state, and national data sets that continue to show stark differences in education access and completion in the U.S. (Muhammad 2010). Correspondingly, we have a rich archive of evidence demonstrating schools and classrooms as places of racialized-colonial practices and curricula; research tracing racialized-colonial policies of separation and exclusion; and decades of data demonstrating disparate practices of funding, resources, training, curricula, infrastructure, and treatment all of which impact what access looks like across U.S. schooling (Cohen and Moffitt 2009). Disparity is evident in national, state, and local school attendance and completion statistics; disciplinary actions and referrals; special education referral and placements; continuing education referrals and placements; and push-out practices (CRDC 2014; Stovall 2013).

We know this data—it is repeated in conference spaces, town hall meetings, and cyclically referred to in media. Education journals produce reams of studies discussing the meanings of this data—debating where the problem lies, critiquing existing policy and practice, arguing paradigmatic or methodological approaches—yet discussion seems to only replicate a narrative of the problem: the existence of disparity in schools. This is data that (should) break(s) our hearts (Pillow 2014b) yet what are we—policy education scholars—doing with and about this data? After years of discussion about the "drop out" or "at risk youth" or the "plight of urban education" do we really not know what to do? Do we really not know what ails us in U.S. school policy and practice?

These questions haunt me and at times leave me exhausted, angry, and ashamed of my own participation in producing scholarship that seems to have little impact, while at the same time I have argued for the importance of working at all levels of intervention—theoretically, methodologically, and in praxis. Yet, as a Feminist scholar, writing and thinking with Women of Color Feminist epistemologies, as a mother of three—the youngest coming to age in a world filled with violence against Black youth—and as a research/scholar who has seen little to no change on young mothers' access to education (Pillow 2004, 2006, 2013), I am feeling a sense of dissonance and urgency to review where policy studies is as a field.

For me, the evidentiary weight of data—the weight of what we know about disparate and unjust conditions in schools and school policy has hit home. Dr. Gloria Ladson-Billing (2006) describes the legacy of education disparities as an "education debt"—something we owe—and here I extend this logic to discuss the "policy debt" occurring in education. Taking this debt and my role and responsibility in it seriously, this essay asks and explores what kind of policy studies will we enact in the face of this debt? What kind of policy studies do we want? And what is/are the purpose(s) of our work?

Working alongside the impetus of Critical Policy Analysis (CPA), I re-turn to feminist policy analysis and specifically Women of Color feminist theory to provide a working example of what this lens can provide to rethink and challenge policy studies in addressing the above questions. Specifically, I provide an overview of four characteristics of Women of Color feminist theory and discuss how these four properties provide necessary interventions in policy studies analysis. Utilizing a working example based upon improving young mothers'[2] access to school, I discuss what it looks like to face the education/policy debt at the policy table—the place of problem solving and policy making—particularly when those impacted by the debt, young mothers, and those charged with "fixing" the debt, social work staff and administrators, are present at the table. Here, Women of Color feminist theory became not simply a new paradigm to try on, but a rethinking necessary to begin to face our policy debt.

1 Women of Color Feminist Theory and Critical Policy Analysis

It could be argued that feminist theorizing made its way into policy studies by the late 1990s (Marshall 1997), however, the radical re-structuring, re-imagining that is part of feminist theorizing has not influentially altered how we do policy studies. Perhaps this is because feminist theorizing has been narrowed to be about gender primarily, creating constructs of other intersectional "add on" categories of race, sexuality, etc. This watering down of feminist theorizing—a neglecting of feminist theories of power, relations and the state—as well as a lack of emphasis on praxis, a uniquely feminist focus on relational responsibilities to do, to put our work to work—renders feminist theory as just another critical paradigm in critical policy studies. Here, I interrupt predominant usages of feminist theory in policy studies by employing the phrase "Women of Color" feminist theory. I acknowledge the potential problematics of this phrasing—essentialism, cooptation—but as explicated below, I use the phrase to emphasize and mark the necessity of radical rethinkings to address policy debt.

Influenced by The Santa Cruz Women of Color Collective's (2014) insistence to retain the phrase "Women of Color" feminisms as a political and social marking and remembering, I utilize Women of Color feminisms to refer to a rich and complex body of theory and literature by Black, Indigenous, Asian, Latina/Chicana, and decolonial/postcolonial theorists and feminists[3] that provide in-depth engagement with the structures and experiences of race, gender, ableism, sexuality, status, and empire/colonialism. While this work can be read alongside

---

[2] I utilize the phrase "young mothers" instead of the commonly used phrase "teen mothers" because it was the preferred wording of those involved in the described project. Young mothers are school age females (ages 13–20) who are/were pregnant and who either have full or part-time custody of their child(ren) or placed their child for adoption. The phrase "expectant/parenting youth" (EPY) is used to differentiate inclusion of young fathers.

[3] See The Santa Cruz Women of Color Collective 2014 essay for a beginning list of scholars this essay pulls upon.

any feminist epistemology, including liberal, material, poststructural, or queer feminisms, Women of Color feminisms provides a significantly different starting place theoretically.

As The Santa Cruz Women of Color Collective (2014) states: "We argue that the formation 'women of color' resonates in feminist and philosophical debates as a critique of and alternative to oppressive, canonical forms of knowledge" (24). In addition to serving as a lens of critique, Women of Color feminisms "enables a way of seeing the world through a lens that refracts light in many ways to reveal a world of possibilities, a world that is constantly shifting and in motion" (The Santa Cruz Women of Color Collective 2014, 24). Women of Color feminisms offers thick descriptions and analytics that acknowledge and theorize the complexities of daily-lived relational experiences. Women of Color feminisms provides analytics to trace how power works across intimate familial, institutional and nation-state relations experienced through social and political discourses, structures, policies, theories, research, and practices.

Women of Color theorizing mobilizes an "always already" theorizing of subjectivity and power; an always already that accounts for histories of colonialism and the intimate relations of power expressed through containments and expressions of gender, race, sexuality, and status (Alexander 2005; Anzaldúa 1987; Lorde 1984; Maracle 1996). As María Lugones (2010) articulates: "We are moving on at a time of crossings, of seeing each other at the colonial difference constructing a new subject of a new feminist geopolitics of knowing and loving" (756). This "new feminist geopolitics" focuses attention on how race, gender, ableism, status, sexuality, and empire/colonialism operate always in cohort together. Such an analytics is key to education policy studies. If, as has long been argued, we acknowledge that education rises out of and is part of colonizing projects (Peterson 1971), then we need analytics that keep the impacts of colonialism in play in relation to for example, racial and gender disparities in school discipline referrals.

Thus, thinking with Lugones, I argue that something different and indispensable occurs when Women of Color feminisms is situated as core ontology and epistemology[4] to centrally think, problematize, and work from. Centering Women of Color theory is different from using Women of Color feminisms as identity work or as intersectional critique. In such usages, Women of Color feminisms is on the side to "real theory," attached as a one-note attempt at including race or inserted as a treatment for gaps in the "real theory." Consider how often such terms are tacked on a prefix to the central real theory: "feminist" policy studies, "queer" policy studies, etc.

This is not to neglect the importance of thinking with the complexities of structural identities. For example, Kimberle Crenshaw's (1989, 1991) development

---

[4]Ontology is concerned with the nature of being, how reality is defined and yields a theory of existence. Epistemology refers to how we know and yields a theory of knowledge. For useful differentiation of feminist epistemology, methodology and method see Harding (1987) and Pillow and Mayo (2011). For discussion of how race and empire impact theory see Dillard (2000) and Pillow (2003).

of "intersectionality" to explain Black women's lives has been highly influential across the social sciences. However, when Crenshaw's complex theorizing of the multiplicities of Black women's lived experiences—always living with tightly woven imbrications of race, class, gender, sexuality, status—is interpreted as a single intersecting point of multiple axis of identities—e.g., Blackness + female as a single intersecting point—the import of Crenshaw's critique is lessened.

Repeated containment of Crenshaw's theorizing led Jennifer Nash (2008) to argue: "The important insights that identity is complex, that subjectivity is messy, and that personhood is inextricably bound up with vectors of power are only an analytic starting point..." (13–14). Or as Cris Mayo (2015) describes:

> When we reach toward intersectionality, we may come to think that we're finally addressing complexity. The simplest point is that we're not there yet. There is as yet only the tentative connection and the troubled subject (p. 251).

Furthermore, recent engagements with intersectionality and Women of Color theorizing note how often intersectionality is used to flatten relations between race and colonialism leading Jaspir Puar (2011) to argue: "categories of the intersectional mantra are the products of modernist colonial agendas and regimes of epistemic violence" (54). When Women of Color theorizing is flattened to "categories of the intersectional mantra" (e.g., gender, race, class), then the potentiality of Women of Color theory to "understand and abolish our extremely uneven global power structures defined by the intersections of neoliberal capitalism, racism, settler colonialism, immigration, and imperialism" (Weheliye 2014, 1) is masked over, ignored and lost.

Women of Color theorizing must be understood as working with intersectionalities, but intersectionalities that are "not there yet," that are in motion, shifting, unable to be explained through a single dot on an axis. Although it is necessary to understand experiences at certain pinpoints—at certain intersecting axes of identity—this pinpoint does not explain, to stay with Crenshaw's example, all of Black women's experiences as gendered, racialized, and sexualized persons impacted by histories and present day vestiges of empire and colonialism. This is an important point for policy studies, as a goal of policy studies is to understand a subject's experiences at a certain policy pinpoint—e.g. female student experiences when re-enrolling in school while pregnant—while at the same time policy studies needs to attend to larger understandings of this student's life overall and the multiple factors impacting her access to education.

If we take seriously Women of Color feminisms complexity of theorizing, then, as Cindy Cruz (2001) states, we will be on a "voyage to a very different epistemological destination" (660) and I would add ontological journey. Where can this different destination and journey take policy studies? What role can Women of Color theorizing play in policy studies facing its policy debts?

Women of Color feminism provides four key characteristics and interventions essential to policy studies and Critical Policy Analysis:

1. A complex analysis of Enlightenment, Western and Colonial thought and the structures, discourses, and policies that arise from these. Women of Color

feminism not only provides a critique of these structures but a radical interruption of western thought, offering specific alternative ontological and epistemological cosmologies that if taken seriously require a reframing of what we know, how we know it, and importantly what we do with our knowing.
2. In this rethinking, Women of Color feminisms develops new forms of relationality through alternative ways of knowing and praxis.
3. Women of Color feminisms at its best always include an interdisciplinary and intersectional analysis of gender, race, ableism, status, sexuality and empire/colonialism; an approach to knowledge that understands and situates constructions of for example gender as always impacted by constructions, surveillances and performances of race/ableism/empire/sexuality. Thus, while we may at times choose to primarily focus on one category, we do not remove the category into a separate silo, but keep a critical complex lens on relations of power. For example, this model allows tracings of how empire (colonialism) impacts racialized heteronormative constructions of family or how deeply constructions of race/ableisms/gender/sexuality are linked to citizenship, human rights policy and state practices.
4. Lastly, Women of Color feminisms is immersed in historical tracings linking what we think of as "the past" to present-day discourses, policies and practices. In earlier work I refer to this as "feminist genealogy" (Pillow 2004)—a meticulous tracing of power through documents, discourses, policies, and embodied evidence of race/ableism/gender/empire/sexualities. In this way Women of Color feminisms provides an active interruption of "epistemological ignorance" (Mills 1997, 2007; Pillow 2012; Sullivan and Tuana 2007); calls for complex analyses of body-mind-spirit, and ways of reading "sideways" (Freeman 2010; Stockton 2009; Pillow 2015a); an engagement with "remembrance pedagogy" (Pillow 2012) and a commitment to knowing our histories in order to understand/decolonize, imagine and survive our futures (Pérez 1999).

These four features of Women of Color feminisms—new ontological/ epistemological frameworks; new forms of relationality and praxis; complex intersectional analysis; and feminist genealogy, epistemological tracings and remembrance praxis—offer the capacity to extend how Critical Policy Analysis (CPA) scholars do education policy studies.

Given this book is focused on CPA and there are excellent overviews of CPA available (see Diem et al. 2014; Young and Diem 2014), I do not review CPA but here take up the "critical" in CPA in order to see how the above four tenets of Women of Color theorizing can work with CPA. As Young and Diem (2014) note: "one of the main goals of CPA is to shed light on how everyday policies, structures, and processes perpetuate and reproduce systems of domination and oppression" (1065). Yet, while the "critical" in CPA is a signal to something being altered, how far away from the root-term—policy analysis—does CPA move? In other words, how "critical" is CPA? Does CPA offer the analytics and call for rethinking ontology and epistemology?

Although CPA has focused attention on, "shed light on", paying attention to everyday lived experiences of power and policy, if existing ontological and epistemological assumptions remain in place, then this critique will be limited. This statement is an acknowledgment that the theoretical associations, constructions and contexts, in which approaches like CPA, exist can limit their analytical power. In other words, if CPA is developed out of and with critical theory, then CPA carries and exhibits the residues of liberal humanist, whitestream (Grande 2003) ways of knowing.

Thus, I suggest that the "critical" in CPA can only be as critical as the theories it is thought with. Atwood and López (2014) make a similar argument when they demonstrate what becomes possible when Critical Race Theory and CPA are thought together. Similarly, Catherine Lugg and Jason Murphy (2014) suggest that queer theory would be most useful to CPA. The question here is not "Which theory is best to use with CPA?" but rather, "What happens to CPA when it is rethought with _____ theory?" "What becomes possible?" "What becomes visible?"

In this move we must be careful to not fall in the additive prefix answer, where, for example, "Feminist policy analysis" or "Queer policy analysis" can too easily be misread as additive identity terms versus theoretical shifts (consider how often policy studies attempts to address its own whitewashed gaps by adding on key terms in-front of methodological frameworks). As someone who likes playing with language and finds power in the well-placed ironic usage or metaphor (Pillow 2002), I am not proposing we stop playing with how we language policy studies, but rather am asking that we attend to the debt that is too often left in place, unmarked, in these moves.

If we accept that the field of policy studies is—like qualitative research—always entrenched in its own colonial history (Denzin and Lincoln 2008; Smith 1999), then the arena of policy studies, including CPA, needs theories that challenge its innate and built-in epistemological and ontological blind spots, which as Charles Mills (1997; 2007) argues are not innocent ignorance's, but purposeful. At times we may want the specificity of analytics that yield critical understanding of race (CRT) or heteronormativity (as Lugg & Murphy describe Queer Theory), but most of us need tools that push us to see the intermeshments of race, gender, ableism, status, sexuality, and colonialism—an overarching theory that keeps all in play. Lugg and Murphy (2014) attest to the importance of CPA utilizing theories that yield "whimsical" reimagining of for example "more equitable policies and school environments" (p. 1196).

In order to interrupt the maintenance normative power of our paradigms and language, I suggest we need to <u>purposefully</u> take up and deeply utilize theoretical analytics, such as Women of Color feminisms, as <u>central</u> to thinking and use CPA "on the side" as methodology. Perhaps policy studies, in its prefix-additive practices, have been confusing and conflating epistemology with methodology and method and the field could use theoretical infusions that take seriously the theoretical importance of race, feminist, queer, or Women of Color theory. Indeed, this was the intent and impetus of early feminist policy studies, not to simply add "feminist" onto "policy" but to use feminist theorizing to absolutely question, dismantle, and reframe the foundations of policy studies (Blackmore 1995; Marshall 1997).

Adding "feminist" to critical policy analysis then would not only, as often argued, create analytics that "concurrently narrows and expands it purposes by focusing on the effects of policy on women" (Mansfield et al. 2014, pp. 1156–1157) but would also provide a deep, radical theoretical shift in policy studies, as explicated in the above four contributions of Women of Color theorizing. In this model of CPA on the side as methodology, key interventions that, in this essay's example, Women of Color feminisms provides can be enacted while utilizing the critical trends in data collection and analysis that CPA provides.

2 Women of Color Feminisms at the Policy Table

So let's turn to what Women of Color feminisms can look like and do in policy studies and here I turn to data and experiences working with agencies that serve expectant and parenting youth (EPY) with the goal of increasing EPY access to and completion of high school.

A few facts to situate the context for this work: (1) although Title IX explicitly addresses the education rights of EPY to date there is NO case law determining what equal access or equal education looks like for EPY; (2) this means each state and each district determines its own policies and practices for EPY; (3) there is very limited data on EPY schooling characteristics and experiences—for privacy reasons most schools do not track EPY separately so they are rolled into other data sets such as "drop-out" or "continuing education." Thus while teen pregnancy has at times been a heated social and political topic of debate, EPY are an absent/presence; and (4) Education scholars are missing in key research and policy impacting EPY with the arenas of Psychology and Social Work dominating social and education policy (Pillow 2004, 2006).

> Foster kid. Teen Mom. Delinquent. Broken. Dropouts. Last chance schools. Aging out. Last chance. Disciplinary referral. At risk. Safety risk. Credit deficient. Language deficient. Culturally deficient. Continuation schools. Last Chance. Incompetent Student. Incompetent Mother. Incompetent. Last Chance—at age 19—last chance.

Such are the terms of engagement EPY face daily in policy and practice. These terms and labels of deficit—found in policy and program text; social media; and in EPY interactions with social service and education professionals—define who is fit and unfit as education and societal subjects. After over ten years of working in New York City with community groups, Young Mother's collectives, and Young Father advocates, the assumptions and discourses impacting EPY have barely shifted, while at the same time youth narratives, attendance, push out and disciplinary referral data continued to demonstrate school-level practices that create barriers to EPY accessing and completing education. A 2013 media campaign in NYC that continued to disparage teen parents (Pérez 2013; Pillow 2013) made it obvious that in order to intervene in policy in meaningful ways, we needed a paradigm shift in thinking about young parents.

In 2013, I had an opportunity to work with an administrative team in the Division of Family and Permanency (DFS) services in NYC Children's Welfare Services. NYC is the largest provider of Children's Welfare services in the U.S. and DFS operates one of the largest foster care and family permanency programs in the country. My role was to observe messaging and interactions in young mother's foster care group home settings; talk with EPY and staff to determine what education messaging was occurring; and determine pathways to improve connections between social services and education for EPY. I also attended DFS team meetings—made up of supervisors, case managers, DFS administrators and EPY, the majority who were African American and Latina.

Observing in the group home settings and listening to young mothers and staff was humbling. The young women in care are the youth considered most "at risk", most deficit—in foster care themselves and young mothers—yet rather than assuming these young women are subjects under care, they speak discourses of awareness and resistance.[5] Staff and administrators of the group homes are the front-line service providers; those who bear the weight and responsibility of enacting a myriad of complex policies and charged with ensuring the safety of the young mother and her child(ren). Similarly sitting around the policy table in DFS, accountability demands were placed alongside critical discussions of existing policies and desires to interrupt deficit practices.

Listening, I was at first surprised by the level of engagement and critique I heard in the group homes and at the DFS policy table and realized I had carried assumptions about who case managers and administrators would be and believe. Seeking to interrupt my own assumptions, I returned to Women of Color feminisms and began to center this relationally and theoretically in my policy work. Many conversations at the DFS policy table focused upon creating new relations, new cultures of education with EPY and staff. Women of Color feminisms became central to this thinking and I found myself bringing in Women of Color readings to share or quotes to spur thinking. This meant we may begin with a quote from Toni Bambara and then turn to a discussion of safety referral policy or move from reading Audre Lorde to look at creating relational education pathways in the young mother's foster care group homes.

Over time, I noticed different kinds of questions were asked about data. Questions about what is left out; what is assumed; and how to get to the embodiment of EPY experiences in schooling. While to critical education policy scholars the shift of impetus in these questions may seem insignificant, for a city/state children's social welfare office that is legally and responsibly bound to quantified data driven policy and evaluation, this was a major shift (Pillow 2014a).

Here a few of the initial results of this process:

- A focus on increasing education training and relational work environments for staff at group homes based on acknowledgement that the staff who have the

---

[5]Resistance here does not refer to "strength" but rather the range of resistances that youth may engage, some of which may seem irresponsible or immature to adults.

most daily hourly contact with EPY are also lowest paid and often do not have education beyond a high school degree. Relational investment in staff came to be seen as key to providing caring education focused environments for EPY;
- Agreement that every meeting that focused on EPY would include 2–4 youth sitting at the table and to hire two EPY to work as DFS research assistants with their offices near DFS staff. These moves, also based on relationality, acknowledged that when we work with, sit with, ride elevators with those we are serving perceptions, assumptions and language change;
- Development of a policy pathways report that included quotes from Women of Color feminisms as the central theoretical impetus and employs relational, catalytic validity and feminist praxis as evaluation measures;
- A re-reading of EPY school data that is challenging Title IX language that EPY are entitled to education "equal to their peers" when initial indications are that the schools EPY are enrolled in are failing EPY's peers—that is, when we look at attendance and completion data at schools where young mother's are placed, young mothers are not underperforming compared to their peers. Across the board some schools have absenteeism rates of up to 60 % on any given day and completion rates below 50 %—pointing to systemic problems youth of color in some boroughs of NYC are facing when attempting to access equal and quality education.

These are beginnings... but in the ruins of data (Pillow 2014b) and amidst lives of youth that are daily-encountering injustices... we need theoretically informed beginnings. I am not suggesting there is some "fix" here; school policy access issues for EPY in NYC have not been solved. I also remain poststructurally theoretically suspicious and could critically unravel all that is being moved forward on (and to some extent I continue to see the benefit of doing such academic mind-work). But, when I was challenged to center Women of Color feminisms at the heart of research, thinking, and analyzing, the thickness of inequities became visible, a visibility that required witnessing (Pillow 2014b) and accounting for; the data became impossible to ignore. Women of Color feminisms fore fronted our policy debt and yielded depths of critique, relational connections and explorations of policy pathways that previously I was not creative, informed or brave enough to pursue.

3 Policy Debt and Policy Studies Obligations

In this essay, I suggest that facing the weight of data surrounding school disparities and injustices, facing the weight and haunting of an education policy debt, will require policy studies to take up and center theoretical tools that speak to deep social, historical constructions and interstitial relationships of gender, ableism, race, status, sexuality, and empire/colonialism. I also suggest that Women of Color theorizing offers education policy studies new ontological and epistemological frameworks that can impact how we think and do policy studies. I need CPA to do the kind of policy work I am invested in—investigations of youth of color, specifically young mothers and EPY access to and completion of quality education in U.S. public schools. However, doing this work without centering theoretical analytics, like Women of Color feminisms, would not only be a gap, it would be irresponsible.

The obvious yet complex embodied experiences of youth in schools—whether pregnant female bodies that literally cannot fit into school desks or the student facing daily micro-aggressions—are essential to understanding school data and policy on push-outs, bullying, disciplinary referrals, school completion and pipelines/pathways. If we have Black youth who continue to ask to live in another country (Pillow 2015a), youth who are publicly shamed (Pillow 2013), and youth who face daily discouragement, and the daily fatigue of being told they do not fit and are not worthy of investment (Pillow 2004, 2006, 2015b), what is our responsibility as policy studies scholars?

Influenced by Dr. Ladson-Billings, I argue that responsibility here requires a facing of the arena of policy study's theoretical research debt; this is our debt—a policy studies debt. Once we acknowledge this debt, additional questions arise:

Does policy study as a field have a responsibility to look closely at its own theories, data productions and practices? To hold itself accountable for deficit discourses and practices of harm in school policy and practice; for continuing micro-aggressions; for patterns, practices and policies that limit access; for patterns of unjust treatment and outcomes and the dissonances and damages these patterns cause? And what would such responsibility look like?

I suggest a first step toward acknowledging policy debt and the above questions require policy studies scholars to critically examine in place theoretical analytics. To directly ask: How am I knowing? Who am I, who is policy studies, thinking with? What tools am I, what tools are policy studies, thinking with? Who and what is produced by these knowing's?

Feminist epistemologies—including queer, race and Women of Color epistemologies—provide theoretical and methodological lens to critically acknowledge and challenge predominant models of knowing while also calling for forms of praxis responsibility, a concern for outcomes, for effects and affects of policy. The call for praxis in feminist and Women of Color theories is a difficult call but should not be ignored. Praxis requires a relationship with theory that focuses on the daily-lived experiences, embodiments, of those named as the policy problem in relation to an obligation of praxis, to think about and put our work to work in ways that are impactful.

Cruz (2001), tracing the importance of Anzaldúa's work argues that Women of Color

> consciousness is not only asking for improved rigor and care in using the logico-scientific methods of inquiry but is also an episteme of hybridity that allows a reading of liminal (or third) spaces and of the methodology of those who occupy such spaces. However, care must be taken to insure that we do not lock into a duel of oppressor and oppressed, but to learn to move beyond the counterstance (661).

Cruz's caution is important to policy studies and critical policy analysis, which too often can fall into us/them theorizing—e.g., young mothers against the "bad" social workers. Cruz also provides the reminder for policy studies to look for more than the counterstance—e.g., writing young mothers as strong resistant heroines and stopping with that counter narrative. Such theorizing has contributed to the current policy debt.

Centering Feminist policy analysis, temporalities, feminist genealogy, Women of Color feminisms—these are the tools I am using to attempt to rethink, intervene and perform praxis in policy settings. The analytics education policy scholars use may be different, but of any tool we pick up questions of utility should be asked—What does this analytic do for us? What does it yield? Where can it go? What can it interrupt? What new forms of knowing and praxis can be possible?

I hope that by keeping such questions circulating, policy studies as a field will seriously take up how it will face and take up the obligations for the policy debt we owe. This is a policy studies that, like Jafari Allen (2012) asks: "what are the best ways to facilitate critical thinking and more ethical, beautiful, and joyful futures for our students (and children, lovers, and friends, wherever we find them) (236)?" That is a policy studies I can live with.

References

Alexander, M. J. (2005). *Pedagogies of crossing*. Durham: Duke University Press.
Allen, J. (2012). Black/Queer/Diaspora at the current conjuncture. *GLQ, 18*(2–3), 211–248.
Anzaldúa, G. (1987). *Borderlands/La Frontera*. San Francisco: Aunt Lute Books.
Atwood, E., & López, G. R. (2014). Let's be critically honest: Towards a messier counterstory in critical race theory. *International Journal of Qualitative Studies in Education, 27*(9), 1134–1154. doi:10.1080/09518398.2014.916011.
Betts, R. B. (1985). *In search of York, the slave who went to the Pacific with Lewis and Clark*. Boulder: Associated Universities Press.
Blackmore, J. (1995). Policy as dialogue: Feminist administrators working for educational change. *Gender & Education, 7*, 293–313.
CRDC—Civil Rights Data Collection (2014). Washington, DC: U.S. Department of Education. http://www2.ed.gov/about/offices/list/ocr/data.html?src=rt/
Cohen, D. K., & Moffitt, S. L. (2009). *The ordeal of equality/did federal regulation fix the schools?* Cambridge: Harvard University Press.
Crenshaw, K. (1989). Demarginalizing the intersection of race and sex: A black feminist critique of antidiscrimination doctrine, feminist theory, and antiracist politics. *The University of Chicago Legal Forum, 140*, 139–167.
Crenshaw, K. (1991). Mapping the margins: Intersectionality, identity politics, and violence against women of color. *Stanford Law Review, 43*(6), 1241–1299.
Cruz, C. (2001). Toward an epistemology of a brown body. *International Journal of Qualitative Studies in Education, 14*(5), 657–669.
Denzin, N. K., & Lincoln, Y. S. (Eds.). (2008). *Collecting and interpreting qualitative materials*. Thousand Oaks: Sage.
Diem, S., Young, M. D., Welton, A. D., Mansfield, K. C., & Lee, P. L. (2014). The intellectual landscape of critical policy analysis. *International Journal of Qualitative Studies in Education, 27*(9), 1068–1090. doi:10.1080/09518398.2014.916007.

Dillard, C. (2000). The substance of things hoped for, the evidence of things not seen: Examining an endarkened feminist epistemology in educational research and leadership. *The International Journal of Qualitative Studies in Education, 13*(6), 661–681.

Freeman, E. (2010). *Time binds: Queer temporalities, queer histories.* Durham: Duke University Press.

Grande, S. (2003). Whitestream feminism and the colonialist project: A review of contemporary feminist pedagogy and praxis. *Educational Theory, 53*(3), 329–346.

Harding, S. (1987). Introduction: Is there a feminist method? In S. Harding (Ed.), *Feminism and methodology* (pp. 1–14). Bloomington: Indiana University Press.

Ladson-Billings, G. (2006). From the achievement gap to the education debt: Understanding achievement in U.S. schools. *Educational Researcher, 35*(7), 3–12.

Lorde, A. (1984). *Sister outsider and other essays.* Boston: Crossing Press.

Lugg, A., & Murphy, J. (2014). Thinking whimsically: Queering the study of educational policy-making and politics. *International Journal of Qualitative Studies in Education, 27*(9), 1183–1204. doi:10.1080/09518398.2014.916009.

Lugones, M. (2010). Toward a decolonial feminism. *Hypatia, 25*(4), 742–759.

Mansfield, K. C., Welton, A. D., & Grogan, M. (2014). "Truth or consequences": A feminist critical policy analysis of the STEM crisis. *International Journal of Qualitative Studies in Education, 27*(9), 1155–1182. doi:10.1080/09518398.2014.916006.

Maracle, L. (1996). *I am woman/a native perspective on sociology and feminism.* Berkeley: Press Gang Publishers.

Marshall, C. (1997). Dismantling and reconstructing policy analysis. In C. Marshall (Ed.), *Feminist critical policy analysis: A perspective from primary and secondary schooling* (pp. 1–42). Washington, DC: Falmer Press.

Mayo, C. (2015). Unexpected generosity and inevitable trespass: Rethinking intersectionality. *Educational Studies, 51*(3), 244–251. doi:10.1080/00131946.2015.1033924.

Mills, C. W. (1997). *The racial contract.* Ithaca: Cornell University Press.

Mills, C. W. (2007). White ignorance. In S. Sullivan & N. Tuana (Eds.), *Race and epistemologies of ignorance* (pp. 13–38). Albany: State University of New York Press.

Muhammad, K. G. (2010). *The condemnation of blackness/race, crime and the making of modern urban America.* Cambridge: Harvard University Press.

Nash, J. C. (2008). Rethinking intersectionality. *Feminist Review, 89*, 1–15.

Puar, J. K. (2011). "I would rather be a cyborg than a goddess"/Becoming-Intersectional in assemblage theory. *PhiloSOPHIA, 2*(1), 49–66.

Pérez, E. (1999). *The decolonial imaginary/writing Chicanas into history.* Bloomington: Indiana University Press.

Pérez, M. (2013). *NYC teen pregnancy campaign bring shaming to bus shelters and cell phones.* http://rhrealitycheck.org/article/2013/03/05/nyc-teen-pregnancy-campaign-brings-shaming-to-bus-shelters-and-cell-phones/

Peterson, P. M. (1971). Colonialism and education: The case of the Afro-American. *Comparative Education Review, 15*(2), 146–157.

Pillow, W. S. (2002). When a man does feminism should he dress in drag? *International Journal of Qualitative Studies in Education, 15*(5), 545–554.

Pillow, W. S. (2003). Race-based methodologies: Multicultural methods or epistemological shifts? In G. Lopez & L. Parker (Eds.), *Interrogating racism in qualitative research methodology* (pp. 181–202). New York: Peter Lang.

Pillow, W. S. (2004). *Unfit subjects: Educational policy and the teen mother.* New York: Routledge.

Pillow, W. S. (2006). Teen pregnancy and education: Politics of knowledge, research, and practice. Politics of education handbook. Lugg C (Ed.), *Educational Policy, 20*(1), 59–84.

Pillow, W. S. (2012). Sacajawea: Witnessing, remembrance and ignorance. *Power and Education, 4*(1), 45–56.

Pillow, W. S. (2013). *SHAME: The New York city teen pregnancy Ad campaign.* Washington, DC: National Women's Law Center.

Pillow, W. S. (2014a). *Invited Keynote. "What Happens when the Feminist Poststructural Theorists Sits at the Policy Table?"* Paper presented at the Poststructural Policy Analysis Workshop, University of British Columbia, Vancouver, British Columbia.

Pillow, W. S. (2014b). *Endarkened witnessing: Practices of love and rage*. Paper presented at the American Education Studies Association Annual Meeting, Toronto, Canada.

Pillow, W. S. (2015a). Mothering a Black son who dreams of another country. Special issue: "From Emmett Till to Trayvon Martin". *Cultural Studies ↔ Critical Methodologies, 15*(4), 316–321.

Pillow, W. S. (2015b). Policy temporality & marked bodies: Feminist praxis amongst the Ruins. *Critical Studies in Education, 56*(1), 55–70.

Pillow, W. S. (2016). *Sex and race in the corps expedition*. In J. Brier and J. Morgan (Eds.), *Connexions: Histories of race and sex in North America* (pp. 203–226). Urbana: University of Illinois Press.

Pillow, W. S., & Mayo, C. (2011). Toward understandings of feminist ethnography. In S. Nagy Hesse-Biber (Ed.), *Handbook of feminist research: Theory and praxis* (2nd ed., pp. 187–205). Thousand Oaks: Sage.

Smith, L. T. (1999). *Decolonizing methodology/research and indigenous peoples*. London: Zed Books.

Smith, W., Hung, M., & Franklin, J. D. (2011). Racial battle fatigue and the miseducation of Black men: Microaggressions, societal problems, & environmental stress. *Journal of Negro Education, 80*(1), 63–82.

Stockton, K. B. (2009). *The queer child, or growing sideways in the twentieth century*. Durham: Duke University Press.

Stovall, D. (2013). Against the politics of desperation: Educational justice, critical race theory, and Chicago school reform. *Critical Studies in Education, 54*(1), 33–43.

Sullivan, S., & Tuana, N. (Eds.). (2007). *Race and epistemologies of ignorance*. Albany: State University of New York Press.

The Santa Cruz Women of Color Collective. (2014). Building on "the edge of each other's battles": A feminist of color multidimensional lens. *Hypatia, 29*(1), 23–40.

Weheliye, A. G. (2014). *Habeas viscus: Racializing assemblages, biopolitics, and Black feminist theories of the human*. Durham: Duke University Press.

Young, M. D., & Diem, S. (2014). Putting critical theoretical perspectives to work in educational policy. *International Journal of Qualitative Studies in Education, 27*(9), 1063–1067. doi:10.1080/09518398.2014.916015.

Afterword

Critical Policy Analysis: Purpose and Practice

This text provides a state of the art in CPA with the stated intention not to survey the critical policy field comprehensively, but to offer roadmaps introducing CPA in a particular context, while recognizing how the global field of policy theorizing has become more important (e.g., Rizvi and Lingard 2010). The text draws on recent innovative methodological approaches to address the global networks that are emerging with the use of critical network ethnography to chart the rise of edu-business; of feminist post structuralist and queer theorizing; and of approaches focusing on the vocabulary of policy texts. Young and Diem's text illustrates that it is about theorizing policy into practice through a multiplicity of approaches and concrete examples because there is no simple theory and method binary. Policy in effect is what gets "enacted" in practice (Ball et al. 2012). Methodology, as this text shows, is the glue that provides the conceptual richness required in contemporary critical policy analysis.

In reading these different theoretical perspectives on critical policy analysis, I am reminded how feminist as other critical research and policy analysis has been sidelined, co-opted and rejected. The relationship between the personal and the political is integral to researching policy, as these chapters illustrate. As a feminist critiquing the field of educational administration, as it was then called in the 1980s before leadership became the dominant lexicon of education reform, policy was inevitably foregrounded in search of a more socially just education. Theorizing and researching policy therefore became a key aspect of my own research (Blackmore 2012, 2014) and teaching of policy studies in educational administration and leadership at Deakin University in Australia. As with these papers, that early work was informed by the then emergent work of Ball (1993) in the UK around the question "what is policy?", feminists such as Carol Bacchi (1996, 2000a, b) who asked "what is the policy problem here?", and discourse theorists such as Fairclough (1992) who focused on the linguistic turn, social change, and the role of the media. Together these theorists made sense of what I was finding in my research on education reform, equity and leadership in particular. It was apparent that how women were positioned as researchers, policy makers, and practitioners was a product of particular dominant discourses about women that circulated within society and education. We needed to develop different methodological approaches to understand how historical context, popular discourses about women and girls, together with organizational structures and processes through which policy was developed, informed how policy was produced, disseminated and articulated into practice. They also marked the beginnings of what is now an established field of policy sociology in education.

As outlined by Young and Diem in the introduction, our early research on gender equity for girls in Australia (Kenway et al. 1998) also led us to critique traditional top down notions of policy as a process in which the problem was defined, informed by research, disseminated and then "implemented." Post-structural theorizing of equity policy texts indicated how they were both informed by, and a product of, multiple often contradictory discourses, beliefs, and desires. As I have argued since, policy texts, once in circulation, could also provide a discourse to be mobilized by practitioners on the ground, offer a language, suggest strategies, and provide a justification for action by teachers and leaders (Blackmore 1999). Policy was therefore a powerful tool for organizational change – whether for better or worse.

Policy can also, as indicated in this text, become a form of symbolic violence, as in the case of gender equity policies that are not supported by leaders, not well-resourced and not evaluated in terms of unexpected effects. Within a performative context of education markets and entrepreneurialism, policy can be used as a rhetorical tool by systems, governments, schools, and universities so they are seen to be doing something but often without the necessary political will and resources to produce the promised impact (Blackmore and Sachs 2007). Within organizations, equal opportunity or affirmative action policies are often expected to be implemented by those without commitment, not well-informed by research, nor offered strategies to produce the desired effect. And as Carpenter illustrates, the "performative act of policymaking" positions education as at fault, failing to achieve economic or social benefits without regard for how education works within economic, social, and political constraints.

Policy analysis, as indicated in this text, increasingly focuses on language use within "policy vocabularies" of success and failure. Carpenter points to the "dramaturgical functions of scripting, staging, setting and performance" mobilized by policy makers and the media to create education as "in crisis," and thus divert attention away from politicians by talking about "turnaround schools" solving economic and social ills. I also have tracked how the language of social justice in policy has changed (Blackmore 2014) and how equity discourses can be co-opted by neoliberal economic and socially conservative oppositional discourses such as that of "recuperative masculinity" (Lingard 2003). Through textual analysis, I charted the shift away from the language of equal opportunity and equity to that of diversity, arguing that the weaker policy discourse of diversity is individualistic and readily aligns with discourses of individual rights or cultural recognition and can therefore be readily coopted by neoliberal discourses which ignore issues around redistributive justice (Blackmore 2006). The power of key concepts in terms of the vocabulary of social justice is evident here. The notion of diversity is more a descriptor of difference and lacks the democratic and legalistic connotations implied by terms such as equality, equity, equal opportunity, or affirmative action that recognize the historical legacies of cultural, racial, as well as gender discrimination.

Feminist critical policy perspectives also are now well established, evident in the earlier work of Catherine Marshall (1997) on policies impacting on schooling and higher education, on gender equity for girls and boys in Australia (Kenway et al. 1998), and in the UK (Arnot et al. 1999). Feminist post structuralism provided a new way of understanding how power is dispersed, of how individual women leaders were positioned differently according to gender, class, and race and how agency was gained through positioning oneself within different contexts. Marshall, Johnson, and Edwards again focus on the key policy problem of how ongoing cultural and systemic factors contribute to the absence of women in executive leadership. In Bacchi's (2000b) terms, they define the problem as not being about women but about context and historical social relations of gender. Significantly, this highlights the conjunction of the "religious turn" of the late twentieth century and the role of the social media in terms of how the conservative right reinforces entrenched gender-based cultural biases. Whiteman, Maxcy and Scribner extend this analysis into the organizational context by unpacking the "institutional logics" that shape how policy is interpreted, either enabling or constraining individual actors in the "micropolitical negotiation of policy enactments," to explain the enduring phenomenom of female underrepresentation in leadership as a system not an individual problem.

The focus of much critical policy work, as indicated by Young and Diem in the introduction, has been on the influence of historical and cultural legacies; asking why a particular policy at this time, what are the sources and relationships of power and hierarchy, and how text, language, and discourse operate in the production, circulation, and dissemination of policy. Brewer and Werts' use of the cultural studies theorist Michel de Certeau to analyze how the notion of consumption in everyday life shifts the focus from power and control by institutional practice to everyday practice. Again, the focus of critical policy analysis is on how policy informs what happens in practice.

Critical policy analysis has also been informed by Critical Race and Indigenous theory by identifying how policies assume and position, and through their language, "the Other" as victims, failures and / or lacking in agency (Ladson-Billings 2004). These chapters illustrate how methodology can identify dominant notions of how parental involvement is defined and practiced with parents constructed through policy over time as choosers, fund raisers, pseudo-literacy teachers, voluntary labour, employers, but also as failures. Policy texts have normative dimensions – good and bad parents – made evident in the targeting of single parent, usually female headed, families. Pillow's Women of Color's example in the text of the "policy debt" presents a strong claim upon policymakers and practitioners to make a difference for such families, but also a clear challenge to researchers as policy activists.

Also made evident is how policy layers reinforce inequality. Milani and Winton's Canadian example shows how fundraising policies produce unexpected inequitable results due to the uneven socio-geographic distribution of wealth between school communities in Canada. This confirms similar critical policy studies on parental involvement in Australia, the UK, and NZ (Blackmore and Hutchison 2010). Inclusive policies at the school level are shaped by system-wide policies in ways that shame, blame, or discourage particular social groups from being involved in their children's education meaningfully as partners with and not against or fearful of teachers. Increasingly, neo-liberal policies of choice are redefining equity as the individual right to choose with little regard to the overall consequences for others who have less choice.

These North American studies show that while context matters in terms of how policies articulate, it is also evident that neo-liberal policies of choice have similar effects. While choice policies have had less impact on the USA where less than 10 % of students go to private schools, charter schools are still in a minority and where in many districts comprehensive local schools still exist, policy studies elsewhere show that choice policies have major effects. Although Free Schools are failing in Sweden, Free School policies are now being advocated in the UK and Australia. In Australia where historically over 30 % of students attend private schools, choice theory originating in the US was popularized through neoliberal governments during the 1990s. Now public funds are being siphoned off to private schools resulting in the residualization of public school systems. In the UK, there is a fragmentation of systems and emergence of privately owned networks of Academies producing a systemless-system (Gunter 2012; Lawn 2013). Educational researchers from a critical policy perspective have indicated how neoliberal policies travelling globally (Rizvi and Lingard 2010) have thus produced greater not less inequality in affluent societies (Raffo et al. 2010). Across all Anglophone countries patterns of socio-economic and racial segregation are now being mapped by policy analysts using quantitative approaches onto residential and geographical segregation (Teese et al. 2007).

Context cannot be ignored by school leaders and teachers, particularly those in high poverty communities as they struggle with increasingly prescriptive policies and regimes of accountability cascading down on them. The multiplicity of conflicting and confusing policies that school leaders confront and negotiate from federal, state and local authorities who seek simple one size fits all solutions adds to the contextual complexity school and university leaders manage on the ground. The tendency for constant restructuring of public school systems in particular and the push towards the privatization of school provision globally in developed and developing economies as global network ethnographies illustrate exacerbates this trend. Yet an OECD study indicates that devolution and school choice policies do not produce better outcomes but on balance does the contrary (Musset 2012).

Analyzing the role of the media in policy formation has become, as I and others (e.g. Blackmore and Thomson 2004; Blackmore and Thorpe 2003) argue, significant in terms of mapping how such policies travel rapidly. Critical policy analysis highlights how the media is a key tool in the production as well as dissemination of policy or "mediatisation" (Lingard and Rawolle 2004). O'Malley and Long in this text utilize Queer Theory to analyze policies in Texas which now are applicable to public schools in terms of a legally determined right. While most principals accept queer young people as not feeling safe in school, they do not feel obligated by law or ethically to undertake professional development that could address issues of endemic bullying and harassment, an area of significant neglect also in university leadership programs. The media, they argue, is central to maintenance of this heteronormative matrix, and how any attempts to include "the Other" as an equal is resisted on the basis that it excludes that group or excludes heterosexuals.

The political activism of Queer Theory is evident in its refusing to accept policy categories of "gendered and sexualized minorities" or normalized discourses and instead to trouble the "implications of cultural production within hetero-normative societies." This requires interrogating codes of knowing in a range of "social, institutional, and professional configurations." This, it can be argued, requires policy activism, a point well made in regard to student voice in Welton, Harris, Altamirano, and Williams' chapter. Rudduck and McIntyre (2007) argued student voice is critical in not only informing school improvement policies. Welton and her colleagues argue that student voice is also a key methodological approach to policy analysis.

Focusing on policy as a mechanism of social change also showed how it was difficult to produce fundamental social change, in part because of how the problem was mis/defined, as Carpenter in this text shows through his use of argumentative discourse analysis (see Bacchi 2000b), the contradictions inherent in policy texts and discourses as well as the resistance, accommodation, and acceptance of policy as policies articulated in and through multiple layers of administration and practice.

This text will contribute significantly to what is now the well-established field of policy sociology in education. The text substantiates the notion that policy can be understood as part of a wider practice-based theory of education. The policy lesson throughout is that CPA as a methodology confirms the view that education is a democratic practice and that social justice and inclusive educational practices should be foregrounded. It raises questions as to the role not only of practitioners but also researchers and policy makers, promoting the view that they not only need to be policy analysts but also policy activists and advocates for social justice through involvement in public policy debates. Atkinson (2000) argues that we undertake policy analysis for three primary reasons: one is policy critique and another policy advocacy, key elements of CPA. The issue is how we as critical policy theorists and researchers undertake her third notion of policy for service to government as who controls education policy is as depicted in this text increasingly in the hands of global policy bodies (e.g. OECD) and non-government organizations.

Burwood, VIC, Australia   Jill Blackmore

References

Arnot, M., David, M., & Weiner, B. G. (1999). *Closing the gender gap: Postwar education and social change*. Cambirdge: Polity.
Atkinson, E. (2000). Critical dissonance and critical schizophrenia: The struggle between policy delivery and policy critique. *Research Intelligence, 73*, 14–16.
Bacchi, C. (1996). *The politics of affirmative action: "Women", equality, and category politics*. London: Sage.
Bacchi, C. (2000a). The see-saw effect: Down goes affirmative action, up comes workplace diversity. *Journal of Interdisciplinary Gender Studies, 5*(2), 65–83.
Bacchi, C. (2000b). Policy as discourse: What does it mean? Where does it get us? *Discourse: Studies in the Cultural Politics of Education, 21*(1), 45–56.
Ball, S. J. (1993). What is policy? Texts, trajectories, and toolboxes. *Discourse: Studies in the Cultural Politics of Education, 13*(2), 10–17.
Ball, S. J., Maguire, M., & Braun, A. (2012). *How schools do policy: Policy enactments in secondary schools*. London: Routledge.
Blackmore, J. (1999). *Troubling women: Feminism, leadership and educational change*. Buckingham: Open University Press.
Blackmore, J. (2006). Deconstructing diversity discourses in the field of educational management and leadership. *Leadership, Educational Management and Administration, 34*(2), 188–199.
Blackmore, J. (2012). Restructuring relations between the state, family, work and education in globalizing economies. *Australian Educational Researcher, 27*(3), 17–35.
Blackmore, J. (2014). 'Wasting talent'? Gender and the problematics of academic disenchantment and disengagement with leadership. *Higher Education Research & Development, 33*(1), 86–99.
Blackmore, J., & Hutchison, K. (2010). Ambivalent relations: Parent and teacher perceptions of parental involvement in school communities. *International Journal of Inclusive Education, 14*(5), 499–515.
Blackmore, J., & Sachs, J. (2007). *Performing and reforming leaders: Gender, educational restructuring & change*. New York: SUNY.
Blackmore, J., & Thomson, P. (2004). Just 'good news'? Disciplinary imaginaries of 'star' school heads. *Journal of Education Policy, 19*(3), 301–320.
Blackmore, J., & Thorpe, S. (2003). Media/ting change: The print media's role in mediating education policy in a period of radical reform in Victoria, Australia. *Journal of Education Policy, 18*(6), 577–596.
Fairclough, N. (1992). *Discourse and social change*. Cambridge: Polity.
Gunter, H. (2012). *The state and education policy. The academies program*. London: Routledge.
Kenway, J., Willis, S., Blackmore, J., & Rennie, L. (1998). *Answering back: Girls, boys and teachers and feminism in schools*. London: Routledge.
Ladson-Billings, G. (2004). Just what is critical race theory and what is it doing in a nice field like education? In G. Ladson-Billings & D. Gillborn (Eds.), *The RoutledgeFalmer reader in multicultural education* (pp. 49–68). London: RoutledgeFalmer.
Lawn, M. (2013). A systemless system: Designing the disarticulation of English state education. *European Education Research Journal, 12*(2), 231–41.
Lingard, B. (2003). Where to in gender policy in education after recuperative masculinity politics? *International Journal of Inclusive Education, 7*(1), 33–56.
Lingard, B., & Rawolle, S. (2004). Mediatizing educational policy: The journalistic field, science policy, and cross-field effects. *Journal of Education Policy, 19*(3), 361–380.
Marshall, C. (1997). Dismantling and reconstructing policy analysis. In C. Marshall (Ed.), *Feminist critical policy analysis: A perspective from primary and secondary schooling* (pp. 1–39). London: The Falmer Press.
Musset, P. (2012). *School choice and equity: Current policy in OECD countries and a literature review* (Working paper 2012: 3). Paris: OECD.

Raffo, C., Dyson, A., Gunter, H., Hall, D., Jones, L., & Kalambouka, A. (Eds.). (2010). *Education and poverty in affluent countries*. London: Routledge.

Rizvi, F., & Lingard, B. (2010). *Globalizing education policy*. London: Routledge.

Rudduck, J., & McIntyre, D. (2007). *Improving learning through consulting pupils*. New York: Routledge.

Teese, R., Lamb, S., & Duru-Bellat, M. (Eds.). (2007). *International studies in educational inequality: Theory and policy*. Dordrecht: Springer.

Index

A
Activism, 68, 84, 85, 89–90, 99, 100, 102, 105, 116, 157, 279
Advocacy, 6, 8, 68, 106, 155–173, 185, 186, 203, 209, 222, 223, 238, 239, 279
Advocacy leadership, 155–173
African American education, 9, 51, 155–173
Agency, 6, 9, 20, 36, 92, 115, 116, 118, 121, 125, 136, 144, 152, 159, 163, 175–189, 238, 239, 268, 277

C
Collaboration, 86, 87, 92, 125, 146, 147, 224
Community, 2, 21, 43, 63, 84, 113, 146, 156, 176, 196, 225, 255, 262, 278
Competition, 24, 93, 124, 145, 147, 197, 203, 208, 209, 216, 228
Concentrated looking, 23
Consumption, 10, 152, 199, 243, 244, 246, 250–257, 259, 277
Context, 1, 4, 5, 7–10, 22, 23, 25, 26, 28, 29, 34–36, 44, 47–50, 56, 57, 59, 63, 65, 66, 68, 70, 74, 83, 84, 86, 87, 89–99, 102, 103, 105, 106, 114, 138, 147, 151, 158, 159, 161, 163–165, 187, 194, 198, 200, 202–208, 216, 220, 221, 232, 237, 244, 246, 249, 253, 254, 257, 267, 268, 275–278
Counter-narratives, 8, 9, 151, 272
Critical democracy, 9, 194, 199, 201–208
Critical policy analysis, x, xi, ix, 1–11, 15, 16, 20, 22–25, 31, 32, 43–59, 65–68, 74, 84, 87, 94, 111–127, 131–148, 152, 156–158, 160, 161, 169, 172, 173, 175–189, 194, 198, 217, 236, 243–259, 262, 265, 266, 268, 272, 275–279
Critical race theory & policy, x, 4, 6, 8–10, 16, 156–161, 163, 172, 173, 267
Critical reflection, 88, 104
Cultural discourse, 131, 137

D
Deconstruction, 23
Democratic subjects, 10, 152, 243–245, 259
Desegregation, 7, 9, 16, 44–55, 58, 59, 156–169, 171, 172
Discourse analysis, x, 6, 9, 10, 15, 16, 25–27, 32, 137, 152, 218, 219, 221, 224, 279
Diversity, 7, 30, 44, 49, 51, 53–59, 64, 70, 97, 145, 146, 152, 171, 200, 203, 205, 276, 277

E
Educational and political leadership and women, 135–137, 141
Educational leadership, x, 8, 16, 29, 49, 64, 67, 76, 78, 101, 131, 135, 139, 140, 166, 187–188
Educational policy, x, 1–4, 6–11, 16, 22, 24, 29, 32, 33, 35–37, 58, 63–78, 84, 89, 122, 126, 152, 158, 172, 224, 236, 253
Education disparity, 262
Epistemology, 1, 3, 10, 23, 25, 26, 67, 68, 151, 188, 248, 253, 262, 264–267, 270, 271
Everyday, 4, 10, 66, 102, 112–114, 118, 127, 152, 159, 163, 225, 236, 243, 244, 246–257, 259, 266, 277

F

Feminism, x, 6, 10, 89, 90, 137, 141, 144–148, 263–272
Feminist critical policy analysis, 6, 15, 31, 131–148
Fundraising policy, 9, 152, 194, 195, 199, 201–208

G

Gender, 4, 22, 29–31, 64–67, 92, 93, 97, 100, 101, 104, 132, 137, 139, 141–148, 160, 198, 200, 263–267, 270, 276, 277, 279
Governed subject, 10, 244–246, 249, 250, 257
Governmentality, 9, 24, 27, 30, 36, 55, 58, 72, 76, 117, 121, 141, 143, 159, 172, 194, 195, 199–206, 208, 209, 217, 219, 222, 223, 230, 232, 235–238, 250, 254, 276, 278, 279

H

Hegemony, 16, 137, 147
Historical analysis, 7, 16, 25–28, 31, 37, 132

I

Immigration legislation, 117, 118, 121
Influence, 9, 19–22, 25–30, 33–36, 44, 47, 48, 56–58, 66, 69, 87, 91–94, 105, 106, 123, 127, 132, 140, 176, 177, 189, 196, 198, 199, 202, 203, 218, 220, 224, 236
Institutional logics perspective, 177
Institutional messages, 180
Interest groups, 24, 137

K

Knowledge, ix, x, xi, 2, 4, 5, 9, 22, 24, 28, 29, 64, 65, 67, 78, 84, 85, 88, 91–93, 101, 107, 112, 116, 119, 120, 137, 151, 152, 161–163, 165, 198, 200–202, 216, 218, 248, 249, 255, 258, 264, 266

L

Latin@ parental engagement, 116
Leadership, 4, 22, 49, 64, 84, 121, 131, 157, 179, 227, 275
Liberal feminism, 90, 264
Linguistic analysis, 218

M

Marketization, 124, 139, 140, 156, 159, 160, 172, 196, 199, 203, 229, 258, 276
Methodology, 5, 15, 16, 33, 48–50, 138, 151, 158, 160–163, 202, 220–224, 264, 267, 268, 271, 275, 277, 279
Micropolitics, 9, 92–94, 99, 100, 103–105, 152, 176, 177, 184, 277

N

Narrative, 69, 71, 77, 101, 112, 116, 132, 162, 222, 225, 262, 272
Neoliberalism, 159, 165, 203
Networks, x, xi, 4, 7, 16, 22, 29–32, 35–37, 93, 100, 105, 125, 126, 176, 177, 180, 181, 185–187, 216, 233, 245, 249, 250, 275, 278
Normalization, 30, 77, 208

O

Ontario, 6, 9, 152, 193–209
Ontology, 176, 178, 181, 183, 264, 266
Oppression, 67, 99, 146, 156, 266
Organizational communication, 177

P

Parental engagement, 8, 115, 116, 118, 122
Parent organizing, 112, 119
Parent positionality, 113
Performativity, 68, 69, 76, 220
Pluralism,
Policy, 2, 19, 44, 63, 84, 111, 131, 156, 175, 194, 215, 243, 262
   actors, 7, 16, 32–37, 65, 68, 69, 152, 201, 202, 223, 245
   design, 9, 48–50
   enactment, 6, 9, 10, 22, 68, 152, 162, 175–189, 244–246, 252, 253, 256–259, 277
   implementation, 7, 9, 23, 36, 43–59, 69, 161, 245, 252, 259
   sociology, 276, 279
   studies, ix, 2, 3, 6, 7, 9, 10, 16, 24, 151, 152, 218–221, 236, 257, 261–272, 278
Politics, 3, 22, 44, 66, 84, 111, 131, 156, 176, 194, 215, 248, 263
Poststructural, 23, 68, 264, 270

Power, 3, 22, 57, 66, 84, 111, 131, 157, 176, 194, 215, 244, 263
Privatization, 159, 199, 203, 278
Privilege, 4, 8, 23, 28, 66, 67, 77, 84, 87, 95, 97–99, 102, 104, 105, 111, 113–115, 126, 127, 147, 167, 178, 188, 217, 235, 236
Progressive, 54, 158, 195, 203, 239, 256

Q
Queer theory, 4, 6, 7, 16, 65, 66, 68, 69, 77, 78, 267, 279

R
Race, 4, 23, 43, 84, 117, 156, 188, 200, 263
Reflexivity, 23, 245
Representation, 11, 27, 29, 30, 65–69, 74–76, 87, 96, 97, 145, 165, 198, 235, 244, 247, 249, 251, 252, 277
Resistance, 4, 23, 95, 101, 102, 104, 116, 157, 165, 183, 245–250, 256–258, 269, 279

S
School
   community relations, 176, 178, 179, 181–183
   fundraising, 193–197, 202–208
   leadership, 139, 141, 144–147, 239
   reform, 83, 84, 88, 92, 95, 96, 106, 113, 122, 123, 172, 224, 229, 236
   turnaround, 84, 185, 217, 237–240, 276
Silence, 30, 67, 76, 78, 99, 101, 137, 144, 147, 201, 253
Social
   construction, 91, 159, 236
   justice, 8, 9, 64, 69–74, 76–77, 84–86, 89, 91, 92, 95, 97–106, 161, 166, 172, 199, 200, 202, 203, 208, 216, 276, 277, 279

Socioeconomic status, 47, 49, 53, 54, 146, 196, 197
State boards of education, 6, 7, 19–37
Student
   assignment, 6, 7, 16, 43–59
   voice, 16, 83–107, 279
Subjectivity, 98, 161, 243, 244, 246, 265
Superintendent, 30, 53, 55, 71, 73, 75, 100, 131, 134–136, 138, 139, 143–145, 147, 157, 182, 226, 228, 239
Symbolism, 27

T
Testing, 9, 58, 123, 157, 164, 195, 256, 258
Title I School Improvement Grant, 10, 35, 152, 217, 218, 220, 222–225, 229, 235–238

V
Values, x, xi, 7, 10, 16, 24, 25, 27, 28, 78, 86, 87, 104, 105, 114, 137, 138, 141, 143–145, 147, 152, 168, 179, 198–202, 205, 207, 208, 220, 227, 236, 250
Voice, 6–8, 16, 32, 47, 57, 83–107, 145–147, 157, 158, 166, 170, 201, 204, 228, 243, 249, 279

W
Women of Color feminisms, 262–271

Y
Youth, 8, 64, 65, 84, 85, 87–93, 101, 102, 105, 106, 159, 163, 165, 169, 171, 261–263, 268–271

Lightning Source UK Ltd.
Milton Keynes UK
UKHW021437030820
367620UK00006B/1668